# WELL SPENT

## How Strong Infrastructure Governance Can End Waste in Public Investment

**EDITORS**

Gerd Schwartz

Manal Fouad

Torben Hansen

Geneviève Verdier

Cover design: IMF Creative Solutions

**Cataloging-in-Publication Data**
**IMF Library**

Names: Schwartz, Gerd, editor. | Fouad, Manal, editor. | Hansen, Torben Steen, editor. | Verdier, Geneviève, editor. | International Monetary Fund, publisher.
Title: Well spent : how strong infrastructure governance can end waste in public investment / editors: Gerd Schwartz, Manal Fouad, Torben Hansen, Geneviève Verdier.
Other titles: How strong infrastructure governance can end waste in public investment.
Description: Washington, DC : International Monetary Fund, 2020. | Includes bibliographical references and index.
Identifiers: ISBN 978-1-51351-181-8 (paper) | 978-1-51353-204-2 (ePub) | 978-1-51353-205-9 (PDF)
Subjects: LCSH: Infrastructure (Economics). | Public investments.
Classification: LCC HC79.C3 W45 2020



Recommended citation: Schwartz, Gerd, Manal Fouad, Torben Hansen, and Geneviève Verdier, eds. 2020. *Well Spent: How Strong Infrastructure Governance Can End Waste in Public Investment*. Washington, DC: International Monetary Fund.

ISBN: 978-1-51351-181-8 (paper)
978-1-51353-204-2 (ePub)
978-1-51353-205-9 (PDF)

Please send orders to:

International Monetary Fund, Publication Services
PO Box 92780, Washington, DC 20090, USA
Tel: (202) 623–7430 Fax: (202) 623–7201
E-mail: publications@imf.org
Internet: www.elibrary.imf.org
www.bookstore.imf.org

# Contents

# Foreword

In recent years, we have had an intensive discussion on infrastructure needs, including their massive size and possible financing options. In contrast, much less attention has been given to *quality* aspects of infrastructure investment, although this is equally important.

Infrastructure investment, only when accompanied by high quality, can fully contribute to sustainable growth and development, for instance through ensuring economic efficiency in view of life-cycle cost. On the other hand, poor quality projects can't reap their full economic benefit. Such investment can also undermine countries' debt sustainability, while causing adverse social and environmental impacts. Furthermore, it may be more vulnerable to natural disasters or to the effects of climate change. Therefore, there is an urgent need for governments to focus more attention on the quality of infrastructure spending. This is the essence of Japan's Quality Infrastructure Investment (QII) initiative.

Based on this initiative, Japan has supported a range of quality infrastructure projects across the globe. Tsubasa ("Wing") bridge in Cambodia is a prime example that I personally have strong attachment to. It has contributed to the country's development by solving a major traffic bottleneck and is now depicted on its banknotes as a symbol of friendship between the two countries.

The value of this QII initiative is worth spreading globally. To this end, Japan put the spotlight on it during its 2019 G20 presidency and led the G20 discussions to the successful endorsement of the "G20 Principles for QII" at the G20 Summit, which set out the G20's aspiration to advance QII.

Now, it is time to implement the QII Principles and doing so will require, as a foundation, strong infrastructure governance—public institutions to plan, allocate, and implement infrastructure investment efficiently and effectively.

I am therefore pleased to have the IMF accompany our quest for advancing QII globally. With its unparalleled analytical strength and deep expertise on infrastructure governance, the IMF has been at the forefront of helping countries' resources to be "well spent" on public investment as the title of this book says. I am convinced that this timely book will help disseminate good practices on infrastructure governance and guide us to better infrastructure outcomes.

I recommend this book to all those—government officials, researchers, investors, practitioners, and others—who have stakes in infrastructure investment. With valuable guidance of this publication, let us gear up our collective action to promote high-quality infrastructure investment and achieve strong, sustainable, balanced, and inclusive growth.

Aso Taro
*Deputy Prime Minister*
*and Minister of Finance, Japan*

# Foreword

Good infrastructure that fosters and supports economic and human development is key to growing the economy, creating wealth, and reducing inequalities. Good infrastructure is a great economic equalizer, advancing access to health, education, and economic opportunities. And, more generally, good infrastructure is a bridge to the future for current and new generations, connecting citizens, facilitating trade, and building resilience against climate change and natural disasters. With the COVID-19 pandemic and its economic fallout still unfolding at the time of writing this Foreword, creating good infrastructure through strong infrastructure governance are more important than ever and key to supporting economic recovery.

Across countries, discussions on infrastructure—the what, why, where, and how much—are closely linked to the Sustainable Development Goals (SDGs), which call for significantly scaling up infrastructure in areas such as health, water, sanitation, energy, and transportation, as well as adapting and fostering resilience to climate change. IMF staff have been actively involved in these discussions, which include estimating the costs of achieving the SDGs, particularly in key infrastructure sectors. The economic recovery from the COVID-19 pandemic will require strong infrastructure governance to ensure that investment spending contributes to high-quality economic growth.

Our work has shown that most countries will find it challenging to meet key public investment needs. A variety of options—raising more revenues, borrowing more, cutting unproductive spending, or getting more private-sector participation—can help to increase infrastructure spending. But all options have limitations and are insufficient on their own. For example, additional borrowing is hampered by high and increasing debt levels.

This book argues that, by addressing inefficiencies and cutting waste in infrastructure spending, governments can get much more out of the public funds they spend. It highlights the urgent need to strengthen infrastructure governance—that is, putting in place the right institutions to plan and implement projects efficiently—to meet priority investment needs. This book also shows what needs to be done and how best to do it, based in part on the IMF's comprehensive approach to assessing infrastructure governance and the almost 60 country public investment management assessments (PIMAs) we have carried out so far.

Drawing on the experience of staff from the IMF and the World Bank, as well as OECD colleagues and experts, the book provides a clear roadmap that shows how countries with limited fiscal space can aspire to spend well and address their key infrastructure bottlenecks. Those who deal with infrastructure issues—governments, development partners, private investors, and civil society—will find this book particularly relevant and interesting. Together we can establish the infrastructure needed to bring about a more wealthy, inclusive, and sustainable future.

Kristalina Georgieva
*Managing Director*
*International Monetary Fund*

# Acknowledgments

This book has been a collective endeavor and has benefited from contributions from both inside and outside the IMF. We thank the contributing authors for their close collaboration and enthusiasm for the topic. The research presented in the book has benefited from the comments by staff of the IMF's Fiscal Affairs Department and other departments. The editors also thank Richard Allen, Guohua Huang, and Eivind Tandberg for their support in reviewing chapters for the book.

Joe Procopio and Rumit Pancholi of the IMF's Communications Department efficiently managed all aspects of the production of the book, and we are grateful for their excellent work. We also thank Nour Chamseddine, Nghiã-Piotr Trọng Lê, Riki Matsumoto, Patrick Ryan, and Sureni Weerathunga for their excellent research assistance in putting together the data used in many chapters of the book. Sasha Pitrof, Young Kim, and Deise Miller Passos Da Silva also provided excellent administrative assistance during the many steps needed to bring the book into completion.

Gerd Schwartz
Manal Fouad
Torben Hansen
Geneviève Verdier

# Contributors

## EDITORS

**Gerd Schwartz** is Deputy Director of the IMF's Fiscal Affairs Department (FAD), where he oversees the department's work on fiscal management, including infrastructure governance. Before joining the IMF, he worked at the European Investment Bank and the Inter-American Development Bank. He earned a PhD in economics from the State University of New York at Albany and has done research on fiscal and financial policy and management issues.

**Manal Fouad**, an Egyptian national, is Chief of FAD's Public Financial Management (PFM) II Division. She is a public finance specialist and has provided advice on fiscal policy and capacity building to governments on macro-fiscal frameworks, fiscal transparency, and infrastructure governance. She oversees PFM capacity-development programs for the Francophone and Lusophone Africa, Asia and the Pacific, and the Western Hemisphere regions. She has held various positions in FAD and the IMF Institute for Capacity Development. She earned a PhD from the Graduate Institute of International Studies and Development in Geneva.

**Torben Hansen** is Deputy Division Chief in FAD's PFM I Division. Since joining the IMF in 2013, he has led capacity development activities focusing on countries in the Middle East, Europe, and Anglophone Africa and participated in analytical work on public financial management, including infrastructure governance. Before joining the IMF, he held senior positions at the Danish Ministry of Finance and the Prime Minister's Office. He earned an MSc in economics from the University of Copenhagen.

**Geneviève Verdier** is Division Chief in the IMF's Middle East and Central Asia Department. She was Deputy Division Chief in FAD's Expenditure Policy Division, where she worked on public expenditure issues and their fiscal and macroeconomic implications. She has held various positions in the IMF's area and functional departments. Before joining the IMF, she was an assistant professor of economics at Texas A&M University and an economist in the Research Department of the Bank of Canada. She earned a PhD from the University of British Columbia. Her work and publications in IMF research and policy publications, books, and peer-reviewed journals cover macroeconomic issues related to public spending efficiency, public investment, sovereign debt restructuring, economic growth, and digitalization.

## AUTHORS

**Richard Allen** is a senior economist in FAD and a senior research associate at the Overseas Development Institute in London. He previously worked with the World Bank, the Asian Development Bank, the Organisation for Economic Co-operation and Development, and the UK Treasury, and was a board member of the European Investment Bank. He has advised governments of more than 60 countries on reforms of public financial management. He is coeditor of the *International Handbook of Public Financial Management*; author of many articles, working papers, technical notes, and book reviews on public finance topics; and co-editor of the IMF's PFM Blog. He earned degrees in economics and public finance from the University of Edinburgh and the University of York.

**Olivier Basdevant** is a senior economist in FAD's Fiscal Operations I Division. He earned a PhD in economics from Sorbonne University in Paris. His publications focus on improving governance and fighting corruption, fiscal policy design, and macroeconomic modeling and forecasting.

**Anja Baum** is an economist in FAD's Fiscal Operations I Division. During her five years in FAD, she has worked on a variety of fiscal and fiscal-related issues, including fiscal rules, revenue mobilization, investment efficiency, corruption, state-owned enterprises, and Sustainable Development Goals (SDGs). Before joining FAD, she spent two years in the IMF's Middle East and Central Asia Department. During her tenure at the IMF, she has supported IMF surveillance and program work in Burundi, Iraq, Madagascar, Vietnam, and the West Bank and Gaza. She earned a PhD in economics from the University of Cambridge and a diploma in economics from the University of Mannheim.

**Mary Betley** is a consultant who provides advice and technical assistance in PFM, public investment and public expenditure management, and budgetary policy and planning. She has assisted governments with reforms of budget and PFM in Africa, Asia, the Pacific, Eastern Europe, and the Balkans. She served as a short-term expert for FAD, the World Bank, the UK Department for International Development, the European Union, and the German Agency for International Cooperation (GIZ). She earned degrees in economics and public finance from the University of Oxford and the University of Warwick, respectively.

**Olivier Bizimana** is a senior economist in the IMF's Research Department. Before joining the IMF in 2015, he was a senior economist in the Global Economics Team at Morgan Stanley in London. He was previously responsible for economic research for the euro area at Crédit Agricole Group in Paris. He has also taught postgraduate courses in macroeconomics at Paris-Dauphine University for five years. His research interests include international finance, monetary policy, macro-financial issues, and business-cycle fluctuations. He earned a PhD and an MPhil in economics from Paris Dauphine University and an MSc in economics and statistics from the École nationale de la statistique et de l'administration Économique (ENSAE) in Paris.

**Andrew Blazey** is Deputy Head of the Budgeting and Public Expenditures Division of the Organisation for Economic Co-operation and Development. His responsibilities include infrastructure investment, public-private partnerships, budget performance and a recent initiative on green budgeting. Before this role, He was Budget Director at the New Zealand Treasury and has managed reforms in investment and infrastructure management, state-owned enterprises, performance initiatives in the public sector, and, most recently, the development of a well-being budget. He has worked at the IMF and in the private sector. He earned an MBA from the Chinese University of Hong Kong.

**Taz Chaponda** is Chief Executive Officer of the Malawi Agricultural and Industrial Investment Corporation. He was a senior economist in FAD from 2016 to 2019, working extensively on infrastructure governance across Africa and Eastern Europe. Before that, he worked for more than 10 years in infrastructure finance with a focus on public-private partnerships in Africa and Asia. In other roles, he served as Head of the Budget Office in the South Africa National Treasury and as an economist at the World Bank country office in Malawi. He earned an MBA from INSEAD business school, an MSc in development economics from the University of Oxford, and a BA in economics from Harvard University.

**Devin D'Angelo** is a research assistant in FAD's Expenditure Policy Division. His work includes research and policy analysis in topics such as income inequality, fiscal policy, and social protection. Before joining the IMF, he earned a BA in economics and applied mathematics from the University of California, Berkeley.

**Eduardo Andrés Estrada**, a Colombian national, is a governance specialist at the World Bank's Governance Global Practice covering Latin America and the Caribbean. He joined the World Bank in 2012 and has participated in the development and implementation of lending operations, as well as preparing analytical reports in public expenditure and public financial management. Before joining the World Bank, he was a consultant at the Inter-American Development Bank and the Organization of American States. In Colombia, he served as an advisor for the House of Representatives and worked in private sector consulting. He earned an MPP in public policy from Georgetown University, and a BA in economics and political science from Davidson College.

**Fabien Gonguet** is an economist in FAD's PFM II Division. His areas of expertise include macro-fiscal forecasting and analysis, infrastructure governance, and fiscal risk management. Before joining the IMF, he worked at the French Treasury, where he focused on revenue forecasts and fiscal policy analysis and on the oversight of multilateral development agencies. He graduated from the École

Polytechnique and ENSAE. He also earned a MSc in international affairs from Sciences Po Paris.

**Nikolay Gueorguiev** is Chief of FAD's Fiscal Operations I Division. An IMF staff member since 2001, he has also worked in the IMF's European and African departments, including as a mission chief for Ukraine, Moldova, Austria, and Slovenia. Before joining IMF staff, he served as Deputy Minister of Finance in Bulgaria and as Advisor to the IMF Executive Director for the group of countries including Bulgaria. He earned a PhD in economics from the University of Maryland, College Park.

**Wei Guo** is a project officer in the IMF's Strategy, Policy and Review Department. He is a PhD candidate and obtained a MSc in economics from the University of Maryland, College Park, and the University of California, Santa Barbara. Before joining the IMF, he worked in the Chief Economist and the Vice President's Office at the World Bank. His research encompasses household finance, shadow banking, firm dynamics, and, more recently, the macroeconomic impact of natural disaster and climate change.

**Jiro Honda** is Deputy Division Chief of FAD's Fiscal Operations I Division. An IMF staff member since 2001, he has also worked in the Finance Department and the African Department, including as Mission Chief for Eswatini, Lesotho, and Namibia and as a liaison with regional institutions. Before joining the IMF, he worked at the Bank of Japan, including as a representative in Hong Kong Special Administrative Region. He earned an MA in international and development economics from Yale University.

**Tannous Kass-Hanna** is an economist in the IMF's Strategy, Policy and Review Department. His work includes analytical and operational projects on inequality and fiscal policy, as well as external sector assessment and debt sustainability analysis in developing countries. His research uses modern macroeconomic theory and tools to investigate the international spillovers of fiscal policy, the effects of policy uncertainty on fiscal policy, and the distributional impact of fiscal policy. He joined the IMF after his doctoral studies in economics at the Toulouse School of Economics in France.

**Roland Kangni Kpodar** is Deputy Unit Chief in the IMF's Strategy, Policy, and Review Department and Senior Fellow at the Foundation for Studies and Research on International Development. He graduated with a PhD in economics from the University of Auvergne in France and, since joining the IMF in 2006, has worked on developing and emerging economies and policy issues, including fiscal, external, monetary, and financial sector issues. His responsibilities also include the institutional relationship with multilateral development banks and comanaging an IMF–Department for International Development project on macroeconomic research in low-income countries. He has published extensively on financial development, poverty reduction, and fiscal issues, including fuel subsidies. He is a national of Togo.

**Nghiã-Piotr Trọng Lê**, a Vietnamese national with Polish roots, is a research officer in FAD's Expenditure Policy Division. He works on topics such as fossil fuel subsidies, costing methodologies for the Sustainable Development Goals, government wage bills, wage premiums, and employment. Before joining the IMF, he worked in economic litigation consulting, specializing in financial services, and in education policy research. He earned BAs in economics and political economy from the University of California, Berkeley, as well as an MSc in public policy from the McCourt School of Public Policy at Georgetown University.

**Tuan Minh Le** is a lead economist at the World Bank. He earned a PhD in public policy from Harvard University. Before joining the World Bank, Dr. Le was consultant at the Public Finance Group, Harvard Institute for International Development, Harvard University, and was an assistant professor of economics at Suffolk University. He has engaged in a broad range of teaching, research, policy advisory consulting, and operations on fiscal policy in all regions. His work focuses on tax policy design, revenue administration, appraisal of development expenditures, and public investment management. Dr. Le has authored numerous published papers and coauthored several books on public investment management, natural resource–led development, and tax reforms.

**Weijen Leow** is a senior financial specialist at the World Bank's Climate Change Group. He jointly leads the Climate Action Peer Exchange program, which supports a coalition of 51 finance ministers in addressing climate change through fiscal policy and financial management. His previous work in the World Bank Group covered urban environmental management, concessional finance and advisory services, and environmental risk management. Between 2011 and 2014, he served as Chief Specialist (Climate Change) at the Ministry of Finance of Singapore and was responsible for resilience and mitigation planning. He earned a degree in chemical engineering from the University of Singapore and an MA in economic development and environment from the Fletcher School.

**Chishiro Matsumoto** is an advisor in FAD, coordinating work on infrastructure governance and engagement with the G20, among others. Before joining the IMF, he held various positions in the Japanese Ministry of Finance, particularly in the Budget Bureau and the International Bureau, where he was involved in policy areas such as national budget formulation, G7/G20, and IMF/multilateral development banks. A national of Japan, he earned a BA in economics from the University of Tokyo, an MSc in finance from the University of Strathclyde, and an MSc in economics from the London School of Economics and Political Science.

**Hiroaki Miyamoto** is an economist in FAD's Fiscal Operations I Division. His primary areas of research are macroeconomics and labor economics. He has published articles on fiscal policies and labor market dynamics at leading journals, including the *Journal of Monetary Economics* and *Review of Economic Dynamics*. Before joining the IMF, he was an associate professor at the University of Tokyo and a professor at the International University of Japan. He earned a PhD in economics from the University of Wisconsin–Madison.

**Tewodaj Mogues** is a senior economist in FAD's Expenditure Policy Division, where she conducts analysis and provides policy advice on topics related to public expenditure. Before joining the IMF in late 2018, she worked for 13 years in the Development Strategy and Governance Division at the International Food Policy Research Institute, where, as a senior research fellow, she led a Consultative Group for International Agricultural Research (CGIAR) research cluster on public investments and institutions. Her fields of expertise include development economics, fiscal federalism, political economy, and agricultural economics. She received an BA in economics from Kalamazoo College and a PhD in Development Economics from the University of Wisconsin–Madison. She is a German national born in Ethiopia.

**Rui Montero** is a technical assistance advisor in FAD's PFM II Division, where he focuses on infrastructure governance, drawing on 27 years of experience. Before joining the IMF in 2018, he spent eight years working on public-private partnerships and infrastructure at the World Bank. Previously, he was infrastructure advisor to the Portuguese Treasury Secretary for more than 10 years and a representative of the Finance Minister of Portugal in steering committees and tender boards for major highway, railroad, tram, and hospital projects. He has extensive experience in multilateral cooperation with governments in Europe, Africa, Asia, and the Americas, including field missions on public investment management assessment, capacitation, and reform.

**Lewis Murara** is a senior economist in FAD's PFM II Division. He has significant PFM experience from governments and international organizations. Before joining the IMF in 2011, he was a public sector management specialist in the World Bank's former Poverty Reduction and Economic Management Network. Previously, he worked for Rwanda's—and was seconded to South Africa's—supreme audit institutions. He graduated from the Economics School of Louvain of the Catholic University of Louvain and the University of Namur in Belgium, and he earned a diploma in public financial management from the Harvard Kennedy School.

**Masahiro Nozaki** is a senior economist in the Australia–New Zealand Division of the IMF's Asia and Pacific Department. He has worked at the IMF since 2003 and joined the Australia team in Fall 2018 after his assignment as Lead Desk for Sri Lanka in the context of an IMF-supported program. He also worked in FAD during 2010–16, focusing on fiscal reforms in Indonesia, Japan, and the Philippines; age-related public spending; fiscal federalism; and energy subsidy reform. His research interests include fiscal policy and social security reforms as well as exchange rate dynamics. He earned a PhD in economics from Brown University.

**Robert Taliercio O'Brien**, an American national, is Regional Director for the Equitable Growth, Finance and Institutions Practice Group in Latin America and the Caribbean at the World Bank. During his 19 years at the World Bank, he has served in a variety of senior positions across three regions. He has designed and led investment and development policy operations, as well as analytical reports, for a range of clients. Before joining the World Bank, he was Lecturer in Public Finance and Manager for Investment Appraisal at the Harvard Institute for International Development. He earned a PhD and an MPP in public policy from Harvard University, an AM in Latin American Studies from Stanford University, and a BA in public and international affairs from Princeton University.

**Sailendra Pattanayak** is Deputy Division Chief in FAD's PFM II Division. Since joining the IMF in 2006, he has advised countries across all income levels on public financial management and fiscal transparency and has led technical assistance missions. Before joining the IMF, he held senior positions in the government of India, including at the Ministry of Finance and the Ministry of Road Transport and Highways, where he handled large infrastructure projects. He has written several papers and has led analytical projects at the IMF on a broad range of fiscal issues. He earned a degree in mechanical engineering from the National Institute of Technology, Rourkela, and MScs in public administration and public policy, respectively, from the École nationale d'administration and Sciences Po Paris.

**Saad Quayyum** is an economist at the IMF's Strategy, Policy and Review Department. He obtained a PhD in economics from the University of Wisconsin–Madison and a BA in economics from Dartmouth College. Before joining the IMF, he worked at the Federal Reserve Bank of Chicago and the State of Wisconsin Investment Board. His research encompasses topics including foreign aid, remittances, trade and diversification, and—more recently—the macroeconomic impact of natural disasters and climate change.

**Carolina Renteria** is Chief of FAD's PFM I Division, responsible for delivering PFM capacity development in Europe, Anglophone Africa, the Middle East, and Central Asia, and for developing a comprehensive PFM analytical agenda. Before joining the IMF, she was Executive Director for Colombia and a group of countries and Lead Economist for Africa at the World Bank. In Colombia, she served as Director of the National Planning Department (Cabinet Member), National Budget Director, and Senior Advisor to the Council of Fiscal Policy. She earned an MSc from New York University in public administration and another from Universidad de los Andes in economic development.

**Isabel Rial** is a senior economist in FAD's PFM I Division. During her 15 years at the IMF, she has worked on a range of cross-country fiscal policy issues, focusing particularly on public investment management, public-private partnerships, and fiscal risks. She has more than 25 years of experience both in the public sector and at the IMF and has consulted for several private sector entities. Before joining the IMF, she was Head of the Fiscal Policy Analysis Division at the Central Bank of Uruguay and was a professor at the Universidad de la República Oriental del Uruguay. Ms. Rial earned a MSc in applied macroeconomics from the Pontifical Catholic University of Chile.

**Fabian Seiderer** is a lead public sector specialist at the World Bank, specialized in PFM and public investment management. He is cochair of the World Bank Community of Practice on Governance of Infrastructure and Public Investment Management. He is currently based in Thailand and has worked on analytics and policy reforms across Africa, the Maghreb and Middle East, South Asia, and now Southeast Asia. His areas of interest are mainstreaming climate in public investment and asset management, and subnational public investment assessments and engagements. He is an economist with an MSc from the University of Bonn, Germany, and from the University of Nanterre and Paris-Sorbonne, France.

**Ashni Singh** is a senior economist in FAD's PFM I Division. He contributes to capacity development in member countries on PFM issues including infrastructure governance. Before joining the IMF, he worked in various public finance capacities in the government of Guyana at both the policymaking and technical levels for more than two decades, including as Minister of Finance from 2006 to 2015 and previously as Director of Budget and Deputy Auditor General. He earned a PhD in accounting and finance from Lancaster University.

**Philip Stokoe** is a senior economist in the Government Finance Division of the IMF's Statistics Department with expertise in international statistical and accounting guidance for public finances. His current role includes analysis of fiscal data and capacity development in fiscal statistics to country authorities. Before joining the IMF five years ago, he worked for the UK Office for National Statistics on classification and related issues for the Public Sector Finances and National Accounts. During this time, he was part of the Government Finance Statistics Advisory Committee that contributed to the production of the IMF's *Government Finance Statistics Manual 2014* and was a vocal participant in Eurostat-led discussions to provide new and improved guidance on government deficit and debt for EU member states.

**Eivind Tandberg** is an infrastructure governance advisor in FAD. He has more than 30 years of experience in public finance, public administration, advisory services, and research. He has previously been Deputy Director General in the

Norwegian Ministry of Finance, Unit Chief at the World Bank, Deputy Division Chief at the IMF, and Director-General in the Oslo city government. He has contributed to assessment and development of public management and governance in 145 countries. He has also participated in the development of several international standards and evaluation frameworks. During the past few years, he has engaged particularly in international work related to infrastructure governance, public investment, governance and budgeting of public institutions, oversight of public corporations, and management of fiscal risks. He has an MSc in economics from the Norwegian School of Economics and Business Administration.

**Dawit Tessema** is an economist at the Development Issues Unit of the IMF's Strategy, Policy, and Review Department. His work focuses on the macroeconomic implications of public investment. Before joining the IMF, he was an economist at the International Food Policy Research Institute and the United Nations Economic Commission for Africa and subsequently served as an economist at the Development Research Department of the African Development Bank (2011–17), working on global economic shock spillovers. He studies at Addis Ababa University and The George Washington University.

**Saji Thomas** is a senior economist in FAD's Fiscal Operations I Division. He has been with the IMF since 2004 and has worked on several countries in sub-Saharan Africa, the Caribbean, the Middle East, and South Asia. Before joining the IMF, he worked in the Research Department of the World Bank. His main areas of research are sovereign debt restructuring, taxation of natural resources, and fiscal rules. He earned a PhD in economics from the University of Minnesota.

**Concepcion Verdugo-Yepes** is a senior economist in FAD's PFM II Division, where she has led and participated in several IMF governance and anticorruption missions. She has worked at the IMF since 2008. From 2008 to 2017, she was an economist in the Legal Department in the Financial Integrity Group. Before joining the IMF, she worked for 10 years in the private sector, developing public-private partnerships in the public infrastructure sector in Spain and Latin America. She has produced numerous articles and contributions on issues related to corruption and financial integrity and significant inputs to IMF policy papers on governance. She earned a PhD in international law and economics from Bocconi University.

**Ha Vu** is a senior economist in FAD's PFM II Division. She has nearly 20 years of experience in public finance, public administration, teaching, and research, including on infrastructure governance. She has provided direct advice on infrastructure governance and PFM in francophone Africa, Asia, Europe, and Latin America, while working at the IMF and earlier at the World Bank. She has also contributed to the development of the IMF's Public Investment Management Assessment framework. She earned a PhD in public policy and public finance from George Mason University.

**Sébastien Walker** is an Economist in FAD's Expenditure Policy Division. He focuses on technical assistance and analytical work in public investment, social spending, and the government wage bill, as well as the broader monitoring of fiscal developments in selected countries in the Middle East and North Africa. He previously worked in the IMF's Africa Department. He earned a BA in philosophy, politics, and economics and an MPhil and PhD in economics from the University of Oxford. In the course of his studies, he taught at the Oxford Department of International Development and at various colleges of the University of Oxford and has completed internships at the IMF, the Bank of England, the UK Financial Services Authority, and some economics consultancies.

**Yuan Xiao** is a senior economist in FAD's Expenditure Policy Division. His work encompasses technical assistance and research on public investment and infrastructure, public-private partnerships, sustainable development goals, and public expenditure management. During his career at the IMF, he has been on country teams covering advanced economies, emerging market economies, and low-income developing countries for both surveillance and program work. He earned a PhD in economics from the University of Michigan.

# Abbreviations

| | |
|---|---|
| AE | *autorisations d'engagement* |
| ASEAN | Association of Southeast Asian Nations |
| CBA | cost-benefit analysis |
| CIT | corporate income tax |
| CONFIS | *Consejo Nacional de Politica Fiscal* (Colombia) |
| CONPES | *El Consejo Nacional de Política Económica y Social* (Colombia) |
| CP | *crédits de paiement* |
| EM-DAT | Emergency Events Database |
| EU | European Union |
| FSGM | Flexible System of Global Models |
| G20 | Group of Twenty |
| GFSM 2014 | IMF *Government Finance Statistics Manual 2014* |
| GMM | generalized method of moments |
| GTOPO30 | US Geological Survey 1996 |
| IPCC | Intergovernmental Panel on Climate Change |
| IT | information technology |
| KOTI | Korea Transport Institute |
| NZTA | New Zealand Transport Agency |
| OECD | Organisation for Economic Co-operation and Development |
| PEFA | Public Expenditure and Financial Accountability |
| PEMANDU | Performance Management and Delivery Unit (Malaysia) |
| PFM | public financial management |
| PFRAM | Public-Private Partnership Fiscal Risk Assessment Model |
| PIM | public investment management |
| PIMA | Public Investment Management Assessment |
| PIP | public investment program |
| PIT | personal income tax |
| PPP | public-private partnership |
| PPPC | *Programa Petrobras de Prevenção da Corrupção* (Brazil) |
| RAI | Rural Access Index |
| SDGs | Sustainable Development Goals |
| UN | United Nations |
| VAT | value-added tax |
| WAEMU | West African Economic and Monetary Union |
| WEO | *World Economic Outlook* |

CHAPTER 1

# Well Spent: How Strong Infrastructure Governance Can End Waste in Public Investment

**Gerd Schwartz, Manal Fouad, Torben Hansen, and Geneviève Verdier**

Public infrastructure is a key driver of inclusive economic growth and development and the reduction of inequalities. Roads, bridges, railways, airports, and electricity connect markets, facilitate production and trade, and create economic opportunities for work and education. Water and sanitation, schools and hospitals improve people's lives, skills, and health. Also, if done right, broad-based provision of public infrastructure can support income and gender equality; help address urgent health care needs (for example, during epidemics); reduce pollution; and build resilience against climate change and natural disasters.

Yet, creating quality—that is, infrastructure that is well-planned, well-implemented, resilient, and sustainable—has often been challenging. Almost all countries have infamous white elephants—major investment projects with negative social returns—that have never delivered on their initial promise. One does not have to search far to come across infrastructure projects that were poorly designed, had large costs overruns, experienced long delays in construction, and/or yielded poor social dividends. Examples of poor project appraisal, faulty project selection, rampant rent seeking and corruption, or lack of funding to complete ongoing projects abound and not only in low-capacity countries. And even perfectly good public infrastructures may deteriorate quickly when maintenance is inadequate, which often reflects a lack of funding or political attention.

Losses and waste in public investment are often systemic. On average, more than one-third of the resources spent on creating and maintaining public infrastructure are lost because of inefficiencies (IMF 2015; and Chapter 3 of this book). These inefficiencies are closely linked to poor *infrastructure governance*—defined as the institutions and frameworks for planning, allocating, and implementing infrastructure investment spending. Estimates suggest that, on average, better infrastructure governance could make up more than half of the observed efficiency losses (Chapter 3).

The need for stronger infrastructure governance for quality investment is widely recognized, and initiatives have been launched to provide guidance on good practice. Yet, although much has been written on what constitutes good infrastructure governance or public investment management, most countries still lack the institutions needed to produce good infrastructure outcomes. Countries frequently stumble over key institutional issues. For example, they may struggle to select projects with the highest social and economic returns and finance projects in a fiscally sustainable way, given limited resources, or struggle to ensure that funding is available as needed throughout project implementation. Budgeting for operations and maintenance costs, ensuring that procurement is transparent and rigorous, or harnessing private sector skills, innovation, and funding without creating undue risks to public finances can also be challenging.

In the wake of *Great Lockdown* and the COVID-19 pandemic, more infrastructure investment and strong infrastructure governance are likely to become even more important (IMF 2020a, 2020b). First, with economic growth turning negative, public investment will have to be part of stimulating weak aggregate demand. For example, in the area of health, the pandemic has revealed a lack of preparedness of many health systems and an urgent need for upgrading health infrastructure that will have to be addressed. Second, countries will emerge from the pandemic with scarce fiscal space, elevated debt levels, large financing needs, and therefore a renewed need to make every dollar count, to ensure the efficiency of investment spending.

This book addresses how resources for public investment can be *spent well.* The overall message is simple: aspirations to end waste in public investment and create better quality infrastructure outcomes have to be met by specific actions on infrastructure governance to reap the full economic and social dividends from public investment.

## QUALITY PUBLIC INFRASTRUCTURE: AN ASPIRATION FOR ALL COUNTRIES

Quality infrastructure plays a crucial role in fostering economic development:

- *Public investment improves delivery of public services and the quality of life of citizens.* Quality infrastructure affects our physical well being at the most basic level. An estimated 2.2 billion people worldwide do not have access to safe water. Their health and livelihoods are at risk from a variety of diseases and epidemics.[1] Research has found that interventions to improve water and sanitation infrastructure have been the most effective in reducing morbidity from these diseases (Freeman and others 2014; Wolf and others 2014; World Health Organization 2016).
- *Public investment connects citizens to economic opportunities by supporting private sector activities.* For example, quality transport infrastructure can

[1] For example, the World Health Organization (2016) estimates that environmental factors, including the availability of sanitary water sources, account for 57 percent of those affected by diarrheal diseases.

reduce travel times and transportation costs significantly (BenYishay and Tunstall 2011), and contribute, among others, to better access to jobs and the facilitation of trade.

- *Public investment is a catalyst for inclusive economic growth and development.* Public investment can increase demand in the short term and productivity in the long term, sometimes even with limited increases in indebtedness, if spending is done efficiently (IMF 2014, 2015; Chapters 2 and 8 of this book).

Infrastructure spending needs are staggering almost everywhere. Low-income developing countries and many emerging market economies have looming infrastructure needs in most sectors. In September 2015, governments assembled at the United Nations agreed on a comprehensive development agenda with 17 Sustainable Development Goals (SDGs) that will require a large scale-up in infrastructure, particularly in water, sanitation and hygiene, energy, and transportation. The estimated total cumulative investment needs to meet the SDGs by 2030 are more than 36 percent of GDP in low-income developing countries and emerging markets (Chapter 4).

Many advanced economies have aging infrastructures and see urgent spending needs for their upkeep and modernization. For example, in the United States, the American Society of Civil Engineers (2017) estimates cumulative spending needs of more than $10 trillion through 2040 to maintain, repair, or rebuild existing infrastructure. In Europe, in November 2014 the European Commission announced an Infrastructure Investment Plan to unlock more than €315 billion for investment spending. In the same year, the IMF (2014) called for an infrastructure spending push to help support both short-term demand shortfalls and longer-term development needs; the OECD (2019) did the same more recently.[2]

In addition, almost all countries face issues related to making their infrastructure more resilient to climate change. Specifically, damage to buildings, transport, energy, and water infrastructures caused by climate change is expected to run into billions (Chapter 15), with small states that are prone to natural disasters being particularly at risk (Chapter 9). In some countries, this is also compounded by daunting infrastructure challenges as a result of wars, prolonged civil strife, or major migration movements.

Meeting these spending needs will be challenging at best. In most countries, spending needs contrast sharply with the resources available to meet them in fiscally responsible and macroeconomically sustainable ways. What are the options?

- *Additional borrowing* is often hampered by already large debt stocks. At $188 trillion-or about 226 percent of global GDP in 2018-global debt levels were at a record high even before the COVID-19 pandemic, with most countries having little room to increase borrowing without risking to put their public debt on an unsustainable path.[3] Even with debt relief, global

[2] See https://oecdecoscope.blog/2019/09/19/growth-is-taking-a-dangerous-downward-turn/.

[3] Global debt data are available from the IMF Global Debt Database: https://www.imf.org/external/datamapper/datasets/GDD.

debt levels are continuing to rise substantially in the wake of the global COVID-19 pandemic.

- *Revenue mobilization* is key to expanding the resource envelope and creating fiscal space but is unlikely to be sufficient in and by itself to generate the resources needed. The median low-income developing country raises about 15 percent of GDP in tax revenue. Gaspar and others (2019) estimate that many countries, including most low-income developing countries, could aspire to increase revenue ratios by about 5 percentage points by 2030. This would certainly help to provide some, albeit not all, of the infrastructure spending needed to achieve key development objectives, like the SDGs. But large and continuous increases in revenue require a strong and sustained government commitment that is sometimes not politically feasible.
- *Private sector participation* in building infrastructure and providing infrastructure services can be an important component of a government's infrastructure strategy but goes hand in hand with significantly increased fiscal risks. Public-private partnerships, for example, can harness private sector innovation and efficiency to improve infrastructure service provision while allowing governments to share project risks with a private partner. But they also usually result in additional debt—both firm and contingent—and are a major source of fiscal risk (see Chapter 11). Bova and others (2016) estimate that the fiscal cost of contingent liabilities in public private partnerships amounted to 1.2 percent of GDP on average for a sample of 80 advanced economies and emerging markets, with a maximum cost of 2 percent of GDP.

In sum, infrastructure needs far exceed the resources that countries can hope to raise in a fiscally responsible and macroeconomically sustainable way. Options for spending more—borrowing, revenue mobilization, and private sector participation—should be considered and assessed, including their fiscal costs and risks. But spending more will not be sufficient to meet the infrastructure needs: governments also need to spend better. Indeed, additional investment spending will only yield the expected results when spending is done efficiently, and quality infrastructure investment is a priority for all countries, particularly as economies emerge from the economic crisis brought about by the COVID-19 pandemic.

## FROM ASPIRATION TO ACTION: THE IMPORTANCE OF INFRASTRUCTURE GOVERNANCE

Weaknesses in infrastructure governance are critical factors behind inefficiencies and poor outcomes. Flyvbjerg (2009) attributed cost overruns and less-than-projected benefits mostly to deliberate optimism bias in project appraisal and planning. Rajaram and others (2014) pointed to a range of reasons for inefficient public investment, including weak interagency coordination processes, projects being driven by political considerations (which disrupts established processes and diminishes the credibility of project appraisal), weak budget systems, challenges in procurement and project implementation, and corruption. IMF (2018) found weaknesses in infrastructure governance to be widespread across the public investment cycle but more prominent in the allocation and implementation stages of public investment, particularly during project appraisal and project selection.

Several chapters of this book describe big infrastructure projects that have gone terribly wrong for one reason or another, including corruption (Chapter 10), fiscal risks that materialize (Chapter 11), poor integration of planning and budgeting (Chapter 12), or insufficient project appraisal and selection (Chapter 13). Also, over the investment cycle, weaknesses in some areas (for example, project implementation) may easily offset strengths in other areas (such as project planning), reflecting that no "production process" is stronger than its weakest link (IMF 2015).

Poor or suboptimal infrastructure outcomes need not be a fact of life, however. Many examples exist where large and complex infrastructure projects have been delivered successfully, particularly in countries with strong frameworks for effective infrastructure governance in place. Chile provides an example of this. Its national investment system—*Sistema Nacional de Inversiones* (SNI)—covers all public bodies and provides a coherent framework for identifying, coordinating, evaluating, and implementing public investments. The system standardizes project presentation formats, establishes explicit application and evaluation processes, provides general and sector-specific methodological guidelines for project appraisal, and introduces a system of "checks and balances" by separating the institution that evaluates projects from the institutions promoting projects (Gómez-Lobo 2012). The Chilean infrastructure governance system has generated cost savings and helped sustain a pipeline of appraised and approved projects that fulfill technical criteria and are eligible for budget funding (World Bank 2006; IMF 2014). Korea and Norway are other examples of countries with strong frameworks for infrastructure governance.

How can countries build strong infrastructure governance? The international community has long emphasized and offered detailed guidance on good practices in infrastructure governance. Most recently, under Japan's presidency in 2019, the Group of Twenty (G20) established a set of quality infrastructure investment (QII) principles (G20 2019), building upon earlier principles established by the Group of Seven (G7) under Japan's presidency in 2016 (G7 2016) and endorsed by the G20 under China's presidency in 2016. Similarly, in 2014, the World Bank set out "eight must-haves" for public investment management to provide guidance on good processes and procedures for managing the infrastructure project cycle (Rajaram and others 2014). The World Bank has used this framework to guide and support country reform efforts. The Organisation for Economic Co-operation and Development (OECD)'s 10-dimensional framework for "Getting Infrastructure Right" also provides guidance on infrastructure-budgeting principles and project management (OECD 2017). These various guidance frameworks first and foremost define aspirations; that is, they set out what countries seeking to produce quality infrastructure should aim for in their infrastructure governance institutions.

In 2015, the IMF launched its Public Investment Management Assessment (PIMA), explicitly designed to support, that is, help countries assess their infrastructure governance institutions in a comprehensive fashion and design a tailored and prioritized action plan (IMF 2015, 2018a). The PIMA provides a framework for assessing infrastructure governance across the full project cycle—the planning, allocation, and implementation stages of public investment—and allows for cross-country comparisons. The PIMA framework is consistent with the various existing guidance frameworks and expands on these by also focusing on the macro-fiscal and budgetary processes in which infrastructure projects are embedded. Using the PIMA framework and the lessons learned from dozens of country PIMAs carried out since 2015, this book seeks to help governments move from aspiration to action, exploring practical solutions to their specific challenges in improving infrastructure governance.

## OVERVIEW OF THE BOOK

The book is divided into three parts. Part I, *Infrastructure, Growth, and Development* (Chapters 2–5), discusses why countries should aspire to invest in public infrastructure, and why it matters to do so in an efficient way. It demonstrates that public investment fosters economic growth and helps countries meet the SDGs when infrastructure governance is strong. It concludes with a presentation of the PIMA framework and lessons learned from PIMAs that have been carried out so far. Part II, *Fiscal Policy for Quality Public Investment* (Chapters 6–9), explores how fiscal policy can help promote, enable, and protect public investment spending. It considers the impact of public investment during periods of expenditure consolidation, examines the effect of fiscal rules, and presents a case study of infrastructure financing in Asia. This part also examines resilience issues in states vulnerable to natural disasters. Part III, *Building Strong Public Investment Institutions* (Chapters 10–15), turns to the foundation of strong infrastructure by establishing good and innovative practices in key areas of infrastructure governance. This part covers critical issues, such as controlling corruption, managing fiscal risks, integrating planning and budgeting, and identifying best practices in project appraisal and selection. It also covers emerging areas in infrastructure governance, such as maintaining and managing public infrastructure assets and building resilience against climate change.

### *Infrastructure, Growth, and Development*

In Chapter 2, Hiroaki Miyamoto, Anja Baum, Nikolay Gueorguiev, Jiro Honda, and Sébastien Walker analyze the macroeconomic impact of public investment. Public investment spending has declined globally in recent years, but this common trend hides large differences in stocks and quality of physical infrastructure assets across countries. The large differences point to the importance of raising the efficiency and productivity of public investment, particularly for countries with insufficient and poor-quality infrastructure assets. The authors suggest that, with more efficient and productive public investment, countries can achieve higher growth, while increasing the level and quality of their infrastructure. In particular, the authors explore how the strength of a country's infrastructure governance system plays a critical role in determining the macroeconomic effects of public investment on economic activity. They find that countries with better governance systems enjoy more positive output effects and fiscal outcomes from public investment, and the effects disappear in countries with weaker governance. They also conclude that the planning and implementation stages of public investment management are particularly important for enhancing the growth impact of public investment.

Infrastructure governance is intrinsically linked to the efficiency of public investment; that is, the ability to improve the volume and quality of infrastructure assets for a given amount of spending. In Chapter 3, Anja Baum, Tewodaj Mogues, and Geneviève Verdier compare the value of public capital and the resulting outcomes in terms of infrastructure volume and quality across countries and provide a measure of the efficiency of public investment spending for more than 160 countries. They find a large median efficiency gap, in which the latter is defined as the percentage difference in infrastructure access and quality for a given level of spending between the median country and the best performers. Over one-third of resources are lost in the public investment process, according to the authors. Improvements in infrastructure governance are crucial in closing this gap. The authors find a robust and significantly positive relationship between efficiency and the strength of a country's infrastructure governance, as measured by the PIMA. Strengthening institutions that manage public investment can therefore play a key role in increasing efficiency: on average, countries could close more than half the efficiency gap if they adopted infrastructure governance and public investment management practices of the best performers.

Increasing efficiency will be critical as countries tackle the 2030 SDG agenda and related ambitious targets for infrastructure. In Chapter 4, Yuan Xiao, Devin D'Angelo, and Nghiã-Piotr Trọng Lê develop methodologies to estimate the investment spending needed to reach the SDGs related to infrastructure in roads and electricity, and in water and sanitation. They find that spending needs are substantial: total cumulative investment needs until 2030 in these three sectors average about 36 percentage points of GDP in emerging markets and low-income developing countries. Estimated investment needs vary significantly across countries depending on their income level but a significant scaling up of public investment spending is required in many countries. For example, until 2030, low-income developing countries would face an annual investment need of about 10 percentage points of GDP, more than two times the current median capital spending of 4.6 percent of GDP. Governments will need to explore policy options for financing the increased spending. Efforts to improve public investment efficiency could affect the size of these spending needs. For example, the authors estimate that improvements in efficiency could reduce annual spending needs by over 1 percentage point of GDP for low-income developing countries. Hence, in addition to exploring financing options, improving public investment efficiency will be crucial to reach the infrastructure-related SDGs.

Part I ends with a presentation of the PIMA framework in Chapter 5, where Taz Chaponda, Chishiro Matsumoto, and Lewis Kabayiza Murara examine the importance of strong infrastructure governance for quality infrastructure investment. They discuss lessons learned from the over 50 PIMAs carried out between 2015 and mid-2019. The chapter shows that all countries, but most notably emerging markets and low-income developing countries, have significant room to improve their infrastructure governance to increase effectiveness in public investment. It argues that large gains can be made by enhancing reforms of the institutions with roles specific to public investment, particularly at the allocation and implementation stages. Whereas countries tend to score better on more general public financial management institutions, such as budget comprehensiveness and availability of funding, they fall short on project appraisal and project selection (early in the public investment cycle), and on monitoring and accounting for assets (later in the cycle). Moreover, infrastructure governance institutions tend to look better on paper than in practice, where gaps in what they can achieve become particularly evident at the implementation stage. This points to the critical importance of having institutions (for example, project selection processes) that are both well designed and function well in practice.

## *Fiscal Policy for Quality Infrastructure Investment*

There is evidence that public investment spending is often cut during episodes of fiscal consolidation, notwithstanding the long and lasting growth benefits attributed to public investment (Chapter 2). In Chapter 6, Tannous Kass-Hanna, Kangni Kpodar, and Dawit Tessema investigate the growth dividends of shifting the composition of government spending toward more public investment during periods of consolidation. The findings suggest that protecting investment spending during fiscal consolidation, although contractionary in the short term, boosts medium- to long-term growth, and so leads to a more sustained reduction in budget deficits. This result, which also holds during good times, underscores the importance of public investment for growth, particularly in countries where initial public investment spending in total government expenditure is low.

In Chapter 7, Olivier Basdevant, Taz Chaponda, Fabien Gonguet, Jiro Honda, and Saji Thomas explore the potential impact of fiscal rules—permanent numerical constraints on fiscal aggregates—on public investment. While fiscal rules may disproportionately affect public investment relative to current spending during fiscal adjustment, the chapter finds that countries with high efficiency in public investment are better at protecting public investment from spending cuts. Therefore, strengthening infrastructure governance can help countries reconcile the fiscal sustainability concerns reflected in their general fiscal rules with the protection of public investment. The chapter also argues that numerical rules can be designed to help countries avoid making undesirable cuts in public investment, especially when the rules are supported by sound public financial management practices, including adequate procedural rules.

Ha Vu, Olivier Bizimana, and Masahiro Nozaki examine public investment needs in emerging and developing Asia in Chapter 8. They assess the need to scale up infrastructure investment in the region and how to deliver it. They first emphasize why emerging and developing Asia would need more and better investment spending to improve infrastructure outcomes and reach the SDGs. They find that financing additional infrastructure spending with higher indirect taxes would be desirable in the long term, particularly in view of the growth-debt trade-off. They also suggest that public investment efficiency in the region needs to be improved to obtain more and better-quality infrastructure for every unit of money spent on infrastructure investment. Countries in emerging and developing Asia should focus reform efforts on their weakest and most critical practices of public investment management, the authors conclude.

Frequencies and levels of damage from natural disasters are expected to rise with climate change, leaving many countries, especially small states, highly vulnerable. Natural disasters destroy lives and livelihoods and also have significant adverse macroeconomic impacts in terms of lower growth and higher debt. They are associated with large recovery costs as significant amounts of public and private infrastructures have to be rebuilt after a disaster. In Chapter 9, Wei Guo and Saad Quayyum explore whether a significant amount of the damages and associated output losses could be avoided by investing in resilient infrastructure. They find that policymakers can save in net present value terms by investing in resilience and avoiding large rebuilding costs. By changing the pattern of support toward building the resilience for infrastructure to withstand damage, countries that are vulnerable to natural disasters can improve investment outcomes, with lower outlays on recovery efforts in the long term. The findings underscore the importance of mobilizing more resources toward building resilience. Given limited fiscal space, not only will countries need to mobilize domestic revenue and prioritize spending but also to spend better and increase the efficiency of capital spending. The international community can play an important supportive role.

## Building Strong Public Investment Institutions

Public investment is particularly vulnerable to corrupt behavior, which may take many forms, including small bribes, kickbacks, collusion, embezzlement, influence peddling, or unlawful beneficial ownership. Sailendra Pattanayak and Concha Verdugo-Yepes demonstrate in Chapter 10 that corruption can occur at any phase of the investment cycle, inflicting different economic costs and requiring different mitigation strategies. They propose a strategy for effectively mitigating corruption risks along the infrastructure cycle that includes a proactive approach to corruption risk management; clear delineation of decision-making authority without conflict of interest; transparent frameworks and criteria for taking infrastructure decisions; effective arrangements to enforce accountability for the decisions taken; a framework for transparent disclosure of relevant information at all key stages; and promotion of integrity in the transactions of private firms/actors involved in public infrastructure. The chapter also identifies specific indicators and "red flags" to improve the detection and sanctioning of corrupt acts, and to alert policymakers and citizens to potential corruption risks.

Public infrastructure projects are typically large and complex, with long planning, implementation, and operational periods, and therefore inherently exposed to uncertainties and risks. Yet, uncertainties and risks receive moderate attention during major investment decisions. Rui Monteiro, Isabel Rial, and Eivind Tandberg demonstrate in Chapter 11 that better risk-management practices can improve outcomes in public infrastructure projects. They review the main sources of risks affecting public infrastructure projects over their entire life cycle and find that a large source of fiscal risk lies in decisions or actions taken by the government, such as inadequate project design, costing techniques, and risk-sharing arrangements. The authors also discuss good practices for assessing, quantifying, and managing risks. They find that all countries have room for strengthening their infrastructure governance frameworks by gradually incorporating a risk-management function.

In Chapter 12, Richard Allen, Mary Betley, Carolina Renteria, and Ashni Singh explore the key role of efficient and well-integrated planning and budgeting functions for building quality infrastructure. The chapter analyzes the evolution and integration of these two key functions of government, considers possible mechanisms to better integrate them, and discusses how they should be organized. The chapter argues that most countries, both advanced and developing, are still struggling to find efficient mechanisms to link their medium- and long-term infrastructure plans within a sustainable fiscal framework. Moreover, establishing planning and budgeting functions that are efficient and effective is much more important than the organizational form of these functions, for which solutions are country dependent. Finally, centralized agencies play a useful role in the strategic planning of infrastructure and mitigating the influence of political factors and the electoral cycle on infrastructure investment.

In Chapter 13, Robert Taliercio and Eduardo Andrés Estrada discuss the key roles that project appraisal and project selection play within the planning and allocation stages of public investment and explore good practice in institutional design of these functions. The authors find that a clear, well-supported appraisal methodology and published project selection criteria, with well-defined processes for project selection, are critical for good infrastructure governance. Undue political influence is an issue in many countries and should be mitigated through rigorous analysis, central ministry scrutiny using clear and transparent procedures, and an independent review of projects before their inclusion in the budget. In low-capacity countries, outsourcing of project appraisal could be considered but should be balanced with the need for in-house capacity building and the development of practical know-how.

Achieving better infrastructure outcomes requires countries to both maintain their assets and manage their overall asset portfolio. Andrew Blazey, Fabien Gonguet, and Philip Stokoe address the little-researched topic of maintaining and managing infrastructure assets in Chapter 14. Based on country examples and empirical evidence, they find that benefits are associated with maintaining and renovating assets, including longer asset life spans, reduced fiscal costs in the medium and long terms, and economic and social benefits for users. The authors also explore a variety of tested mechanisms that can properly provide resources for the maintenance of infrastructure assets. The success of these mechanisms relies on the ability of governments to assess the maintenance needs of an asset from the very beginning, to review its performance regularly, and to adjust actual maintenance spending on a timely basis.

The final chapter of the book goes back to the growing economic and fiscal liabilities that result from the frequency and severity of climate-related extreme weather events. In Chapter 15, Tuan Minh Le, Wei-Jen Leow, and Fabian Seiderer propose an approach that governments could use to adapt their infrastructure governance frameworks to strengthen climate resilience in major stages of public investment management, such as project planning, design, appraisal, selection, and financing. On that basis, they propose that the PIMA framework can be adapted to tackle some relevant climate-change issues. They highlight three key points: first, to avoid overwhelming already-stretched public investment institutions, a focused approach is recommended to assessing and mitigating the most severe climate risks and impacts on major investments; second, upgrading a national public investment system to factor in and mitigate growing climate risks requires a sequenced but holistic approach that includes regulatory, institutional, and operational reforms and provides adequate capacity building; and third, greater institutional cooperation is one of the major preconditions for a functional climate-sensitive public investment management framework.

## REFERENCES

American Society of Civil Engineers. 2017. "Failure to Act: Closing the Infrastructure Investment Gap for America's Economic Future." Reston, VA: American Society of Civil Engineers.

BenYishay, Ariel, and Rebecca Tunstall. 2011. "Impact Evaluation of Infrastructure Investments: The Experience of the Millennium Challenge Corporation." *Journal of Development Effectiveness* 3 (1): 103–30.

Bova, Elva, Marta Ruiz-Aranz, Frederick Toscani, and H. Elif Ture. 2016. "The Fiscal Costs of Contingent Liabilities: A New Dataset." IMF Working Paper 16/14, International Monetary Fund, Washington, DC.

Flyvbjerg, Bent. 2009. "Survival of the Unfittest: Why the Worst Infrastructure Gets Built—And What We Can Do About It." *Oxford Review of Economic Policy* 25 (3): 344–67.

Freeman, Matthew C., Meredith E. Stocks, Oliver Cumming, Aurielie Jeandron, Julian P. T. Higgins, Jennyfer Wolf, Annette Prüss-Ustün, and others. 2014. "Hygiene and Health: Systematic Review of Handwashing Practices Worldwide and Update of Health Effects." *Journal of Tropical Medicine and International Health* 19 (8): 906–16.

Gómez-Lobo, Andrés. 2012. "Institutional Safeguards for Cost Benefit Analysis: Lessons from the Chilean National Investment System." *Journal of Benefit-Cost Analysis* 3 (1): 1–30.

Group of Seven (G7). 2016. "G7 Ise-Shima Principles for Promoting Quality Infrastructure Investment." G7 Ise-Shima Leaders' Declaration, May 27.

Group of Twenty (G20). 2019. "G20 Principles for Quality Infrastructure Investment." G20 Osaka Leaders' Declaration, June 29.

International Monetary Fund (IMF). 2014. *World Economic Outlook: Legacies, Clouds, Uncertainties.* Washington, DC, October.

IMF. 2015. *Making Public Investment More Efficient*. Washington, DC.

IMF. 2018a. *Fiscal Monitor: Capitalizing on Good Times*, April. Washington, DC.

IMF. 2018b. Public Investment Management Assessment—Review and Update. Washington, DC.

IMF. Forthcoming. "Macroeconomic Developments and Prospects in Low-Income Developing Countries." IMF Policy Paper, Washington, DC.

2020a. "The Great Lockdown." *World Economic Outlook*, April. Washington, DC.

________. 2020b. "Policies to Support People During the COIVD-19 Pandemic." *Fiscal Monitor*, April. Washington, DC

Mbaye, Samba, Marialuz Moreno Badia, and Kyungla Chae. 2018. "Global Debt Database: Methodology and Sources." IMF Working Paper 19/11, International Monetary Fund, Washington, DC.

Organisation for Economic Co-operation and Development (OECD). 2017. *Getting Infrastructure Right: A Framework for Better Governance*. OECD, Paris.

OECD. 2019. "Growth Is Taking a Dangerous Downward Turn." Ecoscope Blog, September 19. https://oecdecoscope.blog/2019/09/19/growth-is-taking-a-dangerous-downward-turn/.

Rajaram, Anand, Kai Kaiser, Tuan Minh Le, Jay-Hyung Kim, and Jonas Frank. 2014. *The Power of Public Investment Management: Transforming Resources into Assets for Growth*. World Bank, Washington, DC.

Wolf, Jennyfer, Anette Prüss-Ustün, Oliver Cumming, Jamie Bartram, Sophie Bonjour, Sandy Cairncross, and others. 2014. "Assessing the Impact of Drinking Water and Sanitation on Diarrhoeal Disease in Low- and Middle-Income Settings: Systematic Review and Meta-Regression." *Journal of Tropical Medicine and International Health* 19 (8): 928–42.

World Bank. 2006. *Appraisal of Public Investment: Chile*. Washington, DC: World Bank.

World Health Organization. 2016. "Preventing Disease through Health Environments: A Global Assessment of the Burden of Disease from Environmental Risks." World Health Organization, Switzerland.

# PART I

# Infrastructure, Growth, and Development

CHAPTER 2

# Growth Impact of Public Investment and the Role of Infrastructure Governance

Hiroaki Miyamoto, Anja Baum, Nikolay Gueorguiev, Jiro Honda, and Sébastien Walker

## INTRODUCTION

According to macroeconomic theory, public investment stimulates economic activity through short-term effects on aggregate demand, and it raises the productivity of existing private capital (physical and human). Public investment also encourages new private investment to take advantage of the higher productivity it creates, increasing economic growth (Barro 1990; Barro and Sala-i-Martin 1992; Futagami, Morita, and Shibata 1993; Glomm and Ravikumar 1994; Turnovsky 1997). However, the positive relationship between public investment and growth could turn negative once public capital exceeds a certain threshold, as the burden resulting from financing public capital provision adversely affects economic growth (Barro 1990) or public investment crowds out private investment (Aschauer 1989; Fosu, Getachew, and Ziesemer 2016).

Public investment affects economic growth through two main channels: (1) efficiency (how much a given amount of public investment provides in terms of physical infrastructure) and (2) productivity (how the created physical infrastructure affects the economy).[1]

- *Efficiency*: Not all public investment translates into the same amount of physical infrastructure, meaning that public investment efficiency varies across countries. Many countries receive less value for money than they would have if resources were used more efficiently (see Chapter 3 for more details).
- *Productivity*: Not all new physical infrastructure has the same productive impact on the economy. Even when physical infrastructure is accumulated, its productivity can be eroded by poor project selection and if the created

The authors are grateful to Devin D'Angelo and Clay Hackney for their research assistance.

[1] See, for example, Mandl, Dierx, and Ilzkovitz (2008) for a discussion on the different channels of public investment.

infrastructure contributes little to growth. Good infrastructure governance may lead to better infrastructure quality, with greater beneficial effects (see Chapter 5 for details).

The empirical literature, however, is divided on the significance of the long-term relationship between public investment and economic growth. Aschauer (1989) found that public investment has a strong positive impact on output for the United States. Subsequent studies have shown a positive association between public investment and economic growth but with a smaller magnitude (for example, see Sturm and de Haan 1995). Recently, IMF (2014) and Abiad, Furceri, and Topalova (2016) found a short- and long-term positive and significant effect of public investment on output for advanced economies. For low-income developing countries, Furceri and Li (2017) found a positive effect of public investment on output in the short and medium terms. In contrast, Sturm, Jacobs, and Groote (1999) found a positive and significant short-term effect of public investment on output but did not find any long-term effects. Looking at large public investment boom episodes, Warner (2014, 62) found "very little" evidence supporting the idea that public capital can promote growth beyond the short-term demand effect.

Better infrastructure governance—in other words, stronger institutions to manage public investments—is likely to strengthen the connection between public investment and growth, as broadly supported by empirical findings. Gupta and others (2014) showed that an efficiency-adjusted public capital stock makes a positive and significant contribution to economic growth. IMF (2015) pointed out that countries with stronger infrastructure governance institutions tend to have lower average incremental public-capital-to-output ratios and therefore receive more growth "bang" for their investment "buck"; it also found that countries with higher public investment efficiency receive greater output dividends from public investment.

In contrast, weak infrastructure governance could lead to higher public debt without a growth dividend. Governance problems in project execution may reduce the amount of public capital generated by a unit of public investment, whereas a deficient project selection process could lead to the construction of "white elephants" with minimal contribution to economic activity.[2] More generally, a strong cost-benefit analysis is needed to select and prioritize projects that would meaningfully raise growth without jeopardizing fiscal sustainability.

This chapter analyzes the macroeconomic impact of public investment and explores how the relationships among public investment, economic activity, and fiscal indicators are modified by the strength of a country's infrastructure governance. Stylized facts for public investment and the public capital stock across countries are presented first, followed by an examination of how the strength of a country's infrastructure governance affects the macroeconomic effects of public investment. How the different stages of public investment management affect economic activity is also assessed.

---

[2] The term "white elephant" defines a project for which the cost, particularly that of maintenance, is out of proportion in comparison with its usefulness.

The analysis finds that the strength of a country's infrastructure governance plays a critical role in determining the macroeconomic effects of public investment. Countries with better governance enjoy positive output effects from public investment that countries with weaker governance do not. Regarding public investment management, the planning and implementation stages are important for improving the impact of public investment on economic growth.

## RECENT DEVELOPMENTS OF PUBLIC INVESTMENT

Public-investment-to-GDP ratios across countries differ by income groups.[3] In advanced economies, public investment has steadily declined from an average of 2.4 percent of GDP in the 1990s to a historic low of less than 2 percent after 2010. In low-income developing countries, public investment as a percentage of GDP has been generally increasing since the mid-1990s, at 7 percent in 2018. Emerging market investment levels have historically alternated between 5 and 7 percent of GDP on average (Figure 2.1).

There are equally large differences in the stock of physical infrastructure across country groups (Figure 2.2). The two presented infrastructure indicators (kilometers of roads per capita and electricity consumption) show that both emerging markets and low-income developing countries significantly trail advanced economies in

**Figure 2.1. Trends in Public Investment, 1991–2018**
*(Percent of GDP, simple average of each country group)*

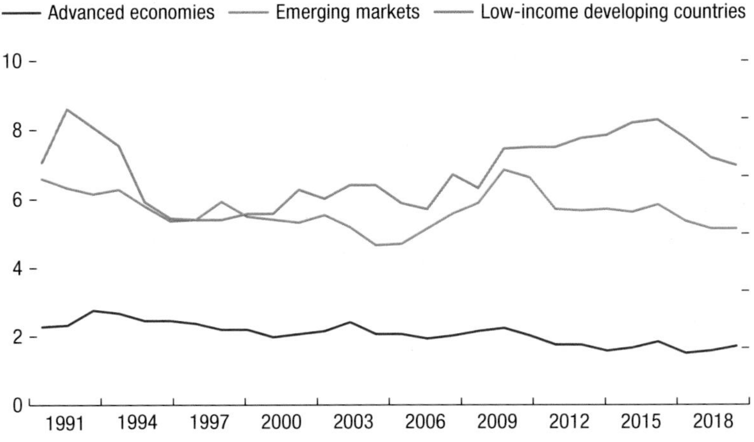


Sources: World Economic Outlook database; and IMF staff estimates.

[3] "Public investment" refers to general government new acquisition of nonfinancial assets as a share of GDP.

**Figure 2.2. Physical Infrastructure, by Income Group, 1990–2016**

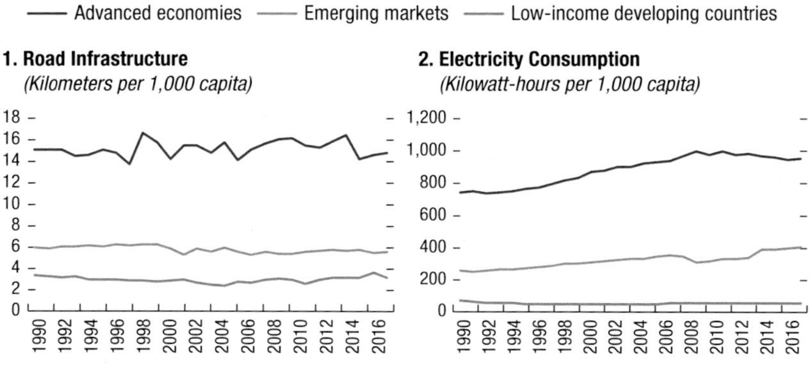

— Advanced economies — Emerging markets — Low-income developing countries

**1. Road Infrastructure**
*(Kilometers per 1,000 capita)*

**2. Electricity Consumption**
*(Kilowatt-hours per 1,000 capita)*

Source: World Development Indicators.

infrastructure provision, despite a consistently larger public-investment-to-GDP ratio. Kilometers of roads per capita have been almost stagnant in all three income groups since 1990, with per capita road stocks of emerging markets and low-income developing countries at a level less than one-third that of advanced economies (Figure 2.2, panel 1). Electricity consumption has equally stagnated at a very low level in low-income developing countries, whereas consumption in advanced economies reached its peak around 2008, and emerging economies continue to increase their consumption (Figure 2.2, panel 2).

Large differences across countries also persist in the quality of infrastructure. Survey-based measures of infrastructure quality, which reflect subjective judgments about the quality of overall infrastructure, suggest that the recent ramping up of public investment in emerging economies and low-income developing countries has helped reduce the perceived disparity in infrastructure across countries.[4] However, these measures also indicate a slight fall in infrastructure quality since the peak in the early 2010s, especially in advanced economies and emerging economies, which may have resulted from the recent fall in investment-to-GDP ratios in those country groups (Figure 2.3, panel 1). Large and persistent disparities between higher- and lower-income countries remain within the coverage of economic infrastructure, such as roads and electricity networks (Figure 2.3, panel 2).

Large differences by income groups (and more among countries) point to the importance of raising the efficiency and productivity of public investment, particularly for those with insufficient and low-quality infrastructure. With more efficient and productive public investment, countries would achieve higher growth while increasing the amount and quality of infrastructure. The next sections analyze the role that public investment management can play in achieving these goals.

[4] The "overall quality of infrastructure" indicator from the World Economic Forum's Global Competitiveness Index data set is used in this analysis. The indicator assesses general infrastructure such as for transport, communications, and energy.

**Figure 2.3. Indicators of Infrastructure Quality and Access**

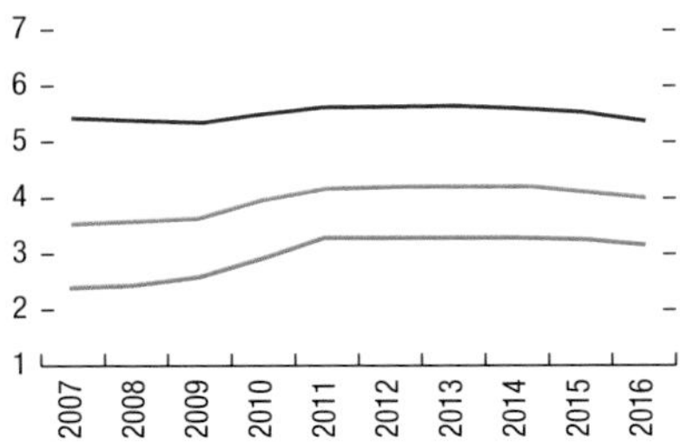


Source: World Economic Forum 2017.
Note: This panel shows the perceived quality of overall infrastructure with the question, "How do you assess the general state of infrastructure (for example, transport, communications, and energy) in your country?" rated from 1 ("extremely underdeveloped—among the worst in the world") to 7 ("extensive and efficient—among the best in the world").

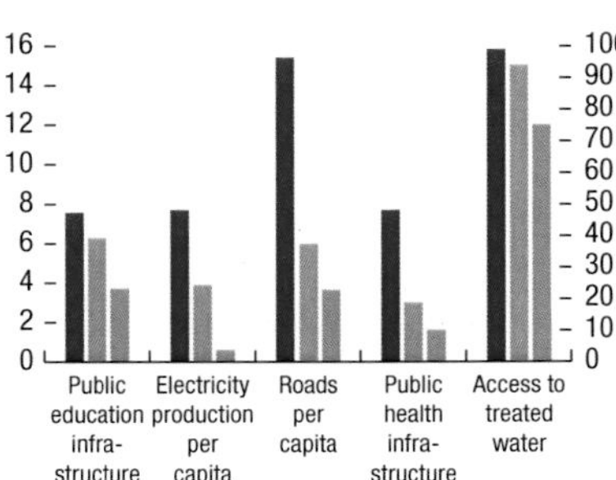


Source: World Development Indicators 2017.
Note: Units vary to fit scale. Left scale: public education infrastructure is measured as secondary teachers per 1,000 persons; electricity production per capita as thousands of kilowatt-hours per person; roads per capita as kilometers per 1,000 persons; and public health infrastructure as hospital beds per 1,000 persons. Right scale: access to treated water is measured as a percentage of the population.

## PUBLIC INVESTMENT, ECONOMIC GROWTH, AND INFRASTRUCTURE GOVERNANCE

This section examines the macroeconomic effects of public investment, controlling for the strength of infrastructure governance in an estimation using the local projection method and public investment forecast errors. Similar to IMF (2014), it examines the impact of public investment shocks—defined as unexpected changes in public investment—on growth, public debt, and private investment by country income groups. It then assesses how the strength of infrastructure governance affects this impact. Our analysis extends the literature on the macroeconomic effects of public investment (IMF 2014; Furceri and Li 2017) in several dimensions, including by examining the macroeconomic effects of public investment shocks in low-income developing countries and adding the influence of countries' infrastructure governance systems, which modifies the baseline results considerably.

### Baseline Results

As a baseline, the examination looks at the macroeconomic effects of public investment shocks by country income groups, without controlling for the strength of countries' infrastructure governance. This chapter focuses on shocks to disentangle the effect of higher public investment itself from the effect of expectations of higher public investment, which generate their own effects. This provides a benchmark for the subsequent exploration of the role of infrastructure governance.

### *Advanced Economies*[5]

Positive public investment shocks raise output (Figure 2.4). A positive public investment shock of 1 percentage point of GDP is associated with an increase in output of about 0.2 percent in the same year and 1.2 percent four years after the shock. This result is in line with other estimates of the public investment multiplier (in, for example, Batini, Eyraud, and Weber 2014). Moreover, public investment shocks have long-lasting effects on output, in line with the hypothesis that an increase in public investment boosts the productive capacity of the economy.

Public debt and private investment, however, are not significantly affected. Higher public investment is not associated with a significant increase in the debt-to-GDP ratio, stemming from two effects: (1) higher investment may not have a significant impact on the government's overall budget, as at least part of the increased spending may be offset by higher revenue or cuts in other spending; and (2) output expands in reaction to the investment shock, as has been noted.[6] Private investment as a share of GDP does not respond to the public investment shock either, as the expansion of output associated with positive public investment shocks outpaces the increase in private investment. This result suggests that higher public investment neither catalyzes nor crowds out private investment. These results are in line with IMF (2014).

### *Emerging Markets and Low-Income Developing Countries*

The impact of public investment shocks on output differs between emerging markets and low-income developing countries (Figure 2.4). In emerging markets, positive public investment shocks increase output in both the short and medium terms. An unanticipated positive public investment shock of 1 percentage point of GDP increases output by about 0.2 percent in the same year and 0.5 percent four years after the shock. This finding is consistent with results in the literature (for example, Furceri and Li 2017). In contrast, the effect of the public investment shock on output is short-lived and weak in low-income developing countries. On impact, output increases by 0.1 percent.[7]

As in advanced economies, there is no statistically significant effect on public debt and private investment, and higher public investment is not associated

[5] When the full sample (advanced economies, emerging markets, and low-income developing countries) is used, the impacts of public investment shocks on the economy are not clear. This is likely due to heterogeneity in macroeconomic impacts of public investment shocks across country income groups.

[6] Although not presented here, the response of the fiscal balance to the positive public investment shock is not statistically significant.

[7] The analysis in Chapter 6 finds that changes in the composition of spending toward greater public investment generally produce strong growth dividends, while the lower the investment efficiency, the lower the expected fiscal multiplier of public investment.

**Figure 2.4. Responses to Unanticipated Public Investment Shocks**

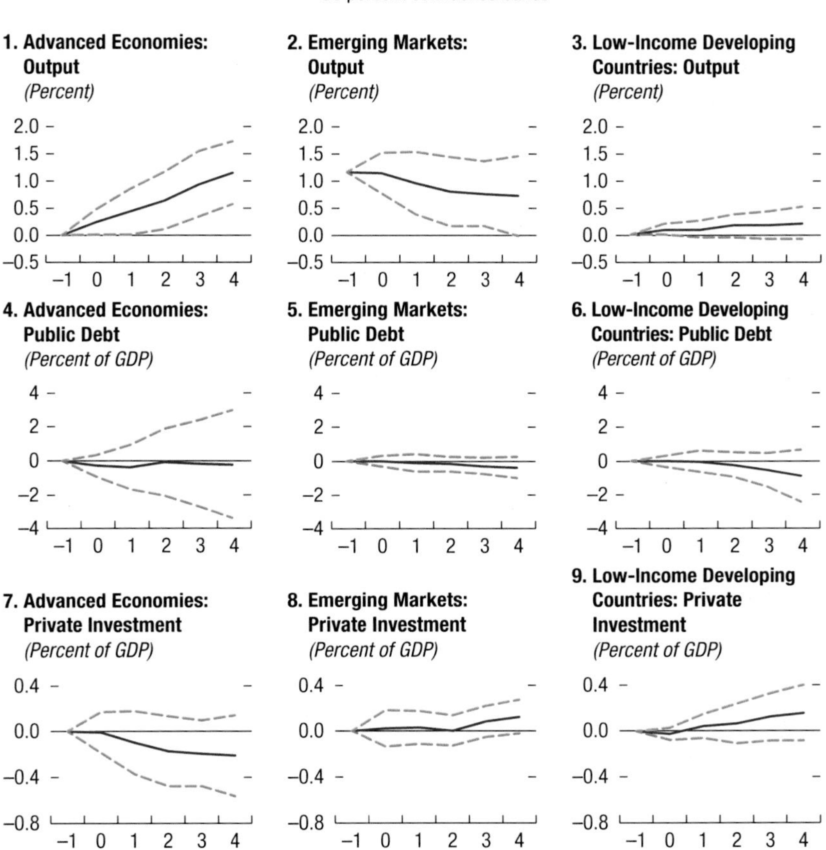


Source: IMF staff calculations.
Note: The x-axis indicates years after the shock at $t = 0$. Shock represents an increase of 1 percentage point of GDP in public investment spending. The sample consists of 107 countries (17 advanced economies, 39 emerging markets, and 51 low-income developing countries).

with an increase in the debt-to-GDP ratio. The results for emerging markets could be understood in the same way as for advanced economies. Because of the higher output associated with the positive public investment shock and the effort to offset part of the investment increase on the deficit, the debt-to-GDP ratio does not increase significantly. For low-income developing countries, the large heterogeneity between countries produces large standard errors that may mask the impact of a public investment shock on public debt. As in advanced economies, private investment does not seem to respond to a public investment shock in both emerging markets and low-income developing countries.

## The Role of Infrastructure Governance

Governance of the public investment process affects the macroeconomic effects of public investment in different ways. As noted, recent studies have indicated that the strength of a country's infrastructure governance plays an important role in determining the connection between public investment and growth (Gupta and others 2014; IMF 2015). A clear picture of how the public investment management process modifies the macroeconomic effects of public investment is warranted to assess the benefits and costs of public investment. The IMF's Public Investment Management Assessment (PIMA) is used for this, measuring the strength of countries' infrastructure governance in emerging markets and low-income developing countries.[8] The PIMA was developed by the IMF to help countries evaluate the strength of their public investment management practices. Because PIMAs have so far been conducted mainly in emerging markets and low-income developing countries, insufficient observations are available for advanced economies in the analyses here. Thus, the World Bank's government effectiveness indicator is used for advanced economies, because of its high correlation with the PIMA for countries where both are available (for details, see Annex 2.1).

Stronger governance in advanced economies results in positive public investment shocks generating better macroeconomic outcomes (Figure 2.5). The analysis shows that in countries with stronger governance, a positive investment shock of 1 percentage point of GDP increases output by about 0.8 percent in the same year, and by 3.2 percent in the medium term.[9] In contrast, in countries with weaker governance, the response of output is, if anything, negative and marginally statistically insignificant. As for public debt, although public investment shocks reduce the debt-to-GDP ratio in countries with stronger infrastructure governance, they increase public debt in countries with weaker governance. The difference in public debt responses between countries with stronger and weaker governance likely reflects differences in responses of the fiscal balance and output. In countries with stronger governance, higher public investment may be accommodated within available resources without significantly affecting the fiscal balance. Furthermore, the higher output associated with a shock reinforces the decline in the debt-to-GDP ratio. Last, in response to an investment shock, private investment tends to increase in countries with stronger governance (possibly through crowding in private investment by improving the productive capacity of the economy), and it declines in countries where governance is weaker. These results are stronger and more significant than the baseline that was shown in Figure 2.4, underscoring the importance of quality

---

[8] See Chapter 5 for more details.

[9] Stronger (weaker) governance is defined based on the value of $z$ in the transition function between governance regimes. If $z$ has a large positive (negative) value, the country is considered to have stronger (weaker) governance (see Annex 2.1).

**Figure 2.5. Effects of Public Investment Shocks in Advanced Economies: The Role of Infrastructure Governance**

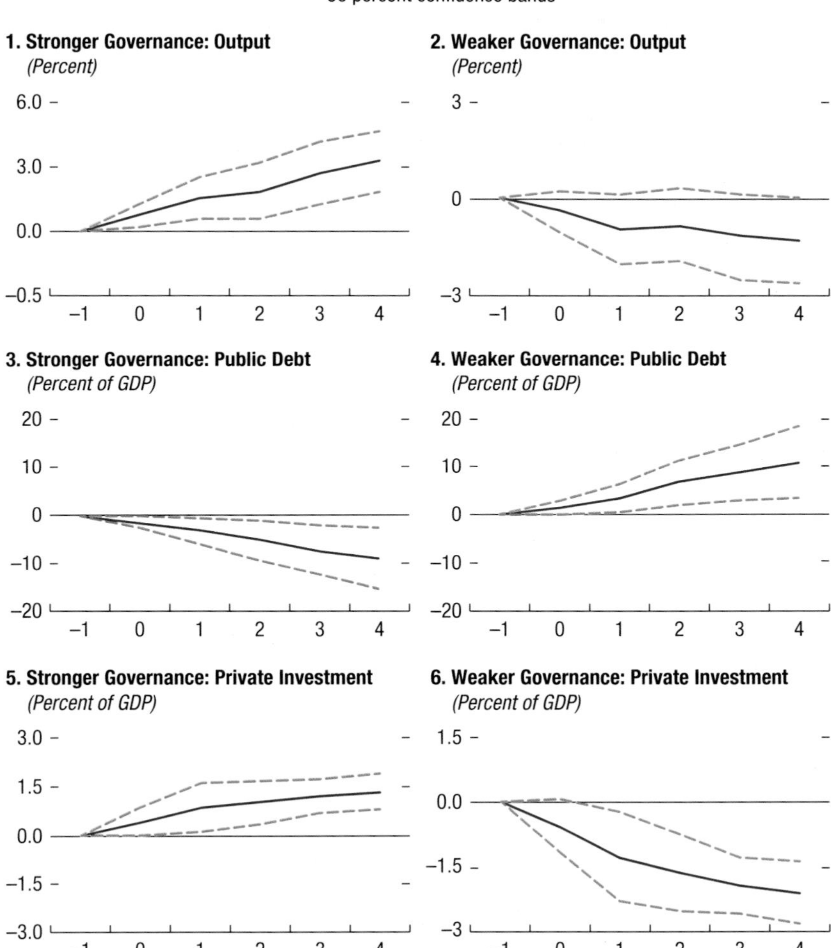


Source: IMF staff calculations.
Note: The x-axis indicates years after the shock, and $t = 0$ represents the year of the shock. Shock represents an increase of 1 percentage point of GDP in public investment spending. The sample size is 507, and the number of countries is 17. Stronger (weaker) governance is defined based on the value of $z$ in the transition function between governance regimes (see Annex 2.1).

infrastructure governance systems for public investment to deliver positive economic outcomes.

The strength of infrastructure governance also matters for the impact of public investment on output in emerging economies and low-income developing countries (Figure 2.6). The results using PIMA show that in countries with stronger

**Figure 2.6. Effects of Public Investment Shocks in Emerging Markets and Low-Income Developing Countries: The Role of Infrastructure Governance**

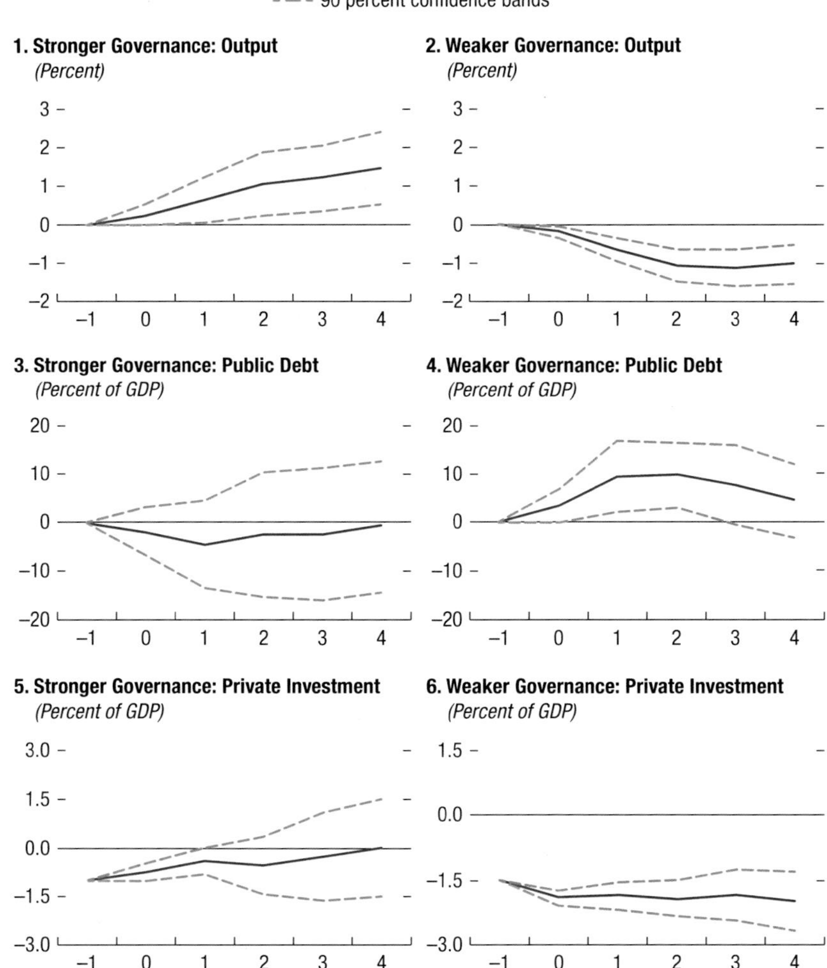


Source: IMF staff calculations.

Note: The x-axis indicates years after the shock, and $t = 0$ represents the year of the shock. Shock represents an increase of 1 percentage point of GDP in public investment spending. The sample size is 792, and the number of countries is 44. Stronger (weaker) governance is defined based on the value of $z$ in the transition function between governance regimes (see Annex 2.1).

governance, positive public investment shocks generate better macroeconomic outcomes. The positive impacts on growth and private investment are larger and debt-to-GDP ratios are not increased. In contrast, output and private investment tend to decline, and public debt tends to rise, in response to an increase in public investment in countries with weaker governance, possibly suggesting problems with project selection and costing, and with the crowding out of private investment.

**Figure 2.7. Effects of Public Investment Shocks on Output**

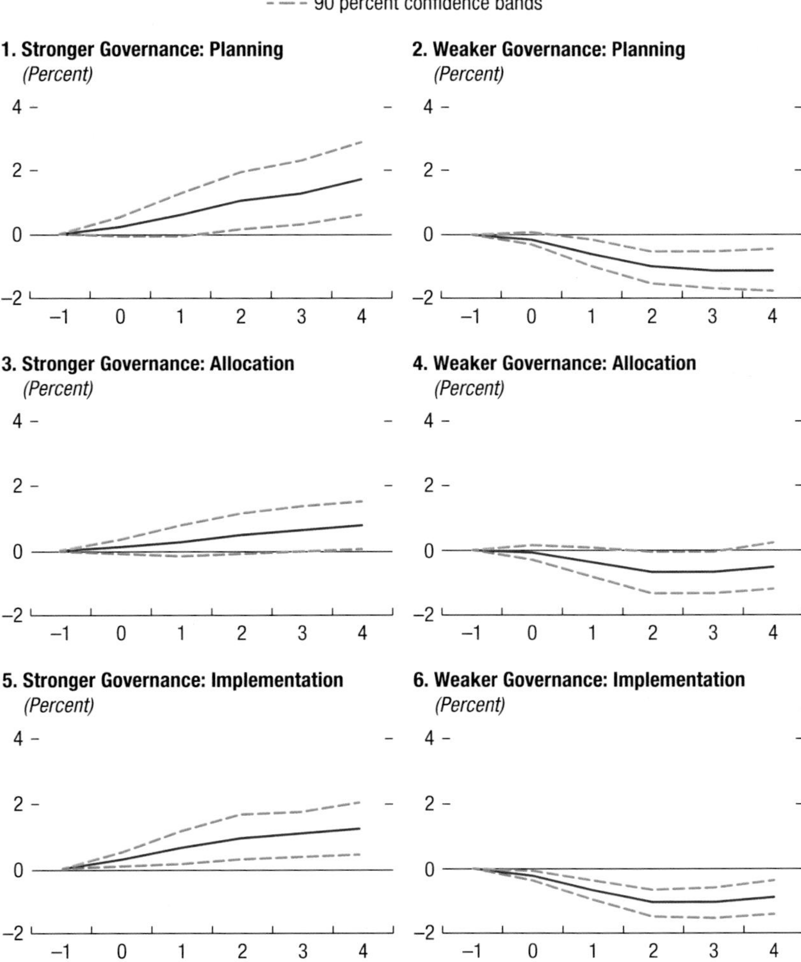


Source: IMF staff calculations.
Note: The x-axis indicates years after the shock, and $t = 0$ represents the year of the shock. Shock represents an increase of 1 percentage point of GDP in public investment spending. The sample size is 792, and the number of countries is 44. Stronger (weaker) governance is defined based on the value of $z$ in the transition function between governance regime (see Annex 2.1).

### Stages of the Public Investment Management Process

The analysis has indicated the important role of infrastructure governance. Next, the investigation turns to how each stage of the public investment management process affects the growth impact of public investment. Using the three PIMA subindicators for each of the three stages of the public investment cycle (planning, allocation, and implementation), further inquiry looks at how the strength of public investment management at each stage of the process affects the growth impact of public investment shocks.

The findings suggest that all three stages are important for the growth impact of public investment (Figure 2.7). At each stage, countries with stronger governance enjoy a positive output effect from public investment; in countries with weaker governance, the output responses are either not statistically significant or negative. This result is important and reasonable, as the three stages are an integral part of the public investment cycle and so interact with each other. A chain is only as strong as its weakest link. Take, for example, where deficiencies in planning affect the allocation and implementation stages of projects. Amid efficient planning, deficiencies in allocation and implementation would also limit the delivery and impact of infrastructure.

## CONCLUSIONS

The strength of infrastructure governance plays a critical role in determining the macroeconomic effects of public investment. Countries with stronger governance achieve a stronger output impact of public investment than do countries with weaker governance. Stronger infrastructure governance helps public investment yield a higher growth dividend by improving investment efficiency and productivity, and it stimulates private sector investment. In contrast, in countries with weak infrastructure governance, crowding out of private investment, higher debt-to-GDP ratios, and significant waste of public money can lead to a negative impact on output even after public investment has been increased.

Public investment supports growth without raising public debt in countries with stronger infrastructure governance. In those countries, increased public investment leads to higher output, in turn raising revenue performance and offsetting some of the deficit increase. In countries with weaker governance, however, the public investment shock is more likely to increase the debt-to GDP ratio—reflecting a weak growth impact of public investment. The analysis in this chapter also finds that private investment tends to increase in countries with stronger governance and decline in countries with weaker governance.

To ensure a positive growth impact of public investment, strengthening each process of public investment management is essential. Separating public investment processes into the three stages (planning, allocation, and implementation), the findings show that all three stages affect the output effects of public investment shocks.

The study draws out two main policy implications. First, countries could significantly improve the growth impact of public investment by strengthening their infrastructure governance. Good infrastructure governance allows public investment to raise output without jeopardizing fiscal sustainability. Second, unless countries with weaker infrastructure governance and investment management improve their institutions and processes before increasing public investment, they risk wasting much of the growth benefit.

## ANNEX 2.1. EMPIRICAL APPROACH

Public investment shocks are identified by using the approach of Auerbach and Gorodnichenko (2012, 2013). In this approach, public investment shocks are identified as forecast errors of public investment. Thus,

$$Shock_{i,t} = PI_{i,t} - PI^{E}_{i,t},$$

where $PI_{i,t}$ is the actual public investment spending as a share of GDP of country $i$ in year $t$, and $PI^{E}_{i,t}$ is the forecast of the public investment spending.[10] Forecasts are taken from the fall issue of the Organisation for Economic Co-operation and Development *Economic Outlook* and October publications of the IMF's *World Economic Outlook* (WEO) for the same year over the period 1985–2017. Because of data limitations, forecasts for advanced economies are taken from the OECD's database, whereas WEO forecasts are used for emerging economies and low-income developing countries.[11] Other macroeconomic variables (real GDP, the debt-to-GDP ratio, and real private investment as a share of GDP) come from various issues of the WEO.

The identified public investment shocks are used to examine the macroeconomic effects of public investment with the local projection method of Jordà (2005):

$$y_{i,t+h} - y_{i,t-1} = \alpha^{h}_{i} + \gamma^{h}_{t} + \beta^{h} shock_{i,t} + \theta^{h} X_{i,t} + \varepsilon^{h}_{i,t} \quad (2.1.1)$$

where $y$ is log of the macroeconomic variable of interest (real GDP, the debt-to-GDP ratio, , and private investment as a share of GDP), $\alpha$ is the country fixed effect, $\gamma$ is the time fixed effect, *shock* is the identified public investment

[10] This methodology overcomes two typical empirical challenges. First, using forecast errors eliminates the "fiscal foresight" problem (for example, see Leeper, Richter, and Walker 2012; and Leeper, Walker, and Yang 2013) because it aligns the information sets of the economic agents with those of the econometricians (see IMF 2014 for details). Second, the forecast error mitigates the endogeneity problem that unanticipated economic conditions may affect the public investment shock. Given that October's forecast has already included information on public investment and economic performance in most of the current year, for endogeneity to be present, public investment should be changed within the same quarter when news on economic conditions is received. However, as Blanchard and Perotti (2002) argued, this is unlikely to occur.

[11] In issues of the *World Economic Outlook*, there are no forecasts of public investment for advanced economies during 2004–08 because of changes in the data aggregation method. As a robustness check, we use different forecasts (spring in the same year and fall in the previous year) and find that the results remain unchanged.

shock, and $X$ is a set of control variables.[12] We estimate equation (2.1.1) for each $h$=0, . . . , 4, where $h$=0 is the year of the public investment shock. We compute the impulse response functions of variables of interest with the estimated $\beta^h$. The confidence intervals associated with the impulse response functions are obtained by the estimated (clustered robust) standard errors of the coefficient $\beta^h$.

We further extend the analyses by allowing the response of the variable of interest to vary with public investment management quality within a regime-switching panel of the form:

$$\begin{aligned} y_{i,t+h} - y_{i,t-1} = {} & \alpha_i^h + \gamma_t^h + \beta_1^h G(z_{i,t})\, shock_{i,t} \\ & + \beta_2^h \left(1 - G(z_{i,t})\right) shock_{i,t} + \theta^h X_{i,t} + \varepsilon_{i,t}^h \end{aligned} \quad (2.1.2)$$

with

$$G(z_{i,t}) = \frac{\exp(-\delta z_{it})}{1 + \exp(-\delta z_{it})}, \quad \delta > 0$$

where $G(\cdot)$ is the transition function and $z$ is an indicator of public investment management, normalized to have zero mean and unit variance. As in IMF (2014), $\delta = 1$.[13] For the indicator $z$, either the PIMA score or the World Bank's government effectiveness indicator are used as measures of infrastructure governance quality. The PIMA score evaluates the strength of public investment management practices at three key stages of the public investment management cycle: planning, allocation, and implementation. To construct the overall PIMA score, 15 subindicators are averaged. However, the countries covered by PIMA are mainly emerging markets and low-income developing countries (with only a few advanced economies). The World Bank's government effectiveness indicator, which accounts for investment and public financial management, is used for advanced economies. This seems reasonable as PIMA and the World Bank's government effectiveness indicator are positively and statistically significantly correlated (correlation = 0.85 for countries where data are available for both indicators).[14]

## REFERENCES

Abiad, Abdul, Davide Furceri, and Petia Topalova. 2016. "The Macroeconomic Effects of Public Investment: Evidence from Advanced Economies." *Journal of Macroeconomics* 50: 224–40.

Aschauer, David Alan. 1989. "Does Public Capital Crowd Out Private Capital?" *Journal of Monetary Economics* 24 (2): 171–88.

[12] Although the local projection method is robust to omitted variables and misspecification (Jordà 2005), we assess the robustness of our results by estimating equation (2.1.1) with control variables including lags of the investment shock and lags of the growth rate of the dependent variable. The results remained qualitatively the same.

[13] The results remain qualitatively unchanged if we use an alternative value of 1.5, as in Furceri and Li (2017).

[14] Similar results are obtained when we use alternative proxies based on "government efficiency" from the World Economic Forum's *Global Competitiveness Report* 2005 through 2017.

Auerbach, Alan J., and Yuriy Gorodnichenko. 2012. "Measuring the Output Responses to Fiscal Policy." *American Economic Journal: Economic Policy* 4 (2): 1–27.

Auerbach, Alan J., and Yuriy Gorodnichenko. 2013. "Fiscal Multipliers in Recession and Expansion." In *Fiscal Policy after the Financial Crisis*, edited by Alberto Alesian and Francesco Giavazzi, 63–98. Chicago: University of Chicago Press.

Barro, Robert J. 1990. "Government Spending in a Simple Model of Endogenous Growth." *Journal of Political Economy* 95: 103–26.

Barro, Robert J., and Xavier Sala-i-Martin. 1992. "Public Finance in Models of Economic Growth." *Review of Economic Studies* 59 (4): 645–61.

Batini, Nicoletta, Luc Eyraud, and Anke Weber. 2014. "A Simple Method to Compute Fiscal Multipliers." IMF Working Paper 14/93, International Monetary Fund, Washington, DC.

Blanchard, Olivier J., and Roberto Perotti. 2002. "An Empirical Characterization of the Dynamic Effects of Changes in Government Spending and Taxes on Output." *Quarterly Journal of Economics* 117 (4): 1329–68.

Fosu, Augustin Kwasi, Yoseph Yilma Getachew, and Thomas Ziesemer. 2016. "Optimal Public Investment, Growth, and Consumption: Evidence from African Countries." *Macroeconomic Dynamics* 20 (8): 1957–86.

Furceri, Davide, and Bin Grace Li. 2017. "The Macroeconomic (and Distributional) Effects of Public Investment in Developing Economies." IMF Working Paper 17/217, International Monetary Fund, Washington, DC.

Futagami, Koichi, Yuichi Morita, and Akihisa Shibata. 1993. "Dynamic Analysis of an Endogenous Growth Model with Public Capital." *Scandinavian Journal of Economics* 95 (4): 607–25.

Glomm, Gerhard, and B. Ravikumar. 1994. "Public Investment in Infrastructure in a Simple Growth Model." *Journal of Economic Dynamics and Control* 18 (6): 1173–87.

Gupta, Sanjeev, Alvar Kangur, Chris Papageorgiou, and Abdoul Wane. 2014. "Efficiency-Adjusted Public Capital and Growth." *World Development* 57 (C): 164–78.

International Monetary Fund (IMF). 2014. *Fiscal Monitor: Public Expenditure Reform—Making Difficult Choices.* Washington, DC, April.

IMF. 2015. *Making Public Investment More Efficient.* Washington, DC. http://www.imf.org/external/np/pp/eng/2015/061115.pdf.

Jordà, Òscar. 2005. "Estimation and Inference of Impulse Responses by Local Projections." *American Economic Review* 95 (1): 161–82.

Leeper, Eric M., Alexander W. Richter, and Todd B. Walker. 2012. "Quantitative Effects of Fiscal Foresight." *American Economic Journal: Economic Policy* 4 (2): 115–44.

Leeper, Eric M., Todd B. Walker, and Shu-Chun Susan Yang. 2013. "Fiscal Foresight and Information Flows." *Econometrica* 81 (3): 1115–45.

Mandl, Ulrike, Adriaan Dierx, and Fabienne Ilzkovitz. 2008. "The Effectiveness and Efficiency of Public Spending." Economic Papers 301, European Economy, European Commission, Brussels.

Sturm, Jan-Egbert, and Jakob de Haan. 1995. "Is Public Expenditure Really Productive? New Evidence for the US and the Netherlands." *Economic Modelling* 12: 60–72.

Sturm, Jan-Egbert, Jan Jacobs, and Peter Groote. 1999. "Output Effects of Infrastructure Investment in the Netherlands, 1853–1913." *Journal of Macroeconomics* 21 (2): 355–80.

Turnovsky, Stephen J. 1997. "Fiscal Policy in a Growing Economy with Public Capital." *Macroeconomic Dynamics* 1 (3): 615–39.

Warner, Andrew M. 2014. "Public Investment as an Engine of Growth." IMF Working Paper 14/148, International Monetary Fund, Washington, DC. https://www.imf.org/external/pubs/ft/wp/2014/wp14148.pdf.

CHAPTER 3

# Getting the Most from Public Investment

Anja Baum, Tewodaj Mogues, and Geneviève Verdier

## INTRODUCTION

Examples of inefficient spending in infrastructure abound in all countries. In the United States, 11 miles of a subway tunnel lie abandoned under the streets of Cincinnati. Residents approved the subway in 1916, but cost overruns meant that it was never completed. Its bond issue was paid off in 1966—at twice the cost of the project, with interest.[1] In Italy, Rome's Vigna Clara railway station, built at a cost of $50 million to transport fans to soccer matches for the 1990 World Cup, was used only for two weeks and shut down in 1993.[2] Williams (2017), analyzing a database of 14,000 development projects in Ghana, found that one-third of projects that start are never completed, wasting on average one-fifth of local government investment. In a sample of Nigerian federal government social sector projects, Rasul and Rogger (2016) found that a quarter were not completed.[3] These are but a few instances of public spending that is not fully reflected in a greater stock of infrastructure assets or improvements in the delivery of public services.

Countries will need to reap the full benefit of their spending to achieve their growth and development goals. Substantial evidence shows that public investment in infrastructure can significantly contribute to economic growth and improve other development outcomes, including those of the Sustainable Development Goals (see Chapter 2 on the investment-growth nexus and Chapter 4 on the goals). Reaching these goals will be challenging. As noted in Chapter 4, total cumulative investment needs in infrastructure between today and 2030 are more than 36 percent of GDP in emerging markets and low-income developing countries. Spending needs are large and financing options are limited:

[1] See https://www.cincinnati-oh.gov/dote/about-transportation-engineering/historical-information/the-cincinnati-subway/.

[2] See https://www.washingtonpost.com/archive/politics/1993/02/28/deepening-scandal-threatens-italian-state/b9cf68d4-f195-44f3-8ac0-45d9ee8a7332/?utm_term=.882e189c658b.

[3] The sample of projects covered 8 percent of the federal government social sector expenditures. Four out of every five of the projects considered were for infrastructure.

- There is little scope to increase *debt financing*. In low-income developing countries, the public debt burden has risen since 2013, and 40 percent of countries in this group face debt-related challenges (IMF 2018b). In advanced economies, debt stands at 105 percent of GDP, a record since World War II (IMF 2018a).
- Increased *domestic revenue mobilization* will cover only part of spending needs, at least in low-income developing countries. Gaspar and others (2019) estimated that in low-income developing countries, an increase in revenue of 5 percent of GDP is ambitious but feasible. Yet, this will be insufficient given the size of the needs.
- *Private sector financing* options are not without fiscal risks. For example, public-private partnerships can provide benefits relative to traditional procurement (such as private sector efficiency and innovation), but their cost must be borne by taxpayers or users and can have explicit or implicit risks and liabilities for governments. (Chapter 11 features a discussion on fiscal risks in infrastructure.)

Boosting the efficiency of public spending—that is, increasing the volume and quality of infrastructure assets without adding to expenditure—can simultaneously tackle the dual challenges of pressing needs and limited financial options. In this balancing act, no effort should be spared to make public investment more efficient—reduce cost overruns, complete ongoing projects, eliminate white elephants and trains to nowhere, and cut opportunities for fraud in the use of public resources.

On average, countries lose more than one-third of their resources in the public investment process, according to estimations made in this chapter. A measure of the efficiency of public investment spending is provided by comparing the value of public capital and resulting outcomes in infrastructure volume and quality across countries. The analysis finds that most countries have an efficiency gap and could substantially increase the return to public investment. Improvements in infrastructure governance are crucial in capturing these gains.

The analysis suggests that the average country could close more than half of the efficiency gap if it adopted the infrastructure governance and public investment management practices of the best performers. The chapter estimates he link between efficiency and the strength of a country's infrastructure governance as measured by the IMF's Public Investment Management Assessment (PIMA; IMF 2018c). The relationship is robust and significant. Indeed, strengthening public investment management institutions can be key to increasing the efficiency of public investment.

## INFRASTRUCTURE AND PUBLIC INVESTMENT EFFICIENCY

Efficiency estimates help assess the degree of inefficiency in public spending. Policymakers are expected to improve social welfare and long-term growth prospects and, in this process, use scarce public resources efficiently. At a time of increased pressure on public balances, analyses that provide guidance on how to make the most out of spending resources take on additional importance. However, providing good guidance is complicated, given that spending data are imperfect, spending outcomes are often ill-defined, cross-country and time-series coverage are limited, and methods to estimate efficiency are flawed. In addition, outcomes may be affected by factors outside the control of policymakers.[4]

Public investment efficiency is defined as the ability to improve the volume and quality of infrastructure assets for a given level of spending. Efficiency is measured through benchmarking—a systematic comparison of the performance of one country's infrastructure outcomes against peers for a given level of spending. For example, if two otherwise similar countries spend the same on roads, the country that ends up with greater kilometers of paved roads is more efficient. While there is abundant literature on benchmarking health and education spending, similar exercises for public investment are scarce (Herrera and Pang 2005; Grigoli and Kapsoli 2013; Albino-War and others 2014; IMF 2015; and Kapsoli and Teodoru 2017; among others).

A country's public investment efficiency is benchmarked relative to an "efficiency frontier." The efficiency frontier is based on the best performers in terms of output (infrastructure outcomes) for any given level of input (cumulative spending or the capital stock). A country on the efficiency frontier is considered "efficient" and assigned a score of 1, whereas a country below the frontier is considered "inefficient" and given a score of less than 1. The further a country is from the frontier the more inefficient it is.[5] The performance of all countries is therefore assessed by measuring distance from this efficiency frontier. This distance is called the efficiency gap.[6] Figure 3.1 illustrates the efficiency frontier based on a single-input (public capital), single-output (infrastructure outcome) model, but estimation methods allow the possibility of multiple inputs and outputs.[7]

Estimates of public investment efficiency are provided for over 100 countries across the income spectrum. For given levels of the public capital stock and GDP per capita (inputs), data are combined on the volume of economic (length of road network, electricity production, and access to water) and social infrastructure (number of secondary teachers and hospital beds), and its quality (derived from the World Economic Forum survey on the quality of infrastructure).[8]

---

[4] Mandl, Dierx, and Ilzkovitz (2008) discusses this.

[5] A hypothetical country that produces no infrastructure outcomes for a given level of input has a score of 0.

[6] The focus of this chapter is on technical efficiency. Countries may efficiently produce the wrong infrastructure—that is, they may be technically efficient while being allocatively inefficient. Estimating allocative efficiency would require comparable cross-country input prices and is outside the scope of the analysis in this chapter.

[7] Figure 3.1 illustrates both input and output efficiency; this chapter focuses on output efficiency estimates.

[8] Roads, electricity, and water receive a large share of public investment, and the public sector also still dominates the provision of social infrastructure. See the Annex for a discussion on data use and treatment.

**Figure 3.1. Investment Efficiency Frontier**

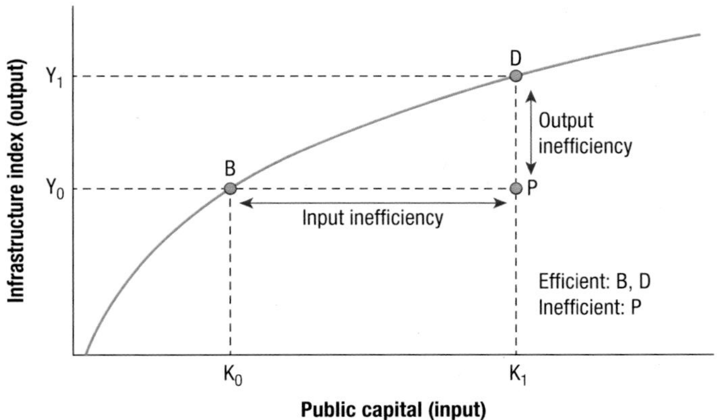


Source: Authors.

The resulting efficiency score is a hybrid indicator, accounting for the volume of economic and social infrastructure and its quality. For robustness, efficiency scores, which are exclusively based on economic infrastructure, are considered.[9] Two methods, described in Box 3.1, are used to estimate efficiency—data envelopment analysis and stochastic frontier analysis.

Estimates in this chapter confirm that there is substantial scope for improving public investment efficiency in most countries. Investment efficiency is estimated for up to 164 countries (using various efficiency score estimation methods), and the results are shown in Figure 3.2. The estimated median efficiency gap is large—over one-third of resources are lost in the public investment process. The gap ranges between 33 percent for the data envelopment analysis estimation and 43 percent for the stochastic frontier analysis (adjusted for skewness), with wide variation across countries around this overall range. Skewness adjustments matter particularly for low-income developing countries, significantly improving the efficiency scores for the top 25th percentile.[10] The different efficiency score outcomes also indicate that the 33 percent average gap resulting from the data envelopment analysis may be a lower bound.

Efficiency varies widely across income groups and regions. In general, the size of the gap shrinks as income rises. For example, as shown in Figure 3.2, panel 1

[9] See Annex 3.3 for data sources and Annex 3.1 for a more detailed discussion of the construction of the efficiency score.

[10] This result is driven by heavy skewness in electricity and road indicators, for which most data from low-income developing countries are clustered on the left of the distribution, leading to overall worse efficiency scores. Skewness adjustment creates normal distributions over all indicators, effectively comparing all indicators in relative terms and reducing this kind of bias. See Box 3.1.

## Box 3.1. Robust Estimation of Spending Efficiency

This box details the methods and data treatment used in this chapter to ensure robustness of the efficiency estimates.

### Methodologies to Estimate Spending Efficiency

There are two families of methodologies to estimate efficiency—parametric and nonparametric. Both estimate a frontier of best performers to identify the efficiency of individual countries relative to a reference set of countries. Each methodology has advantages and disadvantages (and is reviewed in Murillo-Zamorano 2004).

- *Parametric* methods assume a specific functional form for the relationship between spending and outcomes. Efficiency is estimated using econometric methods that require assumptions on the statistical distribution of error terms. For example, stochastic frontier analysis assumes a stochastic relationship between inputs and outputs, allowing the identification of deviations from the frontier as inefficiencies, separating them from measurement error or other noise in the data.
- *Nonparametric* methods are deterministic and based on mathematical programming to identify an "efficient frontier." They do not require assumptions about the distribution of error terms or functional forms. However, all deviations from the frontier are assumed to come from inefficiencies, which makes these models sensitive to the presence of outliers or noise in the data. Data envelopment analysis is—by far—the most widely used method in the nonparametric benchmarking literature (Herrera and Ouedraogo [2018] discusses other nonparametric techniques).

Each method has advantages and disadvantages. Stochastic frontier analysis separates random noise from efficiency; data envelopment analysis incorporates it as part of the efficiency score. The stochastic frontier analysis is estimated using econometric methods; data envelopment analysis directly uses the best-performing countries in the sample to establish the efficiency frontier. IMF (2015) conducted an efficiency estimate analysis for the data envelopment analysis only. Both methods for robustness are presented in this chapter.

### Data Treatment

Some data are corrected for skewness to adjust for the impact of outliers. Some outcome indicators are highly skewed. For example, the observations for electricity production are clustered around low values—a high proportion of low-income countries produce low levels of electricity per capita. However, if there are a few outliers—countries with high production—they will have a disproportionate impact on the aggregate standardized indicator for infrastructure outcomes. The skewness adjustment reduces this effect (see Annex 3.1 for more information on skewness adjustment).

**Figure 3.2. Public Capital and Infrastructure Performance: Hybrid Public Investment Efficiency Score, by Income Level**

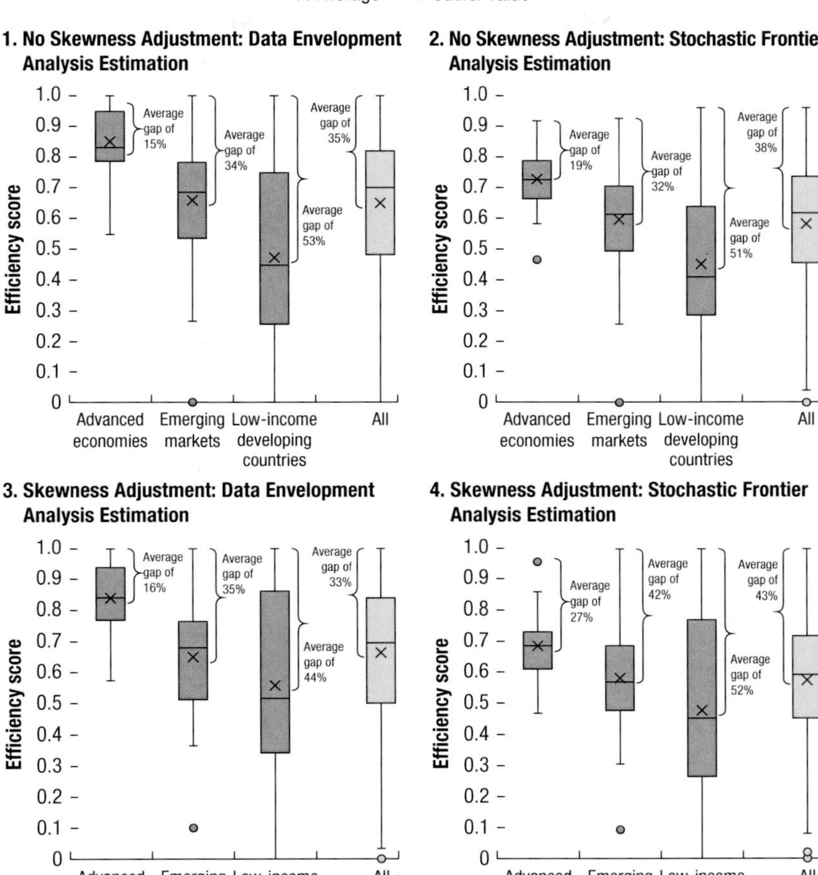


Sources: Feenstra, Inklaar, and Timmer 2015; OECD 2018; World Development Indicators 2018; World Economic Forum 2018; World Economic Outlook database; and IMF staff estimates.

Note: Each box shows the median and the 25th and 75th percentiles, and the whiskers show the nonoutlier maximum and minimum values. Scores range between 0 and 1. The average efficiency gap is computed as the mean percentage difference between the highest and the average efficiency scores. The four panels reflect different combinations of two aspects in the efficiency score derivation methodology.

(data envelopment analysis, nonadjusted efficiency scores), on average, low-income developing countries face an efficiency gap of 53 percent, while emerging markets have a gap of 34 percent, and advanced economies a gap of 15 percent. The range between top and bottom performers declines as income rises. For advanced economies, the maximum efficiency gap ranges from 42 to

49 percent (depending on the method used to derive efficiency scores), and it ranges from 96 to 100 percent for low-income developing countries. Similarly, efficiency gaps in the middle 50 percent of countries—those within the blue and orange boxes in Figure 3.2—vary more across low-income developing countries than across emerging markets or advanced economies. The greater heterogeneity across low-income developing countries suggests that greater scope exists for efficiency improvements in this income group. Regional disparities are prevalent too (Figure 3.3). Average public investment efficiency also varies widely across regions, from an efficiency gap of about 21 percent in Europe to 48 percent in sub-Saharan Africa.

Efficiency gap estimates provide a measure of wasted resources and hint at potential institutional weaknesses. For example, the gap might reflect corruption in the form of cost overruns and bid rigging. Figure 3.4 shows that higher public investment efficiency goes together with lower corruption, measured here as perceived control of corruption. The variance of efficiency scores also declines with declining corruption levels (for a more detailed analysis of the link between corruption and public investment efficiency, see Chapter 10 of this book and IMF 2019). Efficiency gaps could equally reflect weak infrastructure governance institutions, such as weak project design, appraisal, and selection. The next section further explores this link.

**Figure 3.3. Public Capital and Infrastructure Performance: Hybrid Public Investment Efficiency Score, by Region**

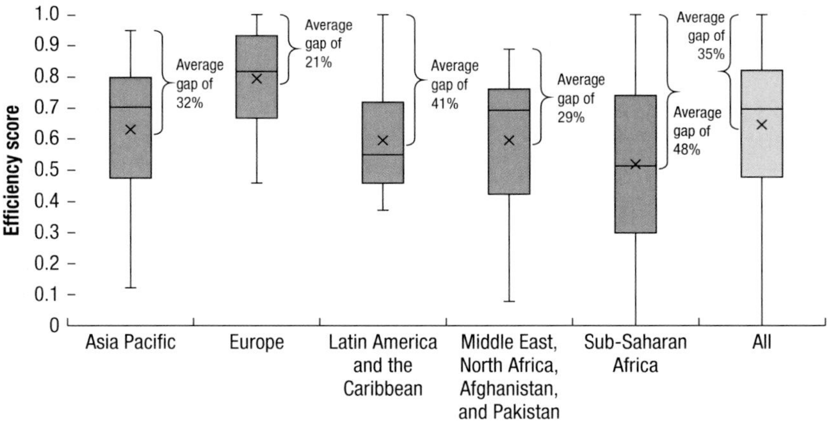


Sources: Feenstra, Inklaar, and Timmer 2015; OECD 2018; WEO 2018; World Development Indicators 2018; World Economic Forum 2018; and IMF staff estimates.
Note: Each box shows the median and the 25th and 75th percentiles, and the whiskers show the nonoutlier maximum and minimum values. Scores range between 0 and 1. The average efficiency gap is computed as the mean percentage difference between the highest and the average efficiency scores. Some groupings with too few countries to be meaningful (North America and the Commonwealth of Independent States) are not shown, but they are included in the "All" country grouping.

**Figure 3.4. Corruption and Public Investment Efficiency**

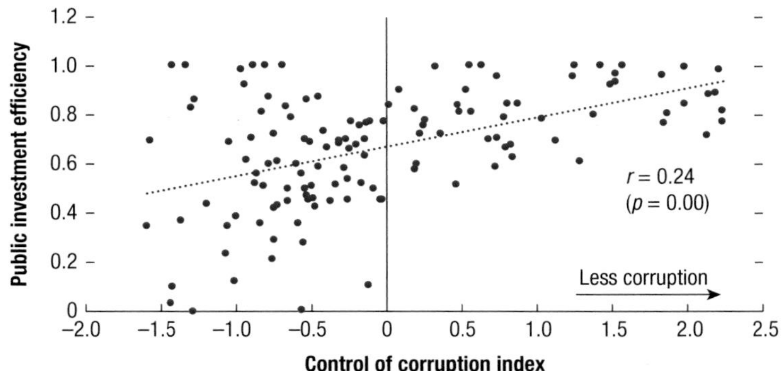


Sources: Worldwide Governance Indicators 2017; and IMF staff estimates.
Note: Efficiency indicators are corrected for skewness and based on the data envelopment analysis methodology.

## INFRASTRUCTURE GOVERNANCE AND EFFICIENCY

The link between infrastructure governance and public investment efficiency is investigated using a regression framework. The analysis assesses how levels of efficiency in public investment spending relate to the quality of public investment management institutions, using the efficiency score estimates described earlier in this chapter and the PIMA effectiveness index.[11]

Fiscal institutions are crucial for economic growth and the efficiency of public spending. Institutional quality has been shown to have a positive impact on economic growth (Aron 2000; Easterly, Ritzen, and Woolcock 2006; Acemoglu and Robinson 2012). As discussed in Chapter 2, additional public investment has a higher growth impact on average in countries with better infrastructure governance. IMF (2015) also established a link between public investment efficiency and infrastructure governance as measured by the IMF's PIMA. Field PIMA missions conducted in the past four years with data collected from 62 countries offer a fresh opportunity to assess the role of infrastructure governance using comparable metrics in a unified framework. The PIMA methodology is discussed in detail in Chapter 5.

The quality of public investment management institutions is highly correlated with estimated measures of public investment efficiency. As shown in Figure 3.5, this relationship holds for efficiency scores based on both overall and economic infrastructure. Advanced economies are set apart as a group of strong performers

[11] See Annex 3.2 for details on the empirical framework.

**Figure 3.5. PIMA Effectiveness and Public Investment Efficiency, by Income Group**

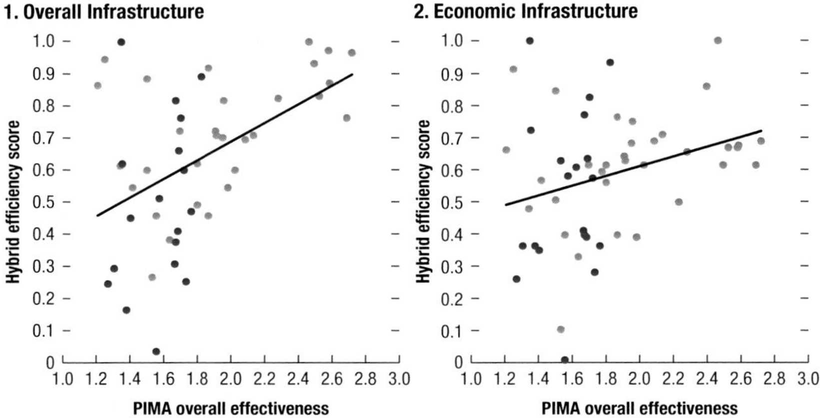


Source: IMF staff calculations.
Note: Efficiency scores are derived using data envelopment analysis and are not adjusted for skewness. PIMA = Public Investment Management Assessment.

in both dimensions of investment management and investment efficiency (Figure 3.5). In contrast, while emerging markets show better results along both parameters than low-income developing countries, significant overlap exists between the two income groups.

The regression analysis shows a statistically and economically significant association between strength of public investment management institutions and public investment efficiency. Figure 3.6 displays the main regression results (the regression coefficient measuring the impact of PIMA on efficiency) when outcome indicators include overall infrastructure (both economic and social).[12] The baseline in Figure 3.6 reflects the scenario with the fewest adjustments—no adjustment for skewness, no additional controls, and estimated using the data envelopment analysis methodology. Additional scenarios are considered for robustness. The analysis makes the following clear:

- *The link between efficiency and PIMA scores is strong and statistically significant.* In terms of magnitude, the estimates suggest that by increasing its PIMA score by one unit (on a scale of 1 to 3), an emerging market economy could rise from the median to the group of best performers for its

[12] See Annex Table 3.2.1 for these and additional results based on further analytical variants.

**Figure 3.6. Infrastructure Governance and Public Investment Efficiency: Increase in Efficiency Associated with a One-Unit Increase in PIMA Score (Overall Infrastructure)**

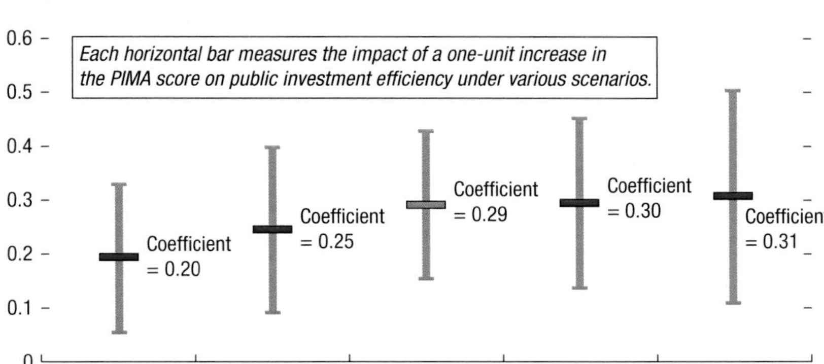


Source: Authors' calculations.
Note: Each horizontal bar represents the coefficient from a separate regression of efficiency scores on PIMA, that is, the figure reflects results from five regressions. Bars are arranged in ascending order of coefficients. The vertical lines indicate 95 percent confidence intervals around the point estimates. Public investment efficiency is measured by the hybrid efficiency score including the quality and volume of overall infrastructure. The baseline result reflects efficiency scores with no adjustment for skewness, estimated using data envelopment analysis, and regression analysis that does not adjust for measurement error and does not control for topography. The other bars correspondingly consider each of these adjustments and variations in estimation methodology. Annex 3.2 discusses the details of the underlying regression analysis and presents results based on additional robustness tests.
PIMA = Public Investment Management Assessment.

income level in efficiency.[13] Estimates are only slightly lower and remain statistically significant when infrastructure outcome indicators are adjusted for skewness. Further assessment of the economic significance of these estimates opens up discussion in the rest of this chapter about how much of the efficiency gap could be closed when public investment management is improved.

- *The results are robust to the estimation method for efficiency.* Although the relationship is somewhat weaker in the regression based on stochastic frontier analysis efficiency scores, regression results are statistically significant for both data envelopment analysis and stochastic frontier analysis estimates.

[13] A one-unit increase in PIMA scores is associated with an increase in the efficiency score by close to 0.3 units across most scenarios in Figure 3.6. To gain perspective on these magnitudes: the one-unit increase in the PIMA score is approximately equal to the difference between the average PIMA scores of low-income developing countries and advanced economies. The associated efficiency gain of 0.3 units is substantive, given that scores only range from 0 to 1.

- *Additional controls do not alter the magnitude of the coefficients.* While efficiency scores account for GDP (see the "Infrastructure and Public Investment Efficiency" section), other factors may affect the efficiency of spending. Additional regressions also control for topography, given that more rugged terrain usually increases the cost of creating infrastructure (in building roads, for example). The result is robust to its inclusion.
- *The results are robust to adjustments for measurement error.* Of the available 62 country PIMAs, 52 were conducted using primary data collected during field missions, while 10 are based on desk assessments based on secondary sources. To correct for potential measurement error in desk assessments, the estimation uses a mission-visit dummy variable as an instrumental variable for the PIMA score.

Sound institutions for public investment also go together with better efficiency in producing economic infrastructure—although by a lesser magnitude than for overall infrastructure. In the analysis so far, consideration has been given to how accumulated public investment translates into infrastructure across multiple

**Figure 3.7. Infrastructure Governance and Public Investment Efficiency: Increase in Efficiency Associated with a One-Unit Increase in PIMA Score (Economic Infrastructure)**

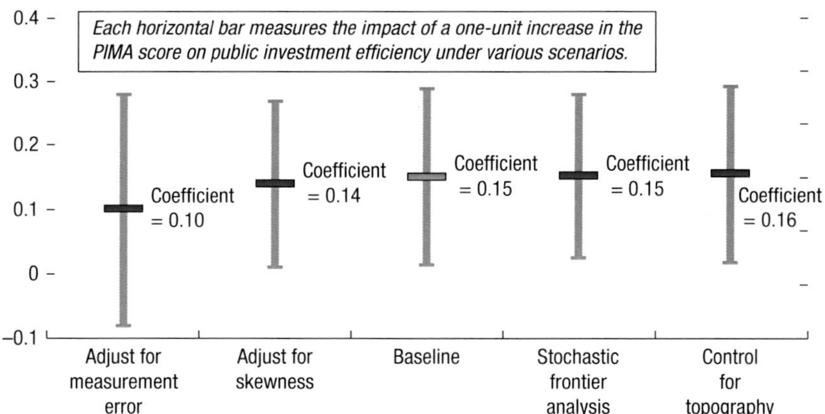


Source: Authors' calculations.
Note: Each horizontal bar represents the coefficient from a separate regression of efficiency scores on PIMA, that is, the figure reflects results from five regressions. Bars are arranged in ascending order of coefficients. The vertical lines indicate 95 percent confidence intervals around the point estimates. Public investment efficiency is measured by the hybrid efficiency score including the quality and the volume of overall infrastructure. The baseline result reflects efficiency scores with no adjustment for skewness, estimated using data envelopment analysis, and regression analysis that does not adjust for measurement error and does not control for topography. The other bars correspondingly consider each of these adjustments and variations in estimation methodology. Annex 3.2 discusses the details of the underlying regression analysis, and presents results based on additional robustness tests.
PIMA = Public Investment Management Assessment.

sectors combined: economic sectors (roads, electricity, water) and social sectors (using proxies for health and education infrastructure). The analysis also considers only the economic sectors, in light of the distinct attention paid to economic infrastructure in many policy settings (Figure 3.7 and Annex Table 3.2.2). There remains a statistically significant association—but of reduced magnitude—between public investment management practices and investment efficiency. The results for economic infrastructure are fairly stable across measures of efficiency and econometric specifications.

Improvements in public investment management could reduce the public investment efficiency gap by half. Figure 3.8 provides a way to assess whether the statistical relationships above are also economically meaningful in magnitude. By how much could countries close the efficiency gap if they improved their public investment management practices? Consider the gains the median country could make by adopting the public investment management practices of the best performers. As shown in Figure 3.8, under the baseline, a country with the median efficiency gap could close more than 53 percent of its gap by adopting the public investment management practices of the country with the 90th percentile PIMA score. The result holds under most scenarios, robust to the measurement of efficiency scores, the estimation method, and the model used in the regression analysis. This suggests that countries could significantly

**Figure 3.8. Share of the Efficiency Gap Reduced by Achieving the PIMA Score of Best Performers, 90th Percentile and Above**

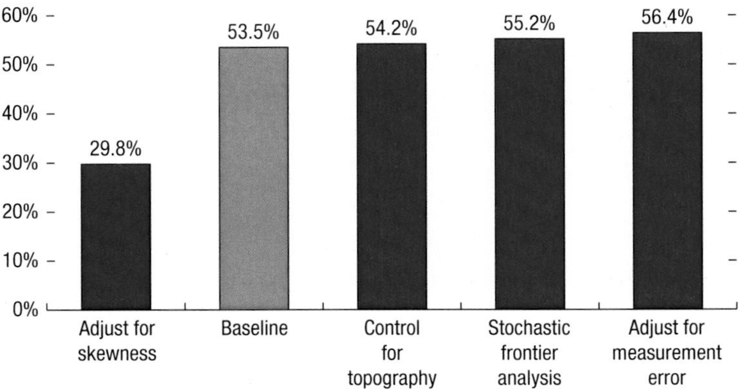


Source: IMF staff calculations.
Note: Results are based on efficiency scores for the quality and volume of overall infrastructure. Best performers are defined as countries at the 90th percentile of PIMA scores. The baseline result reflects efficiency scores with no adjustment for skewness that are estimated using data envelopment analysis, and regression analysis that does not adjust for measurement error and does not control for topography. The other bars correspondingly consider each of these adjustments and variations in estimation methodology. PIMA = Public Investment Management Assessment.

increase the benefits of public investment spending—greater quality and access to infrastructure and resulting higher growth—through improvements in infrastructure governance.

## CONCLUSIONS

This study, which builds on and updates a 2015 report (Box 3.2), finds that more than one-third of resources are lost in the process of managing public investment. Inefficiencies in public investment spending are therefore substantial. This is a nonnegligible source of wasted resources when needs are high and fiscal space is limited.

Better infrastructure governance would raise the efficiency of public investment spending and improve infrastructure outcomes. Adopting the public investment practices of best performers could help countries to close about half their efficiency gap. The data and methods used in this study, while imperfect, help identify priority reform areas.

### Box 3.2. Comparison to Previous Results

This chapter updates the work done in IMF (2015) but uses a more updated and expanded data set and enhances the methodology in the estimation of the following:

#### Efficiency

- *Data.* This chapter uses updated data on the capital stock data and infrastructure outcome indicators (to 2017 or the latest available year). Some indicators are adjusted for skewness to control for outliers (see Box 3.1).
- *Methodology.* As discussed in Box 3.1, the results use both the data envelopment analysis and stochastic frontier analysis methodologies (while IMF 2015 was focused on the former).

#### The Link between Efficiency and Infrastructure Governance

- *Data.* The PIMA sample size is larger (from 25 desk assessments in 2015 to 62 desk and mission assessments in this chapter).
- *Methodology.* The chapter uses additional control for geography (rugged terrain) and possible measurement errors in desk assessments for robustness.

The results are broadly in line with IMF (2015) and confirm that efficiency gaps are sizeable and that public investment management institutions have a role to play in reducing them.

- IMF (2015) found an average efficiency gap of 27 percent, whereas the comparable gap is 35 percent in this chapter's analysis.
- IMF (2015) found that the average country could close two-thirds of the efficiency gap by adopting the public investment management practices of the best performer while the preferred specification used in this chapter suggests a number closer to one-half. Qualitatively, both studies suggest that improving public investment management institutions could dramatically reduce the inefficiency of public investment spending.

Better infrastructure governance also helps to increase fiscal space. Traditional means to increase fiscal space—increasing revenue or reducing spending—should go hand in hand with improvement in infrastructure governance, that is, reforms geared at strengthening relevant fiscal institutions. The IMF's PIMA can help countries identify key sources of inefficiencies across the planning, allocation, and implementation stages of public investment (see Chapter 5 for examples).

Future analytical work should focus on closing gaps in knowledge about the relationship between public investment management and investment efficiency. As more PIMAs become available, the analysis can be extended to a larger sample. A priority would be to close sectoral data gaps. Country-level data on capital spending in transportation, energy, health, and education are scarce. Such data would be particularly useful as they would allow the analysis of sector-specific spending efficiency and help guide policymakers in allocation decisions. Analyses of energy or transportation may be particularly useful as these sectors often constitute a large share of public investment. As a second step, the availability of input prices could help in welfare assessments—not only to determine whether countries are spending well—minimizing costs—but also whether they are allocating spending to sectors that maximize the welfare of their citizens.

## ANNEX 3.1. MEASURING EFFICIENCY USING FRONTIER METHODS

The efficiency analysis is based on evaluating the relationship between infrastructure inputs and outputs. Inputs are measured by the real capital stock and GDP per capita. Infrastructure output is a combined measure of both physical and quality indicators. The physical indicator is a quantitative index combining outcome indicators in various sectors.

The physical indicator may combine pure infrastructure indicators and indicators related to the provision of social services:

- *Pure infrastructure indicators* include the length of road networks (kilometers per capita), access to an improved water source (percent of population) and electricity production (kilowatt-hours per capita). Electricity production and water still receive a large share of public investment (European Investment Bank 2008 and PricewaterhouseCoopers 2014 discuss the composition of public investment spending across infrastructure sectors). Ideally, infrastructure data on ports, railways, and other infrastructure would be added, but country data are still limited, while extensive coverage is needed for the regression analysis.
- *Social sector indicators* are included as the public sector still dominates their provision, usually because of equity considerations as such universal access and social mobility. For example, in education, the public sector accounts for more than half of total investment in both advanced economies and

emerging markets; for health, it ranges from about one-third of investment in selected emerging markets, to about two-thirds in advanced economies, with a significant dispersion across countries (IMF 2015). In addition, especially in developing economies and low-income countries, increases in productivity are closely linked to the expansion in the provision of health and education services (see de la Fuente 2011 for more details). Social sector data used here are the number of secondary teachers and the number of hospital beds, both measured as per 1,000 people.

- Each variable is averaged from the year 2000 until its last available observation. Because each variable is measured on a different scale, all variables are first standardized (following skewness adjustment where needed) and then aggregated as follows:

$$x_i = \frac{1}{5}\sum_{j=1}^{5} \frac{x_{ij} - \bar{x}_j}{\sigma_j}$$

where $x_{ij}$ is the value of the variable $j$ in country $i$, and $\bar{x}_j$ and $\sigma_j$ are the mean and standard deviation of variable $j$ over the considered period.

Several series are adjusted for skewness. Data skewness means that an individual indicator could both lose explanatory power and be overpowering for some countries in the aggregation across indicators. For example, if one or a few countries have much better electricity outcomes than most countries, the distribution of standardized data will be skewed to the left. The electricity outcomes of those outliers will lie far to the right of the distribution. As all data series are standardized, electricity for those few countries would become dominant in the aggregation across indicators (the outcomes of other infrastructure series become less relevant). At the same time, the electricity outcomes for the others would be clustered around a narrow interval on the left of the distribution, making them hard to distinguish, leading to less relevance of the electricity outcomes in the aggregation across indicators. In the present analysis, efficiency scores are both presented in their standard form and adjusted for potential skewness, to examine robustness of results to this variation. Electricity, roads, and water data are corrected for skewness through logarithmic transformations.

The hybrid indicator is constructed by combining the physical indicator with the survey-based qualitative indicator from the World Economic Forum. It obtains an assessment from experts on the general state of infrastructure in each country, generating a rating from 1 (worst) to 7 (best). The hybrid indicator used in the analysis is the arithmetic mean of the two previous indicators (physical and quality) and provides a measure of both the volume and quality of public infrastructure.

The data envelopment and stochastic frontier analyses are then used to estimate investment efficiency scores based on the hybrid indicator and the two inputs: capital stock and GDP per capita. As discussed in the main text, both methodologies have advantages and disadvantages, therefore both are used here. The stochastic frontier analysis needs assumptions on error distributions. Here, it is specified as a normal/half-normal model of the reduced form equation:

$$\ln y_i = f(x_i;\beta) + \varepsilon_i$$
$$\varepsilon_i = \nu_i - u_i$$

where the variable set $x$ is an (m x 1) vector of inputs, here GDP per capita and the public capital stock, and $\beta$ is the corresponding vector of parameters. $v$ is normally distributed with $\left(\nu_i : i.i.d. N\left(0, \sigma_\nu^2\right)\right)$, and the inefficiency term $u$ is specified as a half-normal distribution with zero mean $\left(u_i : i.i.d. N^+\left(0, \sigma_u^2\right)\right)$. The smaller the variance of $u$, the closer the inefficiency terms will be clustered around zero, and the closer the efficiency scores are clustered around one. Efficiency scores based on the hybrid indicator and for both estimation methods cover 130 countries over 2000–17 (unbalanced panel).

## ANNEX 3.2. ASSESSING THE LINK BETWEEN INFRASTRUCTURE GOVERNANCE AND PUBLIC INVESTMENT EFFICIENCY

To determine the association between public investment management institutions and public investment efficiency in the "Infrastructure Governance and Efficiency" section, the following regression framework is used:

$$\theta_i = \alpha + \beta \cdot PIMA_i + \gamma X_i + \varepsilon_i$$

where $\theta_i$ is the efficiency score for country $i$, with variations in its estimations as described in Annex 3.1. $PIMA_i$ refers to the PIMA index value for country $i$, which aggregates public investment management indexes across the three stages of the investment cycle (planning, allocation, and implementation; see Chapter 5 for further details on the PIMA index). The regression includes a control, $X_i$, for the average ruggedness of a country's land surface, as this may affect the efficiency with which public resources are deployed to create infrastructure. Nunn and Puga (2012) developed the index using a global data set from the US Geological Survey (1996). The index sums up, for each country, the squared difference in elevation of each point in a spatial grid from that of its neighbouring points.

Efficiency scores for overall infrastructure are available for 130 countries, while 141 countries have scores for economic infrastructure, and 62 have PIMA indicators. The overlap of observations (countries) with both PIMA values and efficiency scores is 48 and 53 for overall and economic infrastructure, respectively. PIMAs were conducted once for each sample country, with the corresponding missions taking place between 2015 and 2019. The efficiency scores rely on public capital and infrastructure data averaged over time for each country, as described in Annex 3.1. Given that the regressions are therefore of a cross-sectional nature, additional extensive controls were not included, to retain adequate degrees of freedom for the statistical analysis.

The baseline regression is estimated using ordinary least squares.

A variant of the empirical model also takes into account that a subset of the PIMA data (for 10 out of the 62 countries) was collected through desk review rather than through mission visits. An instrumental variable approach is used to mitigate the effect of potential measurement error in desk reviews on the analysis (Hu and Schennach 2008). Specifically, the PIMA index is instrumented with a dummy variable that indicates whether the country's PIMA was derived through field data (dummy takes on the value of 1) or through desk data collection (value of 0). As appropriate for a suitable instrument, this variable is related to the PIMA index that it instruments for but does not independently explain efficiency outcomes (the dependent variable in the

**ANNEX TABLE 3.2.1**

**Cross-Country Regressions: Relationship between Public Investment Efficiency (Overall Infrastructure) and PIMA**

| | | (1) | (2) | (3) | (4) |
|---|---|---|---|---|---|
| | | *Efficiency Scores Using* | | | |
| | | Data Envelopment Analysis | | Stochastic Frontier Analysis | |
| | | *Regression Estimation* | | *Regression Estimation* | |
| | | Ordinary Least Squares | Adjusted for Measurement Error | Ordinary Least Squares | Adjusted for Measurement Error |
| 1. Standard | Public investment management index (PIMA) | 0.29*** | 0.31*** | 0.20*** | 0.17* |
| | | (0.08) | (0.10) | (0.07) | (0.09) |
| | Control for topography | No | No | No | No |
| | No. of countries | 48 | 48 | 48 | 48 |
| | $R^2$ | 0.23 | 0.23 | 0.15 | 0.14 |
| 2. Skew adjusted | Public investment management index (PIMA) | 0.25*** | 0.28*** | 0.17** | 0.15* |
| | | (–0.08) | (–0.10) | (–0.07) | (0.09) |
| | Control for topography | No | No | No | No |
| | No. of countries | 47 | 47 | 47 | 47 |
| | $R^2$ | 0.18 | 0.18 | 0.12 | 0.12 |
| 3. Standard | Public investment management index (PIMA) | 0.30*** | 0.31*** | 0.20*** | 0.18* |
| | | (0.08) | (0.10) | -0.07 | (0.09) |
| | Control for topography | Yes | Yes | Yes | Yes |
| | No. of countries | 47 | 47 | 47 | 47 |
| | $R^2$ | 0.24 | 0.24 | 0.15 | 0.15 |
| 4. Skew adjusted | Public investment management index (PIMA) | 0.25*** | 0.28*** | 0.16** | 0.15* |
| | | (0.08) | (0.10) | (0.07) | (0.09) |
| | Control for topography | Yes | Yes | Yes | Yes |
| | No. of countries | 47 | 47 | 47 | 47 |
| | $R^2$ | 0.18 | 0.18 | 0.12 | 0.12 |

Source: IMF staff calculations.

Note: The figures in each set of row-column combinations result from a separate regression, that is, the table represents results from 16 regressions. Although there are 62 PIMA countries, efficiency scores are available only for 48 of these (the use of the topography control variable and the process of skew adjustment reduces the number of observations by one more unit). Public investment efficiency is measured by the hybrid efficiency score including the quality and volume of overall—that is, economic and social—infrastructure. PIMA = Public Investment Management Assessment.

*$p < 0.1$. **$p < 0.05$. ***$p < 0.01$.

regressions). Results are presented with and without this adjustment for measurement error.

Annex Tables 3.2.1 and 3.2.2 present the regression results that were illustrated in graphical form and discussed in the "Infrastructure Governance and Efficiency" section. They, respectively, show the association of PIMA with investment efficiency for overall infrastructure and for economic infrastructure. The results of the baseline regressions appear in the first column and row of each table, while the other coefficients represent alternative specifications and estimation methods to examine the robustness of the main results.

**ANNEX TABLE 3.2.2**

**Cross-Country Regressions: Relationship between Public Investment Efficiency (Economic Infrastructure) and PIMA**

| | | (1) | (2) | (3) | (4) |
|---|---|---|---|---|---|
| | | *Efficiency Scores Using* | | | |
| | | **Data Envelopment Analysis** | | **Stochastic Frontier Analysis** | |
| | | *Regression Estimation* | | *Regression Estimation* | |
| | | **Ordinary Least Squares** | **Adjusted for Measurement Error** | **Ordinary Least Squares** | **Adjusted for Measurement Error** |
| 1. Standard | Public investment management index | 0.15** | 0.10 | 0.15** | 0.14 |
| | | (0.07) | (0.09) | (0.07) | (0.09) |
| | Control for topography | No | No | No | No |
| | No. of countries | 55 | 53 | 53 | 53 |
| | $R^2$ | 0.09 | 0.08 | 0.10 | 0.10 |
| 2. Skew adjusted | Public investment management index | 0.14** | 0.16* | 0.09 | 0.08 |
| | | (0.07) | (0.09) | (0.06) | (0.08) |
| | Control for topography | No | No | No | No |
| | No. of countries | 52 | 52 | 52 | 52 |
| | $R^2$ | 0.08 | 0.08 | 0.04 | 0.04 |
| 3. Standard | Public investment management index | 0.16** | 0.11 | 0.16** | 0.15* |
| | | (0.07) | (0.09) | (0.07) | (0.09) |
| | Control for topography | Yes | Yes | Yes | Yes |
| | No. of countries | 52 | 52 | 52 | 52 |
| | $R^2$ | 0.12 | 0.11 | 0.14 | 0.14 |
| 4. Skew adjusted | Public investment management index | 0.14** | 0.16* | 0.09 | 0.08 |
| | | (0.07) | (0.09) | (0.06) | (0.08) |
| | Control for topography | Yes | Yes | Yes | Yes |
| | No. of countries | 52 | 52 | 52 | 52 |
| | $R^2$ | 0.09 | 0.09 | 0.04 | 0.04 |

Source: IMF staff calculations.

Note: The figures in each set of row-column combinations result from a separate regression; that is, the table represents results from 16 regressions. Public investment efficiency is measured by the hybrid efficiency score including the quality as well as the volume of economic infrastructure. OLS = ordinary least squares; PIMA = Public Investment Management Assessment.

$^*p < 0.1$. $^{**}p < 0.05$. $^{***}p < 0.01$.

## ANNEX 3.3. DATA SOURCES

| Data Series | Source |
|---|---|
| General government capital stock (2011 purchasing power parity US dollar-adjusted, per capita) | IMF Public Investment and Capital Stock Database |
| GDP per capita | IMF World Economic Outlook |
| Population, total | IMF World Economic Outlook |
| Electricity in terawatt-hours | OECD Library International Energy Agency Electricity Information Statistics |
| Roads per kilometer | International Road Federation |
| Access to treated water (percentage of population) | World Bank World Development Indicators |
| Secondary school teachers | World Bank World Development Indicators |
| Hospital beds | World Bank World Development Indicators |
| Quality of overall infrastructure, 1–7 (best) | World Economic Forum's Global Competitiveness Report |
| PIMA index | IMF's Fiscal Affairs Department PIMA database |
| Ruggedness of topography index, derived from the sum of squared differences in elevation of neighboring points in a spatial grid | Nunn and Puga (2012), based on GTOPO30 (US Geological Survey 1996) |

Note: OECD = Organisation for Economic Co-operation and Development; PIMA = Public Investment Management Assessment.

## REFERENCES


Acemoglu, Daron, and James A. Robinson. 2012. *Why Nations Fail: The Origins of Power, Prosperity, and Poverty*. New York: Crown.

Albino-War, Maria, Svetlana Cerovic, Francesco Grigoli, Juan Carlos Flores, Javier Kapsoli, Haonan Qu, Yahia Said, and others. 2014. "Making the Most of Public Investment in MENA and CCA Oil-Exporting Countries." IMF Staff Discussion Note 14/10, International Monetary Fund, Washington, DC.

Aron, Janine. 2000. "Growth and Institutions: A Review of the Evidence." *World Bank Research Observer* 15 (1): 99–135.

de la Fuente, Angel. 2011. "Human Capital and Productivity." *Nordic Economic Policy Review* 2: 103–32.

Easterly, William, Jozef Ritzen, and Michael Woolcock. 2006. "Social Cohesion, Institutions, and Growth." *Economics and Politics* 18 (2): 103–20.

European Investment Bank. 2008. "Infrastructure Investment, Growth, and Cohesion—Public Investment: Composition, Growth Effects and Fiscal Constraints." *EIB Papers* 13 (1).

Feenstra, Robert C., Robert Inklaar, and Marcel Timmer. 2015. "The Next Generation of the Penn World Table." *American Economic Review* 105 (10): 3150–82.

Gaspar, Vitor, David Amaglobeli, Mercedes Garcia-Escribano, Delphine Prady, and Mauricio Soto. 2019. "Fiscal Policy and Development: Human, Social, and Physical Investment for the SDGs." IMF Staff Discussion Note 19/03, International Monetary Fund, Washington, DC.

Grigoli, Francesco, and Javier Kapsoli. 2013. "Waste Not, Want Not: The Efficiency of Health Expenditure in Emerging and Developing Economies." IMF Working Paper 13/187, International Monetary Fund, Washington, DC.

Herrera Aguilera, Santiago, and Abdoulaye Ouedraogo. 2018. "Efficiency of Public Spending in Education, Health, and Infrastructure—An International Benchmarking Exercise." Policy Research Working Paper 8586, World Bank, Washington, DC.

Herrera, Santiago, and Gaobo Pang. 2005. "Efficiency of Public Spending in Developing Countries: An Efficiency Frontier Approach." World Bank Policy Research Working Paper 3645, World Bank, Washington, DC.

Hu, Y., and S. M. Schennach. 2008. Instrumental Variable Treatment of Nonclassical Measurement Error Models. *Econometrica* 76 (1): 195–216.

International Monetary Fund (IMF). 2015. *Making Public Investment More Efficient.* Washington, DC.

IMF. 2018a. *Fiscal Monitor: Capitalizing on Good Times.* Washington, DC, April.

IMF. 2018b. *Macroeconomic Developments and Prospects in Low-Income Developing Countries—2018.* Washington, DC.

IMF. 2018c. "Public Investment Management Assessment—Review and Update." International Monetary Fund, Washington, DC, May.

IMF. 2019. *Fiscal Monitor: Curbing Corruption.* Washington, DC: IMF, April.

Kapsoli, Javier, and Iulia Ruzandra Teodoru. 2017. "Benchmarking Social Spending Using Efficiency Frontiers." IMF Working Paper 17/197, International Monetary Fund, Washington, DC.

Mandl, Ulrike, Adriaan Dierx, and Fabienne. Ilzkovitz. 2008. "The Effectiveness and Efficiency of Public Spending." Economic Papers 301, European Economy, European Commission, Brussels.

Murillo-Zamorano, Luis R. 2004. "Economic Efficiency and Frontier Techniques." *Journal of Economic Surveys* 18 (1): 33–76.

Nunn, Nathan, and Diego Puga. 2012. "Ruggedness: The Blessing of Bad Geography in Africa." *Review of Economics and Statistics* 94 (1): 20–36.

Organisation for Economic Co-operation and Development (OECD). 2018. IEA Electricity Information Statistics. International Energy Agency. OECD iLibrary.

PricewaterhouseCoopers. 2014. "Infrastructure Development in Asia Pacific (APEC)—The Next 10 Years." PricewaterhouseCoopers, October.

Rasul, Imran, and Daniel Rogger. 2016. "Management of Bureaucrats and Public Service Delivery: Evidence from the Nigerian Civil Service." *Economic Journal* 128: 413–46.

US Geological Survey. 1996. "GTOPO30. Sioux Falls, SD: United States Geological Survey Center for Earth Resources Observation and Science (EROS)." Reston, VA.

World Economic Forum. 2018. *The Global Competitiveness Report 2018*, edited by Klaus Schwab. http://www3.weforum.org/docs/GCR2018/05FullReport/TheGlobalCompetitivenessReport2018.pdf.

Williams, Martin J. 2017. "The Political Economy of Unfinished Development Projects: Corruption, Clientelism, or Collective Choice?" *American Political Science Review* 111 (4): 705–23.

CHAPTER 4

# Infrastructure Investment and the Sustainable Development Goals

Yuan Xiao, Devin D'Angelo, and Nghiã-Piotr Trọng Lê

## INTRODUCTION

The Sustainable Development Goals (SDGs) delineate a comprehensive international agenda for sustainable development by 2030 that has been endorsed by all UN member states and build on the substantial progress achieved under the Millennium Development Goals (UN 2015). The 17 SDGs of the 2030 Agenda for Sustainable Development officially came into force on January 1, 2016. With these new goals universally applied, all countries committed to mobilize efforts aimed at ending poverty, fighting inequality, and reducing climate change over the next 15 years, while ensuring that no one is left behind (Figure 4.1).

Infrastructure development plays a key role in the SDG agenda. The 17 SDGs aim to tackle a wide range of global issues, including those related to poverty, health, education, water and sanitation, energy, inequality, climate, environmental degradation, prosperity, and peace and justice. They include three goals directly related to infrastructure: water, sanitation, and hygiene (SDG 6), energy (SDG 7), and infrastructure and industrialization (SDG 9). Moreover, infrastructure development will have positive spillovers on most other SDGs because every economic and social sector requires good infrastructure for development. Infrastructure is also an important driver of economic growth, which is essential in enlarging a country's revenue base to meet spending needs.[1]

This chapter develops methods to estimate investment spending needs to reach SDGs related to infrastructure and discusses their implications for infrastructure governance in emerging market economies and low-income developing countries. Achieving infrastructure development targets by 2030 requires significant investment and financing. The focus here is on three key sectors—roads, electricity, and water and sanitation—where information is available and quantifiable targets can be defined.

The total cumulative investment needs before 2030 in these three sectors are substantial—at 36.1 percent of emerging market economies' and low-income

[1] An in-depth analysis of the relationship between infrastructure and economic growth features in Chapter 2.

**Figure 4.1. United Nations' Sustainable Development Goals**

Source: United Nations Sustainable Development Goals website.

developing countries' GDP, according to estimates in this chapter. These investment needs vary significantly across both income levels and regions and would require significant scaling up of public investment spending in many countries. Governments and the international community will need to explore policy options to address the challenge to finance the increased spending.

An assessment of countries' current performance on SDGs in infrastructure is a starting point in the discussion in this chapter. Costing methodologies for determining estimated spending needs by income groups and regions for each infrastructure sector are then described in detail. Mobilizing domestic revenues and improving public investment efficiency are also featured as they are crucial considerations in helping countries achieve the SDGs. As noted in Chapter 3, more than one-third of resources are lost in the process of public investment, waste that can be substantially reduced through better infrastructure governance. Public investment management reforms will therefore be a crucial part in reaching SDGs related to infrastructure.

## SDGS IN INFRASTRUCTURE: TAKING STOCK

Tasks for achieving SDGs are distributed unevenly across countries, with larger challenges for developing countries. As Figure 4.2 shows, the median composite SDG index score—a measure that tracks country performance in achieving SDGs—in 2017 is highest for advanced economies at 78 percent and as low as 53 percent for low-income developing countries, with emerging market economies somewhere in between. This suggests there are significant gaps and that more spending will be needed to achieve SDGs in most countries. It is not surprising that higher-income countries tend to have better SDG index scores. In low-income developing countries, not only are the gaps toward reaching SDGs the largest, the group variation in SDG scores is also wider than in other income groups.

**Figure 4.2. SDG Composite Index, 2017**

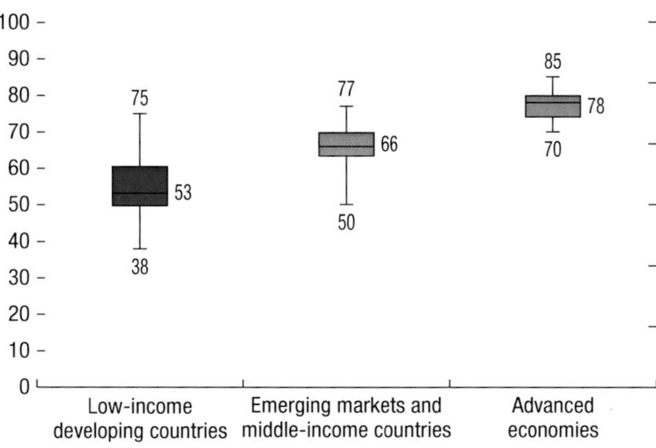


Source: Lafortune and others 2018.
Note: The SDG Index aggregates available data on all individual SDGs into a composite index to provide a quick assessment of how countries are performing relative to their peers. SDG = Sustainable Development Goal.

Similar patterns exist for the three infrastructure-related SDGs (Figure 4.3). Targets, including for infrastructure, include a wide range of quantitative and qualitative performance objectives, and precisely defined targets are in general left for the implementing authorities. As a result, for practical purposes and because of data limitations, the performance measurements and spending-need estimates in this chapter focus only on a subset of the infrastructure-related SDG indicators (Table 4.1).

- *Roads.* As shown in Figure 4.3, panel 1, access to roads in rural areas remains, to different degrees, low in most countries. Low-income developing countries tend to have poor rural road access and road density. World Bank (2019) argues that, given the weak starting positions, universal access to paved roads may not be within reach by 2030 even if countries spend 1 percent of their annual GDP on roads. Overall, the quality of infrastructure (including transportation) is worse in low-income developing countries than in other income groups, and there is a wide variation across countries.
- *Electricity.* There is a long way to universal electricity access in low-income developing countries; by contrast, electricity access is not a significant issue in advanced and emerging market economies (Figure 4.3, panel 2). The variation in electricity access is also noticeably larger in low-income developing countries.
- *Water and sanitation.* Access to safely managed water and sanitation is far from universal, especially in rural areas and in low-income developing countries (Figure 4.3, panels 3 and 4). Significant variation exists for emerging markets and low-income developing countries.

## Figure 4.3. Access to Infrastructure, Selected Indicators

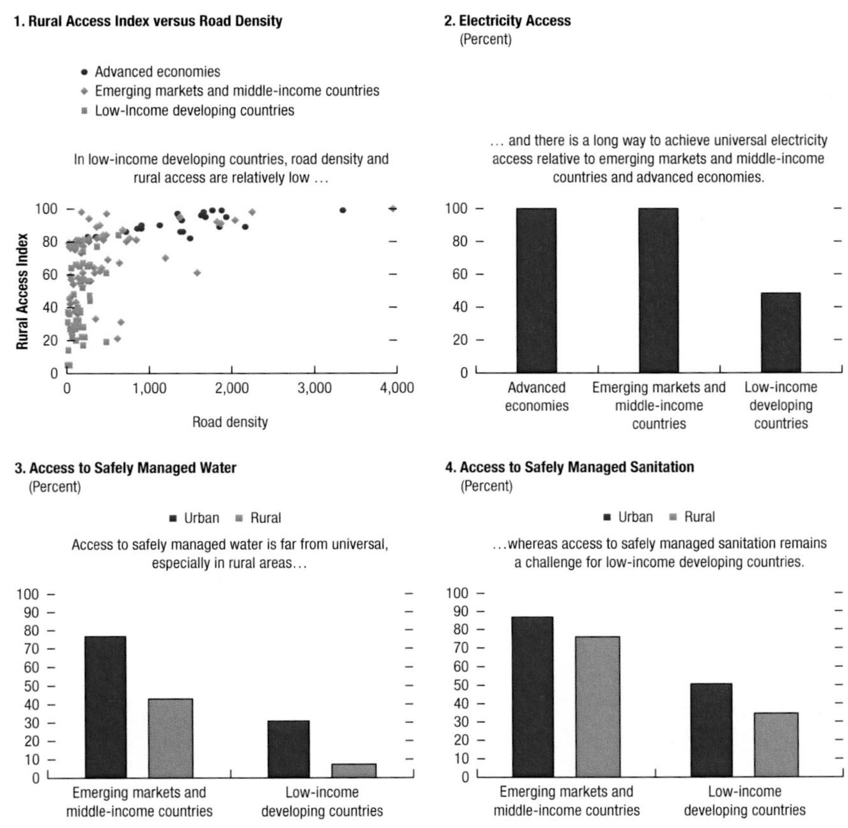


Sources: United Nations SDG indicators; and World Bank Rural Access Index.
Note: SDG = Sustainable Development Goal.

**TABLE 4.1.**

### Infrastructure SDG Targets Considered in This Chapter

| Sector | SDG Target |
|---|---|
| Roads | "Develop quality, reliable, sustainable and resilient infrastructure, including regional and transborder infrastructure, to support economic development and human well-being, with a focus on affordable and equitable access for all." (Target 9.1) |
| Electricity | "By 2030, ensure universal access to affordable, reliable and modern energy services." (Target 7.1) |
| Water and sanitation | "By 2030, achieve universal and equitable access to safe and affordable drinking water for all." (Target 6.1)<br>"By 2030, achieve access to adequate and equitable sanitation and hygiene for all and end open defecation." (Target 6.2) |

Source: United Nations SDGs website.

Note: SDG = Sustainable Development Goal.

## SPENDING NEEDS TO REACH SDGs IN INFRASTRUCTURE

To reach SDGs, it is important to gauge the spending needs of different countries. However, the task is far from straightforward. First, SDG targets include a wide range of quantitative and qualitative performance criteria, and precisely defined targets are not generally agreed upon. Second, measuring performance and calculating the costs requires a substantial amount of information that is often unavailable, especially for emerging markets and low-income developing countries. Third, the costs of implementation are endogenous and depend on factors that include the chosen technologies, country-specific initial conditions and costs, economic and demographic assumptions, and complementary reforms. Fully measuring all aspects of the SDGs is therefore an impossible task. Instead, the attempt in this chapter is to quantify a selected but nonetheless important subset of infrastructure SDGs, making assumptions in estimating the spending needs while acknowledging that the effort should be an evolving process with room for continuous refinement.

Models and methods developed by the IMF and the World Bank are used to estimate spending needs for road and electricity access and for water. Although an important strand of work on infrastructure gaps is apparent, these studies follow an approach motivated by the need to support economic development; they do not directly measure the costs of reaching SDG targets.[2] Bottom-up estimates specifically related to SDG targets on infrastructure are lacking given that the SDG agenda was established just a few years ago and because quantitative targets or indicators for many targets do not exist. This chapter develops a costing methodology for SDGs focusing on access to infrastructure, which is based on the unit cost approach taken in earlier literature about infrastructure gaps. Schmidt-Traub (2015) and Gaspar and others (2019) discuss spending-need estimates for achieving SDGs in a broader set of sectors, including education and health. World Bank (2019) goes beyond costing the access to infrastructure by accounting for climate goals, and explores scenarios based on technological options. Box 4.1 describes the costing methods used in this chapter.

### Investment Spending Needs

Total cumulative investment needs from 2019 to 2030 in the three infrastructure sectors are estimated at around $12 trillion for 121 emerging market economies and low-income developing countries (36.1 percent of their GDP cumulatively). This implies an annual average investment need of about USD 1 trillion (3 percent of GDP) for these countries.[3] As shown in Figure 4.4, on average,

---

[2] See Fay and Yepes (2003) and Global Infrastructure Hub (2017) for examples of this literature.

[3] In the SDG literature, both starting-point GDP and 2030 GDP have been used to express spending needs as percentage of GDP. However, since infrastructure investment will occur continuously to 2030 and beyond, GDP averaging between 2019 and 2030 is used as the denominator throughout this chapter to avoid overrepresenting or underrepresenting the spending needs.

## Box 4.1. Costing Methodology for Roads; Electricity; and Water, Sanitation, and Hygiene

The estimates for the three infrastructure sectors share a common two-step approach.[1] First, an infrastructure gap is defined for a country measuring the distance from the SDG target in the sector. In some sectors, a quantifiable goal (such as universal access) is identified in the SDG. When a clear quantifiable goal is unavailable, the chapter provides a proxy. Second, the cost for closing this gap is calculated based on estimates of sector-specific unit costs found in the literature.

- *Roads*. Because there is no specific numerical UN target for road infrastructure, we operationalize Target 9.1 by using GDP per capita and a rural road access index to measure "economic development and human well-being" (Target 9.1). A target road density—as a function of GDP per capita, population density, and rural road access—is estimated using regression analysis (described in Annex 4.1). Once an infrastructure gap is established, the annual investment needed to close the gap by 2030 is computed given the unit cost—obtained from the literature—to build the road network. Maintenance costs are also included.
- *Electricity*. Because Target 7.1 (universal access) is quantifiable, existing estimates of unit costs are used to calculate the average annual cost to reach universal access while controlling for population growth and maintaining the same initial electricity consumption per user. The need to increase power consumption as economic activity expands is also accounted for.
- *Water, sanitation, and hygiene*. Cost estimates are based on a template developed by the World Bank using the unit cost approach to reach universal access to safely manged water, sanitation, and hygiene services (Hutton and Varughese 2016). The template considers both capital spending and operational costs.

[1] See Annex 4.1 for more details on roads and electricity, and Hutton and Varughese (2016) on water, sanitation, and hygiene.

emerging market economies have an annual investment need of 2.7 percent of GDP until 2030, while for low-income developing countries it is equivalent to 9.8 percent of GDP. To put these figures in context, the median size of capital spending is about 3.6 percent of GDP for emerging market economies and 5.1 percent for low-income developing countries (Figure 4.5). Although the ongoing capital spending will help achieve the SDGs, the remaining investment spending needs estimated in this chapter are still sizeable, especially for low-income developing countries.

SDG spending needs, including the estimated investment needs, vary significantly across income levels and countries (Figures 4.6 and 4.7) and could pose a challenge for lower-income countries. Figure 4.6 displays both infrastructure SDG needs and total SDG spending needs for education, health, and infrastructure, based on estimates in Gaspar and others (2019) and relative to a country's income level (the diameter of the balloon indicates GDP size). Some of the largest spending needs (for both infrastructure and total) occur in the smallest economies. This is not surprising given that low-income countries typically have worse infrastructure, but the pattern does highlight the difficulties that poorer countries face

**Figure 4.4. Total Annual Investment Needs**
*(As a percentage of average GDP)*

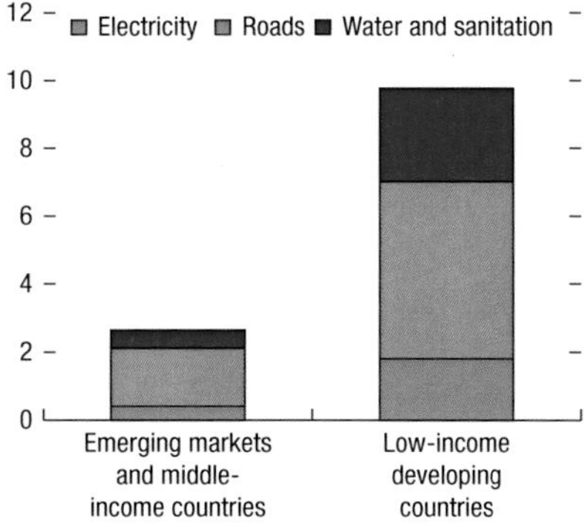


Source: Authors' calculations.

**Figure 4.5. Investment Needs and Budget Spending**
*(As a percentage of average GDP)*

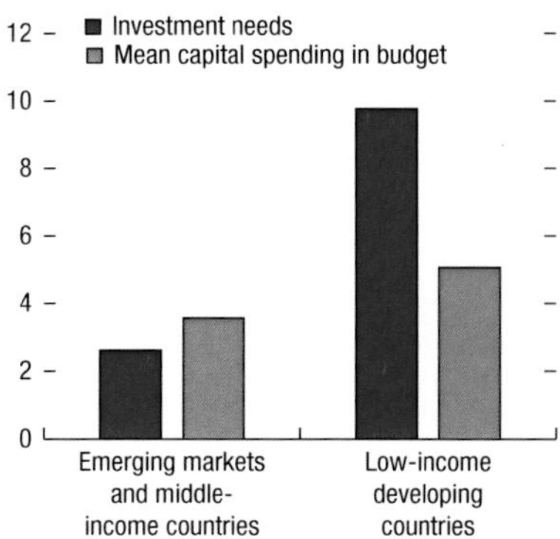


Source: Authors' calculations.

in financing the necessary spending to reach the SDGs. There is also a wide dispersion of investment needs across regions (for emerging market economies and low-income developing countries): the largest investment need is in sub-Saharan Africa, while Europe and Latin America have the smallest need and Asia, the Middle East, and the Commonwealth of Independent States fall in the middle.

**Figure 4.6. Annual Spending Needs, by Size of GDP**
*(As a percentage of average GDP)*

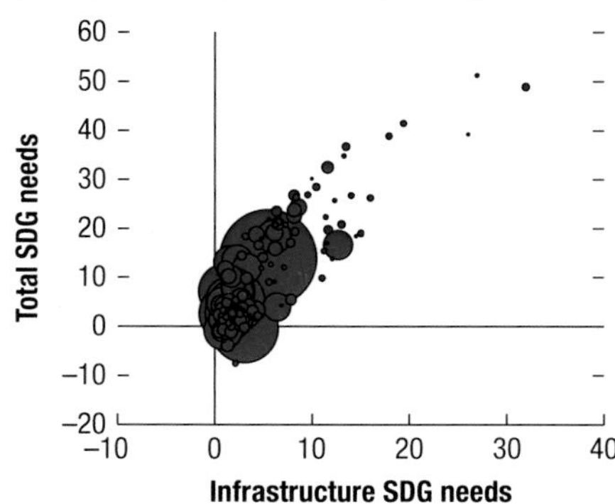


Source: Authors' calculations based on Gaspar and others 2019.
Note: The diameter of the balloon indicates GDP size. SDG = Sustainable Development Goal.

**Figure 4.7. Annual Investment Needs, by Region**
*(As a percentage of average GDP)*

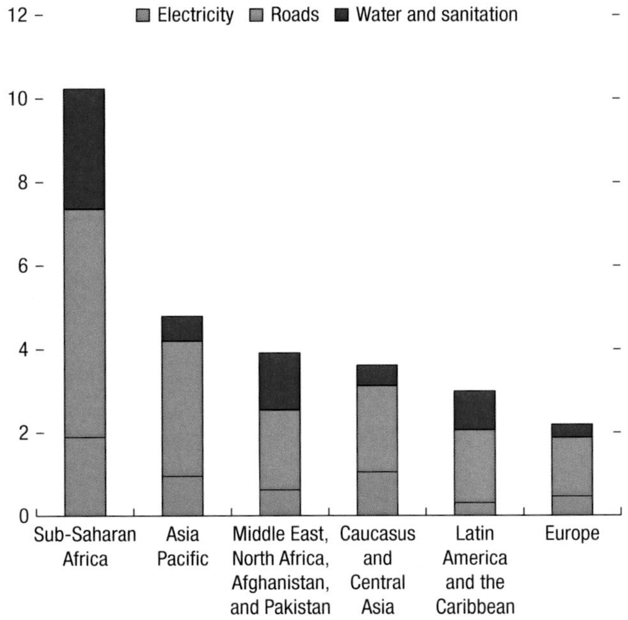

Source: Authors' calculations.

Spending needs in road infrastructure are the largest in both emerging markets and low-income developing countries. As Figure 4.8 shows, emerging markets need average annual investment of 1.7 percent of GDP (1.3 percent of GDP for new construction and 0.4 percent of GDP in maintenance) for roads until 2030, while low-income developing countries need annual investment of 5.2 percent of their GDP (4.1 percent of GDP for new construction and 1.1 percent of GDP in maintenance). These are significant costs, and especially relevant for sub-Saharan Africa, where rural accessibility is of particular concern. In addition, as countries invest to build road networks, maintenance costs will become more important. The model used in this chapter assumes a fixed depreciation rate of road assets, but some studies (for example, World Bank 2019) suggest that maintenance costs can rise to match the amount of new investment in some cases.

Spending needs for universal access to electricity are lower for emerging market economies than for low-income developing countries, but demand-driven investment needs cannot be overlooked. It is estimated that emerging market economies will face an average annual investment need of 0.4 percent of their GDP (0.1 percent of GDP to reach universal access and 0.3 percent of GDP to elevate per user electricity consumption to keep up with economic growth) until

## Figure 4.8. Investment, by Sector

**1. Components of Road Spending Needs**

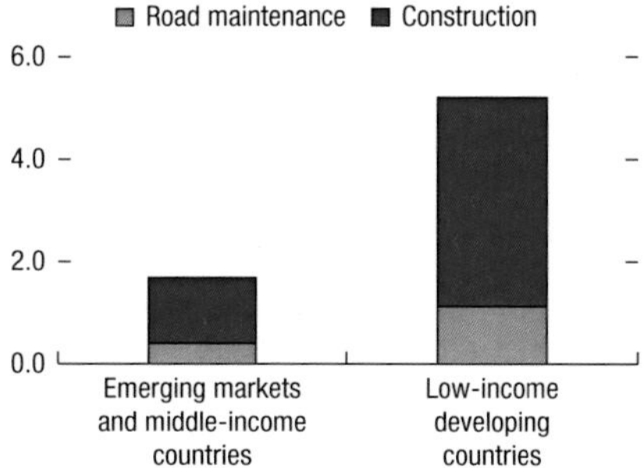


**2. Distribution of Road Spending Needs**

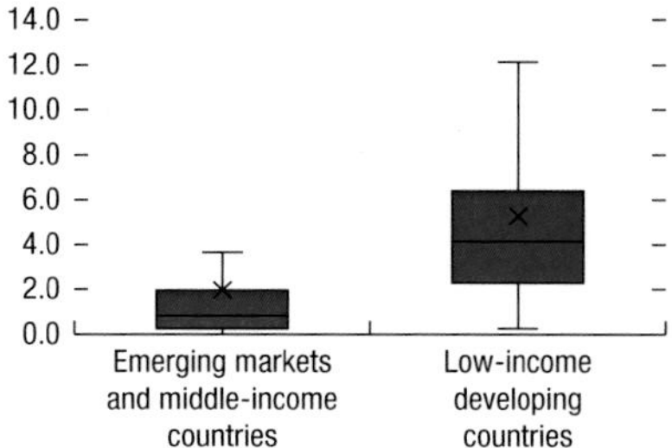


**3. Components of Electricity Spending Needs**

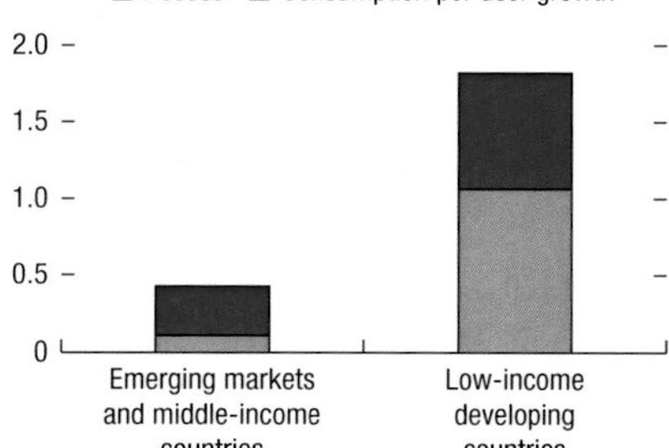


**4. Distribution of Electricity Spending Needs**

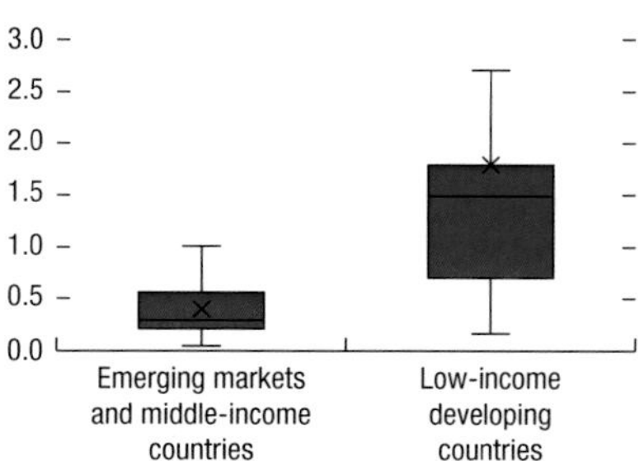


**5. Components of Water and Sanitation Spending Needs**

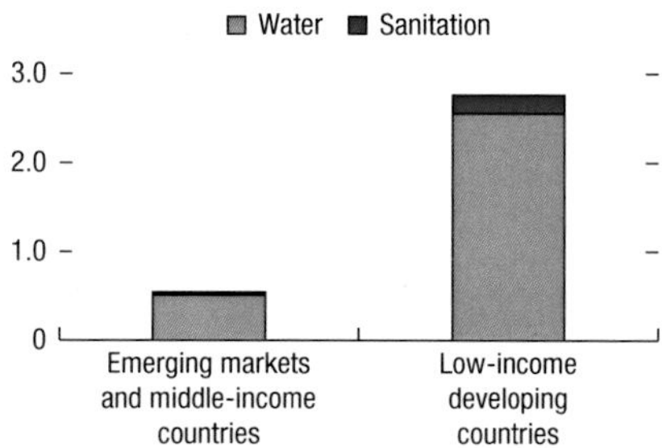


**6. Distribution of Water and Sanitation Spending Needs**

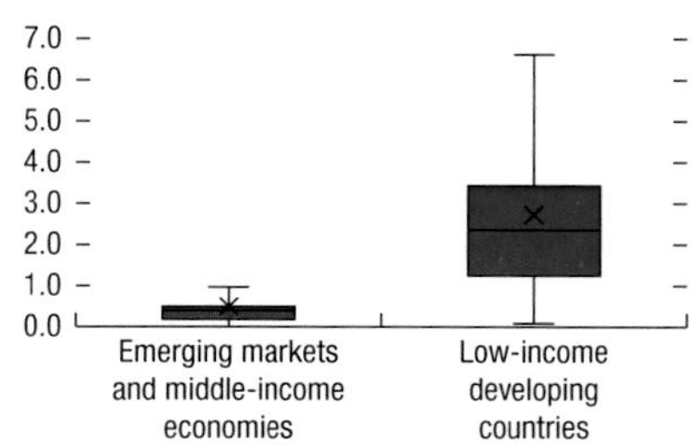


Source: Authors' calculations.
Note: Distributions in panels 2, 4, and 6 show maximum, 75 percent, 25 percent, and minimum values.

2030, while low-income developing countries face an annual investment need of 1.8 percent of their GDP (1.1 percent of GDP to reach universal access and 0.7 percent of GDP to elevate electricity consumption to keep up with economic growth). In emerging market economies, electricity access is not as severe an issue as in low-income developing countries (Figure 4.3). However, more advanced economies tend to have higher power consumption per user. In order to reach aspirations for economic growth, per user electricity consumption may need to increase even when universal access is no longer a concern; for example, in the transition to industrialization while the economic structure shifts toward a more energy-intensive pattern. These investment needs can also be affected by inefficiencies in electricity transmission and country-specific technology in power generation and transmission. World Bank (2019) stresses that operations and maintenance also need to be budgeted for once capital investment is made, to ensure electricity is reliable and affordable.

Investment needs to achieve universal access to safely managed water and sanitation are slightly less than those for electricity access. Average annual spending needs in emerging markets amount to 0.5 percent of their GDP (0.5 percent of GDP for water and 0.01 percent of GDP for sanitation) until 2030, while low-income developing countries face an annual spending need of 2.8 percent of their GDP (2.6 percent of GDP for water and 0.2 percent of GDP for sanitation). As universal coverage requires more than a one-off injection of capital while operation and maintenance in the water sector are especially important, all such costs were included in the estimates.

Our spending-need estimates are comparable to estimates in the literature, but naturally there are caveats in such exercises.[4] Reconciling cost estimates across studies is complicated given differences in the interpretation and inclusion of precise targets, country groupings, spending definitions, specific information available, and years for which estimates are reported. In particular, results from cross-country studies need to be verified and improved by using country-specific information, as governments need to incorporate SDGs into their own national development plans, choose practical development targets, and prioritize among objectives competing for the same resources. Moreover, the unit costs used in the calculations could vary depending on country-specific characteristics, technological choices, and the success of complementary reforms. For example, in country cases in which the methodologies described in this chapter have been applied, some of the unit cost assumptions were based on country-level information.

Efforts to improve public investment efficiency could change the sizes of countries' spending needs. Improvements in infrastructure coverage and quality

[4] As shown in Gaspar and others (2019), other studies tend to find the annual infrastructure spending need for low-income developing countries and emerging markets to be in the neighborhood of $2 trillion (for a wider sectoral coverage than the three sectors examined in this chapter).

**Figure 4.9. Impact of Improving Public Investment Efficiency**
*(Cost as percentage of average GDP)*

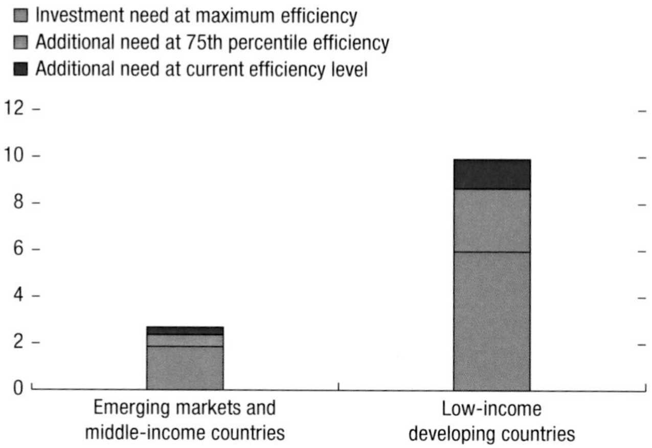

Source: Authors' calculations.

in recent years have been only loosely correlated with public investment, suggesting considerable efficiency loss in public investment in most countries.[5] As seen in Chapter 3, the size of the efficiency gap—the difference between the average country's public investment efficiency and that of best performers—widens as income falls, with a gap of 34 percent in emerging market economies and a gap of 53 percent in low-income developing countries. Reforms could help countries deliver more infrastructure "bang" for their public investment "buck." To illustrate the impact of efficiency gains, suppose emerging markets could improve efficiency such that the resulting average rose to match the current 75th percentile level for the group. Then these economies could reduce their total annual investment needs from 2.7 percent of GDP to 2.3 percent of GDP; if all emerging markets were to reach the maximum efficiency level, then their total annual investment needs would fall to 1.8 percent of GDP (Figure 4.9).[6] Similarly, low-income developing countries could reduce their total annual investment needs from 9.8 percent of GDP to 8.6 percent of GDP if their average efficiency rose to match the current 75th percentile for the group. Were all low-income developing countries to reach maximum efficiency, they could further reduce their total annual investment needs to 5.9 percent of GDP.

[5] See IMF (2015) and Chapter 3 of this book.

[6] Assuming a unitary elasticity of the change in the average unit cost to build the infrastructure, with respect to a change in the efficiency gap.

## IMPLICATIONS FOR REVENUE MOBILIZATION AND PUBLIC INVESTMENT MANAGEMENT

Since the investment needs to achieve infrastructure SDGs are sizeable, successful implementation of the SDG agenda requires strong national ownership to mainstream the SDG strategy into national development plans, investment prioritization, and budget processes. This in turn requires carefully planning the financing options, galvanizing private sector involvement, and managing the associated risks, as well as improving public investment governance and efficiency.

Meeting infrastructure investment needs requires scaling up public investment spending in many countries. Although in some cases the private sector could share the burden of the projected investment, a significant share of spending will necessarily come from the government budget. Therefore, financing the increased spending is a challenge that country authorities and the international community will need to address. Gasper and others (2019) explore some policy options.

- Additional revenue mobilization is the most important source of financing. It is estimated that if countries with tax-to-GDP ratios below the 75th percentile for their income group were to raise them to the 75th percentile, the increase would amount to 5 percentage points of GDP, on average. Adopting a medium-term revenue strategy is key. It would involve the following steps: building a broad-based consensus for medium-term revenue goals; designing a comprehensive tax reform policy, covering its administration and legal framework; committing to sustained political support over many years; and securing adequate resources to support coordinated implementation.
- Structural reforms that boost the level and durability of growth can be used to increase the resources available for investment. These reforms encompass a broad set of areas, including labor and product markets, the financial sector, governance, public finance management, and the business environment.
- Closer cooperation of the international community will help in achieving infrastructure SDGs in low-income developing countries. As mentioned earlier, the investment needs in low-income developing countries and some emerging market economies far exceed what they have been able to spend on public investment on average, and it would be difficult for many countries to rely solely on their own resources. Delivering on existing official development assistance targets would make a substantial contribution to closing the financing gaps.

The private sector can play an important role in infrastructure investment, but private financing is no panacea. Public-private partnerships can deliver infrastructure services more efficiently than can traditional public procurement under certain conditions. A well-designed contract can take advantage of bundling activities from building to operating the infrastructure, as the private partner has an incentive to construct high-quality assets and allocate an appropriate amount of maintenance spending over the lifetime of the asset. In a similar vein, private partners usually have an incentive to finish projects early with public-private partnerships.

However, public-private partnerships are not always more efficient than traditional procurement and entail significant fiscal risks. Privately financed projects will generally face higher financing costs than public sector projects. In addition, given the high contracting costs associated with public-private partnerships, they are only appropriate for large projects, and the quality of service must be measurable. Moreover, although public-private partnerships can help governments to circumvent short-term budget constraints, they do not genuinely create long-term fiscal space and could entail significant fiscal risks, including contingency costs. Therefore, their use will require strengthening public investment management processes and fiscal and legal institutions (navigating the fiscal risks that feature in Chapter 11).

Improvements in public investment efficiency will help to reach the infrastructure-related SDGs. There is significant potential for efficiency gains in public investment for emerging markets and low-income developing countries, since the investment gaps are large. As illustrated in the "Spending Needs to Reach SDGs In Infrastructure" section, if all countries were at their maximum efficiency levels, annual investment costs would be cut by 0.9 percent of GDP for emerging markets and 3.9 percent of GDP for low-income developing countries.

Technological choices among individual sectors will also play an important role in achieving desirable trade-offs among various objectives and result in different costs. For example, World Bank (2019) shows that costs can vary widely with the choice of technology and different pathways used to achieve universal access to safely managed water. In the power sector, there are different strategic choices to deliver different levels of power consumption. In transportation, complementary socioeconomic policies will influence how different modes are delivered and how the sector is organized. These technological decisions will result in different costs and also different levels and quality of infrastructure services.

## CONCLUSIONS

Infrastructure development is a key aspect of the SDG agenda and entails significant investment needs. On average, emerging market economies face an annual investment need of 2.7 percent of GDP for infrastructure (roads, electricity, and water and sanitation) until 2030, while it is 9.8 percent of GDP for low-income developing countries. There is a large variation among countries, and the challenge is especially daunting for low-income developing countries. Gaps in spending on roads dominate the investment needs. These estimates, as in other cross-country studies, should be refined wherever country-specific information is available. Scope exists to improve the methodology in further studies by considering additional factors and information.

In view of the large investment needs, countries need to develop plans to galvanize financing and improve public investment governance and efficiency. Efforts should focus on careful planning of financing options, galvanizing private sector involvement, and managing the associated risks, as well as tapping into foreign aid. Improving public investment governance and efficiency will help to reduce financing needs by increasing the dividends from public investment for a given level of spending.

# ANNEX 4.1. METHODOLOGICAL NOTE ON ESTIMATING COST OF REACHING SDGS ON ROAD AND ELECTRICITY INFRASTRUCTURE

This annex explains the methodology developed at the IMF for estimating the cost of building the road and electricity infrastructure consistent with reaching SDG Target 9.1 and Target 7.1. For the World Bank methodology on costing water, sanitation, and hygiene, see Hutton and Varughese (2016).

## ACCESS TO ROAD INFRASTRUCTURE

A two-step approach is used to estimate the cost for reaching the SDG target related to road access. First, a road infrastructure gap is estimated; and second, the annual investment needed to close the gap by 2030 is computed, given the unit cost to build the road network.

Investment needs to achieve SGD Target 9.1 are envisioned by estimating a target road density based on income, population density, and rural access levels. SDG Target 9.1 states, "Develop quality, reliable, sustainable and resilient infrastructure, including regional and transborder infrastructure, to support economic development and human well-being, with a focus on affordable and equitable access for all." As there is no specific numerical UN target for road infrastructure, the target road density for a country is derived by considering its projected GDP per capita and population density in 2030 and the goal of ensuring adequate access for those in remote locations, which is measured using a Rural Access Index (RAI).[7]

A country's specific target for road density is estimated using elasticities obtained from a regression analysis. Taking a similar approach to the literature for measuring infrastructure gaps (such as for Fay and Yepes 2003), estimates are derived from the following relationship using a cross-section of country-level data:

$$RD_i = C + \beta_1 Y_i + \beta_2 PD_i + \beta_3 RAI_i + \beta_4 X_i + \varepsilon_i,$$

where $RD$ is the log of road density, $Y$ is the log of GDP per capita, $PD$ is the log of population density, $RAI$ is the rural access index, $X$ is a vector of control variables, including the share of agriculture in GDP, share of manufacturing in GDP, and the degree of urbanization. The estimation results, using a cross-section of low-income developing countries and emerging markets, and all countries separately, are shown in Annex Table 4.1.1. Data sources used in the cost estimation are described in Annex Table 4.1.2. The road infrastructure gap is defined as how far a country is from its target road density.

The regression results confirm the positive correlation between road density and GDP per capita, population density, and rural road access. Increasing the RAI by 1 percentage point requires increasing the road density by about 1.7 percent, when using the estimates for low-income developing countries and

[7] The RAI (measured as the percentage of rural households living within 2 kilometers of an all-season road) is developed by the World Bank, and the latest data correspond to 2006. The World Bank is updating the index using a new methodology developed in 2015 (Iimi and others 2016).

**ANNEX TABLE 4.1.1**

**Main Estimated Coefficients**

| | All Countries | Low-Income Developing Countries and Emerging Markets Only |
|---|---|---|
| Number of observations | 86 | 64 |
| Adjusted $R^2$ | 0.7 | 0.7 |
| GDP per capita | 0.176** | 0.127 |
| | (0.0867) | (0.0947) |
| Population | 0.422*** | 0.485*** |
| | (0.0612) | (0.0612) |
| Rural Access Index | 2.413*** | 1.684*** |
| | (0.437) | (0.404) |

Source: Authors' calculations.
Note: Standard errors are in parentheses.
**Significant at the 5% level. ***Significant at the 1% level.

emerging markets, and 2.4 percent using the full sample estimate. This implies that a country with a current access level of 50 percent should have a road density 84–120 percent higher than its current value to increase access to 100 percent. The study finds that the elasticity of road density to GDP per capita is around 0.13 in low-income developing countries and emerging markets. This is similar to the coefficient of 0.14 estimated in Fay and Yepes (2003). Population density also is found to be statistically significant with an elasticity of 0.485 across low-income developing countries and emerging markets, and of 0.422 in the all-country sample. This is about the same as the findings in Fay and Yepes (2003).

Then, the country's specific target is computed and both the investment cost and the associated maintenance cost are calculated. This uses GDP per capita and population density projected for 2030 from World Economic Outlook and UN projections. The RAI is set at a target level,[8] and estimated elasticities are applied to calculate the country's specific target for road density and the corresponding target road length in 2030 ($R^*$). Using the unit cost to build 1 kilometer of road ($C$), the annual average investment cost to reach $R^*$ is as follows:

$$INV = \left(R^* - R_0\right) \cdot C \cdot \frac{1}{T},$$

where $R_0$ is the initial road length and $T$ is the number of years before 2030. For maintenance costs, the assumption is that each year a fraction $\delta$ of the newly constructed road network will need to be replaced. Then, the annual average cost to maintain the new roads would be the following:

$$M = \frac{1}{T} \cdot \delta \cdot \sum_{t=1}^{T-1} INV \cdot t = \frac{\delta \cdot INV \cdot (T-1)}{2}.$$

The unit cost to build 1 kilometer of a two-lane paved road is assumed to be \$487.17, unless a country-specific unit cost is available (World Bank 2013). The

[8] In this chapter, a target RAI ensuring good access is assumed to be 75 percent for those currently below 75 percent and 90 percent of those already above 75 percent.

default depreciation rate $\delta$ is assumed to be 5 percent.[9] To improve the accuracy of the cost estimates, the historical data, unit cost, depreciation rate assumptions, and country-specific targets should be verified and customized based on country information where that is available. The results also need to be interpreted carefully as the road network is only one factor affecting economic and human development, while the location of the roads and road quality are also important for transportation access.

## ACCESS TO ELECTRICITY

The unit cost approach is used to estimate the average annual cost to reach access for 100 percent of households. SDG Target 7.1 states, "By 2030, ensure universal access to affordable, reliable and modern energy services." The average annual cost is estimated as follows:

$$INV1 = \{(1 - a) \cdot P + [P \cdot (1 + g) \cdot T - P]\} \cdot \frac{1}{T} \cdot w \cdot C,$$

where $a$ is the initial fraction of the population with access to electricity, $P$ is the population level, $g$ is the population growth rate, $T$ is the number of years to reach universal coverage, $w$ is the initial level of electricity consumption per user in kilowatt-hours (assumed to be constant), and $C$ is the unit cost to generate and distribute electricity (assumed to be $2,258 per kilowatt) (World Bank 2013b).

In addition, estimates are made for the average annual cost to reach a higher level of consumption per user ($w^*$) in line with economic development. In this case,

$$INV2 = (w^* - w) \cdot P \cdot (1 + g) \cdot T \cdot C \cdot \frac{1}{T},$$

where $w^*$ is assumed to increase with per capita GDP.[10]

**ANNEX TABLE 4.1.2**

Data Sources

| Data | Source |
|---|---|
| GDP and components | IMF World Economic Outlook |
| Population | World Bank World Development Indicators |
| Degree of urbanization | World Bank World Development Indicators |
| Rural Access Index | World Bank Rural Access Index |
| Length of roads (kilometers) | CIA Factbook |
| Area (square kilometers) | World Bank World Development Indicators |
| Unit cost to build roads (dollars per kilometer) | World Bank Global Development Horizons: Capital for the Future (2013) |
| Electricity access | World Bank World Development Indicators |
| Electricity consumption per capita | World Bank World Development Indicators |
| Unit cost including generation and transmission | World Bank Global Development Horizons: Capital for the Future (2013) |
| Data used in the World Bank water template | Hutton and Varughese (2016) |

[9] The literature estimates that the depreciation rate for public capital stock ranges between 2.5 percent and 4.7 percent (see IMF 2015).

[10] The elasticity is assumed to be 0.94, reflecting the estimated correlation.

## REFERENCES

Fay, Marianne, and Tito Yepes. 2003. "Investing in Infrastructure: What Is Needed from 2000 to 2010?" World Bank Policy Research Working Paper 3102, World Bank, Washington, DC.

Gaspar, Vitor, David Amaglobeli, Mercedes Garcia-Escribano, Delphine Prady, and Mauricio Soto. 2019. "Fiscal Policy and Development: Human, Social, and Physical Investments for the SDGs." Staff Discussion Note 19/03, International Monetary Fund, Washington, DC.

Global Infrastructure Hub. 2017. *Global Infrastructure Outlook: Infrastructure Investment Needs—50 Countries, 7 Sectors to 2040.* Sydney: GI Hub.

Hutton, Guy, and Mili Varughese. 2016. "The Costs of Meeting the 2030 Sustainable Development Goal Targets on Drinking Water, Sanitation, and Hygiene." Water and Sanitation Program Technical Paper, World Bank, Washington, DC.

Iimi, Atsushi, Ahmed Farhad, Edward Charles Anderson, Adam Stone Diehl, Laban Maiyo, Tatiana Peralta-Quirós, and Kulwinder Singh Rao. 2016. "New Rural Access Index: Main Determinants and Correlation to Poverty." World Bank Policy Research Working Paper 7876, World Bank, Washington, DC.

International Monetary Fund (IMF). 2015. "Making Public Investment More Efficient." IMF Policy Paper, Washington, DC.

Lafortune, Guillaume, Grayson Fuller, Jorge Moreno, Guido Schmidt-Traub, and Christian Kroll. 2018. "SDG Index and Dashboards—Detailed Methodological Paper." Bertelsmann Stiftung and Sustainable Development Solutions Network, New York.

Schmidt-Traub, Guido. 2015. "Investment Needs to Achieve the Sustainable Development Goals—Understanding the Billions and Trillions." SDSN Working Paper Version 2, Sustainable Development Solutions Network, New York.

United Nations (UN). 2015. "The Addis Ababa Action Agenda of the Third International Conference on Financing for Development." New York.

World Bank. 2013. "Global Development Horizons: Capital for the Future—Saving and Investment in an Interdependent World." Technical Annexes, World Bank, Washington, DC.

World Bank. 2019. *Beyond the Gap: How Countries Can Afford the Infrastructure They Need while Protecting the Planet.* Washington, DC.

CHAPTER 5

# The Public Investment Management Assessment Framework: An Overview

**Taziona Chaponda, Chishiro Matsumoto, and Lewis Kabayiza Murara**

## INTRODUCTION

Efficient, high-quality, and sustainable public investment requires strong infrastructure governance. The link between public investment, infrastructure quality, and sustainable growth has been established elsewhere in this book and in other literature. Strong evidence exists that estimated efficiency gaps are sizeable—on average, countries lose more than one-third of their resources in the public investment process—and that the average country could close more than half the efficiency gap if it adopted best infrastructure governance practices (Chapter 3). Evidence also suggests that countries with better infrastructure governance enjoy positive output effects from public investment, while such impacts disappear in countries where governance is weaker (Chapter 2).

There are several useful guidelines and frameworks to support sound infrastructure governance, but most focus on the project level and pay little attention to the macro effects (see Box 5.1). Although project design and management are key parts of sound infrastructure governance, sound practices to choose the right investments, select the right financing means (including public-private partnerships), and ensure that investments are brought to fruition are macro-critical and essential for achieving overall economic policy goals and managing fiscal risks related to infrastructure.

In 2015, recognizing the need to approach infrastructure governance in a holistic manner, the IMF developed the Public Investment Management Assessment (PIMA) framework to help countries strengthen critical infrastructure governance areas. Given the central role of public investment in promoting growth in a macroeconomically sustainable fashion, the PIMA offers a comprehensive diagnostic tool for assessing the infrastructure governance of countries at all levels of economic development. It identifies areas in need of attention to improve infrastructure governance and points to specific reforms that governments can implement to stretch limited resources and spend better on public investment.

## Box 5.1. Overview of Global Principles and Tools for Infrastructure Governance

The international community has developed various principles and tools to help countries strengthen their infrastructure governance. In June 2019, the Group of Twenty (G20) under Japan's presidency endorsed the G20 Principles for Quality Infrastructure Investment. In these, strengthening infrastructure governance is embraced as one of the six principles to promote quality infrastructure investment based on the shared recognition that "sound infrastructure governance over the life cycle of the project is a key factor to ensure long-term cost-effectiveness, accountability, transparency, and integrity of infrastructure investment" (Ministry of Finance, Japan 2019).

In parallel, international organizations have stepped up efforts to help countries strengthen different aspects of their infrastructure governance. The IMF's Public Investment Management Assessment offers a comprehensive and systemic assessment that allows for comparison of infrastructure governance across countries (IMF 2015; IMF 2018b; IMF and OECD 2019). Several other tools are also available:

- The World Bank has developed a framework for assessing public investment management, which helps countries evaluate the strengths and weaknesses of public investment management practices through eight "must-have" features (Rajaram and others 2014).
- The IMF, jointly with the World Bank, has developed the Public-Private Partnership Fiscal Risk Assessment Model (PFRAM). PFRAM is a tool to assess the potential fiscal costs and risks related to public-private partnership projects, either individually or in a portfolio (IMF and World Bank 2019).
- The OECD published "Getting Infrastructure Right: A Framework for Better Governance" in 2017. This framework lays out governance tools to help policymakers improve the management of infrastructure policy, based on 10 dimensions for how governments prioritize, plan, budget, deliver, regulate, and evaluate infrastructure investment (OECD 2017).

Together, these tools provide a comprehensive approach to helping countries strengthen their infrastructure governance.

On the basis of PIMAs conducted in more than 50 countries, this chapter shows that most countries have much room to improve their infrastructure governance institutions. All countries, irrespective of region or income group, have scope to make improvements in various areas of infrastructure governance, although more so in emerging market economies and low-income developing countries than in advanced economies. On the whole, infrastructure governance institutions tend to be better in design, particularly in the planning stage, than in practice, where weaknesses are particularly evident in the allocation and the implementation stages of public investment. Countries generally score better on more general infrastructure governance institutions that more indirectly affect decision making on public investment, such as budget comprehensiveness and fiscal rules, compared to key infrastructure governance institutions that are specific to public investment decision making, such as project appraisal, project selection and maintenance funding.

**Box 5.2. PIMAs around the World**

PIMAs have become a key tool for helping IMF member countries strengthen their infrastructure governance. From 2015 to October 2019 PIMAs have been conducted in 58 countries[1] across all regions and income levels (Figure 5.2.1). PIMAs and follow-up capacity development activities are conducted by IMF staff in cooperation with staff from other organizations (such as the World Bank, the Inter-American Development Bank, and the Asian Development Bank) and are supported by the IMF's regional capacity development centers.

**Box Figure 5.2.1. Distribution of PIMAs around the World**

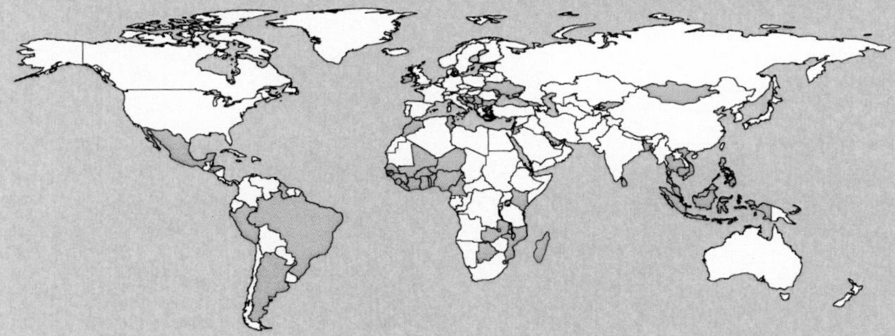

Source: IMF staff.
Note: Shaded countries are those that have conducted PIMAs. PIMA = Public Investment Management Assessment.

[1] For analytical purpose, this chapter uses the results of 52 PIMAs whose reports had been finalized by mid-2019.

The chapter looks at what PIMAs conducted so far have taught us, starting with an overview of the lessons learned from 52 country assessments across the globe finalized by mid-2019 (Box 5.2) and then discusses how governments have used PIMA recommendations to help strengthen their infrastructure governance institutions, often supported by development partners.

## FEATURES OF THE PIMA FRAMEWORK

The PIMA is a comprehensive and standardized framework to assess infrastructure governance in countries across all levels of economic development. PIMAs evaluate the procedures, tools, decision-making and monitoring processes that governments use to provide infrastructure assets and services to the public. PIMAs take a systematic approach to analyzing governance that allows countries to quantify and benchmark their practices against peers. The in-depth analysis, complemented with cross-country comparisons, raises awareness and builds a shared understanding among key stakeholders of required reform actions. This can help countries to develop an overarching strategy for strengthening infrastructure governance that is accessible to policymakers and development partners alike.

**Figure 5.1. Overview of the PIMA Framework**

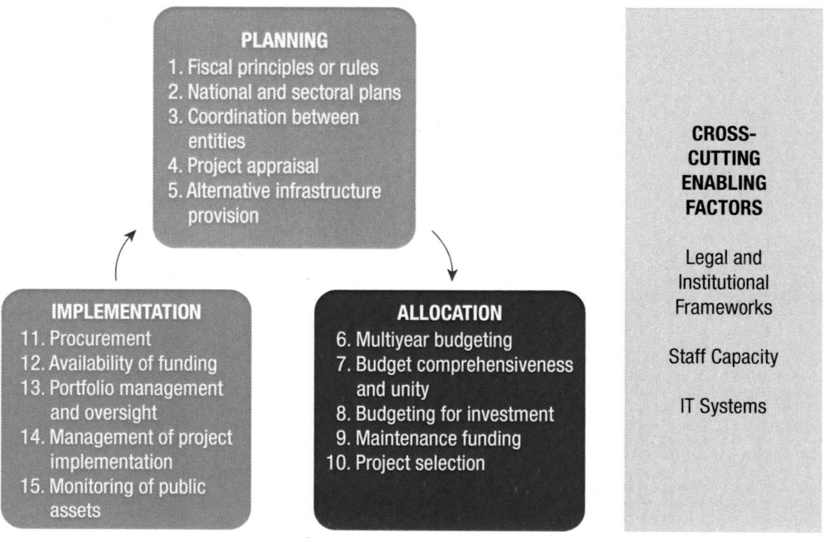


Source: IMF staff based on IMF (2018b).
Note: IT = information technology; PIMA = Public Investment Management Assessment.

PIMAs evaluate 15 institutions, or practices, involved in the three key stages of the public investment cycle (Figure 5.1): (1) planning sustainable investment across the public sector, (2) allocating investment to the right sectors and projects, and (3) implementing projects on time and within budget.[2] All three stages are critical from a macro perspective:

- Planning. Efficient investment planning requires institutions that ensure public investment is fiscally sustainable, effectively coordinated across sectors and levels of government, and properly appraised.
- Allocation. Allocating public investment to the most productive projects requires comprehensive, unified, medium-term budgeting and objective criteria for selecting projects.
- Implementation. Timely and cost-effective implementation of public investment projects requires institutions that ensure projects are fully funded, transparently monitored, and effectively managed throughout their implementation.

Each institution is analyzed along three dimensions that reflect the key features of the given institution, resulting in a total of 45 dimensions. Three possible scores (not met, partially met, or fully met) are assigned to each dimension, and their average within an institution produces a score for that institution. To complete the

[2] For more details, see IMF (2018b).

analysis, PIMAs also include a qualitative assessment of three cross-cutting enabling factors that often impact the overall effectiveness of infrastructure governance institutions: (1) the legal and regulatory framework, (2) IT systems, and (3) general staff capacity. For instance, poor integration of IT systems may limit data sharing on projects. Weak IT systems can have a negative impact across the project cycle, but particularly during implementation, where knowing the correct status of projects, the funds spent, and the condition of individual assets is important for efficient resource use.

A key feature of the PIMA is that it makes a clear distinction between institutional design (what is on paper) and effectiveness (what happens in practice). This is important because what exists on paper may differ from actual practice. For example, a country can establish fiscal rules to set limits on fiscal aggregates, but it might fail to consistently comply with them. Or a country may have developed guidelines for project appraisal that are only applied to a few projects. Low scores in either one or both of these dimensions help inform the reform priorities for the country.

By covering the full public investment cycle in a comprehensive manner, the PIMA also addresses the networked nature of infrastructure governance. In a network, the weakest link determines overall quality. For infrastructure governance, that means that the benefits of having strong institutions in some areas may be jeopardized by weaknesses in other areas. For example, a country may employ high-quality practices for planning public investments, but these will not be effective if insufficient funding is allocated to projects during budget preparation, or if funding gaps during project implementation impede project completion (Box 5.3).

## Box 5.3. Links between Public Investment Management Institutions

Correlations in the strength of different institutions point to the importance of taking a holistic view of the public investment management cycle, as they show complementarities between different stages of the process (Figure 5.3.1).

- Fiscal rules and targets are correlated, although moderately, with a large number of institutions, especially in budget execution, indicating that sound macrofiscal institutions are important for the implementation of projects.
- Countries with strong institutions for project appraisal are generally also strong in project selection, highlighting the benefits of robust project evaluation for project selection.
- Countries that effectively oversee their investment portfolios also tend to have good management mechanisms for individual project implementation, underscoring the importance of proper oversight for project implementation.
- Availability of funding and monitoring of public assets are strongly correlated, indicating the complementarity between cash management and proper accounting and reporting of assets.
- National and sectoral planning correlates weakly with other institutions, suggesting that national and sectoral plans can sometimes be drawn up in a vacuum and in a manner that is not well integrated with budgeting.

**Box 5.3. (*Continued*)**

**Figure 5.3.1. Correlations among Public Investment Management Institutions, 2015–19**

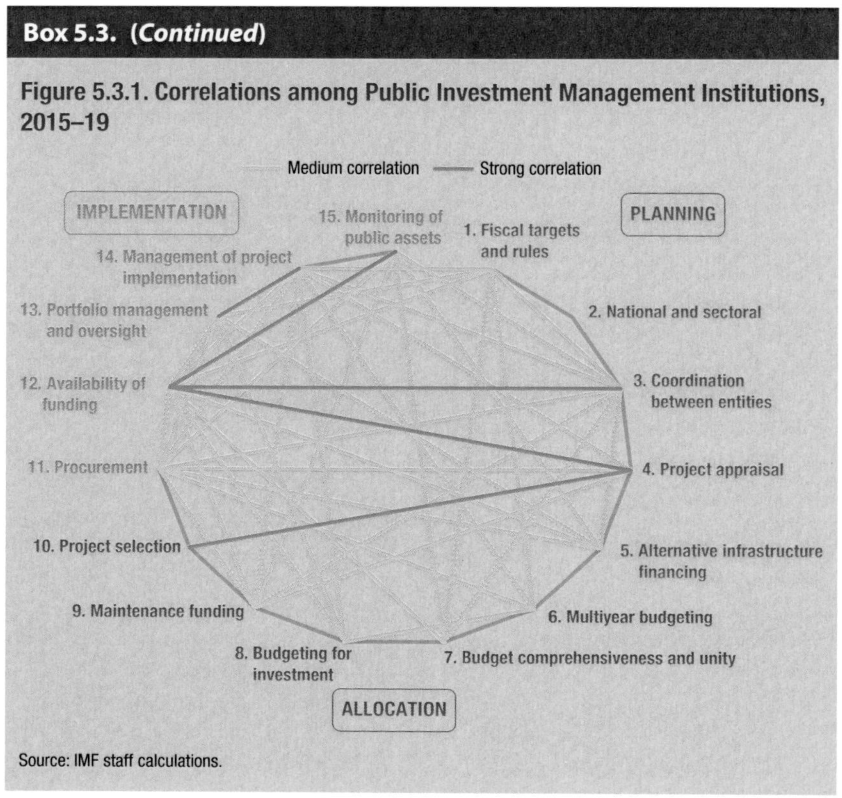


Source: IMF staff calculations.

## BENEFITS OF STRONGER INFRASTRUCTURE GOVERNANCE

The benefits of strong infrastructure governance were established in earlier chapters and include its positive impacts on output (Chapter 2) and efficiency (Chapter 3).

Indeed, evidence shows that stronger infrastructure governance institutions lead to better investment outcomes by raising the efficiency of public expenditure, even as spending declines. Stronger infrastructure governance institutions tend to be associated with lower levels of public investment (Figure 5.2, panel 1), but also translates into higher efficiency (Figure 5.2, panel 2).

Also, stronger institutions are associated with more stable investments and lower perceptions of corruption. As shown in Figure 5.2, panel 3, countries with strong infrastructure governance institutions have less volatile investment flows, suggesting they are less prone to stop-go investment policies. Consequently, more stable investment could lead to better-quality infrastructure. Also, as shown in Figure 5.2, panel 4, stronger infrastructure governance institutions discourage corrupt practices, which is a major risk for large and complex infrastructure projects (see also Chapter 10).

**Figure 5.2. Public Investment Efficiency and Governance Outcomes**

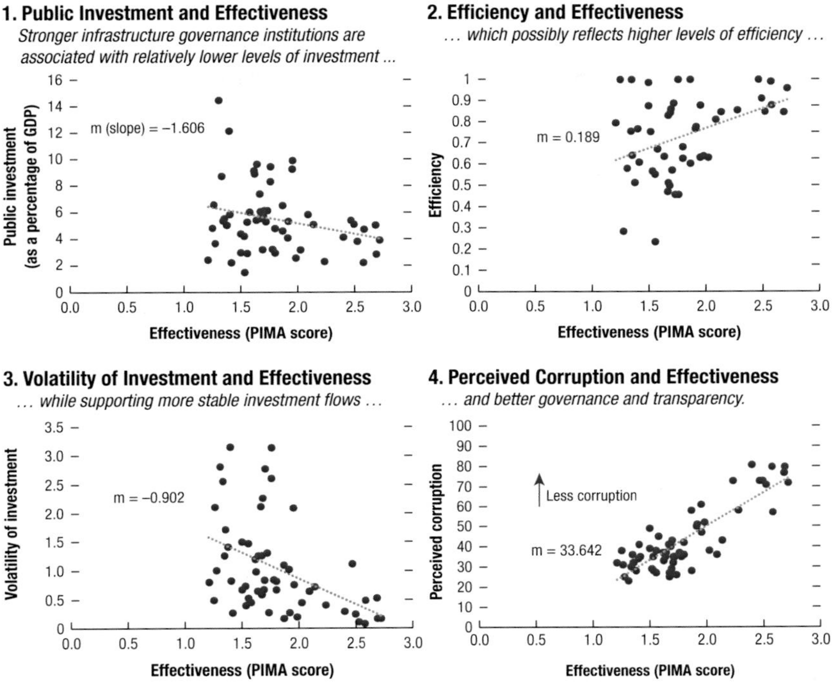

**1. Public Investment and Effectiveness**
*Stronger infrastructure governance institutions are associated with relatively lower levels of investment ...*

Public investment (as a percentage of GDP)
m (slope) = −1.606
Effectiveness (PIMA score)

**2. Efficiency and Effectiveness**
*... which possibly reflects higher levels of efficiency ...*

Efficiency
m = 0.189
Effectiveness (PIMA score)

**3. Volatility of Investment and Effectiveness**
*... while supporting more stable investment flows ...*

Volatility of investment
m = −0.902
Effectiveness (PIMA score)

**4. Perceived Corruption and Effectiveness**
*... and better governance and transparency.*

Perceived corruption
Less corruption
m = 33.642
Effectiveness (PIMA score)

Sources: World Economic Outlook and IMF staff estimates.
Note: In panel 2, efficiency is defined by the Hybrid Public Investment Efficiency Index. See Chapter 3 for details. In panel 3, volatility of investment is measured by the standard deviation of the change in the ratio of public investment to GDP between 2010 and 2015. Panel 4 reflects data from the Corruption Perception Index 2018. PIMA = Public Investment Management Assessment.

## WHAT PUBLIC INVESTMENT MANAGEMENT ASSESSMENTS TELL US ABOUT THE STRENGTH OF INFRASTRUCTURE GOVERNANCE INSTITUTIONS

The PIMAs conducted so far provide valuable insights into the strength of infrastructure governance institutions across countries.

- Countries generally score higher on institutional design than effectiveness, indicating that many countries are not fully translating reforms into practices.
- The gap between institutional design and effectiveness is most pronounced for low-income developing countries, reflecting weak implementation capacity even where sound design features are in place.

- Across the three key stages of the public investment cycle—planning, allocation, and implementation—the lowest effectiveness scores and highest gaps are generally recorded in the allocation and implementation stages, when assets are selected, monitored, and maintained.
- Countries often score more poorly in the key institutions specific to public investment decision making, such as project appraisal, project selection, and maintenance funding, compared to the more general infrastructure governance that more indirectly affect decision making on public investments, such as budget comprehensiveness and fiscal rules.

Overall, the PIMA results show that advanced economies are far stronger in infrastructure governance than emerging market economies and low-income developing countries. Figure 5.3 shows that, on a scale of 1 to 3, emerging market economies and low-income developing countries on average perform far below best practice (a score of 3). However, even advanced economies do not achieve best practice, showing that they too have scope for improvement in selected areas. Much of this chapter focuses on the performance of emerging market economies and low-income developing countries, which have the most to gain from infrastructure governance reforms.

### *Design versus Effectiveness*

Countries generally score higher on institutional design than on effectiveness (Figure 5.4). Overall, countries achieved an average score of 1.9 on institutional

**Figure 5.3. Effectiveness of Public Investment Management, by Income Group, 2015–19**

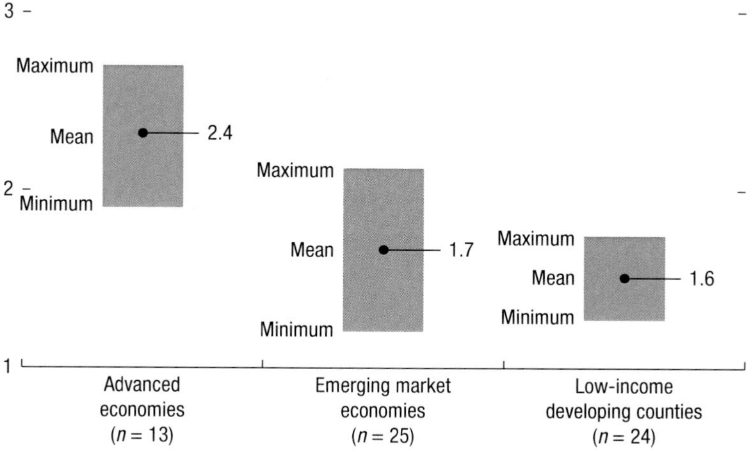


Source: IMF staff calculations based on PIMA reports.
Note: The advanced group includes 10 advanced country desk assessments. Effectiveness is measured on a scale of 1 to 3, with best practice being a score of 3. PIMA = Public Investment Management Assessment.

**Figure 5.4. Institutional Design versus Effectiveness: All Countries, 2015–19**

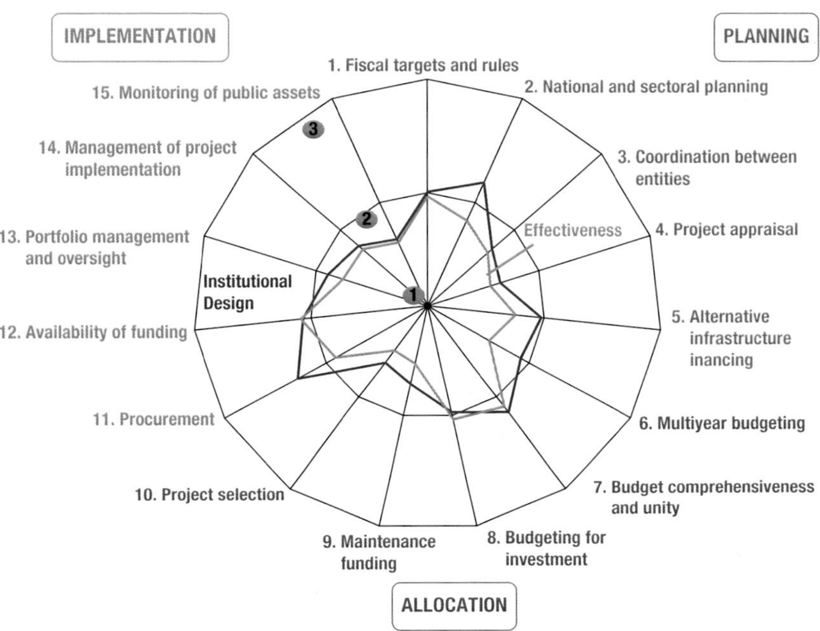


Source: IMF staff calculations based on PIMA reports.
Note: Institutional design and effectiveness are measured on a scale of 1 to 3, with best practice being a score of 3. PIMA = Public Investment Management Assessment.

design compared to 1.8 on effectiveness. This is mostly explained by emerging market economies and low-income developing countries performing worse on effectiveness than advanced economies, perhaps reflecting that the latter have longer experiences in implementing robust infrastructure governance systems and better access to technical and managerial skills.

Emerging market economies and low-income developing countries score lower on effectiveness than on institutional design (Figure 5.5), with low-income developing countries showing the biggest difference between the two. Both groups show similar strength in the planning and allocation stages. However, low-income developing countries fall behind in key aspects of implementation, for example, by failing to provide funding for investment projects in a timely manner, likely because of cash constraints.

The challenges faced by low-income developing countries are frequently related to capacity constraints, particularly in implementing policy reforms. Low-income developing countries have often focused on setting up the legal and regulatory aspects of infrastructure governance and have paid less attention to implementation. They have relatively strong design features in national and sectoral planning, enacting strong public procurement laws and adopting fiscal rules, but weak capacity to undertake

**Figure 5.5. Institutional Design versus Effectiveness, by Income Group, 2015–19**

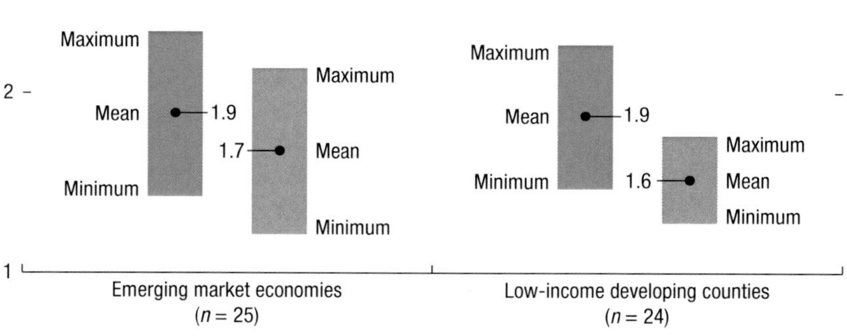


Source: IMF staff calculations based on PIMA reports.
Note: Institutional design and effectiveness are measured on a scale of 1 to 3, with best practice being a score of 3. PIMA = Public Investment Management Assessment.

rigorous project appraisal and selection. For example, while Mali (IMF 2018a) has designed relatively solid systems for project selection, it has yet to implement them fully.

There is scope to strengthen the effectiveness of infrastructure governance across all regions (Figure 5.6). Africa and Europe present the biggest gaps

**Figure 5.6. Average Scores on Institutional Design and Effectiveness, by Region, 2015–19**

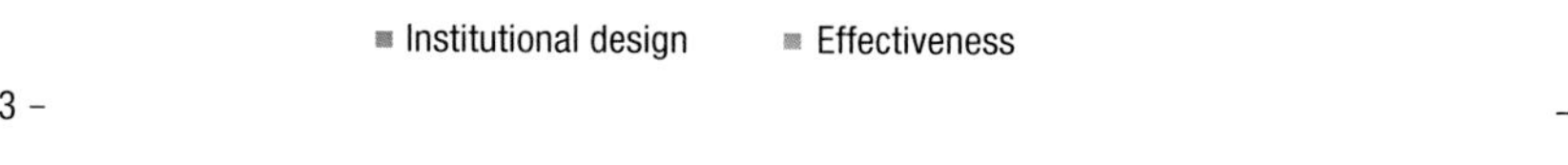


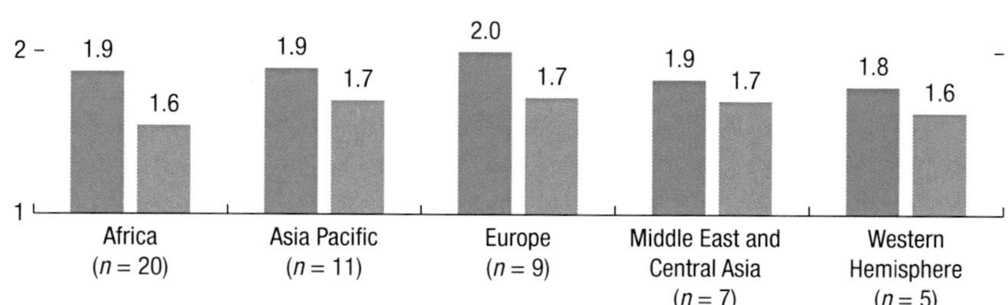


Source: IMF staff calculations based on PIMA reports.
Note: Institutional design and effectiveness are measured on a scale of 1 to 3, with best practice being a score of 3. PIMA = Public Investment Management Assessment.

between design and effectiveness, while Africa and Western Hemisphere present the lowest average effectiveness score. In low-income developing countries, sub-Saharan Africa presents the greatest potential to improve infrastructure governance, pointing to large capacity gaps. The weakest areas include lack of rigorous project appraisal and weak systems to fund and monitor public assets.

### *Strength of Institutions across the Public Investment Cycle*

Gaps between institutional design and effectiveness are evident in all three stages of public investment (Figure 5.7). Countries perform unevenly within each stage of the public investment cycle. At the planning stage, most countries—with a few notable exceptions such as Ireland (IMF 2017) and Mexico—struggle to design and implement robust systems for project appraisal. At the allocation stage, the lowest effectiveness scores are recorded for project selection and maintenance funding. Most countries, including advanced economies, fail to apply a standard methodology for estimating routine and capital maintenance costs. At the implementation stage, the lowest scores was recorded in the monitoring of public assets.

What emerges from this picture is that better scores are often achieved in the early stages of the investment cycle, when countries are setting fiscal targets and rules, and formulating national and sectoral plans. Once in place, these broad frameworks and supporting rules are difficult to translate into effective allocation and implementation because of weaknesses in project selection, maintenance funding, and the monitoring of public assets.

**Figure 5.7. Institutional and Effectiveness Scores, by Stage of Investment, 2015–19**

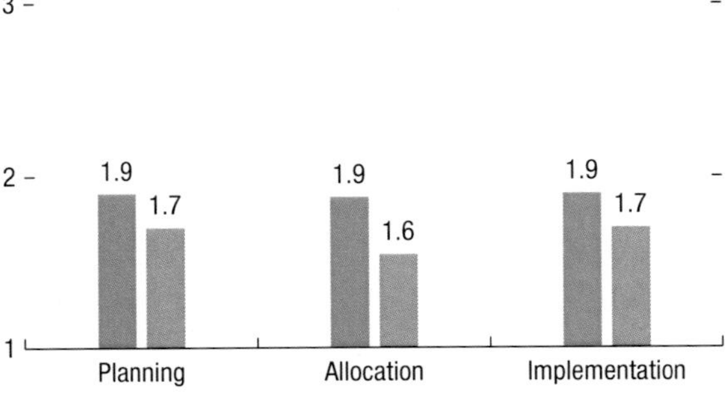


Source: IMF staff calculations based on PIMA reports.
Note: Institutional design and effectiveness are measured on a scale of 1 to 3, with best practice being a score of 3. PIMA = Public Investment Management Assessment.

## *Strongest to Weakest Institutions*

The 15 PIMA institutions can be divided into infrastructure governance institutions that are specific to public investment and more general public financial management institutions that more indirectly affect decision making on public investments. The broader institutions typically score higher than the ones specific to public investment. Figure 5.8 shows that lower scores are observed, on average, in institutions related to project selection, maintenance funding, and project appraisal, areas specific to public investment, while countries tend to fare better in more general public financial management institutions, such as budget comprehensiveness and unity, availability of funding, and fiscal targets and rules. This suggests that countries have paid less attention to institutions whose roles are specific to public investment.

**Figure 5.8. Average Scores for Broader Public Financial Management versus PIM–Specific Institutions**

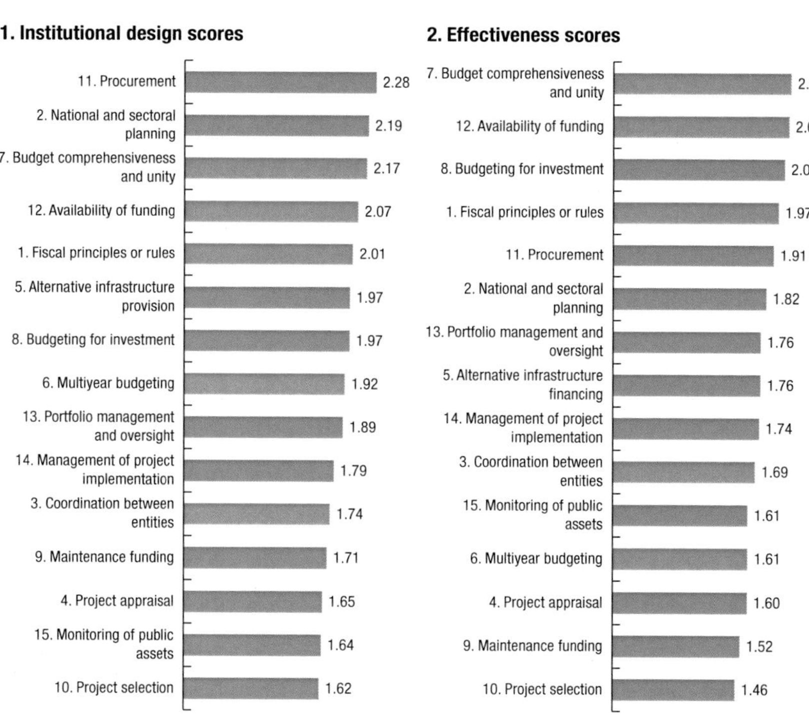


Source: IMF staff calculations based on PIMA reports.
Note: Institutional design and effectiveness are measured on a scale of 1 to 3, with best practice being a score of 3. PFM = public financial management; PIM = public investment management; PIMA = Public Investment Management Assessment.

Project appraisal and selection stand out as two of the most difficult reform areas. Part of the problem is often a lack of funding for these activities and inadequate skills to perform project appraisals. But even where funding is adequate, project appraisal is often rushed because the pressure to deliver quickly leads to shortcuts to get to procurement. Inadequate appraisals, coupled with unwarranted political interference during project selection, can result in poor outcomes.

Monitoring of public assets also stands out as a weakness. Once an asset has been delivered, less attention is paid to maintaining its quality. For example, few countries have a detailed understanding of the number of buildings they have in the public sector, the condition of those buildings, and the maintenance backlog. The same applies to other types of infrastructure.

Advancing reforms of institutions specific to public investment requires closer collaboration between a wide range of players, including ministries of finance, planning ministries, line ministries, and regulatory agencies. Broader public financial management institutions generally fall within the remit of the Ministry of Finance, while reforms of specific institutions rely more on expertise within line ministries and sector regulators. For example, in the energy sector, successful implementation of public investment requires a close collaboration between the Ministry of Finance, the Ministry of Energy, and the energy sector regulator.

## HOW PIMAs ARE USED

How have PIMA recommendations been used to help catalyze country reforms? What follow-up reform actions have countries taken and how has their infrastructure governance been strengthened?

PIMAs produce a set of prioritized recommendations specific to each country and informed by multiple information sources. The assessments draw on information from officials and other stakeholders, and from analysis of available data and documents.

While recommendations cover all stages and reflect the variety of challenges in different countries, the most common PIMA recommendations concern the area of alternative infrastructure financing, as seen in Figure 5.9. Public-private partnerships and investments by state-owned enterprises are often introduced as alternative ways to scale up infrastructure investment by directing resources through channels not restricted by traditional procurement and budget procedures. These alternatives tend to fall outside the budget process and have become major sources of fiscal risk for national budgets (Chapter 11).

In addition, project appraisal and project selection are featured regularly in recommendations, reflecting widespread weaknesses in these areas. One reason for this is that project preparation is costly and oftentimes not adequately funded, particularly in low-income countries where it is not always viewed as an essential part of the planning process. Project selection is often compromised because objective criteria for selection are lacking.

**Figure 5.9. PIMA Recommendations, by Institution, 2015–19**

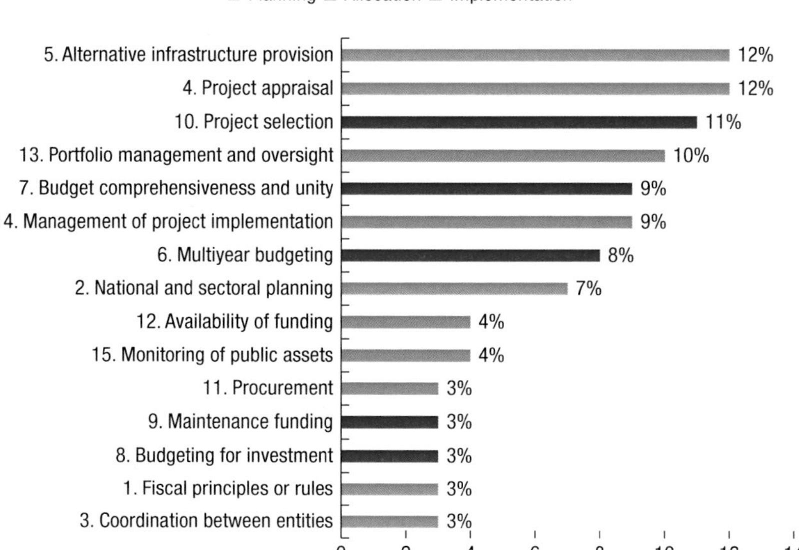


Source: PIMA reports.
Note: IMF staff calculations are based on the recommendations in the 52 PIMA reports. PIMA = Public Investment Management Assessment.

For country authorities, PIMA reports provide a basis for developing reform plans tailored to their needs and prioritized to match their resources and institutional capabilities. The reports bring together in-depth data analyses based on standard charts and qualitative discussions of the key issues. Also, because a consultative approach is followed, which encompasses government ministries and agencies, development partners, and other actors, the reform plans from PIMA assessments typically have broad support.

Many countries have taken actions to implement PIMA recommendations. Some specific examples are presented in Box 5.4.

**Box 5.4. Examples of Infrastructure Governance Reforms from PIMAs**

The PIMA conducted in 2017 in Ireland found infrastructure governance practices were generally high standard, for both institutional design and effectiveness. Nonetheless, a number of recommendations were made to enhance infrastructure governance practices at all stages of the public investment cycle. The National Development Plan 2018–2027, published in February 2018, presented several new measures based on the PIMA recommendations. These include (1) the establishment of an Infrastructure Projects Steering Group, (2) publication of a Capital Tracker, which will become Ireland's primary tool for

**Box 5.4 (*Continued*)**

public transparency on infrastructure projects, priorities, timelines, and performance targets, and (3) improvements in the methods of project appraisal and selection. The government has also reinforced technical processes and staff resources in the Department of Public Expenditure and Review and other government departments dedicated to the appraisal and evaluation of completed investment projects.

In Kenya, the PIMA conducted in January 2017 recommended the establishment of a central public investment management unit to improve coordination among ministries and agencies. It also identified the need for a set of standard project appraisal guidelines to bring consistency across entities. In the months that followed, both reforms were implemented by the government with the support of development partners. The reforms came at a time when President Uhuru Kenyatta announced an escalation of the fight against corruption, which brought greater transparency around large-scale procurement decisions. Such transparency was another area the PIMA had highlighted for action.

From 2012–13, Mongolia experienced a rapid expansion of off-budget spending on public investment, financed by borrowing through the Development Bank of Mongolia. The level of spending, which was volatile, reached nearly 10 percent of GDP and led to a large accumulation of liabilities. Amid declining revenues, Mongolia was unable to sustain this level of spending as it reached the limits of its borrowing capacity. Following the PIMA, authorities transferred the off-budget projects to the state budget and introduced tighter control over the Development Bank of Mongolia's borrowing for new projects. Mongolia also improved project appraisal and selection through a new standard methodology and evaluation criteria, as recommended by the PIMA. This will help to improve the quality of project preparation and contribute to stronger implementation.

Note: PIMA = Public Investment Management Assessment.

## CONCLUSIONS

The PIMA framework helps countries to improve infrastructure governance by identifying targeted reforms that will raise the efficiency and productivity of public investment. PIMAs provide policymakers with comprehensive analysis of strengths and weaknesses in infrastructure governance and how to close the efficiency gaps. However, actions by country authorities are required to bring reforms into effect. For this reason, each PIMA is accompanied by a prioritized reform action plan that includes timelines and reference to the responsible institutions. Most countries score significantly lower on the effectiveness of infrastructure governance institutions than on institutional design. This observation helps to pinpoint where reforms are required most urgently to strengthen infrastructure governance.

Large gains can be made by enhancing reforms of institutions that are specific to public investment. Countries generally score better on more general public financial management institutions, but they fall short on project appraisal and project selection (early in the project cycle) and also on monitoring and accounting for assets (later in the cycle). This often translates into project scope and size being misguided, and maintenance being inadequately funded. Poor maintenance reduces the economic life of valuable capital assets.

More broadly, the PIMA identifies practical ways of determining how to spend limited resources in better ways to improve the efficiency and productivity of public investment. By raising spending efficiency, countries can extract greater value from limited resources, spend less to produce the same or similar outputs, and deliver more stable and higher-quality public services.

## REFERENCES

International Monetary Fund (IMF). 2015. "Making Public Investment More Efficient." IMF Staff Report, Washington, DC, June.

IMF. 2017. "Ireland: Technical Assistance Report—Public Investment Management Assessment." IMF Country Report 17/333, Washington, DC.

IMF. 2018a. "Mali: Technical Assistance Report—Public Investment Management Assessment." IMF Country Report 18/114, Washington, DC.

IMF. 2018b. "Public Investment Management Assessment—Review and Update." IMF Policy Paper, Washington, DC, May.

International Monetary Fund and Organisation for Economic Co-operation and Development. 2019. "OECD/IMF Reference Note on the Governance of Quality Infrastructure Investment." Washington, DC, and Paris.

International Monetary Fund and World Bank. 2019. "PPP Fiscal Risk Assessment Model 2.0 (PFRAM) User Manual." Washington, DC.

Ministry of Finance, Japan. 2019. G20 Principles for Quality Infrastructure Investment. Tokyo.

Organisation for Economic Co-operation and Development (OECD). 2017. "Getting Infrastructure Right: A Framework for Better Governance." Paris.

Rajaram, Anand, Tuan Minh Le, Kai Kaiser, Jay-Hyung Kim, and Jonas Frank (editors). 2014. *The Power of Public Investment Management: Transforming Resources into Assets for Growth.* Washington, DC: World Bank.

# PART II

# Fiscal Policy for Quality Public Investment

CHAPTER 6

# Public Investment over the Fiscal Cycle

Tannous Kass-Hanna, Kangni Kpodar, and Dawit Tessema

## INTRODUCTION

Many countries responded to the global financial crisis by increasing public spending to soften the ensuing economic downturn (IMF 2010; Dhar 2014). Ten years later, public debt has surged to unprecedented levels, prompting calls for fiscal consolidation to rebuild fiscal buffers and curb public debt accumulation. Low-income developing countries in particular must tackle daunting challenges with rising debt vulnerabilities, in part resulting from protracted low commodity prices, leaving no option other than to consolidate.

Faced with limited options to raise revenue significantly in the short term, governments are often forced to rely on expenditure consolidation. However, changes in the composition of government spending during times of fiscal consolidation may affect growth outcomes and ultimately the success or sustainability of the consolidation. Evidence shows that capital spending is often cut during times of fiscal consolidation, despite the lasting benefits for growth attributed to public investment (see Chapter 2). As shown in Figure 6.1, a higher share of public investment in government spending tends to be associated with stronger growth.

The relationship between the size of government and economic growth has been extensively studied (for example, Barro 1990; Glomm and Ravikumar 1997; Ghosh and Roy 2004; Lee and Gordon 2005; Gómez 2007; and Arnold and others 2011). Only a few studies give much attention to the composition of public spending besides its overall size—and they have mixed results. For example, Gemmell, Kneller, and Sanz (2016) and Fournier and Johansson (2016) found that reallocating public spending toward infrastructure and education is conducive to higher long-term output levels in countries of the Organisation for Economic Co-operation and Development (OECD). Gupta and others (2005)

This chapter benefited from financial support from the Macroeconomic Research in Low-Income Countries Project funded by the United Kingdom Department for International Development (DFID, Project ID 60925).

**Figure 6.1. Per Capita Growth and the Share of Public Investment in Total Government Spending in Developing Economies, 2015–17**

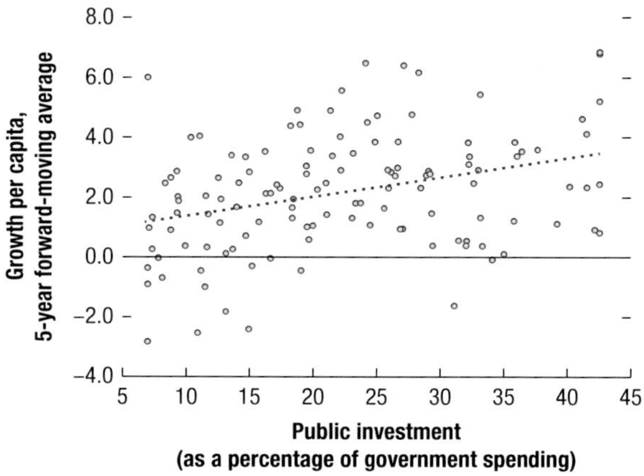

Source: IMF Capital Stock Data Set; and International Financial Statistics.
Note: The y-axis is a 5-year forward-moving average of per capita GDP growth for emerging market and developing economies (see Annex 6.2). Both public investment and 5-year forward-moving averages are averaged over 2015–17.

and Adam and Bevan (2003) have shown that fiscal consolidations achieved through cutting selected current expenditures and raising revenue (respectively) tend to raise medium-term growth rates, and protecting capital expenditures does the same. By contrast, earlier studies such as Devarajan, Swaroop, and Zhou (1996), and Ghosh and Gregoriou (2008) found a positive relationship between the current component of public expenditure and per capita real GDP growth for a group of low-income developing countries spanning the 1970s and 1990s.

This chapter investigates the growth dividends of shifting government spending composition toward more public investment during the fiscal cycle. Fiscal cycles are defined as fluctuations in the primary balance in response to government action or macroeconomic shocks. Using complementary general equilibrium and data-driven models, the findings suggest that protecting investment spending during times of consolidation—although contractionary in the short term—boosts medium- to long-term growth, leading to a more sustained reduction in the budget deficit. However, the growth benefits from rising shares of public investment in total government spending decline beyond a threshold. This result, which also holds during good times, underscores the importance of public investment for growth, particularly in countries with low initial public investment in government expenditure.

The chapter outlines the theoretical model and discusses simulation results of increasing public investment during the fiscal cycle, then presents complementary empirical evidence and some policy implications.

## THEORETICAL MODELING AND SIMULATIONS

Trade-offs between public current expenditure and public investment occur over the fiscal cycle. The associated effects on output can be estimated using simulations of a dynamic stochastic general equilibrium model with the following specifications:

- Households. Consumers spend and save given their budget constraints. The taxes they pay on consumption, as well as labor and capital incomes, finance public expenditure.
- Government. The government uses the collected tax revenue to finance current expenditures (such as wages and salaries) and capital expenditure (such as infrastructure projects).[1]
- Firms. They employ labor and rent capital from households; their production also depends on the government's current expenditures and the stock of public capital. Both types of government spending have a productive impact on output: (1) current expenditures contemporaneously affect output because of spillovers from productive current expenditures (such as health expenditures that raise labor productivity), while (2) capital expenditure creates productivity-enhancing public capital (such as physical and information and communication technology infrastructure).[2]
- Policy simulations. The model is calibrated to mimic a typical developing economy, whose characteristics draw on previous studies and on data used in the empirical section of this chapter (see Annex 6.1). For simplicity, shocks that trigger the need for fiscal consolidation are not analyzed and it is assumed that expenditure restraint is required to achieve this consolidation.

Differences associated with changing the public spending mix—between public current and capital expenditures— are analyzed and quantified and the implications for short-term and long-term growth considered. On one hand, as current expenditures have more immediate effects on economic activity than public investment, spending that is more tilted toward current expenditures amid transient negative shocks would better support short-term growth. On the other hand, public spending tilted toward public investment helps achieve better long-term objectives, although with a more limited short-term impact on growth.

The model simulations in this chapter provide a way to assess which strategy delivers the best outcome. Assuming that a fiscal consolidation equivalent to a

[1] Debt financing of the budget deficit is assumed away for simplicity, as the scope of this chapter lies only in the benefits of varying the spending mix over the fiscal cycle.

[2] The assumption that public expenditure—in infrastructure, research, education, and health services—is productive is widely recognized in the empirical literature (for a survey, see Romp and de Hann 2007). In line with previous studies, public investment is introduced in the form of a change to the public capital stock in the production of the firm (for example, Leeper, Walker, and Yang 2010), whereas current expenditures enter as a flow variable (for example, Aschauer 1989; and Barro 1990).

decrease of 1 percentage point in total government spending to GDP is required, the impact of cutting current and capital spending in response to an increasingly constrained budget is examined over both short and long terms.[3] Two extreme cases are considered. In the first scenario, the burden to deliver needed consolidation falls entirely on current expenditure, meaning that capital spending is fully preserved. In the second scenario, public investment fully adjusts, whereas current expenditure remains unchanged. Focusing on these two extreme cases provides useful insights about the possible macroeconomic outcomes of any intermediate expenditure mix.

The results are illustrated in Figure 6.2. This shows the macroeconomic impact of a 1 percentage point temporary cut in government spending to GDP relative to the steady state. The simulations show notable trade-offs associated with the government spending mix after the shock. A cut in public investment, though maintaining government consumption, produces an almost negligible impact on short-term output as the drop is compensated by a contemporaneous increase in consumption and private investment, hence raising the stock of private capital. However, this comes at the cost of a steadily declining output starting from the fourth year, reaching –0.45 percent of GDP by the end of the time horizon considered (20 years). In contrast, a consolidation that relies entirely on current expenditure, while protecting capital spending, would be contractionary in the short term with a notably contemporaneous drop in output of 0.2 percent of GDP, but output recovers by year three and expands in the long term to stabilize just above 0.2 percent of GDP after 10 years, enough to offset the initial negative impact. Although the short-term growth differential between the two scenarios would argue in favor of cutting public investment, this gap closes within three years and is reversed in the long term to reach around –0.4 percent of steady-state output in 10 years and more than 0.6 percent of GDP by the end of the time horizon.

Given that preserving public spending achieves higher long-term growth, it ensures the durability of fiscal consolidation with sharper medium- and long-term reductions in fiscal deficits (as illustrated in Figure 6.2). This policy approach is naturally favorable when pursuing long-term objectives—such as debt sustainability—which would require a sustainable containment of fiscal deficits. However, it comes at the short-term cost of output contraction. On the other hand, the model illustrates the negligible short-term output benefits from consolidations achieved through cuts to public investment. Although providing limited temporary relief, this approach exacts a steep cost in the form of sustained contractionary pressures on future output and a reversion to initial deficit levels.[4] These results caution against pursuing short-sighted policies to achieve short-term objectives that could be driven by economic or political considerations.

---

[3] It is assumed that the cut in public expenditure is phased out gradually over time, such that its log-linear evolution follows an AR (1) process with a persistence parameter that is set to 0.9 (see Annex 6.1).

[4] The conclusions are broadly similar when running the simulations for a permanent shock to government expenditure.

**Figure 6.2. Impact of a Reduction of 1 Percent in Government Spending on Output and Fiscal Outcomes**

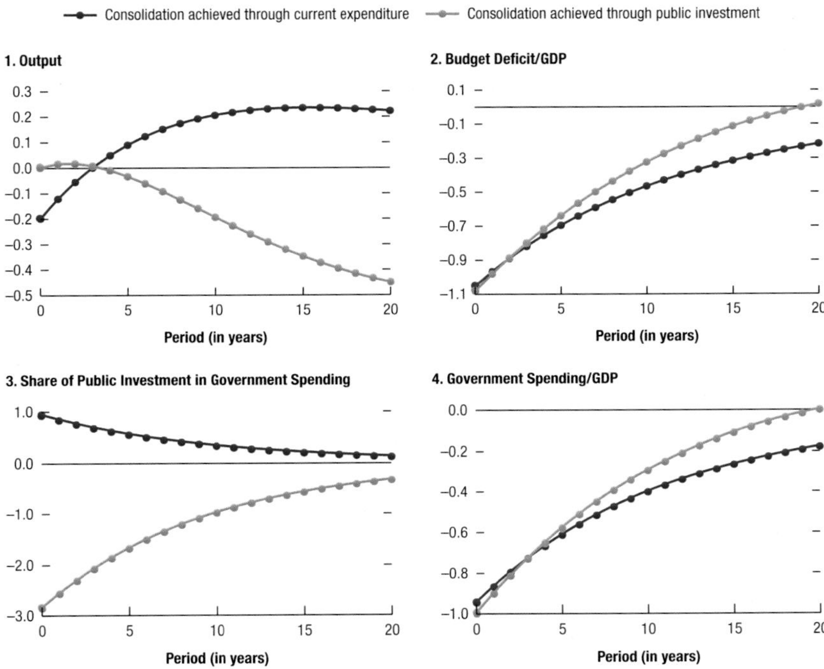


Source: IMF staff.
Note. The y-axis captures the percentage point deviation of the respective variable from its steady-state level.

Some caveats to the analysis are worth noting. Although the parameters of the model are carefully chosen to feature the characteristics of a typical developing country, wide heterogeneity in this income group cannot be ignored; the magnitude of the responses to cuts in current and capital expenditure—as measured by the respective output elasticity—will vary with country-specific circumstances.[5] Another important consideration is the inefficiency of public investment, which is typically sizable in low-income countries (see Chapter 3 for an in-depth discussion). Such inefficiencies—that could result from public investment mismanagement—imply that only a fraction of investment is transferred into public capital (see Dabla-Norris and others 2012; and IMF 2015). Because higher inefficiency means a lower expected fiscal multiplier to public investment, the long-term positive effects on output shown in Figure 6.2 may not materialize.

[5] Therefore, for country-specific studies, the output elasticity of capital and current expenditures must be estimated as accurately as possible (for a survey of the empirical literature, see Romp and de Haan 2007).

## CROSS-COUNTRY EMPIRICAL EVIDENCE

Empirical evidence on the link between the public spending mix and per capita growth during fiscal consolidations complements the analysis, A sample of 155 developing economies spanning 1960–2017 is used. This data-driven approach allows evaluation of the performance of medium-term growth when the public spending mix changes. It presents important advantages over simulation-based methods, notably the ability to (1) exploit a wide data set and extract common trends, (2) control for a larger set of factors that also affect growth, and (3) test nonlinearities in the relationship between growth and spending composition.

The analysis uses a regression that links growth to macroeconomic controls. The model incorporates two main variables: the share of public investment in total government spending and an indicator of fiscal consolidation episodes. The underlying idea is to see if differences in the composition of spending matter when the restoration of fiscal control is needed. The impact on growth of changes to the spending mix is likely to depend on the availability of fiscal space, the health of macro fundamentals, and, broadly, the domestic policy stance over the fiscal cycle. The model accounts for this by including two broad groups of control variables denoted, respectively, as "fiscal space" and "macro-stability" (for details, see Box 6.1).

### Results and Discussion

Changing the spending mix in favor of public investment has strong growth dividends. A simplified version of the empirical model is first estimated without interactions of public investment with fiscal consolidation indicator variables (see Annex Table 6.3.1). After controlling for fiscal space, macroeconomic stability, and fixed effects, the results strongly support the hypothesis that the public spending mix matters for medium-term growth—a finding consistent with earlier findings. Increasing the share of public investment in total government spending from 10 to 20 percent raises medium-term growth by 0.5 percentage point. Interestingly, the results also suggest stronger growth dividends when the share of public investment in spending is low: as the share of public investment grows and reaches around 30 percent of total government spending, its growth dividends marginally decline (Figure 6.3).[6]

This nonlinear relationship persists as more controls are added.[7] This suggests that the public spending mix matters for medium-term growth, more so when public investment accounts for a smaller share of public spending. The intuitive explanation could be that though a higher share of government spending devoted to capital expenditure is good for growth, the return diminishes beyond a threshold, as current expenditure is also needed to maintain a minimum provision of public services.

---

[6] This nonlinearity is captured by including a square term of the share of public investment in spending. The coefficient on this variable is negative and significant.

[7] The inverse min-U test (Lind and Mehlum 2010) fails to reject the existence of a monotone relationship, in all but column 4 in Annex Table 6.3.1, in relation to an inverse U-shaped relationship.

## Box 6.1. Linking Composition of Public Spending to Economic Growth

The regression is specified as follows.

### Dependent Variable

Rich empirical evidence shows that public investment and economic activity do not always move in tandem. For example, Jones (1995) found that every time investment rates increase, countries of the Organisation for Economic Co-operation and Development experience transitory growth effects lasting five to eight years. Therefore, a forward-moving average of per capita real GDP growth is chosen as the dependent variable to capture both the contemporaneous and medium-term growth effects associated with fiscal adjustments (such as changes in the spending mix during consolidation).[1]

### Explanatory Variables

- *Spending mix*. The spending mix is captured by the inclusion of the ratio of capital spending as a share of total government expenditure. To ensure the model specifically captures the impact of changing the public spending mix, the size of total public spending as a ratio to GDP is controlled for.
- *Fiscal space and macroeconomic stability*. The regression covers all four fundamental components of fiscal space: debt sustainability, balance sheet composition, external private sector debt, and market access (IMF 2018). The empirical model captures at least three of these dimensions by using two variables, the *current account balance* and *central bank assets as shares of GDP*. The first measures the extent to which governments can flexibly meet domestic consumption and investment requirements. The second measures the macroeconomic and financial stability provided by central balance sheets. Where payments technology is heavily reliant on currency (rather than on e-transfers), central bank assets are an important buffer to meet payment obligations. This is especially true in low-income developing countries. In contrast, because the asset-side buildup of central bank balance sheets needs to be balanced by an increase in domestic liabilities, there is a chance that some of the benefits gained from asset buildup are offset by some loss in domestic financial intermediation. The degree to which economies minimize vulnerability to external shocks has desirable implications for sustained growth. A wide body of historical evidence ascribes long bouts of low growth and volatility in developing countries to the absence of macroeconomic stability. For the purposes of the study, the stability of macroeconomic outcomes is gauged by a set of controls, including *inflation*, *change in the real exchange rate*, and *government debt* (in percentage of GDP).

### Other Controls

Country and time fixed effects are also included.

Source: IMF staff.
Note: See Annex 6.1 for more details.

[1] This approach is also consistent with Devarajan, Swaroop, and Zou (1996); Ghosh and Gregoriou (2008); and Afonso and Alegre (2011).

**Figure 6.3. The Nonlinear Relation between Spending Composition and Growth**

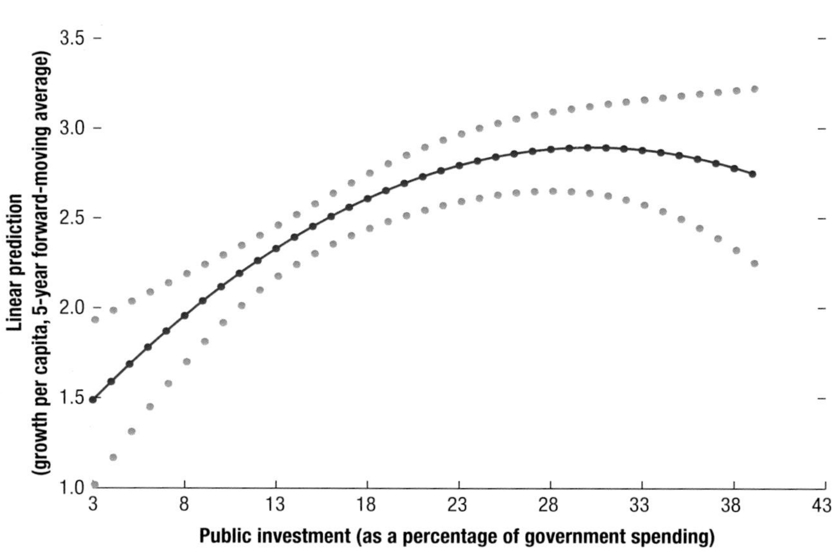


Source: IMF staff.
Note: The figure plots marginal effects from column 4 of Annex Table 6.3.1. It shows the relation between the public spending share of investment and its future growth effect (5-year forward-moving average of growth). All other variables in column 4 are computed at their average.

Moreover, an increase in capital expenditure often translates into an increase in current expenditure because of the knock-on effect of operations and maintenance spending. Underfunding of those outlays can lead to a rapid depreciation of the public capital stock, therefore undermining the expected benefits for growth.

The next step is to investigate whether this relationship holds during good times—when consolidation is not observed—and bad times (when fiscal consolidations are observed). The definitions of fiscal consolidation used in this study largely follow the more recent literature (Von Hagan, Hughes Hallet, and Strauch 2002; Adam and Bevan 2003; Gupta and others 2005). Two narrow definitions of fiscal consolidation are tested. In the first instance, a fiscal consolidation period is defined as events in which primary balances are tightened by at least 1 percent of GDP in two successive years after the primary deficit grew beyond 3 percent of GDP. Countries with a large deficit might need a longer time to rectify the fiscal stance. This is not explicitly accounted for in this definition. Instead of considering longer sequential consolidation, the analysis sticks to the two consecutive year definition, in line with existing literature and for simplicity. The second definition considers any reduction in the primary deficit in two consecutive years after a deficit of 1.5 percent of GDP or higher.

Once again, the spending mix has a significant impact on medium-term growth and depends on the initial spending mix.[8] The inverted U-shaped relationship between the share of public investment in total expenditure and growth holds during the fiscal cycles, in both good and bad times. Panel 1 in Figure 6.4 plots predictions of medium-term growth (see Annex Table 6.3.2, column 4) to illustrate the implications of changing spending compositions in good times and in times of consolidation. The figure suggests that the growth dividend from increased public investment is higher when the initial share of public investment is low. At lower shares of public investment, predicted growth rises sharply. That is because spending shares favor public investment during consolidations. Yet, for a given share of public investment, predicted growth is lower in bad times than in good times. This gap shrinks rapidly and becomes statistically insignificant for higher shares of public spending (Figure 6.4, panel 2). For example, doubling the investment share of public spending to 20 percent from 10 percent increases future growth (5-year moving average) by 0.69 percentage point during good times relative to 1.65 percentage points during consolidations. As the share increases to 30 percent, the growth effects are reduced to 0.33 percent and 0.66 percent, respectively. Growth effects are indistinguishable as the share of investment reaches 35–40 percent.

## Figure 6.4. Importance of Spending-Composition Changes during Consolidation

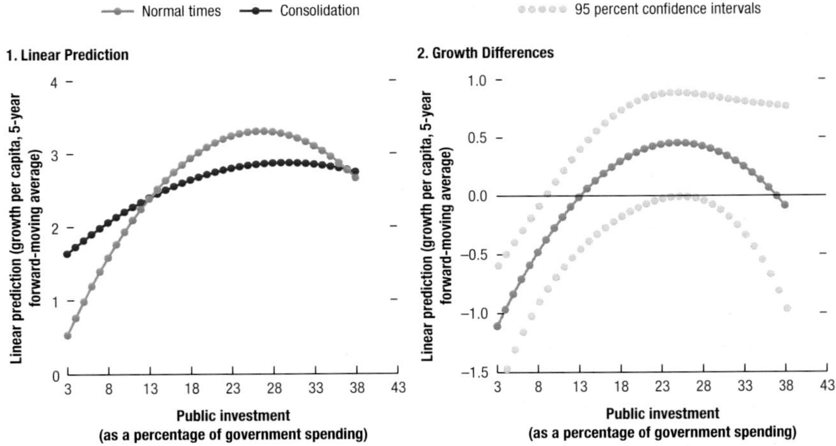


Source: IMF staff.

Note: "Fiscal consolidation" is defined as a reduction of 1 percent of GDP or more in the primary deficit in two consecutive years after the fiscal deficit climbed above 3 percent of GDP. Panel 1 plots predictions of medium-term growth (GDP per capita, 5-year forward-moving average) in the two states (see Annex Table 6.3.2, column 4). Panel 2 plots differences of the growth impacts in the two states. It shows that the spending share of public investment is as important during consolidations as in good times.

[8] Results with interactions between the public spending mix and fiscal consolidation (first definition) are shown in Annex Table 6.3.2.

As shown in Annex Table 6.3.2 (column 3), the impact of fiscal space and macroeconomic stability on growth is broadly in line with expectations. However, while all fiscal space indicators are expected to affect growth positively, central bank assets have a negative impact. A possible explanation could be that a buildup in the asset side of central bank balance sheets requires a similar increase in domestic liabilities, which signals diminished domestic financial intermediation. Controlling for additional growth determinants (human capital, financial development, and trade openness) does not alter the findings (see Annex Table 6.3.3).

Moreover, these results do not change when a broader definition of fiscal consolidation is applied (see Annex Table 6.3.4) or when the sample is expanded to include advanced economies.[9] Figure 6.5 compares the medium-term growth effects of spending compositions in the two states. Again, panel 1 shows that the growth dividend in both states from increased public investment is higher when the initial share of public investment is low, and then declines beyond a threshold. The right panel shows that these growth effects are statistically indistinguishable in the two states for higher shares of public investment.

**Figure 6.5. Importance of Spending-Composition Changes during Consolidation (Using a Broader Definition of "Consolidation")**

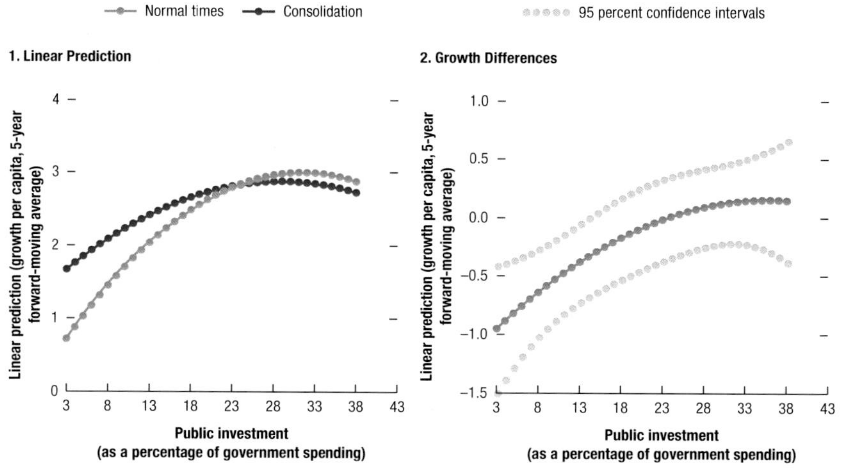


Source: IMF staff.
Note: "Fiscal consolidation" is defined as any deficit reduction when the primary deficit is above 1.5 percent of GDP. Panel 1 plots predictions of GDP per capita in the two states (from Annex Table 6.3.4, column 4). Panel 2 plots predicted growth impacts from the two states. It shows that increasing the investment share of public spending up to a threshold is associated with sharper increases in per capita growth during consolidation (relative to good times). These differences in growth impacts disappear at higher shares of public investment.

[9] Results are not presented here but are available upon request.

## CONCLUSIONS

This chapter investigates the impact of government spending composition on growth during the fiscal cycle. A dynamic stochastic general equilibrium model, calibrated for a hypothetical developing country and empirical estimations, shows that

- A trade-off exists between short-term and long-term growth during consolidation times, as current public expenditures have a more immediate impact on output than public investment. As a result, a cut in public investment barely affects short-term output but proves to be costly in the medium to long term. On the other hand, a consolidation that relies entirely on current expenditure, while protecting capital spending, would be contractionary in the short term, but output recovers quickly and expands sustainably in the long term, fully offsetting the initial negative impact. This also leads to a more sustained reduction in the budget deficit.
- While tilting the composition of spending toward public investment is growth enhancing, the greatest benefits are felt for low initial levels of public investment in government expenditure. As the ratio increases, a diminishing return kicks in beyond a threshold, probably because an excessive crowding out of current expenditure can undermine provisions of other public goods and services, including the maintenance of existing public infrastructure.
- The inverted U-shaped relationship between the share of public investment in total expenditure and growth holds during good times and consolidation periods, with the difference being that, at a given share of public investment, predicted growth is obviously lower in bad times than in good times. This gap phases out as the initial share of public investment increases.

These findings have important policy implications. First, preserving capital spending during a time of consolidation is critical to spurring medium- and long-term growth, and is a key ingredient for a successful and sustainable consolidation. This is particularly relevant for low-income developing countries, which typically have a low ratio of public investment to total spending, and where a growth-friendly consolidation is needed when fiscal sustainability is at stake. Moreover, for these countries, protecting public investment spending in good times is equally as important as in bad times. Nevertheless, it is also important to factor in political economy considerations given that shortsighted policymakers may be tempted to maintain current expenditure because the adverse effects on short-term growth from cutting public investment are limited, even as beyond their horizons this strategy carries very high medium- to long-term costs. As a result, the appropriate expenditure mix should carefully balance the need to support medium- and long-term growth with that of minimizing the negative short-term impact on growth.

## ANNEX 6.1. MODEL DESCRIPTION AND CALIBRATION

A dynamic stochastic general equilibrium model with an infinitely lived forward-looking representative household was used to analyse the data collected for this chapter. The household in turn owns a representative firm employing labor and renting capital to use as factors for production. The government raises revenues through taxes to finance public expenditures in the forms of current productive expenditure and public investment in infrastructure. The model is solved in a decentralized competitive equilibrium by log-linearization around a deterministic steady state.

Annex Table 6.1.1 presents the different parameter values used for the policy simulation. The model is calibrated for a hypothetical economy featuring many characteristics of developing countries. Whereas some parameters are borrowed from previous studies, others are derived from data used in the empirical section.

- The discount rate is set to 0.9, corresponding to a risk-free yearly rate of around 11 percent, and the constant relative risk aversion is set to be equal to 2.5; both are standard measures in the range found in the literature.
- Capital share is set to 0.45, to be consistent with the literature tackling developing countries (for example, García-Cicco, Pancrazi, and Uribe 2010; and Berg and others 2013).
- Government spending to GDP and public investment to government spending are set at 26.5 percent and 24.2 percent, respectively, to match the averages for developing countries using the data set described in the empirical section below.
- Also, the depreciation rate of private capital is set at 0.0985 to target the developing countries' average private investment to GDP of 14.8 percent using the same data set. This depreciation rate also matches the rates used by Berg and others (2013) and yields—along with the risk-free rate—a net rate of return to capital of around 21 percent. That is in the estimated range found for developing countries by Chou, Izyumov, and Vahaly (2016). As for the depreciation of public capital, it is set to be equal to 0.07 to reflect the lower depreciation rate of public capital relative to private capital and to fit the range considered by the literature.

**ANNEX TABLE 6.1.1.**

Parametrization

| Parameter | Description | Value |
|---|---|---|
| $\beta^d$ | Discount rate | 0.9 |
| $\sigma$ | Constant relative risk aversion | 2.5 |
| $\mu$ | Capital share | 0.45 |
| $g_y$ | Government spending to GDP | 26.5% |
| $I^g/G$ | Public investment to government spending | 24.2% |
| $\delta$ | Depreciation rate of private capital | 0.0985 |
| $\delta^g$ | Depreciation rate of public capital | 0.07 |
| $\alpha$ | Production elasticity to public capital | 0.12 |
| $\beta$ | Production elasticity to public consumption | 0.04 |
| $\tau^k$ | Capital tax | 30% |
| $\tau^c$ | Consumption tax | 16% |
| $\rho$ | Persistence of government spending shock | 0.9 |

Source: IMF staff.

- Arslanalp and others (2010) reviewed the literature on public capital and growth. They estimated the production function for countries in the Organisation for Economic Co-operation and Development compared with those outside the group and found a year-over-year production elasticity of 0.12 for OECD countries.[10] This estimate also fits the range used in the literature tackling developing countries. Also, the model adds a productive public current expenditure; the elasticity of production is set so this component of government spending is one-third that of public capital, to reflect its lower productivity.
- The capital tax rate is set to 30 percent and the consumption tax rate is set to 16 percent to be consistent with corporate tax rates and VAT rates in developing countries, particularly in low-income countries. The labor income tax rate is set to balance the budget in a steady state.

## ANNEX 6.2. DATA AND EMPIRICAL MODEL SPECIFICATION

Data are used for a sample of 155 developing countries over 1960–2017 (see Annex Tables 6.2.1 and 6.2.2) to estimate the following model:

$$g_{it} = \alpha_i + \alpha_t + \alpha_j + \beta_1 \frac{P^I_{it}}{G_{it}} + \beta_2 \frac{G_{it}}{Y_{it}} + \gamma FISCSPC + \phi MACROSTAB$$

$$+ \eta SHOCK + \partial_1 \frac{P^I_{it}}{G_{it}} \times SHOCK + \xi_{it} \qquad (6.2.1)$$

The dependent variable $g_{it}$ is a five-year forward-moving average of real per capita GDP growth. The moving average is constructed by attaching different weights to different years. The fourth and fifth years are given relatively higher weights (31.25 percent) compared to the first three years (each 12.5 percent) to account for lags between public investment and capital buildup. The left-hand side variables include country and time fixed effects $\alpha_i$ and $\alpha_t$, the public investment share

**ANNEX TABLE 6.2.1.**

Data Sources

| Variable | Data Source |
|---|---|
| Public investment, % of government expenditure | Fiscal Affairs Department Capital Stock Data Set |
| Government expenditure, % of GDP | World Economic Outlook |
| Government stability | World Bank Governance Indicators |
| Current account balance, % of GDP | International Financial Statistics |
| International debt issues, % of GDP | Financial Soundness Indicators |
| Central bank assets, % of GDP | Financial Soundness Indicators |
| Private investment, % of GDP | World Bank Data |
| Inflation | World Economic Outlook |
| Real effective exchange rate change, year-over-year | International Financial Statistics |
| Gross debt, % of GDP | World Economic Outlook |

Source: IMF staff.

[10] Arslanalp and others (2010) estimated the production function's elasticity to public capital using 1- and 10-year specifications. They estimated an elasticity of 0.12 in the short-term specification and 0.26 in the long-term one for non-OECD countries, and 0.13 and 0.08, respectively, for OECD countries.

**ANNEX TABLE 6.2.2.**

## Emerging Market and Developing Economies Sample

| East Asia and Pacific | Europe and Central Asia | Latin America and the Caribbean | | Middle East and North Africa | South Asia | Sub-Saharan Africa | |
|---|---|---|---|---|---|---|---|
| Brunei Darussalam | Albania | Anguilla | Paraguay | Algeria | Afghanistan | Angola | Madagascar |
| Cambodia | Armenia | Antigua and | Peru | Bahrain | Bangladesh | Benin | Malawi |
| China | Azerbaijan | Barbuda | St. Kitts and Nevis | Djibouti | Bhutan | Botswana | Mali |
| Fiji | Belarus | Argentina | St. Lucia | Egypt | India | Burkina Faso | Mauritania |
| Indonesia | Bosnia and Herzegovinia | The Bahamas | St. Vincent and the Grenadines | Iran | Maldives | Burundi | Mauritius |
| Kiribati | Bulgaria | Barbados | Suriname | Iraq | Nepal | Cabo Verde | Mozambique |
| Lao P.D.R. | Croatia | Belize | Trinidad and Tobago | Jordan | Pakistan | Cameroon | Namibia |
| Malaysia | Georgia | Bolivia | Uruguay | Kuwait | Sri Lanka | Central African | Niger |
| Marshall Islands | Hungary | Brazil | Venezuela | Lebanon | | Republic | Nigeria |
| Micronesia | Kazakhstan | Chile | | Libya | | Chad | Rwanda |
| Mongolia | Kosovo | Colombia | | Morocco | | Comoros | Senegal |
| Myanmar | Kyrgyz Rep. | Costa Rica | | Oman | | Republic of Congo | Seychelles |
| Nauru | FYR Macedonia | Dominica Rep. | | Qatar | | Democratic Republic | Sierra Leone |
| Palau | Moldova | Dominica | | Saudi Arabia | | of the Congo | Somalia |
| Papua New Guinea | Montenegro | Ecuador | | Syria | | Côte d'Ivoire | South Africa |
| Philippines | Poland | El Salvador | | Tunisia | | Equatorial Guinea | South Sudan |
| Samoa | Romania | Grenada | | United Arab | | Eritrea | Sudan |
| Solomon Islands | Russian Federation | Guatemala | | Emirates | | Eswatini | São Tomé and Príncipe |
| Thailand | Serbia | Guyana | | Yemen | | Ethiopia | Tanzania |
| Timor-Leste | Tajikistan | Haiti | | | | Gabon | Togo |
| Tonga | Turkey | Honduras | | | | The Gambia | Uganda |
| Tuvalu | Turkmenistan | Jamaica | | | | Ghana | Zambia |
| Vanuatu | Ukraine | Mexico | | | | Guinea | Zimbabwe |
| Vietnam | Uzbekistan | Nicaragua | | | | Guinea-Bissau | |
| | | Panama | | | | Kenya | |
| | | | | | | Lesotho | |
| | | | | | | Liberia | |

Source: IMF staff.

of government expenditure $\frac{P^I_{it}}{G_{it}}$, the GDP share of government spending $\frac{G_{it}}{Y_{it}}$, and sets of controls for "fiscal space" *FISCSPC* and "macro-stability" *MACROSTAB*. *SHOCK* is a dummy variable capturing episodes of fiscal consolidation when the primary balance improved by a threshold amount.

A forward-moving average of per capita real GDP growth is chosen as the dependent variable to capture both the contemporaneous and medium-term growth spurts associated with fiscal adjustments (such as spending mix during consolidation).[11] The impact on growth of such changes to the spending mix are likely to depend on the availability of fiscal space and the health of macro fundamentals and, broadly, the domestic policy stance over the fiscal cycle. The model accounts for this by including two broad groups of control variables denoted, respectively, "fiscal space" and "macro-stability."

Key components of fiscal space include debt sustainability, balance sheet composition, external private sector debt, and market access (IMF 2018). Two variables in the empirical model capture at least three of these dimensions (the current account balance and central bank assets as shares of GDP). The first measures the extent to which governments can flexibly meet domestic consumption and investment requirements. The second measures the macroeconomic and financial stability provided by central balance sheets. On the one hand, where payment technology is heavily reliant on currency (rather than e-transfers), central bank assets are an important buffer to meet payment obligations. This is especially true in low-income developing countries. On the other hand, because asset-side buildup of central bank balance sheets needs to be balanced by an increase in domestic liabilities, there is a chance that some of the benefits gained from asset buildup are offset by some loss in domestic financial intermediation.

The degree to which economies reduce vulnerability to external shocks to a minimum has desirable implications for sustained growth. A wide body of historical evidence ascribes long bouts of low growth and volatility in developing countries to the absence of macroeconomic stability. For the purposes of the study, the stability of macroeconomic outcomes is gauged by a set of controls, including inflation, change in the real exchange rate, and government debt (percentage of GDP).

The model incorporates two variables of interest: the share of public investment in total government spending and an indicator of fiscal consolidation episodes. The underlying idea is to see if differences in the composition of spending matter when fiscal control needs to be restored to that of good times. To ensure that the model specifically captures the impact of changing the public spending mix, the size of total public spending as a ratio to GDP and a range of country and time fixed effects are also controlled for.

Furthermore, fiscal consolidation episodes are incorporated with the dummy variable *SHOCK*. Two definitions are considered, drawing on recent literature (Von Hagan, Hughes Hallet, and Strauch 2002; Adam and Bevan 2003; Gupta and others 2005). First, a fiscal consolidation period is defined as events when

[11] This approach is consistent with Devarajan, Swaroop, and Zou (1996); Ghosh and Gregoriou (2008); and Afonso and Alegre (2011).

primary balances tightened by at least 1 percent of GDP in two successive years after the primary deficit grew beyond 3 percent of GDP. The second definition considers any reduction in the primary deficit in two consecutive years after a deficit of 1.5 percent of GDP or higher.

Additional fixed effects $\alpha_j$ are included to capture state dependence of medium growth performance. These include fragile country fixed effects, commodity exporter fixed effects, and IMF income group fixed effects. These fixed effects account for *peace dividends* in postconflict economies, and conditional convergence and structural growth volatility in resource-dependent economies.

## ANNEX 6.3. GROWTH EFFECTS FROM CHANGING COMPOSITIONS OF SPENDING

**ANNEX TABLE 6.3.1.**

Growth Effects from Composition of Spending

| | (1) | (2) | (3) | (4) | (5) |
|---|---|---|---|---|---|
| Public investment, % of government expenditure | 0.06*** | 0.13*** | 0.14*** | 0.14*** | 0.13*** |
| | (0.010) | (0.043) | (0.044) | (0.040) | (0.038) |
| (Public investment, % of government expenditure)$^2$ | | −0.00* | −0.00** | −0.00*** | −0.00*** |
| | | (0.001) | (0.001) | (0.001) | (0.001) |
| Government expenditure, % of GDP | | | 0.01 | 0.02 | 0.04* |
| | | | (0.019) | (0.018) | (0.019) |
| Government stability | | | 0.17*** | 0.14*** | 0.12*** |
| | | | (0.044) | (0.043) | (0.047) |
| Current account balance, % of GDP | | | | −0.03** | −0.00 |
| | | | | (0.016) | (0.017) |
| Central bank assets, % of GDP | | | | −0.11*** | −0.05 |
| | | | | (0.030) | (0.032) |
| Private investment, % of GDP | | | | | 0.06*** |
| | | | | | (0.020) |
| Inflation | | | | | −0.01 |
| | | | | | (0.011) |
| Real effective exchange rate change, year-over-year | | | | | 0.01 |
| | | | | | (0.009) |
| Gross debt, % of GDP | | | | | −0.02*** |
| | | | | | (0.005) |
| Constant | 0.85*** | 0.10 | −1.36* | −0.70 | −1.10 |
| | (0.232) | (0.502) | (0.772) | (0.807) | (0.950) |
| No. of observations | 2,969 | 2,969 | 2,253 | 1,984 | 1,681 |
| $R^2$ | 0.52 | 0.52 | 0.54 | 0.58 | 0.64 |
| Country fixed effects | Yes | Yes | Yes | Yes | Yes |
| Year fixed effects | Yes | Yes | Yes | Yes | Yes |
| IMF income fixed effects | Yes | Yes | Yes | Yes | Yes |
| Commodity exporter fixed effects | Yes | Yes | Yes | Yes | Yes |
| Fragile fixed effects | Yes | Yes | Yes | Yes | Yes |
| Maximum inverse U-curve | — | 47.11 | 36.58 | 33.34 | 34.25 |
| U-test (P>\|t\|) | — | — | 0.237 | 0.085 | 0.117 |

Source: IMF staff.

Note: The dependent variable is a forward-moving average of per capita real GDP growth. Robust standard errors appear in parentheses. The hypotheses of the inverse U-test are as follows: $H_0$: relationship is monotonic or U-shaped; $H_1$: relationship is inverse U-shaped. The maximum inverse U-curve is the threshold at which increasing the share of investment has no growth benefits. The U-test determines whether the threshold is statistically significant. IMF income group fixed effects are dummies for low-income developing countries and emerging market economies. The fragility fixed effects row captures countries with Country Policy and Institutional Assessment scores of 3 or lower.

***$p < 0.01$. **$p < 0.05$. *$p < 0.1$.

**ANNEX TABLE 6.3.2.**

## Composition of Spending during Fiscal Consolidation

| | (1) | (2) | (3) | (4) |
|---|---|---|---|---|
| Public investment, % of government expenditure | 0.12*** | 0.13*** | 0.13*** | 0.12*** |
| | (0.043) | (0.044) | (0.039) | (0.037) |
| (Public investment, % of government expenditure)$^2$ | −0.001 | −0.002** | −0.002** | −0.002** |
| | (0.001) | (0.001) | (0.001) | (0.001) |
| Consolidation | −2.63*** | −2.91*** | −3.33*** | −2.50*** |
| | (0.669) | (0.756) | (0.813) | (0.553) |
| Public Investment × Consolidation | 0.18*** | 0.19*** | 0.26*** | 0.19*** |
| | (0.060) | (0.067) | (0.070) | (0.054) |
| Public Investment$^2$ × Consolidation | −0.003** | −0.003** | −0.004*** | −0.003*** |
| | (0.001) | (0.001) | (0.001) | (0.001) |
| Government expenditure, % of GDP | | 0.01 | 0.02 | 0.03* |
| | | (0.019) | (0.018) | (0.019) |
| Government stability | | 0.17*** | 0.13*** | 0.12*** |
| | | (0.043) | (0.042) | (0.046) |
| Current account balance, % of GDP | | | −0.03* | −0.001 |
| | | | (0.016) | (0.017) |
| Central bank assets, % of GDP | | | −0.11*** | −0.05 |
| | | | (0.030) | (0.032) |
| Private investment, % of GDP | | | | 0.06*** |
| | | | | (0.020) |
| Inflation | | | | −0.01 |
| | | | | (0.012) |
| Real effective exchange rate change, year-over-year | | | | 0.01 |
| | | | | (0.009) |
| Gross debt, % of GDP | | | | −0.02*** |
| | | | | (0.005) |
| Constant | 0.28 | −1.14 | −0.54 | −0.97 |
| | (0.500) | (0.765) | (0.786) | (0.931) |
| No. of observations | 2,969 | 2,253 | 1,984 | 1,681 |
| $R^2$ | 0.52 | 0.54 | 0.59 | 0.64 |
| Country fixed effects | Yes | Yes | Yes | Yes |
| Year fixed effects | Yes | Yes | Yes | Yes |
| IMF income fixed effects | Yes | Yes | Yes | Yes |
| Commodity exporter fixed effects | Yes | Yes | Yes | Yes |
| Fragile fixed effects | Yes | Yes | Yes | Yes |

Source: IMF staff.

Note: The dependent variable is a forward-moving average of per capita real GDP growth. "Fiscal consolidation" is defined as a total of 1 percent GDP reduction in the primary deficit in two consecutive years after a fiscal deficit of 3 percent of GDP or higher. Robust standard errors appear in parentheses. IMF income group fixed effects are dummies for low-income developing countries and emerging market economies. The fragile fixed effects row captures countries with Country Policy and Institutional Assessment scores of 3 or lower.

***$p < 0.01$. **$p < 0.05$. *$p < 0.1$.

**ANNEX TABLE 6.3.3.**

## Composition of Spending and Growth during Good and Bad Times: Additional Control Variables

| | (1) | (2) | (3) | (4) |
|---|---|---|---|---|
| Public investment, % of government expenditure | 0.12*** | 0.16*** | 0.16*** | 0.16*** |
| | (0.043) | (0.061) | (0.061) | (0.049) |
| (Public investment, % of government expenditure)$^2$ | −0.00 | −0.00** | −0.00** | −0.00** |
| | (0.001) | (0.001) | (0.001) | (0.001) |
| Consolidation | −2.63*** | −2.64** | −3.24*** | −2.14*** |
| | (0.669) | (1.026) | (1.014) | (0.810) |
| Consolidation × Public Investment, % of Government Expenditure | 0.18*** | 0.23** | 0.30*** | 0.23*** |
| | (0.060) | (0.094) | (0.097) | (0.073) |
| Consolidation × (Public investment, % of government expenditure)$^2$ | −0.00** | −0.00** | −0.01*** | −0.00*** |
| | (0.001) | (0.002) | (0.002) | (0.001) |
| Government expenditure, % of GDP | | −0.00 | 0.01 | 0.02 |
| | | (0.027) | (0.027) | (0.024) |
| Government stability | | 0.19*** | 0.18*** | 0.14*** |
| | | (0.063) | (0.056) | (0.049) |
| Human Capital Index | | 0.05 | 0.37 | 1.63 |
| | | (2.195) | (2.170) | (1.821) |
| Financial depth | | 0.07* | 0.07* | 0.08*** |
| | | (0.035) | (0.037) | (0.028) |
| Trade openness | | 0.00 | 0.01 | 0.00 |
| | | (0.008) | (0.007) | (0.007) |
| Current account balance, % of GDP | | | 0.01 | 0.01 |
| | | | (0.021) | (0.023) |
| Central bank assets, % of GDP | | | −0.00 | 0.06 |
| | | | (0.059) | (0.053) |
| Private investment, % of GDP | | | | 0.03 |
| | | | | (0.029) |
| Inflation | | | | 0.01 |
| | | | | (0.016) |
| Real effective exchange rate change, year-over-year | | | | 0.01 |
| | | | | (0.009) |
| Gross debt, % of GDP | | | | −0.03*** |
| | | | | (0.006) |
| Constant | 0.28 | −2.22 | −3.30 | −5.40 |
| | (0.500) | (5.409) | (5.338) | (4.527) |
| No. of observations | 2,969 | 840 | 792 | 766 |
| $R^2$ | 0.52 | 0.72 | 0.74 | 0.78 |
| Country fixed effects | Yes | Yes | Yes | Yes |
| Year fixed effects | Yes | Yes | Yes | Yes |
| IMF income fixed effects | Yes | Yes | Yes | Yes |
| Commodity exporter fixed effects | Yes | Yes | Yes | Yes |
| Fragile fixed effects | Yes | Yes | Yes | Yes |

Source: IMF staff.

Note: Robust standard errors appear in parentheses.

*** $p < 0.01$. ** $p < 0.05$. * $p < 0.1$.

**ANNEX TABLE 6.3.4.**

## Robustness Test with Second Definition of Consolidation

| | (1) | (2) | (3) | (4) |
|---|---|---|---|---|
| Public investment, % of government expenditure | 0.12*** | 0.13*** | 0.16** | 0.18*** |
| | (0.042) | (0.044) | (0.063) | (0.064) |
| (Public investment, % of government expenditure)$^2$ | −0.00 | −0.00** | −0.00* | −0.00** |
| | (0.001) | (0.001) | (0.001) | (0.001) |
| Consolidation | −1.74*** | −1.92*** | −2.44** | −1.15 |
| | (0.512) | (0.586) | (0.922) | (0.809) |
| Public investment consolidation | 0.11** | 0.11** | 0.16* | 0.05 |
| | (0.046) | (0.053) | (0.079) | (0.067) |
| (Public Investment)$^2$ × Consolidation | −0.00* | −0.00 | −0.00 | −0.00 |
| | (0.001) | (0.001) | (0.001) | (0.001) |
| Government expenditure, % of GDP | | 0.01 | 0.01 | 0.05* |
| | | (0.019) | (0.029) | (0.028) |
| Government stability | | 0.17*** | 0.14** | 0.15*** |
| | | (0.043) | (0.056) | (0.053) |
| Current account balance, % of GDP | | | −0.05* | −0.01 |
| | | | (0.024) | (0.025) |
| International debt issues, % of GDP | | | −0.04** | −0.04** |
| | | | (0.015) | (0.017) |
| Central bank assets, % of GDP | | | −0.14*** | −0.07* |
| | | | (0.046) | (0.037) |
| Private investment, % of GDP | | | | 0.07* |
| | | | | (0.037) |
| Inflation | | | | −0.02 |
| | | | | (0.017) |
| Real effective exchange rate change, year-over-year | | | | 0.02 |
| | | | | (0.012) |
| Gross debt, % of GDP | | | | −0.03*** |
| | | | | (0.009) |
| Constant | 0.28 | −1.09 | 0.20 | −1.10 |
| | (0.492) | (0.766) | (1.310) | (1.559) |
| No. of observations | | | | |
| $R^2$ | 2,969 | 2,253 | 991 | 884 |
| Country fixed effects | 0.52 | 0.54 | 0.62 | 0.68 |
| Year fixed effects | Yes | Yes | Yes | Yes |
| IMF income fixed effects | Yes | Yes | Yes | Yes |
| Commodity exporter fixed effects | Yes | Yes | Yes | Yes |
| Fragile fixed effects | Yes | Yes | Yes | Yes |

Source: IMF staff.

Note: The dependent variable is a forward-moving average of per capita real GDP growth. "Fiscal consolidation" is defined as any reduction in the primary deficit in two consecutive years after a fiscal deficit of 1 percent of GDP or higher. Robust standard errors appear in parentheses. IMF Income group fixed effects are dummies for low-income developing countries and emerging market economies. The fragile fixed effects identify countries with Country Policy and Institutional Assessment scores of 3 or lower.

***$p < 0.01$. **$p < 0.05$. *$p < 0.1$.

## REFERENCES

Adam, Christopher, and David Bevan. 2003. "Staying the Course: Maintaining Fiscal Discipline in Developing Countries." *Brookings Institution Trade Forum* 1: 167–214.

Afonso, António, and Juan Alegre. 2011. "Economic Growth and Budgetary Components: A Panel Assessment for the EU." *Empirical Economics* 41 (3): 703–23.

Arnold, Jens Matthias, Bert Brys, Christopher Heady, Åsa Johansson, Cyrille Schwellnus, and Laura Vartia. 2011. "Tax Policy for Economic Recovery and Growth." *Economic Journal* 121: 59–80.

Arslanalp, Serkan, Fabio Bornhorst, Sanjeev Gupta, and Elsa Sze. 2010. "Public Capital and Growth." IMF Working Paper 10/175, International Monetary Fund, Washington, DC.

Aschauer, David. 1989. "Is Public Expenditure Productive?" *Journal of Monetary Economics* 23 (2): 177–200.

Barro, Robert. 1990. "Government Spending in a Simple Model of Endogenous Growth." *Journal of Political Economy* 98 (5): 103–26.

Berg, Andrew, Rafael Portillo, Shu-Chun S. Yang, and Luis-Felipe Zanna. 2013. "Public Investment in Resource-Abundant Developing Countries." *IMF Economic Review* 61 (1): 92–129.

Chou, Nan-Ting, Alexei Izyumov, and John Vahaly. 2016. "Rates of Return on Capital across the World: Are They Converging?" *Cambridge Journal of Economics* 40 (4): 1149–66.

Dabla-Norris, Era, Jim Brumby, Annette Kyobe, Zac Mills, and Chris Papageorgiou. 2012. "Investing in Public Investment: An Index of Public Investment Efficiency." *Journal of Economic Growth* 17: 235–66.

Devarajan, Shantayanan, Vinaya Swaroop, and Heng-Fu Zou.1996. "The Composition of Public Expenditure and Economic Growth." *Journal of Monetary Economics* 37 (2): 313–44.

Dhar, Sanjay. 2014. "IMF Macroeconomic Policy Advice in the Financial Crisis Aftermath." Independent Evaluation Office of the IMF BP/14/07, International Monetary Fund, Washington, DC.

Fournier, Jean-Marc, and Åsa Johansson. 2016. "The Effect of the Size and the Mix of Public Spending on Growth and Inequality." OECD Economics Department Working Paper 1344, Organisation for Economic Co-operation and Development, Paris.

García-Cicco, Javier, Roberto Pancrazi, and Martin Uribe. 2010. "Real Business Cycles in Emerging Countries?" *American Economic Review* 100 (5): 2510–31.

Gemmell, Norman, Richard Kneller, and Ismael Sanz. 2016. "Does the Composition of Government Expenditure Matter for Long-Run GDP Levels?" *Oxford Bulletin of Economics and Statistics* 78 (4): 522–47.

Ghosh, Sugata, and Andros Gregoriou. 2008. "The Composition of Government Spending and Growth: Is Current or Capital Spending Better?" *Oxford Economic Papers* 60 (3): 484–516.

Ghosh, Sugata, and Udayan Roy. 2004. "Fiscal Policy, Long-Run Growth, and Welfare in a Stock-Flow Model of Public Goods." *Canadian Journal of Economics* 37 (3): 742–56.

Glomm, Gerhard, and B. Ravikumar. 1997. "Productive Government Expenditures and Long-Run Growth." *Journal of Economic Dynamics and Control* 21 (1): 183–204.

Gómez, Manuel A. 2007. "Optimal Tax Structure in a Two-Sector Model of Endogenous Growth." *Journal of Macroeconomics* 29 (2): 305–25.

Gupta, Sanjeev, Emanuele Baldacci, Benedict Clements, and Erwin R. Tiongson. 2005. "What Sustains Fiscal Consolidations in Emerging Market Countries?" *International Journal of Finance and Economics* 10: 307–21.

International Monetary Fund (IMF). 2010. "Strategies for Fiscal Consolidation in the Post-Crisis World." IMF Departmental Paper 10/08, Washington, DC.

IMF. 2015. "Making Public Investment More Efficient." IMF Policy Paper, Washington, DC, May.

IMF. 2018. "Assessing Fiscal Space: An Update and Stocktaking." IMF Policy Paper, Washington, DC, June.

Jones, Charles. 1995. "Time Series Tests of Growth Models." *Quarterly Journal of Economics* 110 (2): 495–525.

Lee, Young, and Roger H. Gordon. 2005. "Tax Structure and Economic Growth." *Journal of Public Economics* 89 (5–6): 1027–43.

Leeper, Eric, Todd Walker, and Shu-Chun S. Yang. 2010. "Government Investment and Fiscal Stimulus." *Journal of Monetary Economics* 57 (8): 1000–12.

Lind, Jo Thori, and Halvor Mehlum. 2010. "With or Without U? The Appropriate Test for a U-Shaped Relationship." *Oxford Bulletin of Economics and Statistics* 72 (1): 109–18.

Romp, Ward, and Jakob de Haan. 2007. "Public Capital and Economic Growth: A Critical Survey." *Perspektiven der Wirtschaftspolitik* 8: 6–52.

Von Hagen, Jürgen, Andrew Hughes Hallett, and Rolf Strauch. 2002. "Budgetary Consolidation in Europe: Quality, Economic Conditions, and Persistence." *Journal of the Japanese and International Economies* 16 (4): 512–35.

# CHAPTER 7

# Designing Fiscal Rules to Protect Investment

**Olivier Basdevant, Taz Chaponda, Fabien Gonguet, Jiro Honda, and Saji Thomas**

## INTRODUCTION

Public investment supported by strong infrastructure governance can have a significant economic growth impact, as documented in Chapter 2 and in the literature such as Lucas (1988) and Romer (1990). Countries therefore should allocate adequate resources for public capital spending to meet their national development goals. In doing so they should ensure that capital spending is embedded in a stable and predictable fiscal framework, such as a fiscal rule, to avoid detrimental cycles of boom and bust in public investment.

Under numerical fiscal rules, however, public investment can be an easy target for spending cuts. Numerical fiscal rules impose a long-lasting constraint on fiscal aggregates (Kopits and Symansky 1998; IMF 2005, 2009), such as government debt, the budget balance,[1] or expenditures (Box 7.1).[2] By constraining excessive deficits, fiscal rules can build and preserve fiscal space to achieve the main objectives of the government (IMF 2018) and support a stable and predictable fiscal framework. That said, when fiscal rules constrain overall spending, this may also lead to investment cuts, especially in times of fiscal adjustment, as capital spending is easier to change than other less discretionary and more politically sensitive types of expenditure. This is an unintended and distortionary effect, as short-term constraints lead to actions that harm long-term growth. Indeed, this chapter finds that numerical fiscal rules are often associated with lower levels and higher volatility of public investment.

Given these conditions, this chapter has two critical findings.

1. Countries with high efficiency in public investment (see Chapter 3) are better at protecting public investment from spending cuts. Accordingly,

The authors are grateful to Eslem Imamoglu for her research assistance.

[1] The budget balance is referred to as the difference between government revenues and spending of each year.

[2] Balassone and Franco (2000), Creel, Monperrus-Veroni, and Saraceno (2009), and Schaechter and others (2012) also discussed the role of fiscal rules in ensuring sustainable levels of public investment.

## Box 7.1. Fiscal Rules: Basics

Fiscal rules, by constraining discretionary options for policymakers, can foster fiscal responsibility. While fiscal rules are typically numerical in form (for example, a deficit ceiling), successful implementation of such rules is usually supported by procedural rules (such as on the design of the budget preparation process; see IMF 2009) and broader fiscal institutions (having independent oversight through fiscal councils is an example given in IMF 2013). Over the past two decades, the use of fiscal rules has spread worldwide from a handful of advanced economies in the 1990s to a large number of countries across all income groups (IMF 2017). Many countries now have multiple fiscal rules in place; budget balance rules, for example, are often combined with debt rules. Fiscal rules are often embedded in a fiscal responsibility law, which provides legal basis for the rules. Taken together, numerical and procedural rules complement each other in promoting fiscal responsibility.

Numerical fiscal rules are defined by the fiscal indicator they target, such as debt, budget balance, expenditure, or revenue rules (Annex 7.1 and IMF 2009).[1] While numerical rules can foster fiscal discipline, they have also been criticized for unduly constraining other fiscal objectives, including public investment (Eyraud and others 2018). Some countries have aimed to introduce more flexibility with the so-called golden rules, which aim to protect public investment by removing this type of spending from the definition of the targeted deficit (Blanchard and Giavazzi 2004). Moreover, following the global financial crisis countries have established new rules or overhauled existing ones, leading to the so-called second-generation fiscal rules, which typically include expenditure rules or fiscal effort rules (Eyraud and others 2018). Building on sound public financial management systems, these rules are crafted to target objectives that are more under the control of fiscal authorities (for example, by focusing on cyclically adjusted fiscal balances) and to better protect public investment. Overall, second-generation rules can fulfill fiscal discipline objectives without hampering the countercyclical role of fiscal policy (Eyraud and others 2018).

Procedural rules, together with other fiscal institutions, are essential to achieve the objectives of numerical rules. They consist of procedures for the budgetary process that establish good practices, raise predictability, and improve transparency (Kopits and Symansky 1998), sometimes as part of fiscal responsibility laws. These laws may, for instance, require the government to prepare and present a fiscal policy statement that sets out medium-term fiscal objectives and a medium-term fiscal framework, including budgetary expenditure ceilings. It is also common to have provisions on the reporting of fiscal outcomes to promote transparency, such as a requirement for the government to publish accurate and timely midyear and end-of-year fiscal reports. Furthermore, well-defined numerical rules typically include escape clauses, defining procedures as to when the application of rules should be suspended, and how and when it would be reinforced. In addition, fiscal institutions such as fiscal councils, which are often tasked with monitoring the implementation of numerical rules, have proven to be equally supportive of the broader objectives of fiscal rules (IMF 2013).

---

[1] Advantages and disadvantages are associated with each type of numerical rule, according to Cangiano, Curristine, and Lazare (2013).

even with fiscal rules in place, strengthening infrastructure governance can help countries address fiscal sustainability concerns and still protect public investment.

2. Numerical rules can be designed to prevent undesirable cuts in public investment, especially when supplemented by sound practices for public financial management (PFM), including adequate procedural rules. Further, good infrastructure governance, particularly medium-term fiscal and budget frameworks and arrangements to protect capital appropriations during project implementation, is key to fostering public investment efficiency and performance (IMF 2015).

## THE IMPACT OF NUMERICAL FISCAL RULES ON PUBLIC INVESTMENT

Fiscal rules frequently do not treat public investment differently from recurrent expenditure (IMF 2015). As noted, this can lead to excessive cuts in capital spending, especially during adjustment periods (IMF 2018). To examine the impact of fiscal rules on public investment, the level and volatility of public investment is first contrasted between countries with and without fiscal rules. Next, the impact of different types of fiscal rules is examined, along with how the results are influenced by supporting fiscal institutions and procedural rules.

### Numerical Rules Associated with Lower Investment and High Volatility

Drawing on the IMF's Fiscal Rules Dataset (2017), the level and volatility of public investment in countries with fiscal rules is explored. Countries with numerical fiscal rules (on expenditure, budget balances, and public debt, for example) are compared with those that do not have numerical rules.[3,4] The following are key findings:

- Numerical fiscal rules are associated with slightly lower levels of public investment. On average, the level of public investment in countries with numerical fiscal rules is 0.2–0.5 percent of GDP lower than in those without fiscal rules (Figure 7.1). This holds for all income groups and is consistent with literature that has criticized fiscal rules (especially first-generation rules) for overly constraining public investment (IMF 2018). Indeed, as noted, the discretionary nature of public investment can make it an easy target for adjustment-driven cuts to maintain fiscal targets.

[3] The data set covers 96 countries with fiscal rules. See Annex 7.2.

[4] These stylized facts do not suggest any causality between fiscal rules and public investment.

**Figure 7.1. Public Investment, by Income Group, 1985–2015**
*(Percent of GDP, average, total of 150 countries)*

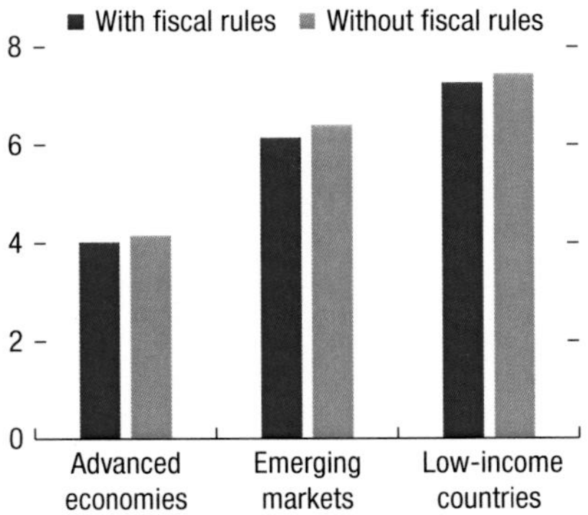


Sources: Country authorities; and IMF staff estimates.

**Figure 7.2. Public Investment Volatility, by Income Group, 1985–2015**
*(Average, standard deviation of public investment to GDP of five years, total of 150 countries)*

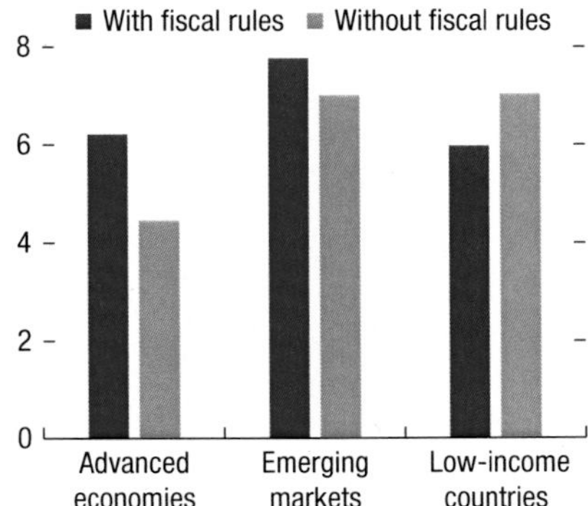


Sources: Country authorities; and IMF staff estimates.

- Under fiscal rules, public investment is more volatile in advanced economies and emerging market economies than in others. For these country groups, numerical fiscal rules tend to be accompanied by higher investment volatility, as measured by the standard deviation of public investment in terms of GDP (Figure 7.2), suggesting that public investment may be subject to spending adjustments to comply with the numerical fiscal rules. In low-income countries, however, fiscal rules tend to be accompanied by lower volatility of public investment, though the difference is small.
- When large spending cuts are needed, low-income countries and emerging markets with fiscal rules tend to rely more on cuts in public investment. Examining episodes of annual spending cuts of more than 1 percentage point of GDP, contributions to these cuts by capital and recurrent spending can be estimated (Figure 7.3). In advanced economies and emerging markets, spending cuts of this magnitude are driven by recurrent spending, while the contribution by capital spending is more limited.[5] That pattern is reversed in low-income countries. When comparing countries with and without numerical fiscal rules, cuts in capital spending are more pronounced in emerging markets and low-income countries. In advanced

[5] The presence of automatic stabilizers could be a factor, particularly in advanced economies.

**Figure 7.3. Composition of Spending Cuts, by Income Group, 1985–2015**
*(Median, contributions to total spending cuts of all episodes, in percent, total of 156 countries)*

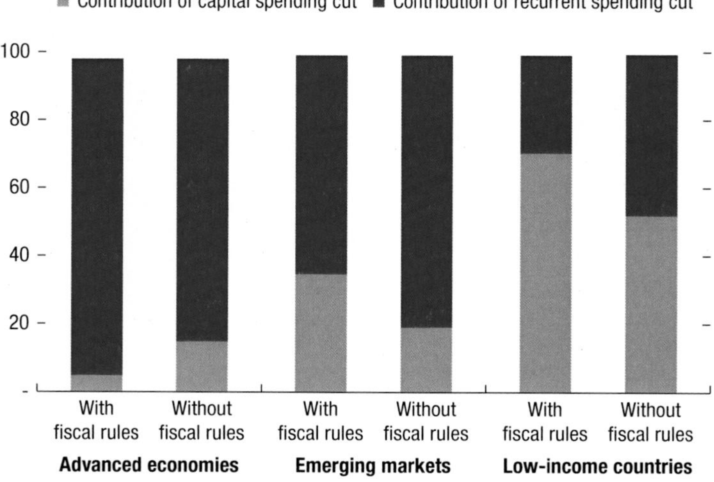


Sources: Country authorities; and IMF staff estimates.

economies the opposite is true, because they tend to have strong PFM systems and a more predictable medium-term budget framework, which limits cuts to public investment. This finding for emerging markets and low-income countries is in line with the presumption that fiscal rules can suppress capital spending (IMF 2018).

## The Impacts of Numerical Rules on Public Investment

Next, the impact of different fiscal rules on the level and volatility of public investment is examined.[6] For this, econometric estimates of the impact of different combinations of fiscal rules are produced using a generalized method of moments (GMM) methodology.[7] The model includes macroeconomic variables, numerical fiscal rules, supporting fiscal institutions, and procedural rules as explanatory variables. Expenditure rules and debt rules are the focus

[6] Given a limited sample size, the results are not always consistent across all sample groups and thus should be interpreted with caution.

[7] GMM estimation is better suited to estimating dynamic panel models when there are endogeneity and reverse feedback effects from dependent to explanatory variables.

for the numerical fiscal rule.[8] Annex 7.2 describes the methodology in more detail. In line with the recent literature (Eyraud and others 2018), debt rules and expenditure rules appear to be associated with lower investment (Annex Table 7.3.1).

The resulting estimates, examined by income group, point to a negative impact of debt rules on the level of public investment in emerging markets, while the impacts are insignificant in advanced economies and low-income countries. This may reflect strong PFM systems in advanced economies (such as for the selection of quality investment projects and the capacity for adequate medium-term planning), which could dampen the negative impact on public investment; in low-income countries, donor financing of public investment may limit the negative impact of numerical fiscal rules. The negative impact could also be an indication that fiscal rules are less effective in low-income countries, as they may exist "on paper" but are not adhered to or have no effect on policymaking. Some supporting fiscal institutions and procedural rules can have a negative impact on the level of public investment: reporting requirements on compliance with the rules and the presence of a fiscal council might make fiscal rules more effective, rendering fiscal consolidation more binding and leading to a reduction in public investment.

It is interesting to note that countries with high efficiency in public investment[9] tend to better preserve public investment, even with fiscal rules. In these countries, the negative impact of fiscal rules on investment disappears (Figure 7.4). This suggests that the potentially negative effect of fiscal rules can be mitigated with improved quality and effectiveness of public investment, which can be achieved through improvements in infrastructure governance. In other words, preservation of capital investment could be supported with fiscal rules with more emphasis on strong procedures and other institutions, which are at the foundation of second-generation rules.

A few countries have implemented golden rules, but these have not shown any ability to contribute effectively to a higher level of public investment despite their theoretical appeal (Box 7.2). The analysis in this chapter suggests that golden rules may have a negative impact on investment, particularly in advanced economies, primarily because of weaknesses in their design: golden rules, by overlooking fiscal sustainability per se, are vulnerable to having their implementation altered once sustainability is at risk and to calls for a fiscal adjustment (OECD 2008; Valencia 2015). However, the number of countries with such rules is limited (mostly advanced economies), and the empirical finding on golden rules

[8] Results for countries with other fiscal rules (budget balance) were not robust, perhaps because of collinearity with debt and expenditure rules.

[9] Investment efficiency is defined as achieving the accumulation of public physical assets (in both quantity and quality) in a cost-efficient manner (see Chapter 3 for more detail). In the regression equation we introduced an interaction term between fiscal rules and the investment efficiency of the country. We find that higher-efficiency countries tend to preserve public investment even under fiscal rules (Annex Table 7.3.1).

**Figure 7.4. Estimated Impacts on the Level of Public Investment with Fiscal Rules**

*(Estimated coefficient, all countries)*

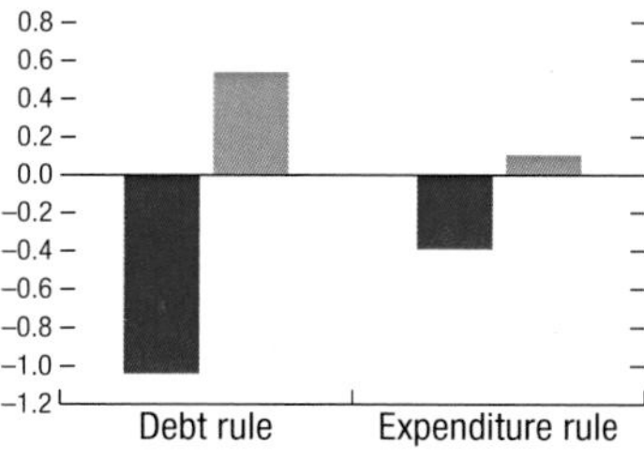


Sources: Country authorities; and IMF staff estimates.

**Figure 7.5. Estimated Impacts on the Volatility of Public Investment with Debt Rules, by Income Group**

*(Estimated coefficients)*

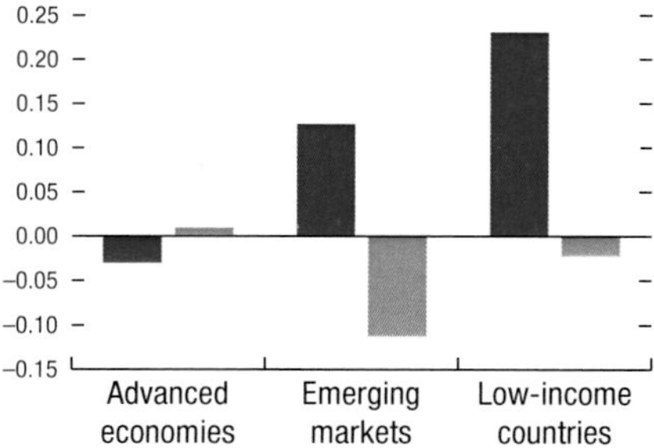


Sources: Country authorities; and IMF staff estimates.

## Box 7.2. Country Experiences with Golden Rules

### Mexico, 2009

In 2009, the government excluded capital expenditures made by the national oil company and the state-owned electricity company from the nominal budget balance. This impeded an appropriate assessment of the fiscal stance and contributed to adverse public debt dynamics (Valencia 2015).

### Germany, 1969–2010

Until 2011, a golden rule (IMF 2017) was in place for the central government, restricting the use of borrowing for public investment, unless an adverse and unexpected shock required borrowing to cover part of recurrent spending. *Länder* had similar requirements in their constitutions. The rule was abandoned because it proved ineffective at slowing the buildup of debt (OECD 2008).

### United Kingdom, 1998–2007

The United Kingdom had two fiscal rules in place: a golden rule (although defined over the economic cycle to give more flexibility) and a debt ceiling of 40 percent of GDP. While the objectives were sound, the rules failed for two main reasons. First, the rules did not provide adequate room during bad times, as the UK got closer to its debt ceiling, which subsequently pushed for a fiscal adjustment hardly compatible with the golden rule. Second, the compliance requirement was primarily based on an assessment of the anticipated fiscal stance over the economic cycle, with a limited correction mechanism after in case of adverse events. The compliance requirement led to an increase in debt which, by the time the rule was abandoned, had become significantly above the threshold of 40 percent of GDP.

(Annex 7.3) is hardly conclusive. Overall, unless golden rules are complemented with an overarching numerical rule on public debt, they are vulnerable to creating unsustainable debt dynamics (IMF 2018).

Our analyses also confirm that, controlling for other variables, numerical (debt) rules are generally associated with higher volatility of investment (Annex Table 7.3.2).[10] Particularly, this is the case for emerging markets and low-income countries, reflecting the intuition that when faced with fiscal consolidation under fiscal rules, public investment is an easy candidate for spending cuts because of its discretionary nature. When adjusted for efficiency, however, debt rules are associated with lower volatility of investment in emerging markets and low-income countries (Figure 7.5), which suggests that fiscal rules in countries with higher investment efficiency tend to improve the predictability and stability of public investment (and thus contribute to lower volatility). In advanced economies, we did not find a significant effect on volatility in the presence of fiscal rules, likely because these countries tend to have strong PFM systems. Finally, escape clauses and fiscal transparency are associated with lower volatility, particularly in advanced economies and low-income countries, suggesting that these practices contribute to a more stable environment for investment. Fiscal responsibility laws do not have a significant impact on the volatility of public investment.[11]

## DESIGN OF FISCAL RULES TO PROTECT QUALITY PUBLIC INVESTMENT

Fiscal rules can be combined with mechanisms aimed at protecting public investment. In exploring how, the discussion turns to (1) specific types of numerical fiscal rules, and (2) infrastructure governance practices that could mitigate the unintended impacts of rules on public investment.

### Numerical Fiscal Rules to Better Protect Public Investment

Second-generation rules—removing excessive rigidity of fiscal rules—can better protect public investment from cuts, primarily because they allow flexibility throughout the economic cycle (Eyraud and others 2018). However, they also come at the cost of greater complexity and capacity requirements, notably on PFM systems and procedural rules. Two types of second-generation fiscal rules are often highlighted as being more "investment friendly" for their capacity to protect spending during downturns, and have become increasingly popular:

- *Expenditure rules.* These can protect investment as they are designed specifically to protect spending throughout the implementation of medium-term

[10] Volatility is measured as the five-year rolling average volatility of public investment to GDP.

[11] According to the literature, there is mixed evidence on the impact of fiscal responsibility laws on fiscal outcomes (Corbacho and Schwartz 2007; Caceres, Corbacho, and Medina 2010).

fiscal objectives (IMF 2018). They offer an avenue to "blend" numerical targets with medium-term budget frameworks, by setting expenditure ceilings consistent with the targets, which can then be applied throughout budget preparation and implementation (see the discussion in the next paragraph). However, expenditure rules are not flawless either: recurrent spending is by nature harder to cut than investment spending and can still leave the bulk of the adjustment to fall on public investment during bad times, like other numerical rules (Guerguil, Madon, and Tapsoba 2017).

- *Fiscal effort rules.* Usually defined through the cyclically adjusted balance or the structural balance,[12] these can also better protect investment, primarily by bringing flexibility to deficit rules. Adopting a deficit rule (adjusted for the economic cycle and for one-off factors) can in principle generate similar guidance to that of expenditure rules, as it can also be operationalized into expenditure ceilings. Fiscal effort rules also have the advantage of being broader in scope by factoring in cyclical adjustment on the revenue side.

These second-generation fiscal rules may be less suitable for countries with capacity constraints. Though expenditure rules or cyclically adjusted deficit rules can offer a framework for preserving public investment, they also have their challenges, as they assume that countries are subject to well-defined cycles, and that there is adequate institutional capacity to implement fiscal policies adjusted for cyclical economic fluctuations, ideally cast within a medium-term framework. Both assumptions can be overly demanding for countries with limited capacity. In such cases, a ceiling on current expenditures to avoid crowding out public investment, combined with a simple budget balance rule, may be preferable (IMF 2018). Such rules would have the advantage of focusing on preserving fiscal sustainability in low-income countries, which typically lack fiscal space and tend to be more vulnerable to shocks.

## Infrastructure Governance Practices to Strengthen the Predictability of Public Investment

As shown in previous section, in countries with high efficiency in public investment (for example, through better PFM practices), the negative impact of fiscal rules can be mitigated. Good PFM practices—including those pertaining to medium-term budgeting and infrastructure governance—can help mitigate any harm that fiscal rules might otherwise do to public investment. Such practices, which are embedded in the Public Investment Management Assessment (PIMA) tool (Chapter 5), help governments better plan public investment, give protection or priority to capital spending, and ensure the sound execution of the capital budget. For countries with numerical fiscal rules, medium-term planning and budgeting combined with procedures that protect appropriations

[12] The structural balance is the cyclically adjusted balance further adjusted for one-off measures.

for capital spending can help mitigate the negative impact of numerical rules on public investment. This chapter's analysis of PIMA scores from a cross-country sample of 25 countries (14 emerging markets and 11 low-income countries) that have implemented at least one type of numerical fiscal rule supports that view.

As most public investment projects are multiyear endeavors, countries with strong infrastructure governance tend to plan and budget their capital spending over a long time horizon, contributing to more predictable capital spending. Not only can such practices mitigate the negative effect of fiscal rules on investment levels, they may also reduce investment volatility.

- *Strategic planning.* Many emerging markets and low-income countries prepare medium-term investment strategies as part of their national development planning. Under best practice, these strategies contain realistic investment priorities, cost estimates, and clear objectives for each sector, while being consistent with the fiscal constraints. PIMA scores for countries with numerical fiscal rules show that advanced national and sectoral planning practices are associated with higher investment (Figure 7.6); however, the analysis does not find that such practices impact volatility.
- *Medium-term budgeting.* Medium-term fiscal and budget frameworks bring investment strategies into effect in a fiscal environment that complies with

**Figure 7.6. Level of Public Investment, with Effective "National and Sectoral Planning"**
*(Percent of GDP, 2010–15 average)*

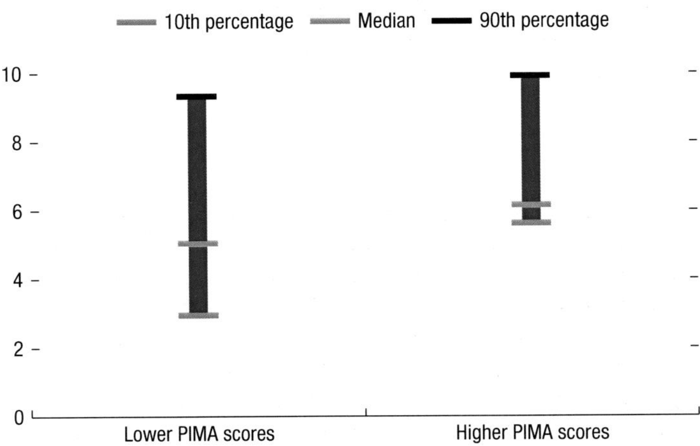


Source: IMF staff estimates.
Note: PIMA effectiveness scores for Institution 2 ("National and Sectoral Planning") for a sample of 25 countries with at least one numerical fiscal rule. On a scale of 0–10, below 5 represents lower PIMA scores and 5 and above represent higher PIMA scores. PIMA = Public Investment Management Assessment.

the numerical rules. By presenting investment envelopes in line with available fiscal space, as well as detailed fiscal policy measures, the medium-term fiscal framework creates expectations about how the government intends to operationalize its development plans. Medium-term budget frameworks also provide sector ministries with some predictability on their medium-term capital appropriations—in some countries, multiyear appropriations are even voted into law (see Box 7.3). PIMA scores indicate that in countries with fiscal rules, robust medium-term budgeting practices increase investments and reduce volatility (Figure 7.7).

Medium-term planning and budgeting can be undermined by regular budget revisions from one year to the next, and by in-year adjustments to appropriations. To guard against this, several procedural rules on the use of budget appropriations have been developed to protect budget allocations to capital projects. Usually set in budget system laws, they include communicating on multiyear commitments, setting limitations on transfers of appropriations from capital to current spending, and giving explicit priority to ongoing capital projects (instead of starting new

### Box 7.3. Multiyear Appropriations in West African Economic and Monetary Union Countries

The West African Economic and Monetary Union (WAEMU) comprises eight member countries (Benin, Burkina Faso, Côte d'Ivoire, Guinea-Bissau, Mali, Niger, Senegal, and Togo). All countries have agreed to meeting a set of "convergence criteria" since 2001 (revised in 2014), including a debt rule and a deficit rule. To support enforcement, WAEMU adopted six directives in 2009 aimed at setting a "harmonized fiscal framework" across member countries. This includes advanced public financial management practices such as medium-term fiscal and budget planning, program budgeting, and transparency requirements. Despite initial delays, all directives have now been transposed into national laws.

One key reform of the harmonized fiscal framework is the introduction of a double budget appropriation system, comprising regular annual budget appropriations—*crédits de paiement* (CP)—and multiyear commitment authorizations—*autorisations d'engagement* (AE). Both types of appropriation are voted by parliaments every year. Advanced economies are required to allow the government to sign a multiyear contract or to commit public monies for several years, while CPs are required to allow accountants to pay the bills. Therefore, to be executed, each expenditure item requires both types of appropriation. This double appropriation system (which has also been implemented in France since 2006) is especially useful to protect investment spending, which often necessitates multiyear commitments. When fully operational, the system facilitates monitoring of future spending needs associated with ongoing projects, and so it complements traditional cash accounting and supports implementation of the fiscal rules.

The implementation of the AE-CP framework in WAEMU has started in all countries but is not yet fully effective. Such a reform requires significant capacity building (both in finance ministries and in line ministries) and necessitates development of information technology systems to monitor commitments. However, thanks to the reform, WAEMU countries' practices for the protection of capital spending are on average already ahead of those in other low-income countries, and close to the average practices of emerging market economies (see Figure 7.3.1).

**Box 7.3 (*Continued*)**

**Figure 7.3.1. Effectiveness of "Investment Protection" in West African Economic and Monetary Union Countries**
*(Average PIMA score, scale 0–10)*

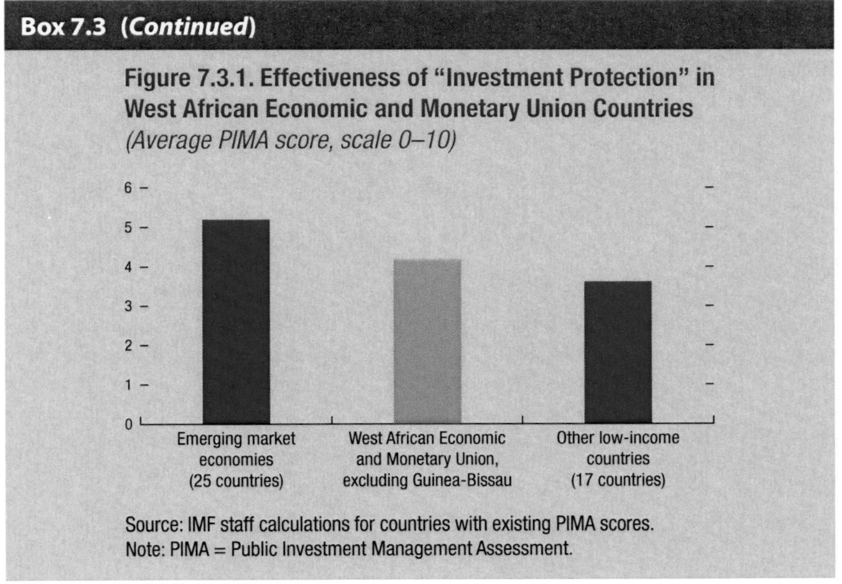


Source: IMF staff calculations for countries with existing PIMA scores.
Note: PIMA = Public Investment Management Assessment.

**Figure 7.7. Level and Volatility of Public Investment with Effective Medium-Term Budgeting**
*(Percent of GDP, 2010–15 average)*

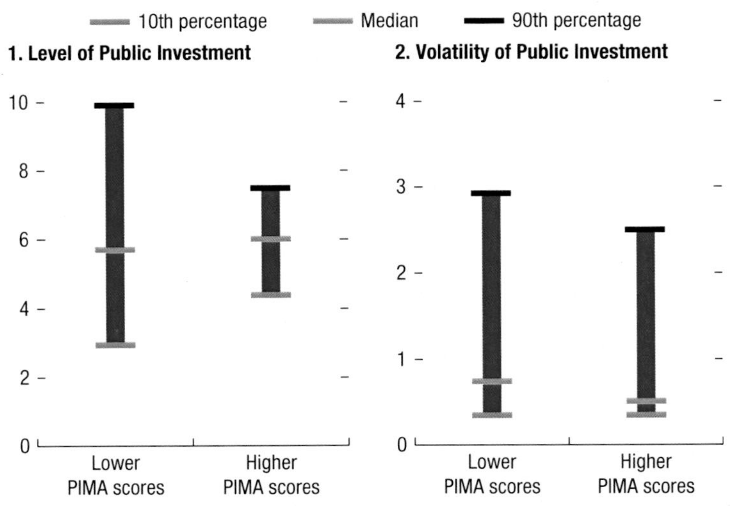


Source: IMF staff estimates.
Note: PIMA effectiveness scores for Institution 6 ("Multiyear Budgeting") for a sample of 25 countries with at least one numerical fiscal rule. On a scale of 0 to 10, below 3.3 represents lower PIMA scores and 3.3 and above represent higher PIMA scores.
PIMA = Public Investment Management Assessment.

**Figure 7.8. Level of Public Investment, with Effective "Budgeting for Investment"**
*(Percent of GDP, 2010–15 average)*

**Figure 7.9. Volatility of Public Investment, with Effective "Implementation" Practices**
*(Percent of GDP, 2010–15 average)*

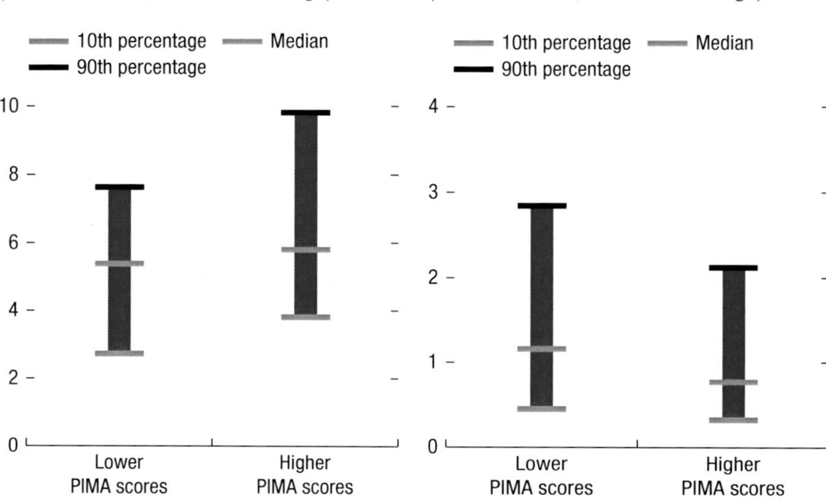


Source: IMF staff estimates.
Note: PIMA effectiveness scores for Institution 8 ("Budgeting for Investment") for a sample of 25 countries with at least one numerical fiscal rule. On a scale of 0 to 10, below 5 represents lower PIMA scores and 5 and above represent higher PIMA scores. PIMA = Public Investment Management Assessment.

Source: IMF staff estimates.
Note: Average PIMA effectiveness scores for Institutions 11 to 15 ("Implementation") for a sample of 25 countries with at least one numerical fiscal rule. On a scale of 0 to 10, below 3.3 represents lower PIMA scores and 3.3 and above represent higher PIMA scores. PIMA = Public Investment Management Assessment.

ones). PIMA scores for countries with numerical fiscal rules suggest that strong practices in these areas are associated with higher investment levels (Figure 7.8); however, on their own, they do not seem to reduce investment volatility. Other infrastructure governance practices pertaining to the sound implementation of investment projects—such as competitive procurement or making sure that funding is available when needed—appear to be more important in dampening volatility (Figure 7.9).

## CONCLUSIONS

Rigid implementation of numerical fiscal rules can come at the cost of lower public investment. The analyses in this chapter indicate that the level of public investment can be lower in countries with fiscal rules, particularly in emerging markets. This supports the intuition that public investment can be an easy adjustment target because it has a smaller political cost than other spending. However, the unintended drawback of fiscal rules on public investment can be addressed by second-generation fiscal rules and strong infrastructure government institutions, helping to prevent persistent cuts in investment that may hamper long-term growth prospects and eventually increase fiscal vulnerabilities.

Numerical fiscal rules may also lead to higher volatility of public investment, possibly hindering a stable flow of capital spending. This chapter finds that fiscal rules, particularly debt rules, on average, are associated with higher investment volatility, particularly in emerging markets and low-income countries. Such impacts, however, are reversed in countries that have high investment efficiency. With fiscal rules, stability of public investment can also be promoted by supporting fiscal institutions and through procedural rules, such as reporting requirements on compliance with fiscal rules or having a fiscal council.

Second-generation fiscal rules—removing excessive rigidity of rules—offer a way to protect public investment, though at the cost of greater complexity and capacity requirements. Such rules typically require (1) more complex rules that address broader procyclicality issues, and (2) strong infrastructure governance. As the first requirement is often challenging for countries with capacity constraints, countries may opt for simpler numerical rules, which underscores the need for supporting infrastructure governance institutions to protect the efficiency of public investment.

To support the predictability of public investment while securing fiscal sustainability objectives, countries with fiscal rules should strengthen infrastructure governance. Key practices can help to reduce volatility and sustain public investment without compromising fiscal sustainability objectives. Specifically, countries should focus on medium-term fiscal planning and budgeting, combined with procedures that protect appropriations for capital spending and ensure that project funding is made available in line with approved capital budgets.

# ANNEX 7.1 A SIMPLE TAXONOMY OF FISCAL RULES

**ANNEX TABLE 7.1.1.**

A Simple Taxonomy of Fiscal Rules

| | | Success Factors | | | |
|---|---|---|---|---|---|
| | Sustainability versus Investment | Simplicity[10] | Flexibility[10] | Built-In Correction Factor[11] | Quality of Public Financial Management[12] |
| First-generation rules[1] | | | | | |
| Debt | | | | | |
| Debt ceiling[2] | Sustainability | + | – | No | Basic |
| Debt brake[3] | Sustainability | + | Neutral | Yes | Basic |
| Budget balance | | | | | |
| Deficit ceiling[4] | Sustainability | + | – | No | Medium |
| Golden rule[5] | Investment | + | + | No | Medium |
| Revenue rule[6] | Balanced | + | Neutral | Yes | Medium |
| Second-generation rules[7] | | | | | |
| Expenditure rule[8] | Balanced | + | + | Yes | Advanced |
| Fiscal effort rule[9] | Balanced | – | + | Yes | Advanced |

Source: IMF staff estimates.

[1] First-generation rules refer to fiscal rules that were largely in place before the global financial crisis.

[2] Debt rules generally set a limit, in percentage of GDP, on the level of public debt. However, they do not provide guidance for fiscal policy when debt is well below its ceiling.

[3] Debt-brake rules aim to address the lack of guidance when debt is far below the ceiling, with an automatic deficit correction mechanism triggered when debt reaches a certain level.

[4] Deficit-ceiling rules can be defined on the headline deficit or the deficit "over the cycle." Often, they are coupled with debt-ceiling rules, with the deficit objective supporting the debt objective.

[5] Golden rules set a target on the deficit (either the headline level or the cyclically adjusted one) but exclude public investment from the scope of the rule.

[6] Revenue rules are primarily used in resource-rich countries, to guard the budget against large fluctuation of commodity prices, by adopting price-smoothing formulas. In principle, these rules offer an avenue to build buffers in good times and reduce procyclicality, especially on the investment side. However, they have been of limited effectiveness in practice.

[7] Second-generation rules are more flexible rules introduced in the aftermath of the crisis, which attempted to address flexibility and enforceability issues (Hodge, Kim, and Lledó 2018).

[8] Expenditure rules usually set limits on expenditure in absolute terms, growth rates, or percentage of GDP. They can be helpful in protecting automatic stabilizers on the revenue side, thus leaving room for automatic stabilizers to operate. However, because in their simplest form they would not tackle fiscal sustainability well (as they exclude revenue from the definition), they would need to be coupled with another rule (for example, a debt brake) or factor in the revenue side. (The European expenditure benchmark caps the growth rate of expenditure net of new revenue measures.)

[9] Fiscal effort rules are typically rules set on the cyclically adjusted deficit (possibly also adjusted for one-off measures). The advantage of such a rule versus targeting a headline deficit is that a cyclically adjusted balance objective is a variable less vulnerable to exogenous shocks and therefore fiscal authorities can have more control over them.

[10] + = more flexible/simple; – = less flexible/simple.

[11] A key feature of second-generation rules is the presence of built-in corrective mechanisms.

[12] Quality of public financial management systems requirement. Advanced: second-generation rules typically require strong public financial management systems, particularly to address adjustments for the economic cycle. Medium: some key public financial management systems are needed to be well functioning, such as a well-established budget system. Basic: suitable even for countries with limited public financial management capacity.

## ANNEX 7.2. EMPIRICAL METHODOLOGY

All macro variables (GDP, debt, investment, and trade openness) are from the World Economic Outlook database. Fiscal rules and related variables are from the new IMF Fiscal Rules Dataset, which provides systematic information on the use and design of fiscal rules, covering both national and supranational fiscal rules in 96 countries from 1985 to 2015. The data set covers four types of rules: budget balance rules, debt rules, expenditure rules, and revenue rules, applying to the central government, the general government, or the public sector. It also presents details on various characteristics of rules, such as their legal basis, coverage, escape clauses, and enforcement procedures, and takes stock of key support features, including independent monitoring bodies and fiscal responsibility laws.

Different combinations of fiscal rules are tested using a generalized method of moments (GMM) methodology to address endogeneity issues related to public investment. The GMM model generally follows the methodology used in Dabla-Norris and Srivisal (2013).

$$V_{it} = \beta_0 V_{it-1} + \beta_1 FR_{it} + \beta_2 X_{it} + \varepsilon_{i,t}$$

This is where $V$ is either the change in the level of public investment or a measure of public investment volatility[13] at time $t$ for country $i$; $FR$ is a dummy variable for countries adopting fiscal rules; $X$ is a set of other control variables; and $\varepsilon$ is the error term. In addition to the various types of fiscal rule variables, the control variables are macroeconomic variables that could also have an impact on public investment, such as

- GDP per capita—to control for the level of development and institutions;
- Gross public debt—public investment may act to smooth out movements in public debt;
- Private investment—as a substitute for public investment;
- Trade openness—higher trade openness could facilitate public investment.

Because the information on procedural fiscal rules is limited, the analysis focused on two rules linked to supporting fiscal institutions (fiscal responsibility laws and fiscal councils) and rules pertaining to strict procedures (such as escape clauses and fiscal transparency through fiscal reporting). To address concerns that public investment may be endogenously influencing GDP growth or other control variables, a GMM system (Blundell and Bond 1998) is used. As is now standard in the literature, a panel data set is constructed by transforming the time series data into nonoverlapping five-year averages. The analysis used one or two time-period lagged variables of dependent variables as instruments.

[13] Investment volatility was calculated as the standard deviation of the five-year public investment.

## ANNEX 7.3. RESULTS

**ANNEX TABLE 7.3.1.**

Generalized Method of Moments Model on Level of Public Investment

| | Numerical Rules Only | | | | Numerical and Supporting Fiscal Institutions and Procedural Rules | | | |
|---|---|---|---|---|---|---|---|---|
| | All | Advanced Economies | Emerging Markets | Low-Income Countries | All | Advanced Economies | Emerging Markets | Low-Income Countries |
| Expenditure rule | −0.390** | −0.506 | −0.455** | 0 | 0.119 | 0.298 | 0.149 | |
| Debt rule | −1.043* | 0.319 | −0.465*** | 0.178 | 0.122 | 1.099 | −0.160* | 0.651 |
| Investment Efficiency × Expenditure Rule | 0.497** | 0.573 | 0.592** | 0 | | | | |
| Investment Efficiency × Debt Rule | 1.584* | −0.161 | 0.171 | −0.318 | | | | |
| Golden rule | −0.142 | −0.280** | −1.219 | −0.542 | −0.915*** | −1.684* | −0.200 | |
| Level of investment = L | 0.235* | 1.016*** | 0.239*** | 0.921*** | 0.269*** | 0.900*** | 1.017*** | 0.0212 |
| Nominal GDP | 0.0937 | −0.0173 | −0.00377 | 0.0878** | 0.0827* | 0.297 | −0.0176 | 0.127 |
| Gross public debt | −0.00147* | −0.000396 | −0.00696*** | 0.00312*** | −0.00110** | 0.00321 | −0.00335*** | 0.000662 |
| Per capita income | −4.67e−06 | 9.16e−06 | -6.71e−06*** | −1.80e−06 | -3.39e−06 | 2.48e−06 | -9.57e−06*** | 1.37e−05 |
| Level of private investment | 0.0170* | 0.0189** | −0.00296 | −0.00281 | 0.00361 | −0.0160 | 0.0377*** | −0.00709 |
| Escape clause | | | | | −0.103 | −0.0614 | −0.144 | −1.335 |
| Fiscal council | | | | | −0.417* | 0.0274 | −0.106 | 0.153 |
| Fiscal transparency | | | | | −0.431*** | −0.924 | 0.160 | −1.021 |
| Constant | | | | | | −0.693 | −0.208 | |
| Observations | 412 | 54 | 212 | 214 | 412 | 54 | 281 | 163 |
| Number of countries | 134 | 17 | 68 | 51 | 134 | 17 | 69 | 49 |
| AR(2) *p* value | 0.12 | 0.32 | 0.1 | 0.03 | 0.04 | 0.79 | 0.59 | 0.06 |

Note: Standard errors are in parentheses.
***$p < 0.01$. **$p < 0.05$. *$p < 0.1$.

**ANNEX TABLE 7.3.2.**

## Generalized Method of Moments Model on Volatility of Public Investment

| | Numerical Rules Only | | | | Numerical and Supporting Fiscal Institutions and Procedural Rules | | | |
|---|---|---|---|---|---|---|---|---|
| | All | Advanced Economies | Emerging Markets | Low-Income Countries | All | Advanced Economies | Emerging Markets | Low-Income Countries |
| Expenditure rule | −0.0774 | −0.0448 | −0.0752 | 0 | 0.0601 | −0.0502*** | 0.101 | |
| Debt rule | 0.131*** | −0.0374 | 0.125** | 0.231*** | 0.0673 | −0.0860** | 0.0558 | 0.226*** |
| Investment Efficiency × Expenditure Rule | 0.0790 | −0.0191 | 0.165* | 0 | | | | |
| Investment Efficiency × Debt Rule | −0.188*** | 0.0163 | −0.237*** | −0.253** | | | | |
| Golden rule | −0.0430 | −0.0130 | −0.0793 | 0.113** | −0.0606 | −0.0132 | −0.0690 | |
| Per capita income | -3.95e−07 | −1.99e−06 | 1.30e−07 | −2.73e−05** | -1.41e−07 | −4.96e−07 | 2.46e−07 | -2.68e−05** |
| Volatility of investment | −0.0253 | −0.0871 | 0.0493* | −0.0478 | −0.0255 | −0.00916 | 0.0453 | −0.0499 |
| Nom final GDP | 0.000186 | 2.36e−05 | −8.06e−05 | 0.000217 | 0.000201 | 6.87e−05 | −0.000112 | 0.000271 |
| Volatility of private investment | 0.810*** | 1.014*** | 0.738*** | 0.944*** | 0.814*** | 1.035* | 0.7503*** | 0.939*** |
| Escape clause | | | | | −0.0732 | 0.0783** | −0.00519 | −0.209** |
| Fiscal council | | | | | −0.0596* | −0.0637** | −0.0289 | −0.0585 |
| Fiscal transparency | | | | | −0.0922 | 0.0403 | −0.140** | −0.312** |
| Constant | 0.148* | 0.0248 | 0.152 | 0 | 0.161*** | −0.000655 | 0.139 | 0.113** |
| Observations | 548 | 42 | 288 | 218 | 548 | 42 | 288 | 218 |
| Number of countries | 138 | 17 | 70 | 51 | 138 | 17 | 70 | 51 |
| AR(2) $p$ value | 0.03 | 0.07 | 0.03 | 0.09 | 0.06 | 0.20 | 0.02 | 0.09 |

Note: Standard errors are in parentheses.
***$p < 0.01$. **$p < 0.05$. *$p < 0.1$.

## REFERENCES


Balassone, Fabrizio, and Daniele Franco. 2000. "Public Investment, the Stability Pact and the 'Golden Rule.'" *Fiscal Studies* 21 (2): 207–29.

Blanchard, Olivier, and Francesco Giavazzi. 2004. "Improving the SGP through a Proper Accounting of Public Investment." CEPR Discussion Paper 4220, Center for Economic Policy Research, Washington, DC.

Blundell, Richard, and Stephen Bond. 1998. "Initial Conditions and Moment Restrictions in Dynamic Panel Data Models." *Journal of Econometrics* 87 (1): 115–43.

Caceres, Carlos, Ana Corbacho, and Leandro Medina. 2010. "Structural Breaks in Fiscal Performance: Do Fiscal Responsibility Laws Have Anything to Do with Them?" IMF Working Paper 10/248, International Monetary Fund, Washington, DC.

Cangiano, Marco, Teresa Curristine, and Michael Lazare. 2013. *Public Financial Management and Its Emerging Architecture*. Washington, DC: International Monetary Fund.

Corbacho, Ana, and Gerd Schwartz. 2007. "Fiscal Responsibility Laws." In *Promoting Fiscal Discipline*, edited by Manmohan S. Kumar and Teresa Ter-Minassian, 58–105. Washington, DC: International Monetary Fund.

Creel, Jérôme, Paola Monperrus-Veroni, and Francesco Saraceno. 2009. "On the Long-Term Effects of Fiscal Policy in the United Kingdom: The Case for a Golden Rule." *Scottish Journal of Political Economy* 56 (5): 580–607.

Dabla-Norris, Era, and Narapong Srivisal. 2013. "Revisiting the Link between Finance and Macroeconomic Volatility." IMF Working Paper 13/29, International Monetary Fund, Washington, DC.

Eyraud, Luc, Xavier Debrun, Andrew Hodge, Victor Duarte Lledó, and Catherine Pattillo. 2018. "Second-Generation Fiscal Rules: Balancing Simplicity, Flexibility, and Enforceability." IMF Staff Discussion Note 18/04, International Monetary Fund, Washington, DC.

Guerguil, Martine, Pierre Madon, and René Tapsoba. 2017. "Flexible Fiscal Rules and Countercyclical Fiscal Policy." *Journal of Macroeconomics* 52: 189–220.

Hodge, Andrew, Young Kim, and Victor Duarte Lledó. 2018. "The Emergence of a Second Generation of Fiscal Rules." Technical Background Note of the IMF Staff Discussion Note, "Second-Generation Fiscal Rules: Balancing Simplicity, Flexibility, and Enforceability." IMF Staff Discussion Note 18/04, Interational Monetary Fund, Washington, DC.

Ilzetzki, Ethan, Enrique G. Mendoza, and Carlos A. Vegh. 2010. "How Big (Small?) Are Fiscal Multipliers?" NBER Working Paper 16479, National Bureau of Economic Research, Cambridge, MA.

International Monetary Fund (IMF). 2005. *Fiscal Responsibility Laws*. Washington, DC.

IMF. 2009. *Fiscal Rules—Anchoring Expectations for Sustainable Public Finances*. Washington, DC.

IMF. 2013. *The Functions and Impact of Fiscal Councils*. Washington, DC.

IMF. 2015. *Making Public Investment More Efficient*. Washington, DC.

IMF. 2017. *Fiscal Rules Dataset*. https://www.imf.org/external/datamapper/FiscalRules/map/map.htm.

IMF. 2018. *How to Notes: How to Select Fiscal Rules—A Primer*. Washington DC.

Kopits, George, and Steven A. Symansky. 1998. *Fiscal Policy Rules*. IMF Occasional Paper 162. Washington, DC: International Monetary Fund.

Lucas, Robert. 1988. "On the Mechanics of Economic Development." *Journal of Monetary Economics* 22: 3–42.

Organisation for Economic Co-operation and Development (OECD). 2008. *OECD Economic Surveys: Germany*. Paris: OECD.

Romer, Paul. 1990. "Endogenous Technological Change." *Journal of Political Economy* 98 (5): S71–S102.

Schaechter, Andrea, Tidiane Kinda, Nina Budina, and Anke Weber. 2012. "Fiscal Rules in Response to the Crisis—Toward the 'Next-Generation' Rules. A New Dataset." IMF Working Paper 12/187, International Monetary Fund, Washington, DC.

Valencia, Fabien. 2015. "Strengthening Mexico's Fiscal Framework." IMF Country Report: Selected Issues 15/314, International Monetary Fund, Washington, DC.

# CHAPTER 8

# Boosting Infrastructure in Emerging Asia

Ha Vu, Olivier Bizimana, and Masahiro Nozaki

## INTRODUCTION

Infrastructure is essential to support sustainable and equitable growth in emerging and developing Asia. More and better-quality infrastructure is needed for countries in the region to maintain economic growth, advance to high-income levels, keep pace with profound economic and demographic changes, provide better services to citizens, and achieve Sustainable Development Goals (SDGs).

Policymakers considering building up the infrastructure stock need to look at potential macroeconomic and fiscal consequences. Boosting spending on infrastructure can raise growth in the short term by stimulating aggregate demand. It can also shore up potential growth in the long term as better infrastructure promotes the economy's productivity. Nonetheless, the spending boost can result in higher fiscal deficits and public debt if financed by borrowing, which can also crowd out private investment. Alternatively, a tax-financed spending boost can prevent increasing public debt, but the growth stimulus can be dampened by higher taxes on domestic demand or labor supply. The growth-debt trade-off inherent in financing infrastructure spending can be a key consideration for policymakers.

Whereas public investment can be an important catalyst for economic growth, the benefits depend crucially on how it is managed. Countries that are less efficient in public investment get less growth impact from boosting infrastructure spending (IMF 2015; Chapter 3 in this book). Inefficiencies are often due to weaknesses in public investment management. Improvements in infrastructure governance practices can help countries obtain the most economic benefits from their public investment. In this regard, emerging and developing Asian countries need to know how to improve governance practices to more effectively translate public investment into productive infrastructure.

This chapter accounts for these conditions in analyzing how emerging and developing Asian countries can build more and better infrastructure in an effective and efficient way.

The next part of the chapter assesses the region's infrastructure needs, looking at the current state of infrastructure, reviewing historical developments in infrastructure spending, and analyzing the efficiency of public investment. It finds that emerging and developing Asian countries would need more and better public investment to improve infrastructure outcomes and reach SDGs.

After that, the chapter focuses on how to meet infrastructure needs. Using macroeconomic model simulations, the chapter analyzes whether an infrastructure spending boost should be financed by tax increases or government borrowing and finds that in the long term, the growth-debt trade-off could be resolved by financing with higher indirect taxes. The benefit of improving public investment efficiency in raising long-term growth is highlighted. How to improve public investment management in Asia is then discussed, drawing on Public Investment Management Assessments (PIMAs) by the IMF in 11 Asian countries. The discussion finds that there is substantial scope in the region for improving the appraisal and selection of infrastructure projects, the funding of maintenance spending, multiyear budgeting, and monitoring of public assets. Key policy and institutional recommendations form the conclusion.

## THE STATE OF INFRASTRUCTURE AND PUBLIC INVESTMENT IN ASIA

Public investment has been higher in Asia than in other regions over the past 25 years. Government investment as a share of GDP in emerging and developing Asia (even when excluding China) was higher than all other regions during the 1990s and has always been above the average of emerging and developing Europe and Latin America and the Caribbean (Figure 8.1). It was also higher than emerging markets and low-income developing countries during 1990–2011 (Figure 8.2).

Government investment as a share of GDP in emerging and developing Asia was high during 1990–96 (at 8.5 percent, on average) but started decreasing after the 1997 Asian financial crisis. China has had even higher public investment than the rest of the region.[1] A pickup in infrastructure investment through public-private partnerships (PPPs) has been insufficient to compensate for the decrease in government investment spending.[2]

However, infrastructure outcomes in emerging and developing Asia are still lagging. According to survey-based measures, the infrastructure quality score in emerging and developing Asia is below emerging and developing Europe and the Middle East and North Africa (Figure 8.3). Perceptions are that infrastructure quality has stagnated since 2012, after converging with emerging markets until 2012 (Figure 8.4).

---

[1] Government infrastructure investment in China peaked at 32 percent of GDP in 1993, then decreased but still stayed high over the past couple of decades. It fell to 25 percent in 1997 following the Asian financial crisis, then 18 percent in 2007 during the global financial crisis and has hovered around 15 percent in recent years.

[2] In the last decade, a growing proportion of infrastructure services in Asia has been delivered through public-private partnerships (PPPs), though with significant differences across countries. Many PPP contracts were signed before the Asian financial crisis and after the 2007 global recession. The average nominal value of contracts reached 1.8 percent of GDP in 1998 and 2.2 percent in 2012.

**Figure 8.1. General Government Investment, by Region**
(Percent of GDP)

Sources: World Economic Outlook data; and IMF staff estimates.

**Figure 8.2. General Government Investment, by Income**
(Percent of GDP)

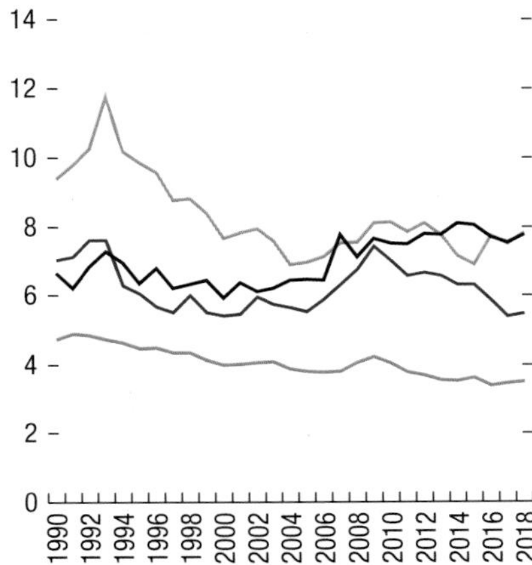


Sources: World Economic Outlook data; and IMF staff estimates.

**Figure 8.3. Perception of Infrastructure Quality, by Region, 2017**

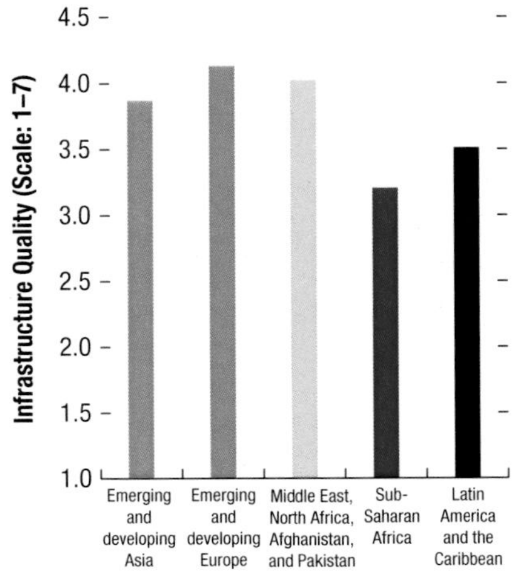


Source: World Economic Forum 2017.

**Figure 8.4. Perception of Infrastructure Quality, by Income, 2006–17**

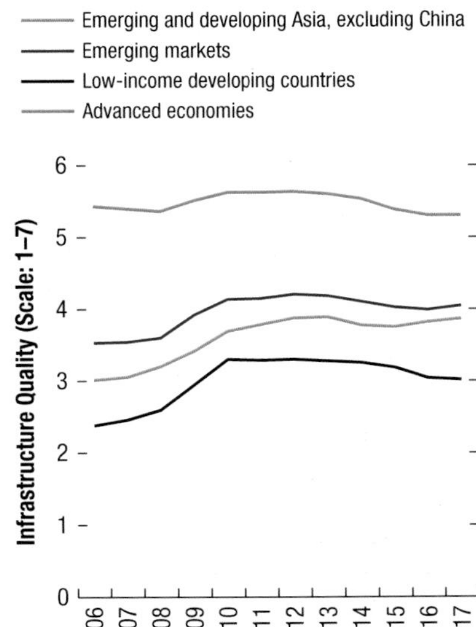


Source: World Economic Forum 2017.

**Figure 8.5. Measures of Infrastructure Access**

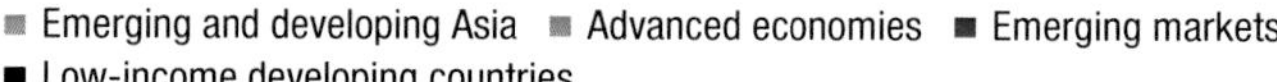


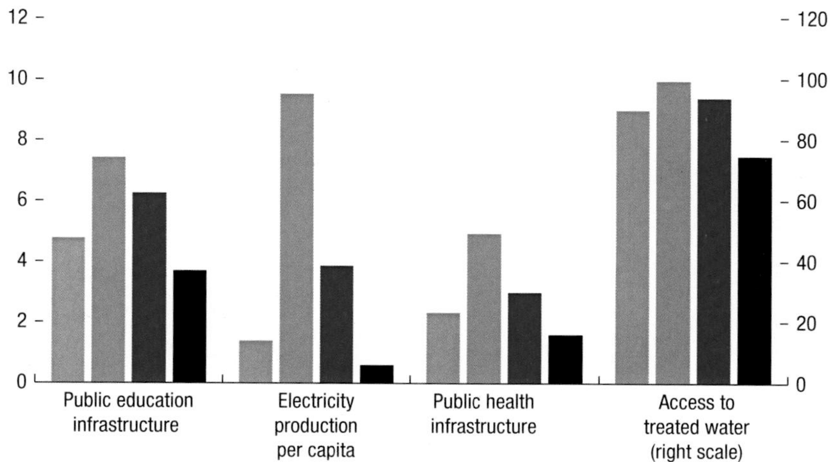


Source: World Development Indicators 2017.
Note: Units vary to fit scale. Left scale: education infrastructure is measured as secondary teachers per 1,000 persons; electricity production as kilowatt-hours per 1,000 persons; and health infrastructure as hospital beds per 1,000 persons. Right scale: access to water is measured as percentage of population.

Physical measures of infrastructure also suggest emerging and developing Asia still lags behind emerging markets in the coverage of education infrastructure and electricity, and somewhat less so in access to public health infrastructure and water (Figure 8.5).

Therefore, emerging and developing Asia would need to improve the infrastructure outcomes of public investment spending. On average, countries lose over one-third of their resources in the public investment process owing to inefficiencies (see Chapter 3).[3] This efficiency gap relative to best performers is smaller than observed in low-income developing countries but larger than the performance of emerging markets and advanced economies (Figure 8.6). This suggests there is scope to improve the efficiency of public investment spending.

In addition, emerging and developing Asia would need large investment spending to reach the SDGs. Chapter 4 in this book estimates that on average, Asian countries would need additional annual infrastructure investment of about 5 percent of GDP in water, roads, and electricity by 2030 to meet the SDGs. Currently, annual

[3] The IMF has developed a methodology for estimating the efficiency of public investment. This is explained in Chapter 3. Simply stated, the estimate of a country's performance is based on an index of infrastructure outcomes compared with its per capita public capital, or cumulative spending on public investment. A "frontier," which consists of the countries achieving the highest output per unit of input, is drawn. The efficiency gap measures the relative difference between a country's performance and the best performers.

**Figure 8.6. Public Investment Efficiency Scores**

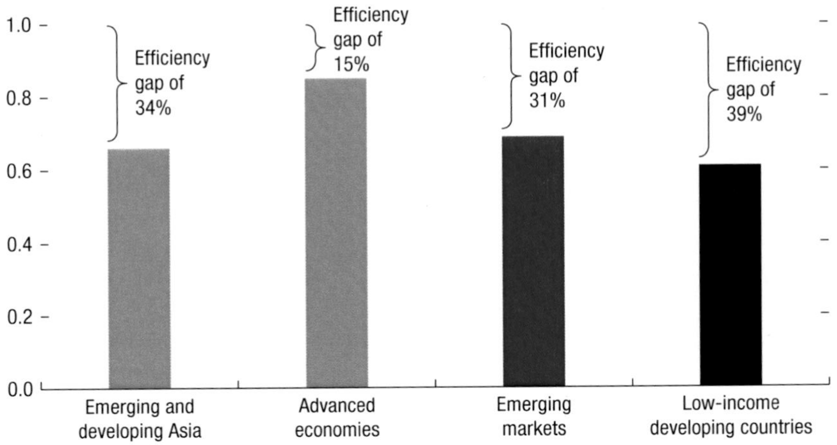

1.0
0.8
0.6
0.4
0.2
0.0

Efficiency gap of 34%
Efficiency gap of 15%
Efficiency gap of 31%
Efficiency gap of 39%

Emerging and developing Asia
Advanced economies
Emerging markets
Low-income developing countries

Source: Authors' calculations based on Chapter 3 of this book.
Note: The efficiency gap measures the relative difference between a country's performance and best performers.

government investment of about 7 percent of GDP in emerging and developing Asia covers all sectors, not just the three sectors. The needs for emerging and developing Asia are the second-largest of the five regions in the world, only below those for sub-Saharan Africa. The road sector in emerging and developing Asia would need the highest additional investment of over 3 percent of GDP (Figure 8.7).

**Figure 8.7. Infrastructure Investment Needed to Achieve Sustainable Development Goals**
*(Percent of average GDP)*

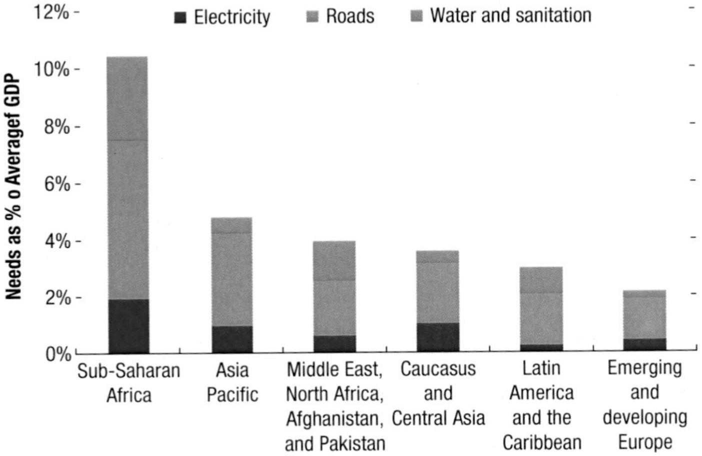

12%
10%
8%
6%
4%
2%
0%

Needs as % o Averagef GDP

■ Electricity ■ Roads ■ Water and sanitation

Sub-Saharan Africa
Asia Pacific
Middle East, North Africa, Afghanistan, and Pakistan
Caucasus and Central Asia
Latin America and the Caribbean
Emerging and developing Europe

Source: Authors' calculations based on Chapter 4 of this book.

More and better investment spending in emerging and developing Asia could also lead to higher GDP growth. Chapter 2 suggests that increased investment spending in countries with better infrastructure governance leads to higher output.

## HOW INFRASTRUCTURE SPENDING IN ASIA CAN BE BOOSTED

Policymakers needing to build infrastructure can benefit from knowing whether increased public infrastructure spending should be financed through higher taxes or borrowing. This question is addressed through the lens of the growth-debt trade-off in emerging and developing Asian countries, using macro-model simulations for selected countries, and by analyzing the macroeconomic benefit of making public investment management more efficient. The final part of the discussion looks at how to improve public investment management institutions in emerging and developing Asia, building on the PIMAs that IMF has conducted in the region.

### Should Infrastructure Spending Increases Be Financed by Tax Measures or Borrowing?

The macroeconomic effects of public infrastructure improvement in Asia are evaluated using the IMF's Flexible System of Global Models (FSGM). The FSGM is an annual, multiregion, general equilibrium model of the global economy combining both micro-founded and reduced formulations of various economic sectors. In the model, total consumption consists of spending both from households that can save and from those who can only consume out of current income. Firms produce goods and services using labor and their holdings of private capital. The government purchases final goods directly, including consumption and investment goods, and makes transfers to households through various tax instruments. Monetary authorities set interest rates to achieve an inflation target in the medium term.

The FSGM is particularly well suited to analyze the macroeconomic effect of a ramp-up in public infrastructure spending. Indeed, government investment, in addition to affecting aggregate demand directly, also cumulates into the stock of public infrastructure, raising the economy wide level of productivity. The accumulation of public investment into public capital varies to some extent from country to country, depending on the efficiency of public investment management. Moreover, the model is set up so that the economy responds significantly to fiscal policy in both the short and the long terms. The FSGM's theoretical structure and simulation properties are laid out in Andrle and others (2015).[4] The simulations

[4] This analysis uses the Asia and Pacific Department Model, a module of the Flexible System of Global Models (FSGM), which contains individual blocks for 15 Asian countries and 9 additional regions that represent the rest of the world (Annex 8.1).

are undertaken for six countries: India, four ASEAN economies (Indonesia, the Philippines, Thailand, Vietnam), and one small frontier economy (Sri Lanka).

The simulations assume a permanent increase in public investment of 1 percent of GDP phased in over five years, with varying financing scenarios. Though large infrastructure needs are apparent in the region, a 1 percent increase in public investment is used for simplicity and comparison across countries. Hence, the simulations show a conservative estimate of potential output gains. Moreover, given that the simulations assume a permanent shock, a more ambitious government investment program would significantly weaken public finances, would require sizable tax hikes that may not be politically feasible and/or would require combining alternative sources of funding such as through PPPs. Macroeconomic implications depend on how the investment increase is financed, particularly whether it is financed by tax or debt.[5] The simulations consider four scenarios:

- *Scenario A: Tax financing through higher VAT.* The fiscal cost of the public investment increase is fully offset by a hike in indirect taxes, which would be equivalent to a VAT. This would imply a hike in the tax rate of about 1.3–1.7 percentage points.
- *Scenario B: Tax financing through higher income tax.* The fiscal cost is fully offset by a hike in direct taxes, split evenly between personal income tax (PIT) and corporate income tax (CIT). This would imply an increase in the PIT rate of about 0.8 percentage point and a rise in the CIT rate ranging from 2.0 to 3.9 percentage points, depending on countries.
- *Scenario C: Debt financing with a standard reaction of the interest rate to higher debt.* The public investment increase is fully financed by borrowing rather than by higher taxes.[6] Because this would have an adverse effect on the interest rate and borrowing costs, the simulations assume an increase in the risk premium by 3 basis points per unit increase in the ratio of public debt to GDP (the debt-to-GDP ratio).[7]

[5] The scope to finance infrastructure spending by rationalizing current expenditure is low in emerging and developing Asia, given generally low government expenditures and countries' need to increase social spending.

[6] In the FSGM, this scenario is implemented by adjustment of the fiscal deficit target to the additional discretionary spending assumed in the policy experiment. In Scenarios C and D, the fiscal balance is affected by the cycle, reflecting the effects of automatic stabilizers, while general lump-sum transfers adjust to cover the increased debt-service costs associated with a permanently higher deficit. In principle, any expenditure or fiscal instrument in FSGM can be used for automatic adjustment toward the deficit target; general lump-sum transfers are used because they have the least distortionary effects.

[7] The risk premium is exogenous in the FSGM and calibrated based on the increase in the debt-to-GDP ratio to better reflect the crowding-out effect of government debt. The assumption of 3 basis points is based on Kumar and Baldacci (2010), who find that appropriate risk-premium elasticities would be in the range of 3–5 basis points for a panel of advanced and emerging market economies. The conservative value of 3 basis points here is motivated by most of the selected economies having low debt-to-GDP levels (with the notable exceptions of Sri Lanka and India).

**TABLE 8.1.**

**Growth-Debt Trade-Off with a Sharp Increase in Public Investment**

| | Scenario A: Tax Financing through Higher Vat | Scenario B: Tax Financing through Higher Income Tax | Scenarios C and D: Debt Financing with a Reaction of the Interest Rate to Higher Debt |
|---|---|---|---|
| Benefits | • A sharp increase in public investment raises growth because of fiscal multiplier effects and higher public capital stock.<br>• By construction, fiscal balance is unchanged, as the spending increase is offset by higher VAT collection. | • The increase raises growth because of fiscal multiplier effects and higher public capital stock.<br>• By construction, fiscal balance is unchanged, as the spending increase is offset by higher income tax collections. | • The increase raises growth because of fiscal multiplier effects and higher public capital stock. |
| Costs | • Dampens private consumption, partially offsetting the growth impact of higher public investment. | • Dampens investment and labor supply and demand, partly offsetting the growth impact of higher public investment. | • Fiscal deficit and public debt increase over time.<br>• Higher borrowing costs crowd out private investment and depress capital stock, dampening the growth impact of higher public investment. |

Source: Authors.

- *Scenario D: Debt financing with a benign reaction of the interest rate to higher debt.* A higher deficit would still lead to an increase in borrowing costs but at a lower elasticity of the risk premium at 1 basis point (rather than 3 basis points in Scenario C).

The macroeconomic benefits and costs of a sharp increase in public investment can be considered through the lens of growth-debt trade-off. Table 8.1 shows the benefits and costs by scenarios.

- Under tax-financed scenarios (budget neutral), the fiscal balance is unchanged, as the public investment increase is financed with higher consumption taxes. By contrast, under debt-financing scenarios, the fiscal balance worsens and public debt rises in parallel with the increase in public investment. This raises the government's borrowing cost, as higher public debt raises the risk premium.
- The increase in public investment lifts growth in the short and long terms. In the short term, higher aggregate demand raises output through multiplier effects. In the long term, higher public investment raises the public capital stock, boosting productivity. The resulting rise in the marginal productivity of capital and labor stimulates private investment and labor demand, also stimulating private consumption.
- The output gains are dampened as agents react to higher taxes or borrowing costs. In the tax-financed scenarios (A and B), higher taxes weaken private demand in the short term, partially offsetting the growth stimulus from

higher public investment spending. Whereas a VAT hike negatively affects private consumption, higher CIT and PIT rates, which weigh on firms' investment and labor demand and discourage labor supply, are generally more distortive than a VAT hike. IMF (2013) finds that corporate income taxes have the most negative effect on growth, followed by labor income taxes, then indirect taxes, and finally property taxes.

- In the debt-financing scenarios (C and D), the rise in the government's borrowing costs crowds out private investment and depresses the private capital stock over time, dampening growth in the short and long terms. This effect is weaker in Scenario D, where the assumed elasticity of the risk premium to public debt is lower.

Simulation results shown in Figure 8.8 quantify the growth-debt trade-off for each of the six economies. The figures plot simulated outcomes for real GDP and the debt-to-GDP ratio, showing the difference from the status quo (that is, without an infrastructure spending increase) in 3 years and 10 years after the beginning of the sharp increase in public investment. The 3- and 10-year outcomes represent short-to-medium-term effects and long-term effects. The key findings are as follows:

- The sharp public investment increase raises real GDP in all countries and in all scenarios. In the short-to-medium term, a boost in aggregate demand from multiplier effects is not fully offset by a weakening in private consumption or investment. The net impact on output in the short-to-medium term is larger for Vietnam (0.2–0.4 percent depending on scenarios) than for the rest of the economies (0.1–0.3 percent).[8] In the long term, the positive growth feedback from the higher public capital stock kicks in, while domestic demand recovers. The net long-term effect on output is large for Vietnam (2.0–3.0 percent), relatively small for Indonesia (0.5–1.2 percent), and between 1.0 percent and 2.0 percent for the rest. Overall, countries with higher initial government investment efficiency record the largest cumulative increase in real GDP in the long term.[9]
- Among tax-financed scenarios, the output boost in the short-to-medium term and the long-term is larger when the public investment increase is financed by a VAT hike (Scenario A) than by an income tax hike (Scenario B), in line with the expectation that a VAT hike would be the less distortive. Similarly, among debt-financing scenarios, the output boost is stronger under Scenario D than under Scenario C, because the former assumes a

[8] The implied short-term fiscal multiplier is 0.5 for India, 0.3 for Indonesia, 0.3 for the Philippines, 0.3 for Sri Lanka, 0.4 for Thailand, and 0.3 for Vietnam. They are in line with the estimates presented in the IMF Technical Note on fiscal multipliers (Batini and others 2014).

[9] The calibration of the parameter of public investment efficiency is based on the combination of long-term output elasticity of government investment (see Ligthart and Suárez 2005) and estimates of the survey-based quality indicators published in the IMF policy paper "Making Public Investment More Efficient" (2015).

## Figure 8.8. Growth-Debt Trade-Off with a Sharp Increase in Public Investment

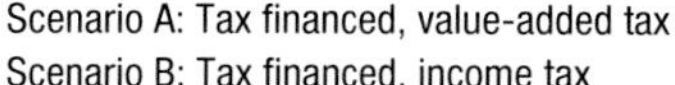


**1. India: Short-to-Medium-Term Effect**

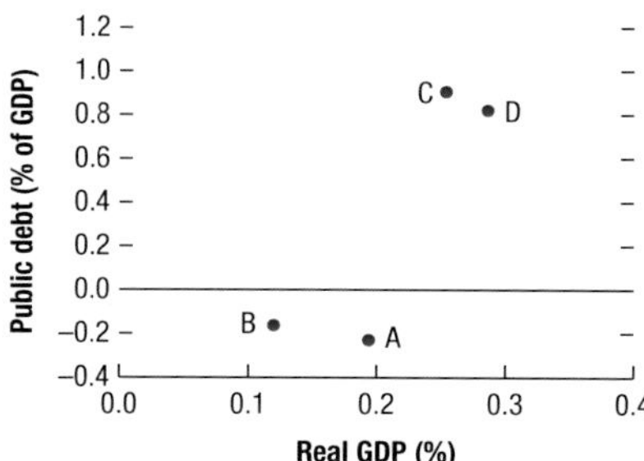


**2. India: Long-Term Effect**

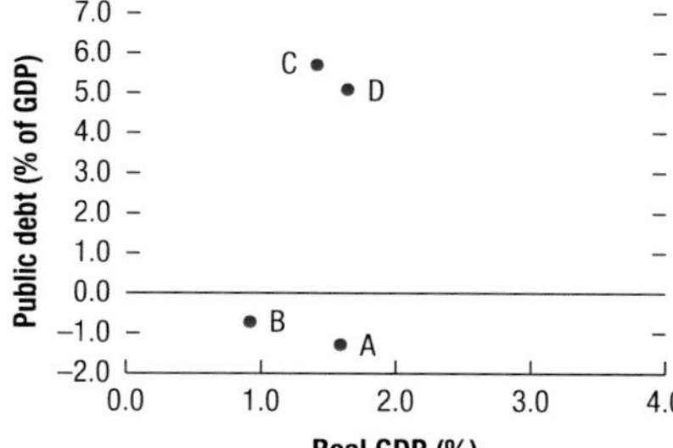


**3. Indonesia: Short-to-Medium-Term Effect**

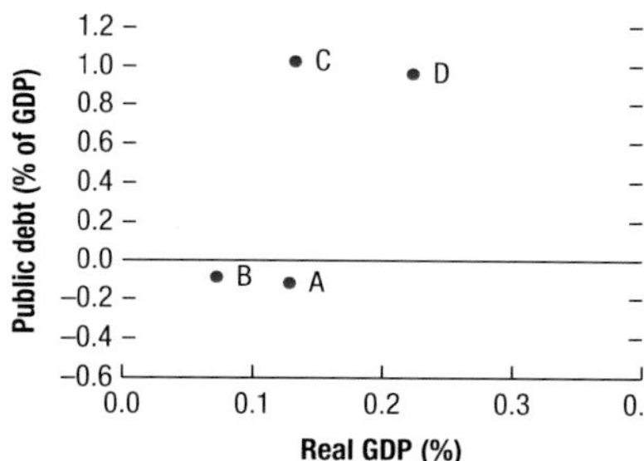


**4. Indonesia: Long-Term Effect**

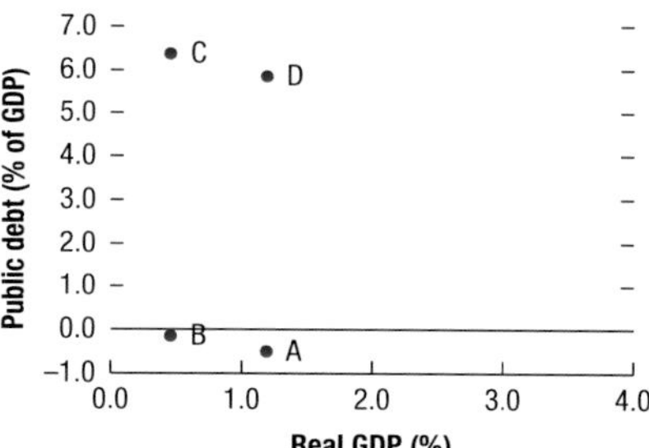


**5. Philippines: Short-to-Medium-Term Effect**

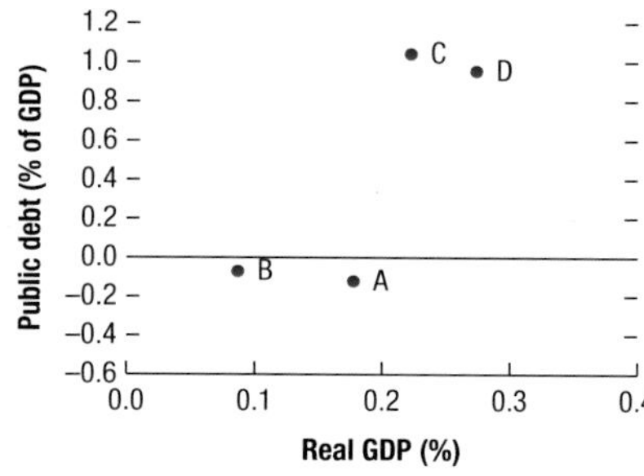


**6. Philippines: Long-Term Effect**

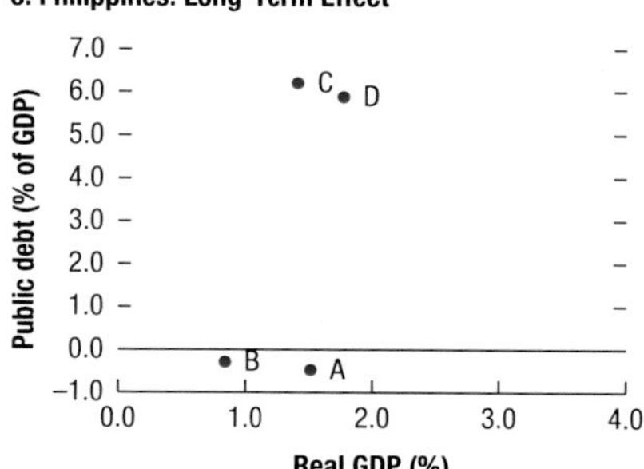


Source: IMF staff calculations from Flexible System of Global Models simulations.
Note: The panels in the figure plot simulated outcomes for Scenarios A, B, C, and D, showing the difference, as a percentage of GDP, from the status quo (that is, without a sharp increase in infrastructure spending) in real GDP levels and public debt (for example, a positive value for Scenario A means that the outcome is larger under the scenario than under the status quo). The short-to-medium-term effect represents the difference 3 years after the start of the spending boost, and the long-term effect is set at 10 years.

**Figure 8.8. Growth-Debt Trade-Off with a Sharp Increase in Public Investment *(continued)***

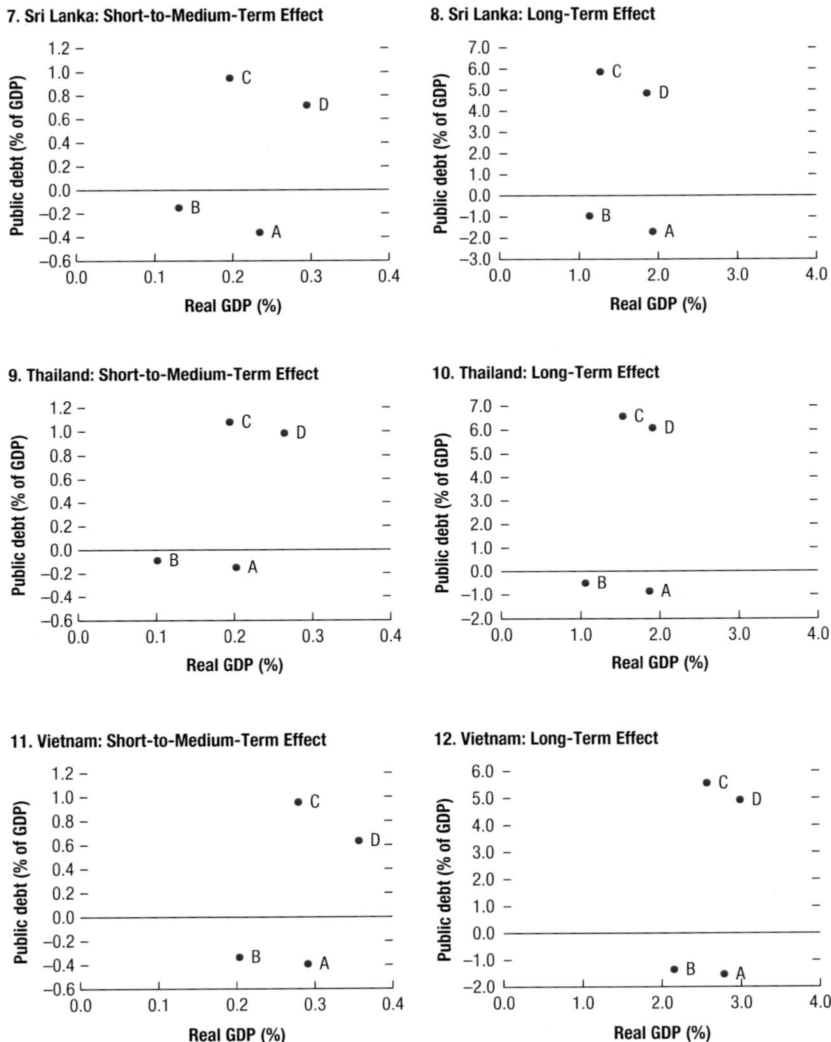


Source: IMF staff calculations from Flexible System of Global Models simulations.
Note: The panels in the figure plot simulated outcomes for Scenarios A, B, C, and D, showing the difference, as a percent of GDP, from the status quo (that is, without an infrastructure spending boost) in real GDP levels and public debt (for example, a positive value for Scenario A means that the outcome is larger under the scenario than under the status quo). The short-to-medium-term effect represents the difference 3 years after the start of the spending boost, and the long-term effect is set at 10 years.

more benign reaction of the interest rate to debt increase, limiting the weakening in private investment.

- As expected, the ratio of public debt to GDP rises in debt-financing scenarios (C and D) by 5–7 percentage points in the long term. On the other hand, tax-financing scenarios (A and B) see a slight decrease in the debt-to-GDP ratio, reflecting higher GDP levels owing to the sharp increase in public investment, while the fiscal balance remains unchanged.

## Which Financing Option Would Better Address the Growth-Debt Trade-Off: Tax Financed or Debt Financed?

- In the short-to-medium term, a debt-financed public investment boost would achieve higher multiplier effects than a tax-financed boost, as long as the resulting increase in borrowing costs can be contained.[10] Because the larger multiplier effects are associated with higher public debt, the scenario with debt-financed public investment (Scenario D) may still not be preferred to the VAT-financed scenario (Scenario A).
- In the long term, however, the relative attractiveness of debt financing (Scenario D) diminishes, as the output boost under Scenario D is broadly the same as under VAT-financing (Scenario A) in all countries. This is because even a benign increase in risk premium associated with a rising debt-to-GDP ratio in Scenario D damps down private investment over time, reducing output gains in the long term. Scenario A achieves a relatively high output boost with no increase in public debt, while the public debt increases in Scenario D. This suggests that VAT-financing is superior to debt financing in solving the growth-debt trade-off in the long term.

Policymakers would also need to be mindful of the negative impact of VAT rate increases on income inequality. Indirect taxes such as VAT may be regressive; that is, they levy a higher burden (relative to income or expenditure) on the poor than on the rich. While income inequality is not captured by the model here, the regressive impact can be reduced in that the accompanying infrastructure spending boost is pro-poor (for example, developing local roads that improve accessibility of rural areas). The regressive impact can be ameliorated by strengthening public spending that benefits the poor relatively more, such as for education, health care, and targeted social safety nets.

The growth-debt trade-off can be lessened by the growth payoff of improving public investment efficiency. The output boost from a public investment increase would be large in a country with high public investment efficiency, because it would be able to build more infrastructure with a given amount of

[10] For all countries, the short-and-medium-term output boost is slightly larger in Scenario D than in Scenario A, whereas it is broadly comparable between Scenarios C and A.

**Figure 8.9. The Effect of Higher Public Investment on Real GDP, Year 10**
*(In percent deviation from control)*

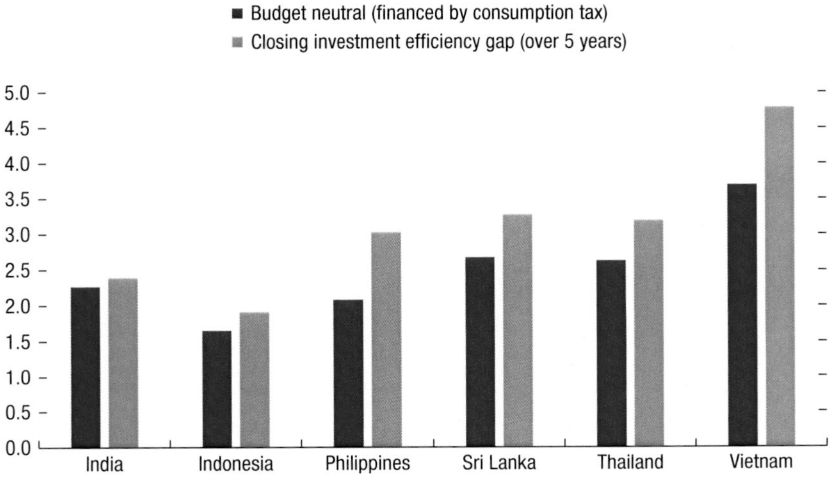

Source: IMF staff calculations.

public investment. In addition, the resulting rise in productivity raises labor demand and wages, further lifting private consumption in the long term. To illustrate these, FSGM simulations are conducted to gauge output gains from closing the public investment efficiency gap under the VAT-financing scenario (A) in each of the six countries. Results reported in Figure 8.9 show that closing the efficiency gap over five years would boost the year-10 output by 0.6–1.1 percentage points, with an exception of India and Indonesia where the improvement is only 0.1–0.3 percentage point.

## How Can Public Investment Efficiency Be Improved in Asia?

Strengthening infrastructure governance can help countries improve public investment efficiency. Analysis in Chapter 3 suggests that the average country loses about 30 percent of the returns on its investment to inefficiencies in its public investment management processes, with substantial scope for improving public investment efficiency across income groups. Improvements in public investment management can help countries reduce more than half of their inefficiency gap.

Emerging and developing Asian countries could improve infrastructure governance by focusing reform efforts on their weakest and most critical practices of public investment management. The initial results of the PIMAs for 11 countries

**Figure 8.10. Institutional Strength and Effectiveness of Public Investment Management in Emerging and Developing Asia**

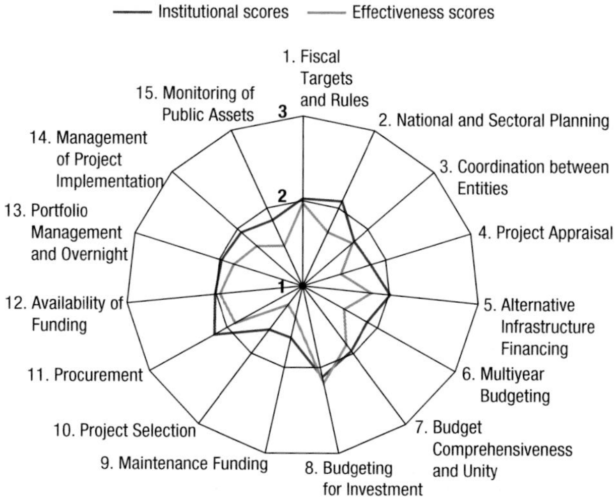

Source: IMF Public Investment Management Assessment missions, 2015–19.

in Asia[11] show that most public investment management practices in the region have good *institutional strength* (Figure 8.10). However, effectiveness in their *implementation* is generally lower.

The average of PIMA scores in Asian countries are mostly in the middle range. Institutional strengths lie mostly in the planning and implementation phases, where three out of five practices each meet at least medium scores. These scores reflect the somewhat good practices in fiscal framework and rules that provide overall targets for fiscal policy, the planning of national and sectoral public investments, the use of alternative financing means for infrastructure such as PPPs, the procurement law and regulations, the availability of funding within a budget year, and the general oversight of the infrastructure investment portfolio. However, Asian countries, on average, have weaker institutional strength in several other public investment management practices. These include the coordination between the central government and local governments as well as oversight of infrastructure investments by state-owned

[11] The IMF has conducted PIMA missions in 11 countries in Asia and the Pacific: Bangladesh, Indonesia, Kiribati, Malaysia, Maldives, Mongolia, the Philippines, Sri Lanka, Thailand, Timor-Leste, and Vietnam. Also see the PIMA background and methodology in Chapter 8.

enterprises, project appraisal and selection, maintenance funding, and monitoring of public assets.

Within Asia, while emerging markets and low-income developing countries share certain similarity in public investment management institutions, several distinct strengths and weaknesses are apparent. Financing for capital spending is usually made in a timelier manner in emerging markets. This helps sectoral ministries plan and commit expenditure on capital projects in advance based on more reliable cash flow forecasts. In contrast, because of lack of funding and weak capacity of cash management low-income developing countries often have cash rationing, leading to delays of project implementation. However, low-income developing countries are stronger than emerging markets in Asia in several practices such as procurement of major projects and budgeting for investment. Many major projects in low-income developing countries are funded by international organizations, which generally have competitive and transparent procurement. Budgeting for investment in low-income developing countries often protects capital investment by allowing multiyear contracts and being more restrictive in shifting funding from capital to current expenditure during budget execution.

Public investment management practices in Asia are generally better in the planning and implementation phases but worse in the allocation phase than in other regions. Clear areas of comparative strength for Asia are in fiscal rules, coordination between entities, alternative infrastructure financing in the planning phase, and in procurement, the availability of funding, and portfolio and project management during implementation. In the allocation phase, shortcomings in Asia include the practices of budget comprehensiveness and unity, and maintenance funding. Asian economies share common weaknesses with the rest of the world in project appraisal and selection, multiyear budgeting, and monitoring assets.

The least effective public investment management institutions in Asia are involved in appraising and selecting projects, maintenance funding, multiyear budgeting, and monitoring of public assets. Not only is design strength already low but effectiveness in implementation is even lower.

- *Project appraisal*: Most countries in the sample have weak mechanisms for project appraisal. Major projects are often not subject to rigorous technical, economic, and financial analysis (7 out of 11 countries in the sample). Time to evaluate major projects is often insufficient and often no standard appraisal methodology is applied (5 out of 11). Low-quality appraisal makes it difficult to choose between competing projects and often leads to delays in implementation.
- *Project selection*: Most of the countries (7 out of 11) do not have an effective review of major projects by a central ministry before projects are included in the budget. Project selection is often not transparent, and it lacks clear and published criteria (7 out of 11). Nearly all countries (9 out of 11) lack

a pipeline of already-vetted projects that is used for selecting projects for inclusion in the budget.

- *Maintenance funding*: More than half of the countries lack a standard methodology for estimating needs and funding for routine maintenance and major improvements of infrastructure assets. Most (5 out of 7) do not have information on funding for routine and capital maintenance by a ministry or agency responsible for it but aggregate such spending.
- *Multiyear budgeting*: Nearly all of the countries (9 out of 11) do not publish projections about overall or disaggregated capital spending by a ministry or sector over a three- to five-year horizon. Almost all (10 out of 11) do not have multiyear ceilings on capital expenditure by ministry, sector, or program. Nearly half of the countries (5 out of 11) do not publish projections about the total construction cost of major capital projects.
- *Monitoring of public assets*: Asset registers in more than half of the countries (6 out of 11) are neither comprehensive nor updated regularly. Most of the countries (7 out of 11) do not include the value of nonfinancial assets in government financial accounts and do not record the depreciation of fixed assets in operating statements.

While emerging and developing Asian countries address common infrastructure governance weaknesses, they could also learn from successful practices in the region. These include fiscal rules that support fiscal sustainability in Indonesia, national and sectoral strategies guiding investment allocation in Vietnam, the strong PPP framework in Timor-Leste, an effective mechanism to protect ongoing investment projects in the Philippines, e-procurement in Bangladesh, practical portfolio monitoring in Malaysia, and comprehensive asset monitoring in Mongolia (see Box 8.1). While lessons can be learned among peers in the region and the world, each country would have to implement specific reforms, with their sequencing and solutions dependent on the country's situation.

### Box 8.1. Examples of Good Public Investment Management Practices in Emerging and Developing Asia

- *Fiscal targets and rules*: In Indonesia, fiscal policy is guided by statutory limits on general government deficit and debt. These rules have served Indonesia well in achieving fiscal responsibility and ensuring debt sustainability. A medium-term fiscal framework with major fiscal aggregates provides adequate top-down input into the budget formulation.
- *National and sectoral planning*: In Vietnam, the government prepares a large number of national and sectoral strategies for public investment, most being published and clearly linked. The recently adopted Law on Planning is meant to streamline the sectoral and national planning process. The overall medium-term investment plan framework, which has been developed by the Ministry of Planning and Investment in accordance with the Public Investment Law and in cooperation with the Ministry of Finance, aims to determine the overall funding framework.

**Box 8.1 (*continued*)**

- *Alternative infrastructure financing:* In Timor-Leste, the public-private partnership decree-law provides a comprehensive overview of the government's approach to identification, development, selection, and implementation of these partnerships. This includes criteria for assessing and selecting projects, and requirements for value-for-money reviews of project proposals. The methodology ensures that relevant risks and liabilities—explicit and contingent—are identified and systematically recorded. The partnerships process is managed by a dedicated unit in the Ministry of Finance. Public-private partnerships have been used to mobilize private sector knowledge and experience in the implementation of complex projects, rather than as a financing mechanism.

- *Budgeting for investment:* In the Philippines, a two-tier budgeting approach protects funding for ongoing projects in the annual budget and over the medium term. Annual budget estimates for ongoing projects (Tier 1) are first prepared by line agencies, discussed with the Department of Budget and Management during Tier 1 hearings, and then approved by the Development Budget Coordination Committee and included in a published budget priorities framework. The allocation of new spending is discussed during later hearings about new projects (Tier 2 hearings). In addition, outlays are appropriated on an annual basis with multiyear obligation authority for new projects. Multiyear commitments are included in the budget documentation.

- *Procurement:* In Bangladesh, the web-based electronic government procurement system, e-GP, covers procurement of works, goods, and services. The methods used in e-GP have been largely competitive. The public has access, through the e-GP website, to tender documents, bid statistics, and summary contract data relating to each tender and to key performance information covering all tenders announced. The e-GP has the capability to produce analytical reports and publishes on its website a quarterly performance indicators report, covering 42 indicators. A data dashboard and a civil engagement feature will allow the public to provide feedback on contract implementation.

- *Portfolio management and oversight:* In Malaysia, a project monitoring system called SPP II assists the government in gaining effective oversight of all projects. The system generates reports that ministries and agencies can use for weekly monitoring, as well as producing monthly reports to help senior management. Yearly monitoring reports are generated to enable politicians to have a condensed view of the progress and status of all projects. Reports are simple to understand and can be interpreted by technical, financial, and political personnel. There is no wasted information to clutter the system.
- *Monitoring of public assets:* In Mongolia, comprehensive asset surveys are conducted every four years for all nonfinancial assets, including infrastructure. The State Local Property Management System, a manually updated software system, keeps track of assets. Tangible assets, including buildings, construction, roads, and bridges, are reported in the balance sheets. They are valued initially at acquisition cost and subsequently depreciated in accordance with International Public Sector Accounting Standards. Depreciation of fixed assets is captured in the government income statement, using depreciation methods allowed by IPSAS 17.

Source: IMF Public Investment Management Assessment missions, 2015–19.

## CONCLUSIONS

This chapter assesses the need to scale up infrastructure investment in emerging and developing Asia and how to deliver it. Reviews of past developments, cross-country comparisons, and simulation-based analyses lead to four key messages.

First, emerging and developing Asia needs more and better investment spending to improve infrastructure outcomes and reach SDGs. Infrastructure quality in the region has stagnated since the early 2010s at a level below other regions, while public capital stock has decreased relative to GDP since 2000. Emerging and developing Asian countries have sizable infrastructure spending needs, estimated at about 7 percent of the region's GDP in 2030, to meet the SDGs. Infrastructure investment through PPPs picked up in the mid-2000s but has not offset the decline in government infrastructure spending.

Second, in emerging and developing Asia, financing an infrastructure spending boost with higher indirect taxes would be desirable in the long term in view of a growth-debt trade-off. Macroeconomic model simulations for India, Indonesia, the Philippines, Sri Lanka, Thailand, and Vietnam suggest that it matters how an infrastructure spending boost is financed. In the short-to-medium term, assuming a benign borrowing risk premium, the growth pickup would generally be higher with debt financing than with tax financing. With debt financing resulting in higher public debt, policymakers face a growth-debt trade-off. Among tax options to finance the spending boost, indirect taxes such as VAT are less distortive and generate more economic growth than income taxes. In the long term, the size of the growth pickup does not differ between VAT financing and debt financing, although VAT achieves a slight decrease in the debt-to-GDP ratio. While VAT financing would be a preferable option for policymakers for the long term, they would need to be mindful of its negative impact on income inequality, which can be dealt with by strengthening public spending that brings relative strong benefits to the poor, such as education, health care, and targeted social safety nets.

Third, emerging and developing Asia can benefit from improving public investment efficiency, which helps produce more and better-quality infrastructure for every unit of money spent on infrastructure investment. The region's public investment is generally less efficient than in advanced and emerging market economies. Model-based simulations for the countries selected in this chapter suggest that a reduction in the public investment efficiency gap would substantially increase the size of the long-term expansion in output from an infrastructure spending boost, thus helping to resolve the growth-debt trade-off.

Fourth, emerging and developing Asian countries could enhance public investment efficiency by focusing reform efforts on their weakest and most critical practices of public investment management. PIMAs by the IMF for 11 of the region's countries suggest that the design of institutions dealing with public investment management is relatively strong but the countries' implementation of infrastructure projects is less effective. Specifically, emerging and developing Asia would have substantial scope for improving the appraisal and selection of projects, the funding of maintenance spending, multiyear budgeting, and monitoring of public assets. Emerging and developing Asian countries can also learn from the good practices of their peers.

## ANNEX 8.1. ASIA AND PACIFIC DEPARTMENT MODEL SIMULATION RESULTS

The macroeconomic effects of public infrastructure improvement in Asia are evaluated using the Asia and Pacific Department Model, a module of the Flexible System of Global Models (FSGM), which contains individual blocks for 15 Asian countries and nine additional regions that represent the rest of the world. The simulations are undertaken for India, four Southeast Asian economies—Indonesia, the Philippines, Thailand, and Vietnam—and one small frontier economy—Sri Lanka (see Annex Figures 8.1.1 through 8.1.6).

### Assumptions

The simulations assume a permanent increase in public investment of 1 percent of GDP phased in over five years. Monetary policy responds endogenously to the shock by following a standard monetary policy rule, whereby interest rates are adjusted as inflation and the output gap change.

The baseline simulations are carried out assuming that agents learn about the policy step by step—and that the policy is fully credible only after five years (imperfect foresight).[12]

As the macroeconomic implications differ depending on how investment spending is financed, the policy experiments are assessed under two financing scenarios: budget neutrality (tax financed) and debt-financing scenarios.

Under the budget neutrality scenario, any fiscal cost of the policy push is offset by an increase in revenue that keeps the deficit target unchanged. In the tax-financed scenario, two forms of financing are considered: (1) an increase in indirect tax (consumption tax—VAT) of 1 percent of GDP and (2) a hike in direct taxes split evenly between personal income tax (PIT) and corporate income tax (CIT)—0.5 percent of GDP respectively.

Under the debt-financing scenario, the deficit target adjusts to the additional discretionary spending assumed in the policy experiment. Under this scenario, general lump-sum transfers only adjust to cover the increased debt-service costs

[12] Alternative experiments also explore the cases in which policies are assumed to be fully credible—that is, the entire path of implementation is known to economic agents at the beginning of the shock (perfect foresight). In this alternative scenario (perfect foresight), policies have sizable short-term effects, as agents fully internalize the impact of the policies at the time of their announcement and frontload spending accordingly.

associated with a permanently higher deficit.[13] In both financing scenarios, the fiscal balance is affected by the cycle (reflecting the effects of automatic stabilizers).

Moreover, given that the debt-financed public investment increase can raise borrowing costs, the experiments incorporate the assumption of a risk premium associated with rising public debt as a proportion of GDP. As the orders of magnitude of the increase in the risk premium are uncertain, two calibrations are examined. The baseline debt-financing scenario sets the risk premium at 3 basis points per unit increase in the debt-to-GDP ratio. This assumption is based on Kumar and Baldacci (2010) who find debt elasticities in the range of 3–5 basis points for a panel of advanced and emerging market economies. This conservative value is motivated by debt-financing most of the selected emerging Asian economies having low debt-to-GDP levels (with the notable exception of Sri Lanka and India). An alternative calibration assumes that the risk premium increases by 1 basis point per unit increase in the debt-to-GDP ratio.

The implications of improving the efficiency of public investment within each financing scenario are also assessed. According to the IMF's Public Investment Efficiency Indicators, there is scope for improvement in most of the selected Asian emerging economies. We compare a scenario of unchanged efficiency (baseline) with a subscenario of improved efficiency. We evaluate the effects of closing the public investment efficiency gap, as measured by the survey-based quality efficiency indicator, over five years.

## Results: Macroeconomic Effects of Boosting Public Investment

The increase in public investment lifts real GDP in the short and long terms in both the tax-financed and the debt-financed scenarios. The output gains differ, however, depending on how the public investment spending is financed. The most significant output gains in the long term are generated under the consumption-tax-financing scenario. Hence, as a baseline scenario for the tax-financed variant, a consumption tax increase is preferred over direct taxes (both CIT and PIT), as it has the least long-term distortionary effects on capital and labor supply. The 1 percent of GDP permanent increase in consumption tax assumed to finance public investment spending implies a tax-rate hike of about 1.3–1.7 percentage points. For all selected Asian emerging economies, the increase in real GDP is more muted in the long term when direct taxes are raised, as they hamper private investment and capital stock. Moreover, higher CIT and PIT weigh, to a lesser extent, on private consumption in the short term, as they

[13] In principle, any expenditure or fiscal instrument in FSGM can be used for automatic adjustment toward the deficit target. General lump-sum transfers are used because they have the least distortionary effects.

discourage firms' labor demand and posttax wages to households. By contrast, with the notable exception of Vietnam, a hike in indirect taxes (VAT) discourages private consumption in the short term.

It should be noted also that direct-tax financing—split evenly between PIT and CIT—generates smaller output gains than deficit financing with a low risk premium (a 1 basis point per unit increase in the debt-to-GDP ratio) in the medium and long terms.

Under the baseline tax-financed scenario (consumption tax), the public investment push leads to significant output gains in the long term. Higher public investment raises the public capital stock, which boosts general productivity of the economy. The resulting rise in the marginal productivity of capital and labor stimulates private investment and raises labor demand. This lifts private consumption in the long term. In the short term, however, the increase in taxes dampens private consumption, partially offsetting the stimulating impact of higher public investment spending. Inflation is higher in the short and medium term, owing to positive output gaps, but converges to baseline in the long term given a stabilizing monetary policy.

Exports increase in this scenario as a response to higher production and the real exchange rate depreciation. The real net export position improves in the long term, as demand for imports is dampened by higher costs. The current account balance is permanently weaker relative to baseline because of a lower income balance, reflecting a deteriorating net foreign asset position.

All in all, the rise in public investment financed with consumption taxes results in cumulative increases in real GDP of between 3.5 percent and 7.0 percent in the long term. Countries with higher calibrated values for efficiency record the largest cumulative increase in real GDP in the long term: Vietnam displays the largest gains (7.2 percent), followed by Sri Lanka (5.9 percent), Thailand (5.7 percent), India (5.4 percent), and the Philippines (4.6 percent). The public investment scale-up has the smallest impact in Indonesia (3.6 percent).

The long-term effect on real GDP of a deficit-financed increase in public investment is more muted. The adverse effects on output become apparent as the risk premium associated with a higher debt-to-GDP ratio rises. In the short-to-medium term (5 to 10 years), for most of the selected economies, deficit financing with a low risk premium generates as much output gains as the tax-financed scenario. The GDP impact is more muted under the baseline deficit-financed scenario (3 basis points per unit increase in the debt-to-GDP ratio) because the rise in government borrowing costs crowds out private investment and depresses the capital stock. However, private consumption is higher. Labor supply expands by more than in the tax-financed scenario, as households need to work more to offset the lower transfers required to stabilize public debt in the long term. For most of the selected emerging Asian economies, the current account balance deteriorates in the short-to-medium term and improves in the long term in the baseline deficit-financed scenario, as the reduction in net savings in the public sector is more than offset by the increase in net savings in the private sector. A lower increase in the risk premium (1 basis point per unit increase in the debt-to-GDP ratio) has a smaller dampening effect on private investment, and hence on real GDP in the long term. As a result, the current account balance in the scenario with a lower risk premium deteriorates permanently because of the lower income balance, as households substitute foreign assets for domestic assets.

Overall, the long term GDP impact of higher public investment in the baseline deficit-financing scenario is particularly more muted in Indonesia, Sri Lanka, and Thailand (about 1.5 percentage points lower than in the tax-financed scenario). These are economies in which deficit financing crowds out the most private capital in the long term.

Under the tax-financed scenario, the general government balance target is unchanged, while the debt-to-GDP ratios improve slightly in the short-to-medium term, reflecting the impact of higher output, and converge to steady state in the long term. By contrast, in the baseline deficit financing scenario—by assumption—the deficit target–to-GDP ratios rise by the same amount as public investment spending, while the debt-to-GDP ratios increase significantly, by about 15 percentage points in most of the selected economies, in the long term. Thailand registers the largest increase in the GDP-to-debt ratio in the long term (23 percentage points), reflecting a lower inflation rate.

Eliminating the inefficiency in public investment generates additional output gains in both the tax-financed and the deficit-financed scenarios. Closing the public investment efficiency gap would add between 1.0 and 1.8 percentage points to real GDP in the long term. The largest additional GDP gains are observed in Vietnam (2.0 percentage points) and the Philippines (2.0 percentage points), followed by Sri Lanka (1.3 percentage points), Thailand (1.2 percentage points), and Indonesia (0.6 percentage point). India, which is close to the efficiency frontier, records the smallest additional GDP gains in the long term (0.3 percentage point).

## Annex Figure 8.1.1. Macroeconomic Effects of Boosting Public Investment in India

*(One percent of GDP over five years)*

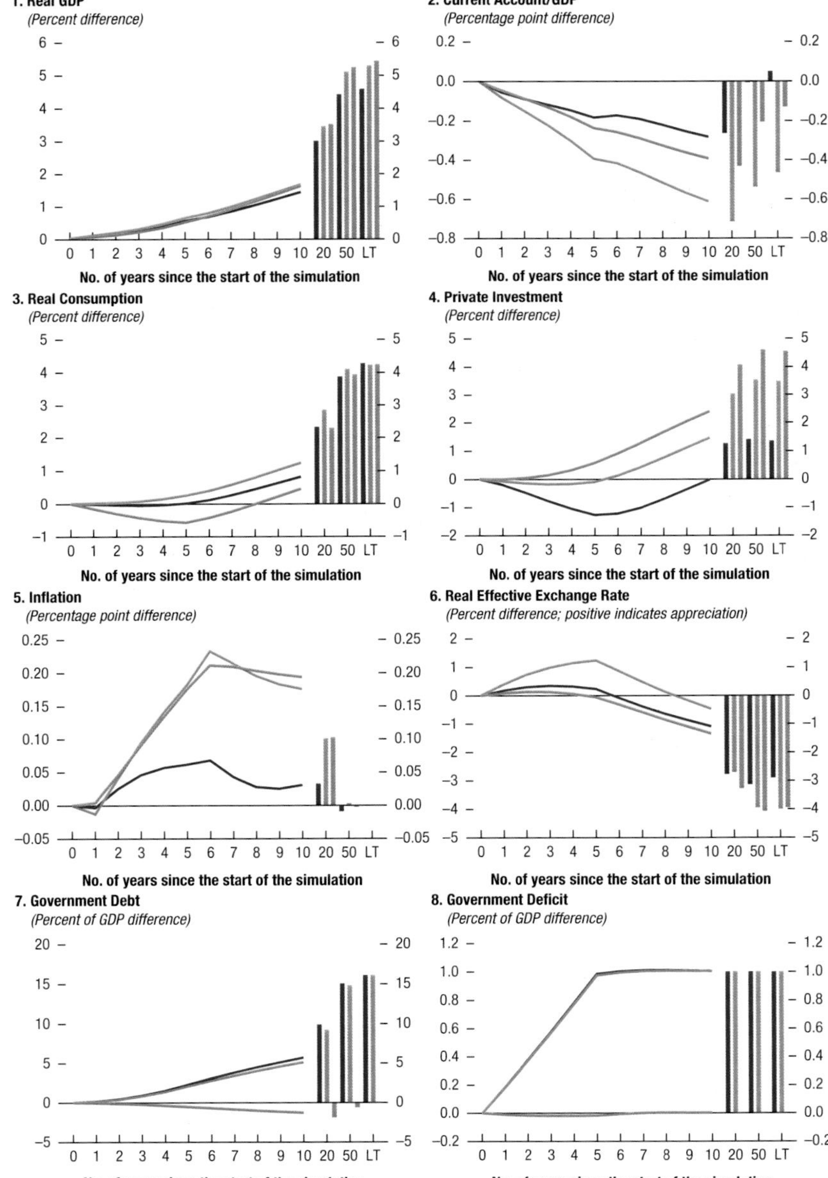


Source: IMF staff calculations from Flexible System of Global Models simulations.
Note: "LT" refers to the steady-state value.

## Annex Figure 8.1.2. Macroeconomic Effects of Boosting Public Investment in Indonesia

*(One percent of GDP over five years)*

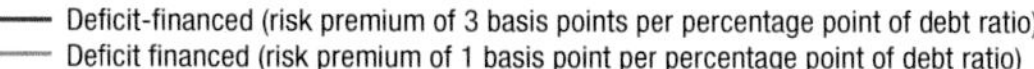

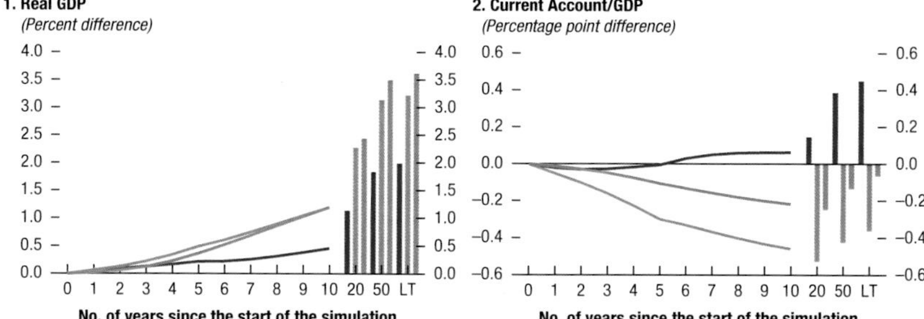


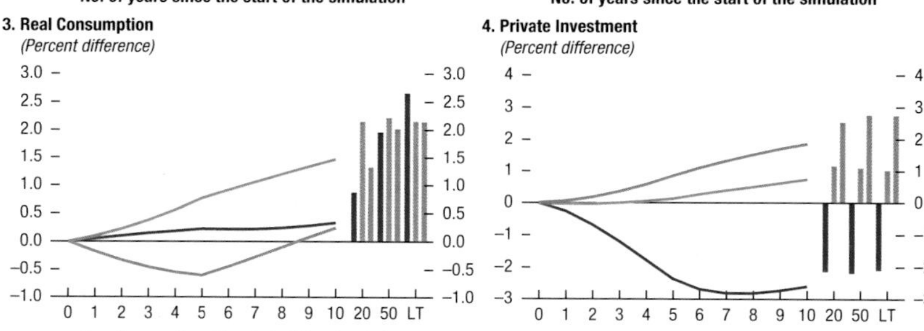

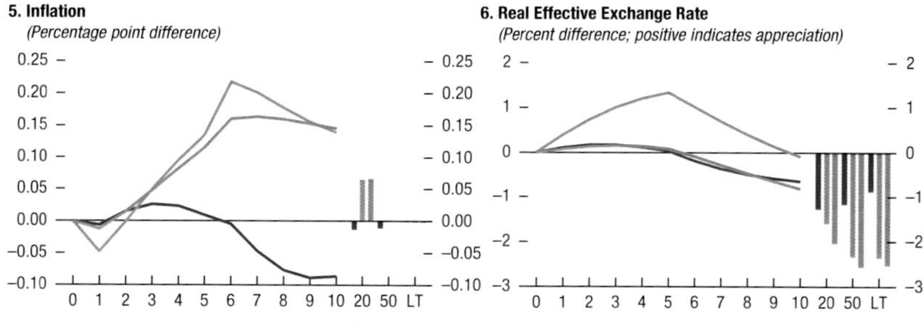


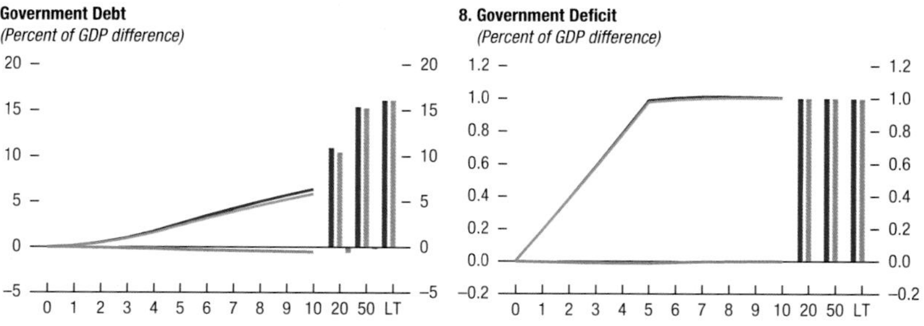


Source: IMF staff calculations from Flexible System of Global Models simulations.
Note: "LT" refers to the steady-state value.

## Annex Figure 8.1.3. Macroeconomic Effects of Boosting Public Investment in Thailand

*(One percent of GDP over five years)*

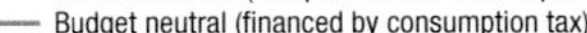

Deficit-financed (risk premium of 3 basis points per percentage point of debt ratio)
Deficit financed (risk premium of 1 basis point per percentage point of debt ratio)
Budget neutral (financed by consumption tax)

**1. Real GDP**
*(Percent difference)*

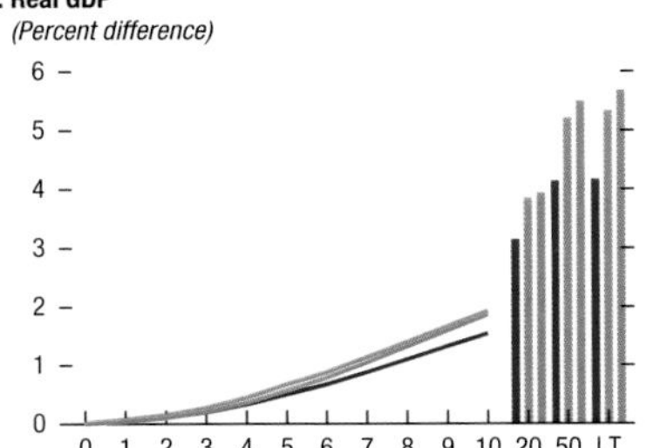


**No. of years since the start of the simulation**

**2. Current Account/GDP**
*(Percentage point difference)*

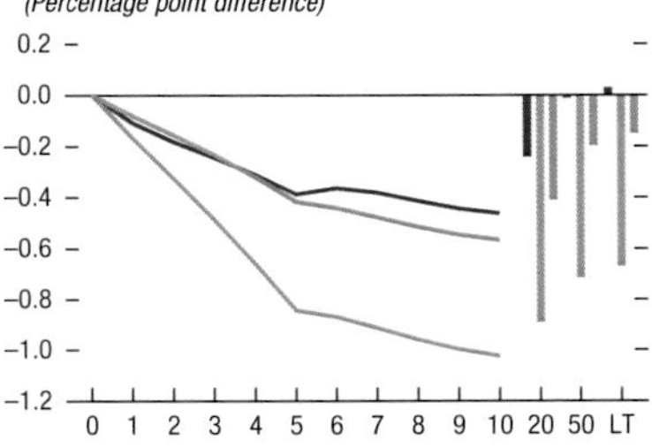


**No. of years since the start of the simulation**

**3. Real Consumption**
*(Percent difference)*

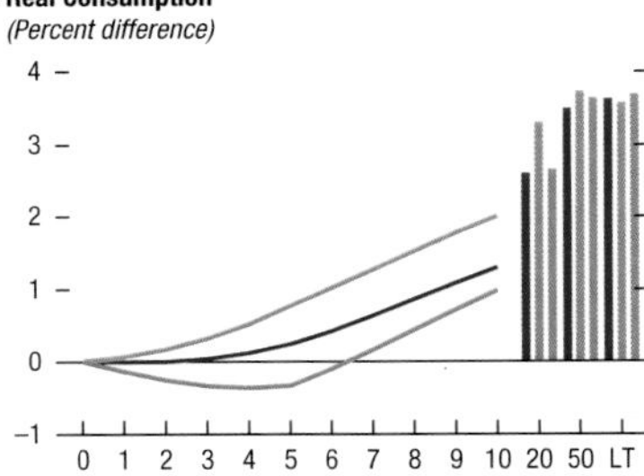


**No. of years since the start of the simulation**

**4. Private Investment**
*(Percent difference)*

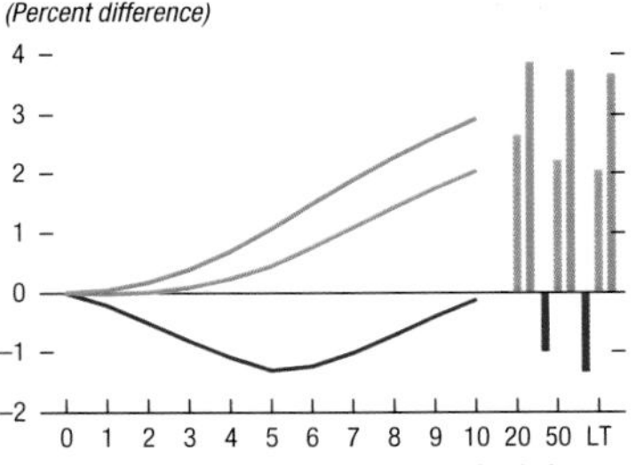


**No. of years since the start of the simulation**

**5. Inflation**
*(Percentage point difference)*

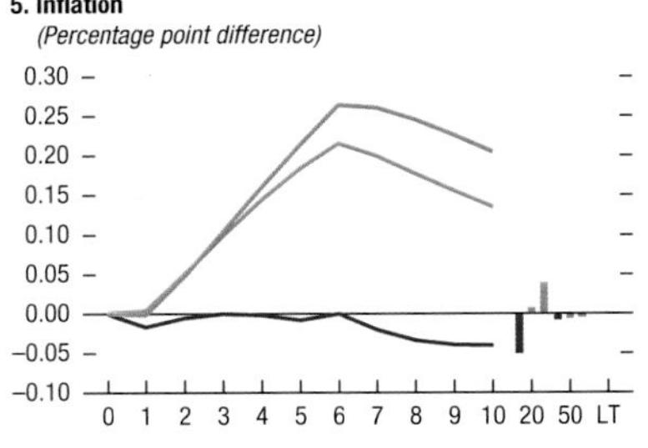


**No. of years since the start of the simulation**

**6. Real Effective Exchange Rate**
*(Percent difference; positive indicates appreciation)*

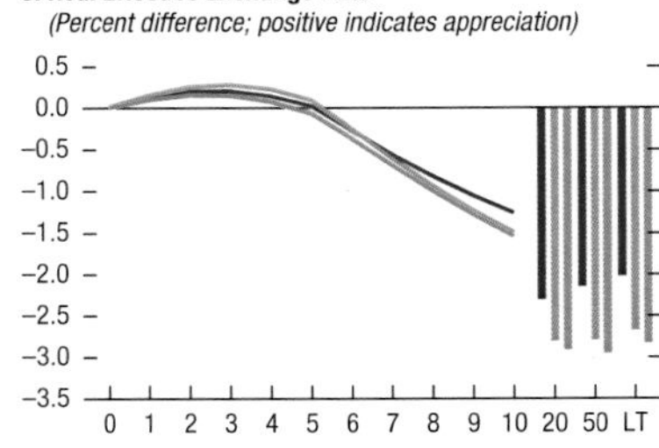


**No. of years since the start of the simulation**

**7. Government Debt**
*(Percent of GDP difference)*

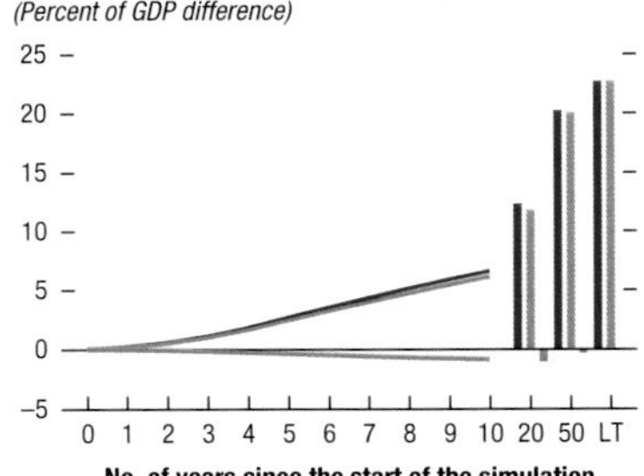


**No. of years since the start of the simulation**

**8. Government Deficit**
*(Percent of GDP difference)*

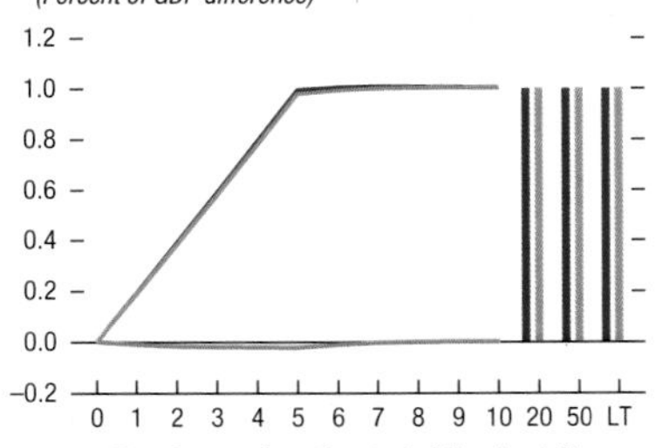


**No. of years since the start of the simulation**

Source: IMF staff calculations from Flexible System of Global Models simulations.
Note: "LT" refers to the steady-state value.

## Annex Figure 8.1.4. Macroeconomic Effects of Boosting Public Investment in Vietnam

*(One percent of GDP over five years)*

Deficit-financed (risk premium of 3 basis points per percentage point of debt ratio)
Deficit financed (risk premium of 1 basis point per percentage point of debt ratio)
Budget neutral (financed by consumption tax)

**1. Real GDP**
*(Percent difference)*

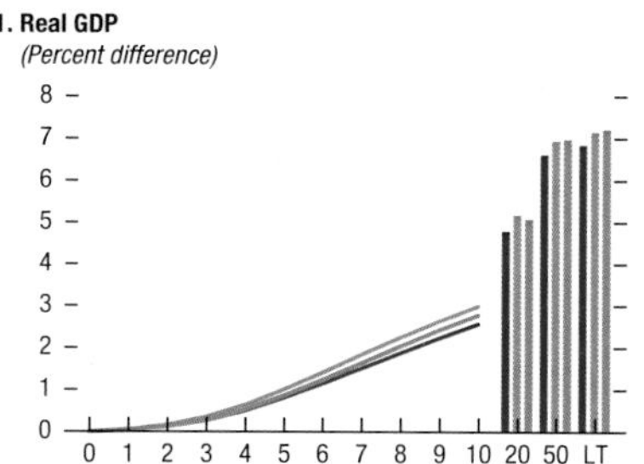


**2. Current Account/GDP**
*(Percentage point difference)*

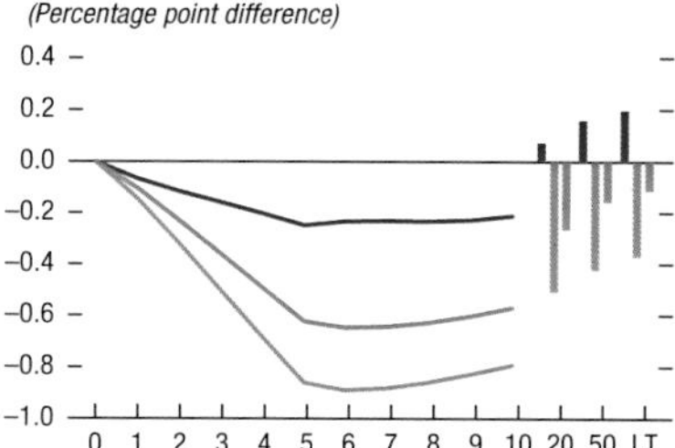


**3. Real Consumption**
*(Percent difference)*

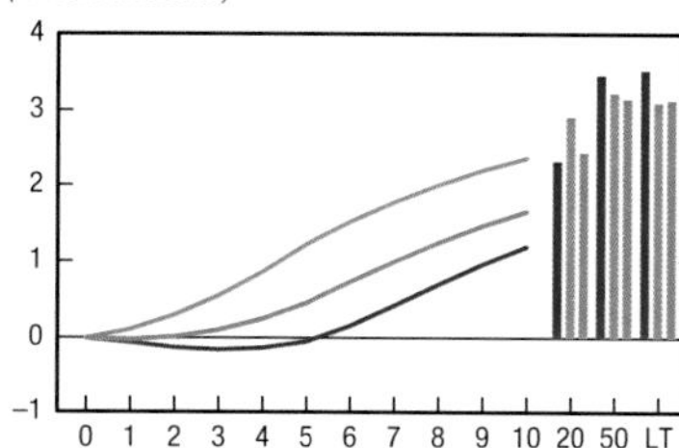


**4. Private Investment**
*(Percent difference)*

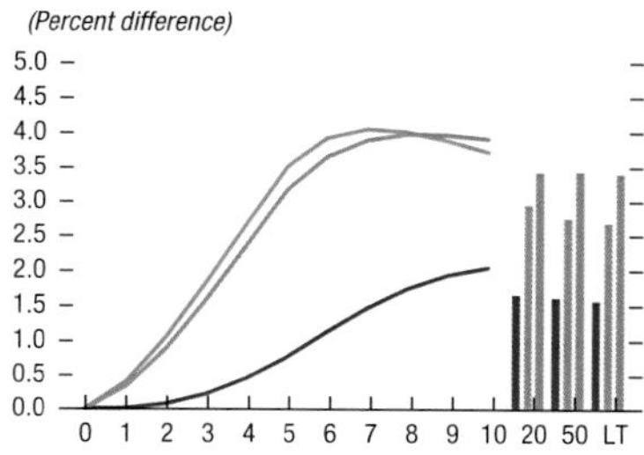


**5. Inflation**
*(Percentage point difference)*

0.30
0.25
0.20
0.15
0.10
0.05
0.00
−0.05
−0.10
0 1 2 3 4 5 6 7 8 9 10 20 50 LT
No. of years since the start of the simulation

**6. Real Effective Exchange Rate**
*(Percent difference; positive indicates appreciation)*

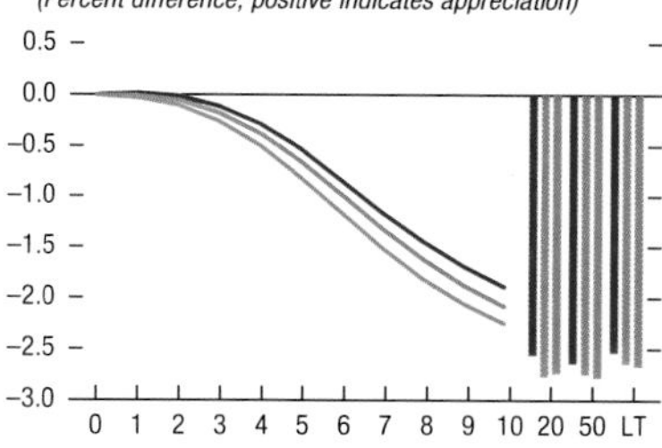


**7. Government Debt**
*(Percent of GDP difference)*

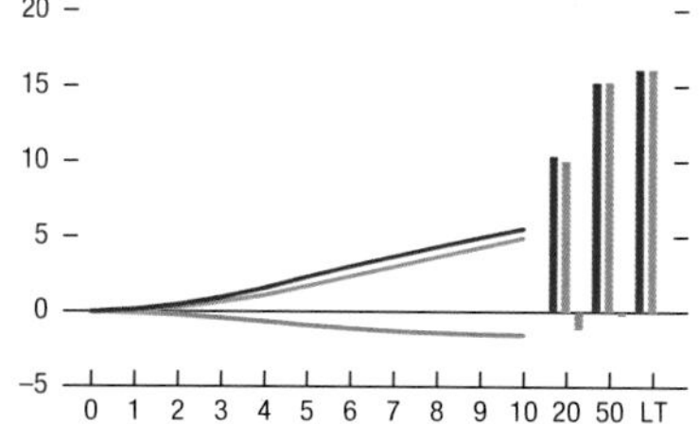


**8. Government Deficit**
*(Percent of GDP difference)*

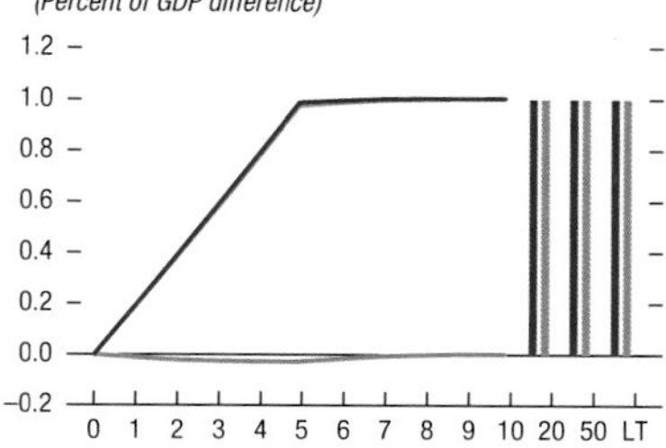


Source: IMF staff calculations from Flexible System of Global Models simulations.
Note: "LT" refers to the steady-state value.

**Annex Figure 8.1.5. Macroeconomic Effects of Boosting Public Investment in the Philippines**

*(One percent of GDP over five years)*

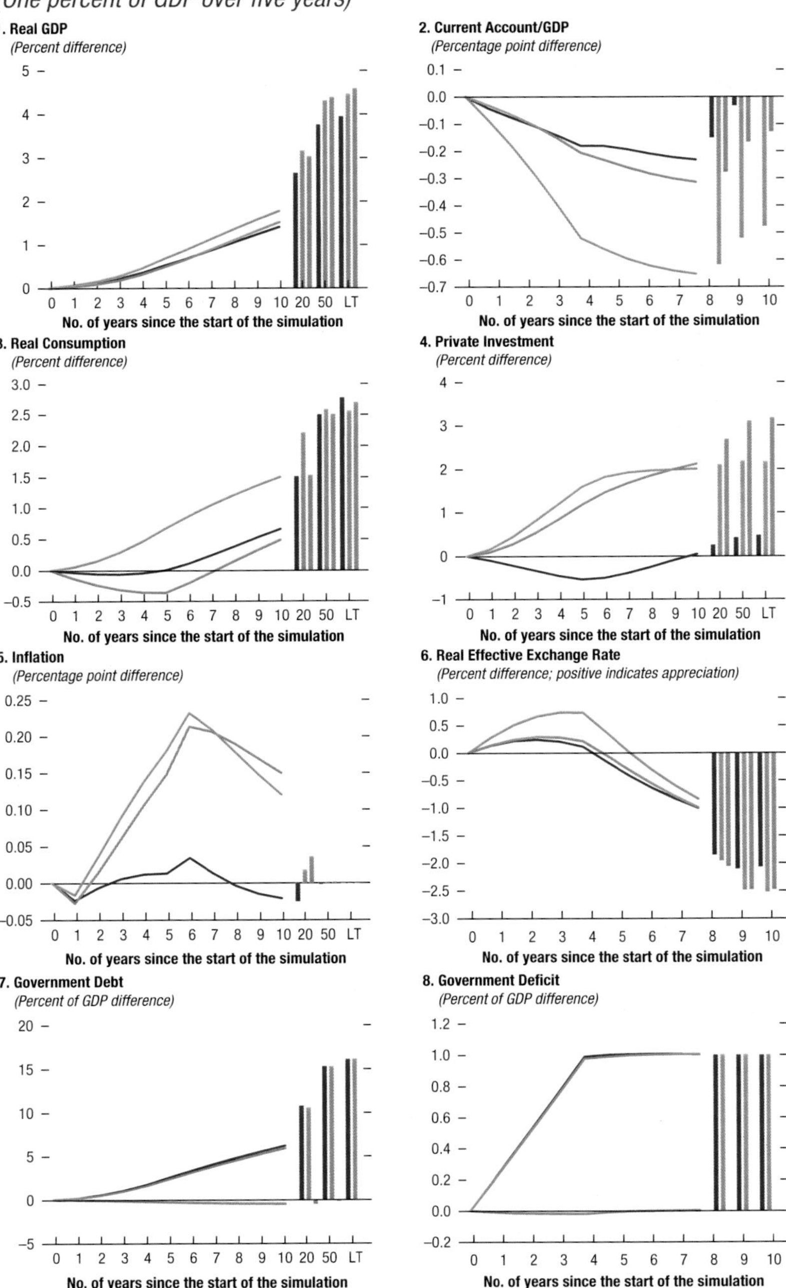


Source: IMF staff calculations from Flexible System of Global Models simulations.

Note: "LT" refers to the steady-state value.

## Annex Figure 8.1.6. Macroeconomic Effects of Boosting Public Investment in Sri Lanka

*(One percent of GDP over five years)*

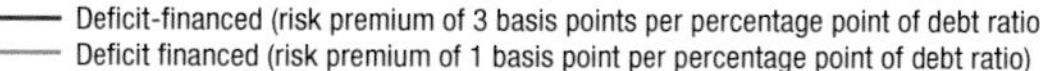


**1. Real GDP**
*(Percent difference)*

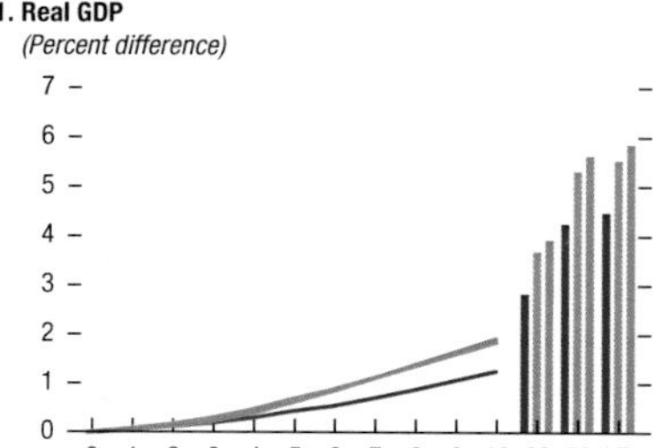


**2. Current Account/GDP**
*(Percentage point difference)*

0.4
0.2
0.0
−0.2
−0.4
−0.6
−0.8
0 1 2 3 4 5 6 7 8 9 10 20 50 LT
No. of years since the start of the simulation

**3. Real Consumption**
*(Percent difference)*

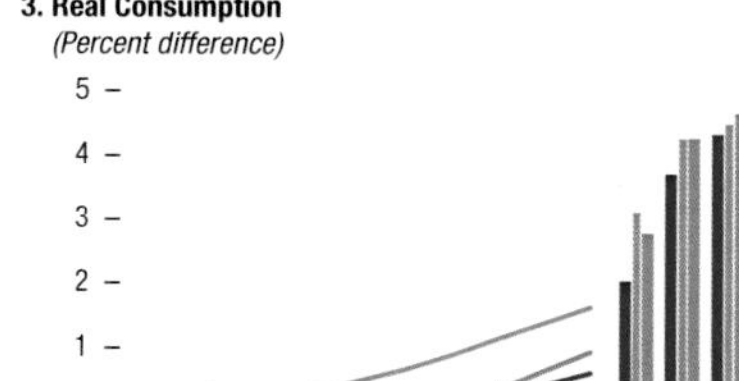


**4. Private Investment**
*(Percent difference)*

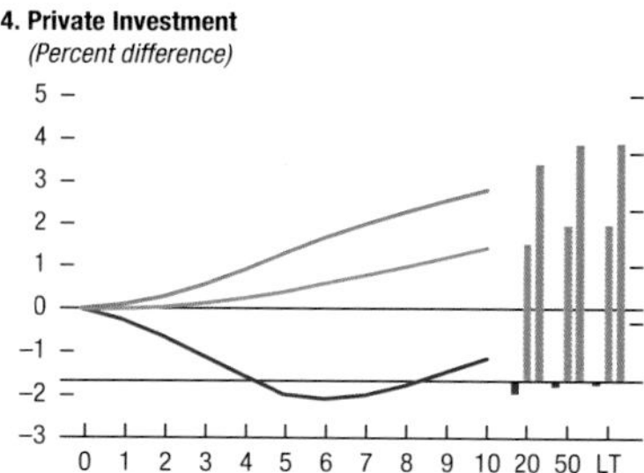


**5. Inflation**
*(Percentage point difference)*

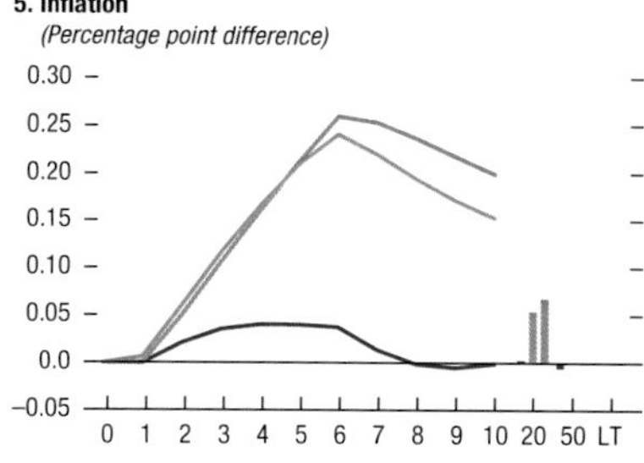


**6. Real Effective Exchange Rate**
*(Percent difference; positive indicates appreciation)*

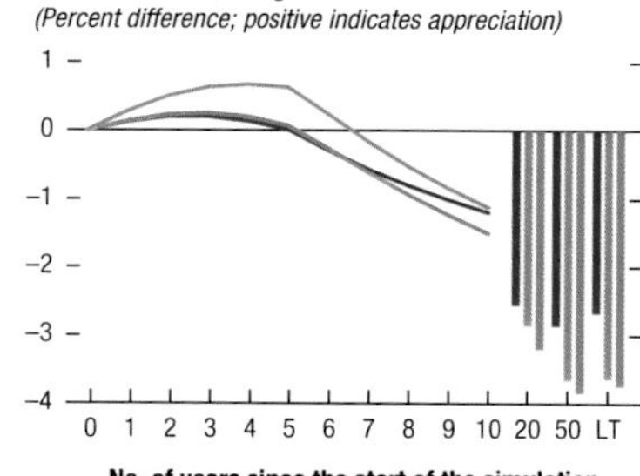


**7. Government Debt**
*(Percent of GDP difference)*

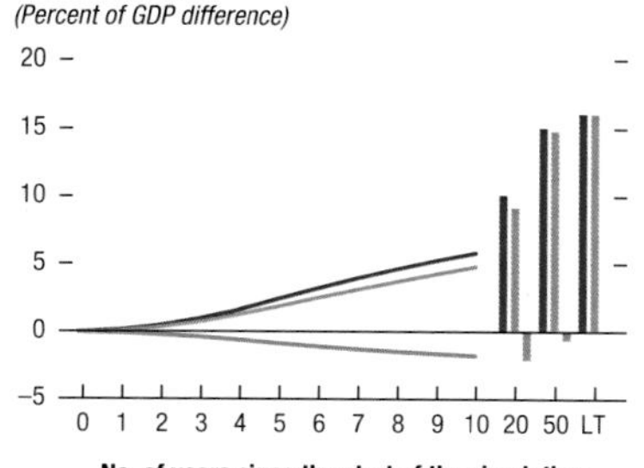


**8. Government Deficit**
*(Percent of GDP difference)*

1.2
1.0
0.8
0.6
0.4
0.2
0.0
−0.2
0 1 2 3 4 5 6 7 8 9 10 20 50 LT
No. of years since the start of the simulation

Source: IMF staff calculations from Flexible System of Global Models simulations.
Note: "LT" refers to the steady-state value.

## REFERENCES

Andrle, Michal, Patrick Blagrave, Pedro Espaillat, Keiko Honjo, Benjamin L Hunt, Mika Kortelainen, René Lalonde, and others. 2015. "The Flexible System of Global Models—FSGM." IMF Working Paper 15/64, International Monetary Fund, Washington, DC.

Batini, Nicoletta, Luc Eyraud, Lorenzo Forni, and Anke Weber. 2014. "Fiscal Multipliers: Size, Determinants, and Use in Macroeconomic Projections." IMF Technical Notes and Manuals 2014/04, International Monetary Fund, Washington, DC.

International Monetary Fund (IMF). 2013. *Fiscal Monitor: Taxing Times*. Washington, DC, October.

IMF. 2015. "Making Public Investment More Efficient." IMF Policy Paper, Washington, DC.

IMF. 2018. "Public Investment Management Assessment: Review and Update," IMF Staff Report, Washington, DC.

Kumar, Manmohan S., and Emanuele Baldacci. 2010. "Fiscal Deficits, Public Debt, and Sovereign Bond Yields." IMF Working Paper 10/184, International Monetary Fund, Washington, DC.

Ligthart, Jenny E., and Rosa M. Martin Suárez. 2005. "The Productivity of Public Capital: A Meta Analysis." Working Paper, Tilburg University.

CHAPTER 9

# Building Resilience to Natural Disaster in Vulnerable States: Savings from Ex Ante Interventions

**Wei Guo and Saad Quayyum**

## INTRODUCTION

The frequency of natural disasters is expected to rise with climate change, along with the damage they do. This leaves many countries, especially small states, highly vulnerable. The number of Category 4 and 5 storms in the North Atlantic is expected to increase by 45 to 87 percent over the course of 21st century (Knutson and others 2013), and weather events such as floods, coastal inundation, drought, and cyclones are expected to intensify in the Pacific (World Bank 2017). These patterns will exacerbate economic challenges for small island nations in the Caribbean and the Pacific, where average annual damage from these disasters as a percentage of GDP are typically four to five times higher than in other countries (IMF 2019). For example, Dominica was devastated by a hurricane in 2017, with damage done equal to more than 200 percent of GDP, only two years after being by hit by a hurricane that cost the country nearly 100 percent of GDP.

These natural disasters not only destroy lives and livelihoods, but also do significant harm to economic growth and national debt. Noy and Nualsri (2007), Noy (2009), Raddatz (2009), Loayza and others (2012), and Bayoumi, Quayyum, and Das (forthcoming) documented the adverse effect of natural disaster on growth. Lee, Zhang, and Nguyen (2018) found that large disasters a have significant negative effect on growth and fiscal and trade balances among small Pacific island nations. Strobl (2012) explored the impact of hurricanes in the Central America and Caribbean regions and found that on average they lead to reduction in growth of 0.83 percent in the year of impact.

These disasters are associated with large recovery costs as significant stocks of public and private infrastructure have to be rebuilt (IMF 2018b). Given the large size of these shocks and limited fiscal space in disaster-vulnerable countries, much of the recovery costs are often financed by official development assistance from the international community (IMF 2019).

A significant amount of the damage and associated output lost could be avoided through investment in building resilient infrastructure in vulnerable areas before the next disaster strikes (in other words, an ex ante intervention). However, financing for this is insufficient. United Nations Environment Programme (2016) reported that adaptation needs are at least two to three times the available international public financing. Donor support for vulnerable countries is heavily skewed toward postdisaster recovery.[1] Domestic financing for resilience building is also limited, as many of the vulnerable countries have high public debt or high-priority development needs.

This chapter explores whether building resilience is cost effective. In other words, whether the benefits are sufficient to justify the upfront costs. It uses a dynamic stochastic general equilibrium model to explore intertemporal trade-offs and the benefits of building resilience, focusing on six countries especially vulnerable to natural disasters—Antigua and Barbuda, Dominica, Fiji, Haiti, St. Lucia, and St. Vincent and the Grenadines. The following two policy options for policymakers over a 20-year span are explored:

1. Take no resilience actions before a disaster occurs.
2. Spend a constant fraction of GDP in building resilient infrastructure in non-disaster years.

The exercise assumes that countries are hit by disasters of various sizes over 20 years based on the historical frequency of these shocks. It also studies a scenario in which the frequency of disaster increases because of climate change.[2]

The cost of rebuilding public infrastructure after a disaster is found to be larger in the first scenario than in the second, as the stock of infrastructure is less resilient. Policymakers can save in net present value terms by investing in resilience before a disaster and so avoid large rebuilding costs. According to the model used, the average savings for the six island nations considered (net of additional cost of investing in resilience) in the baseline is 10 percent of initial-year GDP over 20 years and increases up to 14 percent of GDP if the frequency of disasters rises. In addition, countries benefit from lower output losses in the event of a disaster, which averages to about 4 percent of initial-year GDP in net present value terms. The average increases to about 6 percent of initial-year GDP in the scenario in which the frequency of disaster increases.

The findings underscore the importance of mobilizing more resources toward building ex ante resilience. As noted in Chapters 3 and 4, for many vulnerable states, financing for such investments will be limited by available fiscal space. Countries will not only need to mobilize domestic revenue and prioritize spending, but also spend better and increase the efficiency of capital spending. The international community can also play a role. By changing the pattern of support toward building resilience, donors can not only increase welfare in disaster-vulnerable

[1] See IMF (2016) for a detailed discussion on international financing of natural disasters and climate change.

[2] In this scenario, the country is hit by one additional large natural disaster exceeding 20 percent of GDP damage in the 20-year period.

countries but can also expect to save in the long term from lower outlays on recovery efforts in disaster-vulnerable countries.

This work is related to the literature exploring the impact of public investment on growth such as Barro (1990), Barro and Sala-i-Martin (1992), and Futagami, Morita, and Shibata (1993). It is also related to papers on the macroeconomic and fiscal impact of natural disaster. Such papers include Cavallo and Noy (2011), Cavallo and others (2013), and Bevan and Cook (2015). Finally, the analysis here is closely related to Marto, Papageorgiou, and Klyuev (2018), which employed a similar model to study how small developing states could build resilience to and recover from natural disasters while maintaining debt sustainability. In particular, Marto, Papageorgiou, and Klyuev (2018) explored how much grant financing is required to ensure debt sustainability, and how donor support for resilience can improve debt profile. Nevertheless, the following analysis departs from that in some key assumptions. It assumes resilient capital is more expensive than nonresilient capital, which creates an intertemporal trade-off for policymakers in choosing what kind of capital to invest in. It also introduces multiple shocks that are calibrated to a country's own history in terms of frequency and size—which also play an important role in the intertemporal trade-off. Furthermore, it assumes that countries have borrowing constraints, which is common among disaster-vulnerable small states, many of which have high debt or are at high risk of debt distress (IMF 2019).

## STYLIZED FACTS

The number of natural disasters per year has been steadily increasing since the early 1990s (Figure 9.1; Chapter 14). In 2017, the number of disasters reported was more than double that of 1992. With climate change, this trend is likely to

**Figure 9.1. Frequency of Natural Disasters: 1980–2017**

- Geophysical events (earthquakes, tsunamis, volcanic activity)
- Meteorological events (tropical cyclones, extratropical storms, convective storms, local storms)
- Hydrological events (floods, mass movement)
- Climatological events (extreme temperatures, droughts, forest fires)

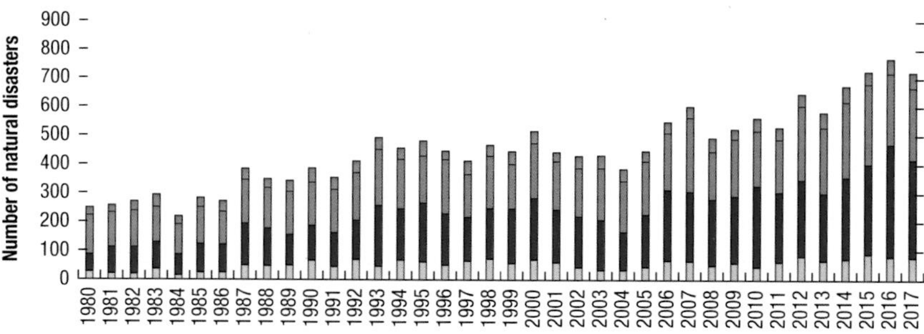


Source: Munich Re Group.

continue. These disasters cause significant damages, especially for small states. The average annual effect of natural disasters for small Caribbean and Pacific states ranges between 2.0 percent and 3.0 percent of GDP, which is about four to five times higher than for larger countries (see Figure 9.2, panel 1).

Large natural disasters have significant macroeconomic impact—reducing growth and pushing up debt. Disasters that cause damage exceeding 20 percent of GDP are followed by a decline in growth of about 3 percentage points on

## Figure 9.2. Impact of Natural Disasters and Disaster Aid Allocation

**1. Damage from Natural Disasters**
(1980–2017)

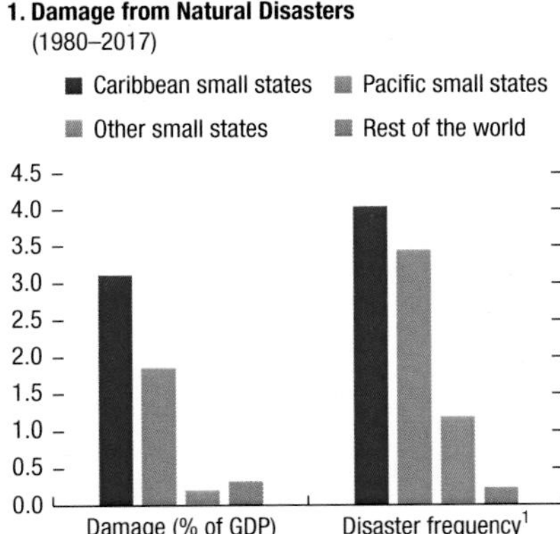


Sources: EM-DAT; WEO; and IMF staff estimates.
[1]Frequency is the annual average of all natural disaster incidents from 1980–2017 per 10,000 square kilometers of land area.

**2. Impact of Large Disaster on GDP per Capita[2]**

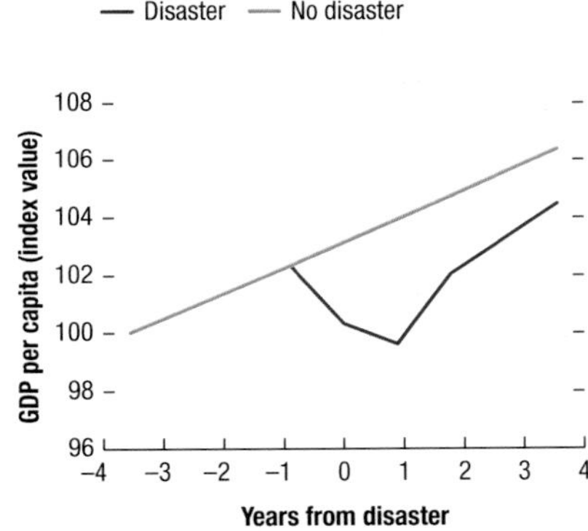


Sources: EM-DAT; and IMF 2019.
[2]Disasters with damage greater than 20 percent of GDP; based on average growth rate from 15 episodes in developing countries between 1991 and 2016.

**3. Public Debt around Large Disaster[3]**
(Damage >20% of GDP)

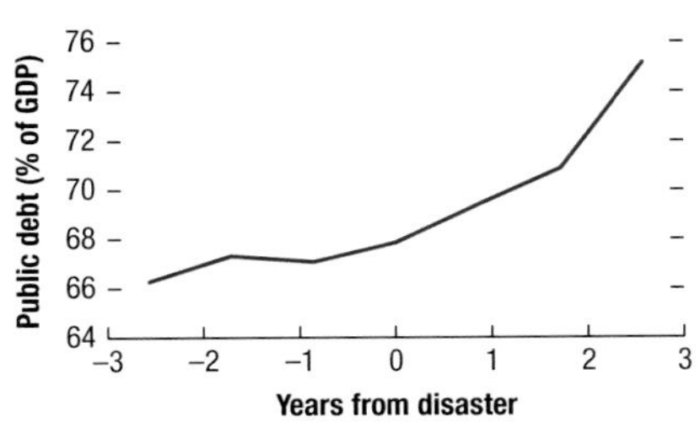


Sources: EM-DAT; and IMF 2019.
[3]Average public debt for 11 episodes of large natural disasters in developing countries between 1992 and 2016 for which data are available.

**4. Allocation of Disaster-Related Development Assistance**
(Average, 1990–2010)

Emergency response and reconstruction
Disaster prevention and preparedness

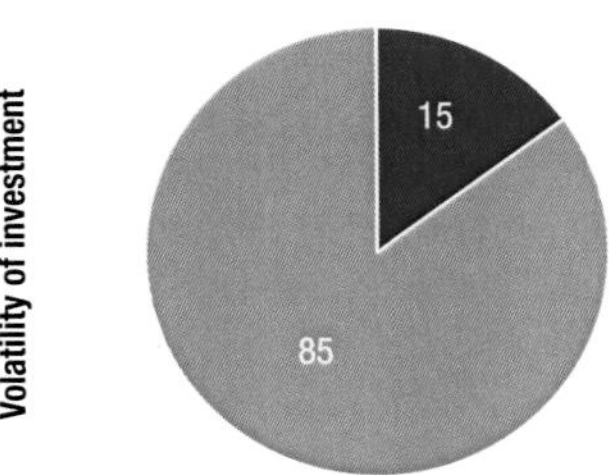


Source: Disaster Aid Tracking database.

Note: EM-DAT = Emergency Events Database; WEO = World Economic Outlook.

**Box 9.1. Fiji's Efforts to Build Ex Ante Resilience to Natural Disaster and Climate Change**

Fiji is particularly vulnerable to natural disasters. Tropical storms and floods cause about 5 percent of GDP damage annually, but damage can be as high as 20 percent of GDP, as it was for Tropical Strom Winston in 2016. The government has been steadily increasing investment in resilience, from about 4 percent of its annual budget in 2013 to about 10 percent in fiscal year 2016/17.

Recently Fiji conducted a climate vulnerability assessment to identify the investment needed to improve resilience to natural disasters and climate change. It has estimated these investment needs to be about 100 percent of GDP over 2018–2027, of which about half is on top of funds already earmarked in existing plans.

Increased spending to improve infrastructure is central to Fiji's strategy to mitigate climate change, with transportation infrastructure getting the highest amount. It also envisages large investment in flood-risk management and coastal protection. These investments are expected to not only improve resilience to natural disasters but also improve livelihoods and productivity.

To finance resilience building, the government instituted the new Environmental and Climate Adaptation Levy in 2017, which is expected to yield 1 percent of GDP. Moreover, in November 2017 Fiji issued its first sovereign bond for financing climate and environmental resilience projects, becoming the first developing country to pursue such an initiative. Between 2011 and 2014, Fiji received about $10 million (about 0.25 percent of GDP) in concessional finance per year from multilateral and bilateral donors for climate resilience and disaster-risk management. It will need continued and additional support from donors to achieve its ambitious resilience plans.

Source: Government of Fiji, World Bank, and Global Facility for Disaster Reduction and Recovery 2017.

average (Figure 9.2, panel 2) and increase debt by about 8 percent of GDP (Figure 9.2, panel 3). However, considerable heterogeneity is seen across countries, depending on initial conditions and size of the shock. In Dominica for example, growth is estimated to have collapsed to –9 percent in 2017–18 after Hurricane Maria in 2017.[3]

Building resilience is expensive. Estimates for total investment needed for climate adaptation vary significantly across countries and depend on risk tolerance. The Climate Change Policy Assessment for Belize (IMF 2018a) assesses the need for resilient investment at 28 percent of GDP.[4] The climate vulnerability assessment for Fiji estimates costs to be about 100 percent of GDP over 10 years (see Box 9.1).[5] Table 9.1 shows the cost of adaptation for some Pacific island nations.

Donor support is at present heavily skewed toward postdisaster support instead of building ex ante resilience (Figure 9.2, panel 4). In 1990–2010, 85 percent of aid for disaster-related expenses was allocated to postdisaster recovery and humanitarian

[3] The estimated growth is the average of the two years based on IMF (2018a).

[4] Climate Change Policy Assessments are joint World Bank and IMF exercises carried out as pilots for assessing policy gaps in mitigation and adaptation strategies to climate change.

[5] The climate vulnerability assessment was prepared by the Government of Fiji with assistance from the World Bank to assess interventions and investments needed to make the country climate resilient.

**TABLE 9.1.**

**Costs of Resilience in 2020s, in Selected Pacific Countries**
*($ millions per year at 2018 international prices)*

| Country | Adaptation Costs for Coastal Protection | | Costs of Protecting Infrastructure from High Temperature and Rainfall | Cost of Adaptation to Higher Cyclone Winds for Public Buildings | | Total ($, Millions) | | Total (Percent of 2018 GDP) | |
|---|---|---|---|---|---|---|---|---|---|
| | Low | High | Average | Low | High | Low | High | Low | High |
| Fiji | 78 | 253 | 23 | 150.7 | 163.5 | 252 | 440 | 4.6 | 8.1 |
| Kiribati | 14 | 46 | 22 | – | – | 36 | 68 | 17.7 | 33.3 |
| Marshall Islands | 14 | 46 | 9 | 17.2 | 19.3 | 41 | 75 | 19.9 | 36.5 |
| Micronesia | 7 | 22 | 16 | 16.8 | 19.1 | 39 | 57 | 11.6 | 16.9 |
| Palau | 2 | 10 | 5 | – | – | 7 | 15 | 2.3 | 4.7 |
| Samoa | 4 | 16 | 9 | 21.4 | 27.0 | 35 | 53 | 4.0 | 6.0 |
| Solomon Islands | 89 | 308 | 20 | – | – | 109 | 328 | 7.9 | 23.8 |
| Tonga | 9 | 31 | 10 | 25.0 | 27.5 | 44 | 68 | 10.0 | 15.7 |
| Vanuatu | 40 | 143 | 8 | 34.4 | 38.3 | 82 | 189 | 8.6 | 19.8 |
| Total | 257 | 875 | 122 | 265.5 | 294.7 | 645 | 1,292 | 9.6 | 18.3 |

Sources: World Bank 2016; and IMF staff estimates.

assistance. Only about 15 percent went toward building resilience. Climate financing is four times more focused toward mitigation than adaptation activities.

## THE POLICY EXPERIMENT

### The Setup

This section analyzes the returns of investment in resilient infrastructure, how they vary with economic and climate change parameters, and whether they are sufficiently high in net present value terms to cover the costs of investment. For this purpose, we use a multisector dynamic stochastic general equilibrium model to study the trade-off in building resilience. The model is a small open economy in which households purchase agricultural and manufacturing goods as well as services. There are five types of households: unskilled, skilled, government employees, entrepreneurs, and farmers. Households take prices and government policies as given. The government chooses tax policy and spending levels, including public investment. It can invest in infrastructure that is resilient and is not. The former is more expensive but is more durable.[6] The latter is cheaper but depreciates at a higher rate when there is a natural disaster. Details of the model can be found in Annex 9.1 and in Guo and Quayyum (forthcoming).

[6] For illustrative purposes, we assume resilient infrastructure is 10 percent more expensive than non-resilient infrastructure, while Marto, Papageorgiou, and Klyuev (2018) assumed costs are the same, and Guerson and others (forthcoming) assumed resilient infrastructure costs 20 percent more. The robustness of results is tested by varying this assumption.

**Figure 9.3. Damage from Natural Disasters: 1980–2017**
(Annual average, percent of GDP)

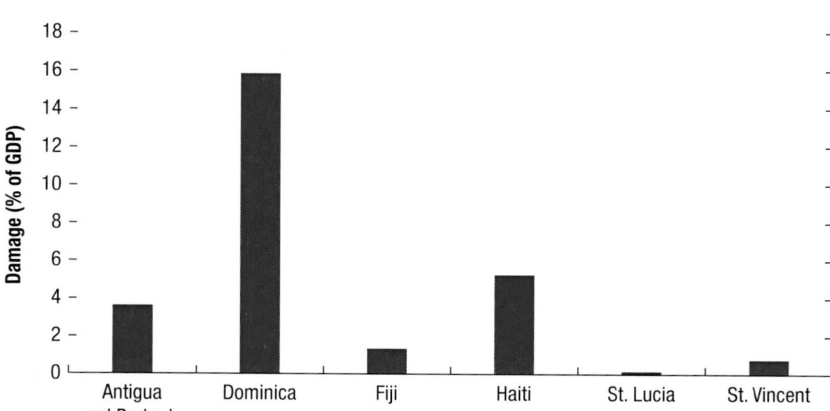


Source: IMF staff calculations, based on EM-DAT data.
Note: EM-DAT = Emergency Events Database.

The model is calibrated to six disaster-vulnerable economies.[7] Country-specific data from this group inform assumptions made about the sizes of various sectors (for example, agriculture and manufacturing), factor endowments and allocation (for example, initial wealth, skill distribution of the labor force), the types of goods consumed by households, tax rates, disaster frequency, and damage (see Annex 9.2). Features of the production function, the labor participation rates, and depreciation of capital were estimated using national data.[8]

The disasters that hit countries can be divided into three types: small, medium, and large. Small disasters cause damage of less than 5 percent of GDP, medium disasters cause damage of 5 percent to 20 percent of GDP. Large disasters cause damage exceeding 20 percent of GDP. Table 9.2 shows the frequency of different-sized disasters for the six countries.

The depreciation rate for resilient and nonresilient capital varies with the size of shock. Small and medium shocks do not increase depreciation of resilient infrastructure over its nondisaster rate. Resilient capital depreciates when hit by a large shock, but at a rate lower than nonresilient capital would depreciate under a similar size of shock.[9] In contrast, nonresilient capital depreciates in the face of all shocks.

[7] These countries suffered average annual damage of 0.4 to 16 percent of GDP (see Figure 9.3).

[8] The discount factor was borrowed from the literature and set to 0.9.

[9] For simplicity, it is assumed that resilient and nonresilient capital depreciate at the same rate in nondisaster years.

**TABLE 9.2.**

**Frequency of Disaster, Based on Experience over a 20-Year Period**

| | Small | Midsize | Large |
|---|---|---|---|
| Antigua and Barbuda | 1 | 1 | 1 |
| Dominica | 2 | 1 | 3 |
| Fiji | 10 | 3 | |
| Haiti | 6 | 1 | 1 |
| St. Lucia | 4 | 0 | 1 |
| St. Vincent and the Grenadines | 2 | 2 | 0 |

Source: IMF staff calculations, based on EM-DAT data.
Note: Disaster size is based on the scale of damage (*small* refers to less than 5 percent of GDP damage; *midsize* refers to 5 percent to 20 percent of GDP damage; *and large* refers to GDP damage exceeding 20 percent).
Note: EM-DAT = Emergency Events Database.

## Policy Scenarios

The model described in this chapter is used to study and compare the following two scenarios:

- *No action.* The government does not invest in resilient capital but invests only in nonresilient capital to offset the depreciation of capital. However, when there is a natural disaster, the government rebuilds the damaged infrastructure with resilient capital. The cost of rebuilding is financed entirely by foreign grants.[10]
- *Build resilience.* The government chooses to invest in resilient capital to offset the depreciation of capital.[11] Given that resilient capital is more expensive, this requires additional financing of about 1 percent of GDP in nondisaster years. The additional financing is assumed to come from donor grants or a combination of grants and higher tax revenue. When there is a natural disaster, the destroyed infrastructure is rebuilt using resilient capital financed through grants, like in the previous scenario.

# KEY INSIGHTS

While policymakers spend about 1 percent of GDP in nondisaster years in the "build resilience" scenario, they save significantly in years when the countries are hit by disasters. Figure 9.4 shows the path of additional public investment for St. Vincent and the Grenadines under the two scenarios. In the "no action" scenario, no additional investment is made in nondisaster years (the orange line remains at zero). St. Vincent and the Grenadines faces two simulated medium-sized disasters and two small disasters over the 20-year period based on the simulation starting from a nondisaster year. After 20 years, the simulations would be back to the

[10] Many of the disaster-vulnerable countries, especially in the Caribbean, are fiscally constrained (see IMF 2019) and rely heavily on donor support after a disaster. For the sake of simplicity, it is assumed that the rebuilding costs are all donor financed.

[11] It is assumed that the investment rates are the same in the two scenarios.

**Figure 9.4. Additional Public Spending on Infrastructure: St. Vincent and the Grenadines**

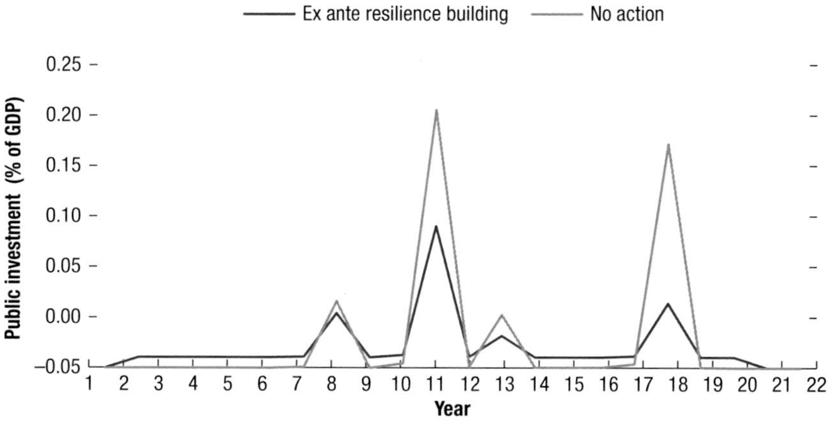

Source: IMF staff calculations, based on simulation for a period of 20 years.

initial status for a new circle so that the situations in period 1 are identical to other situations after period 20. These can be seen in the four spikes in public investment. The blue line shows the path of public investment for a scenario in which policymakers invest in resilience. In nondisaster years, the blue line is higher than the orange line because of additional expenditure in resilience. However, the spikes in public investment are much smaller in disaster years.

The difference in public spending between the two scenarios is calculated, along with the net present value of the difference as a percentage of initial-year GDP for each of the six countries.[12] This is shown in Figure 9.5. For all six countries, the savings in lower recovery costs in disaster years from resilience building outweigh the additional expenses incurred in nondisaster years over the 20-year period. Net savings under the baseline scenario vary between 3 percent and 20 percent of the recipient's GDP. The largest savings are in Fiji, which has the highest incidence of large disasters. The net savings increase significantly when one large disaster is added to the 20-year period, varying between 9 percent and 22 percent of GDP across the six countries.[13]

Moreover, significant gains come from lower output losses in disaster years from building resilience beforehand. When public capital is more resilient, productive capacity shrinks less and fewer output disruptions occur. The gains range from 2 percent of initial-year GDP in St. Vincent and the Grenadines to about 8 percent of initial-year GDP in Dominica, where large disasters have been

[12] A discount factor of 5 is used for the net present value calculations.

[13] These savings are independent of whether the spending on resilience is financed through grants or a combination of grants and tax revenue.

**Figure 9.5. Savings from Building Ex Ante Resilience and Avoiding Large Recovery Costs**
(Net present value, as a percent of first year's GDP)

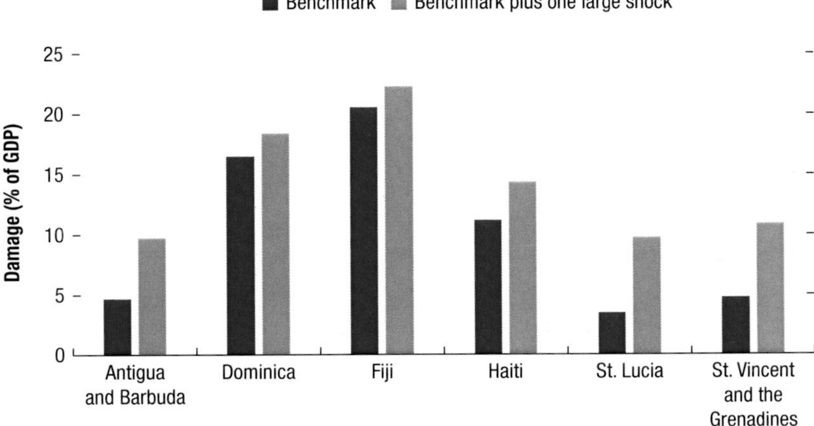


Source: IMF staff calculations, based on simulation for a period of 20 years.

frequent in recent years (Figure 9.6). If a higher frequency of disasters is assumed, the gains range from about 4 percent of GDP in Fiji to over 8 percent in Dominica. These numbers are based on a scenario in which the additional investment needed for building resilience is financed through external grants. When VAT rates are raised to pay part of the higher cost of resilience, the output gains

**Figure 9.6. Gains from Lower Output Loss from Building Ex Ante Resilience**
(Percent of first year's GDP, net present value)

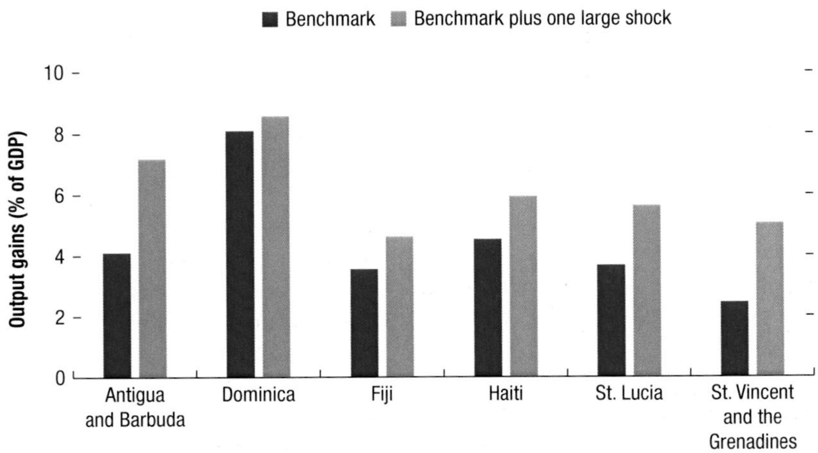


Source: IMF staff calculations, based on simulation for a period of 20 years.

**Figure 9.7. Additional Saving with Higher Productivity of Public Investment**
(Percent of GDP)

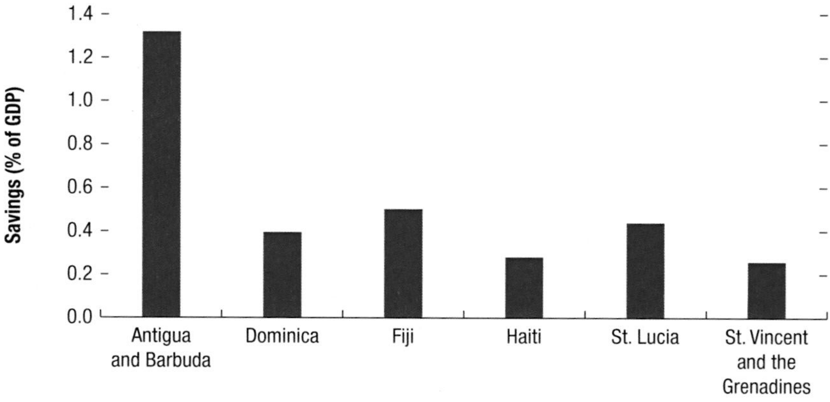

Source: IMF staff calculations, based on simulation.

are only marginally smaller (less than 0.5 percent of GDP), but consumption drops significantly.[14]

Improving the efficiency of investment spending could significantly increase the gains from investment in building resilience. As noted in Chapter 3, improvements in infrastructure governance can impact the efficiency of spending significantly—countries can boost the quality and volume of infrastructure with limited increases in spending. In the model in this chapter, this can be captured through the production function. A test is carried out to determine how better public infrastructure governance affects the returns from investment in building resilience in vulnerable areas by increasing the productivity of public capital—better infrastructure governance would increase the response of output to an increase in the capital stock. In general, this leads to stronger output gains from investing in resilience. In particular, increasing the elasticity of output of public capital from 0.14 in the baseline to 0.2 leads to output gains in excess of the baseline estimates of between 0.3 percent of GDP (in St. Vincent and the Grenadines) and 1.3 percent of GDP (in Antigua and Barbuda). This is shown in Figure 9.7.[15]

[14] In this scenario about one-third of the cost of building resilience is borne by the vulnerable countries by increasing the VAT rate. Increasing the burden-sharing ratio through higher taxes lowers GDP, but only marginally, in the model.

[15] In the baseline, it is assumed that a 1 percent increase in public capital leads to a 0.14 percent increase in output, based on data from Dominica. In the new scenario, the assumption is that a 1 percent increase in public capital leads to a 0.2 percent increase in output, based on the average estimate in Arslanalp and others (2010) for countries that are not members of the Organisation for Economic Co-operation and Development.

## POLICY IMPLICATIONS

The results support switching resources toward building resilience in countries that are vulnerable to natural disasters. By spending more on resilience, policymakers can expect to save on postdisaster recovery in disaster-vulnerable countries. As a significant part of the postdisaster recovery costs in small vulnerable states is usually financed by donors, they could expect to save on costs by providing more resources for resilience building.

Vulnerable countries and donors would need to take significant steps to raise financing necessary to build resilience. Donor assistance is particularly important. Concessional financing, preferably grants, would help countries build resilience while ensuring debt sustainability. Climate funds—which are also financed by the international community—are another source of funding but would need to improve access for projects by simplifying some of their administrative requirements, which many disaster-vulnerable states find cumbersome.[16] However, country authorities will also need to generate fiscal resources through stronger domestic revenue mobilization and possibly switching low-priority expenditure toward resilience building. Countries will also need to spend better and improve efficiency of public spending (through better governance).

## ANNEX 9.1. MODEL SETUP AND PARAMETERS

The model consists of a small open economy with three consumption goods: agriculture, manufacturing, and services. There are five types of households: unskilled, skilled, government employees, entrepreneurs, and farmers. Households solve dynamic optimization problems taking prices and government policies as given. In addition to consumption decisions, the different participants of the economy make decisions that affect output and incomes, taking into account uncertainty from natural disasters:

- *Unskilled households.* Choose to work for farmers or in the informal sector.
- *Skilled households.* Choose to work for entrepreneurs or to migrate.
- *Government employees.* Choose to work for the government or to migrate.
- *Farmers.* Hire labor to produce agriculture goods and invest.
- *Entrepreneurs.* Hire labor for the formal manufacturing and services sector and invest.

Three goods are produced: (1) agriculture (produced by farmers), (2) manufacturing (produced by entrepreneurs), and (3) services (produced by entrepreneurs in the formal sector and by unskilled workers in the informal sector). Services are produced by both the formal and the informal sectors.

As input for the production function, the agriculture sector uses unskilled labor and capital. The manufacturing sector employs skilled labor and invests in

[16] Climate funds provide financing for climate mitigation and adaptation activities.

capital to produce manufacturing goods. Production in the services sector can be formal using skilled labor or informal using unskilled labor. Agriculture and manufacturing goods are tradable and sold domestically or internationally, while service goods are nontradable and sold only domestically.

Households decide how much to consume of each good. In addition, skilled households have an occupational choice; they decide the share of time devoted to work in the domestic formal sector and the share time devoted to work abroad.[17] Unskilled households also have an occupational choice between working in the agriculture sector or working in the informal sector. Government workers have a similar occupational choice, since they can receive a public sector wage or migrate and work abroad.

The possibility of labor migration is a key feature of the model, with important macroeconomic implications. The model allows households to choose between working in the local economy, or migrating to work in other countries and sending back remittances. Notice that this is a macro-critical feature for small states and small open economies, including in the Caribbean, Central America, and Asia Pacific. Migration typically has a significant impact on both the quantity and the quality of labor, given that migration can be skill biased. For example, Dominica's population has shrunk in recent years despite an average natural growth rate, with emigration being more prominent for high-skilled workers, at 80 percent of the population. These skilled workers contribute to the economy by sending remittances, of around 5 percent of GDP per year.

Farmers own their capital and decide how much unskilled labor to hire and how much to invest in capital to produce the agriculture goods. Entrepreneurs also own capital; they decide how much skilled labor to hire to produce formal services and manufacturing and invest in capital that is used as an input on the production of manufacturing goods.

The government sector includes a granular menu of fiscal policy instruments. The government collects tax revenue (VAT, corporate taxes, and personal income tax) and nontax revenue (mainly through citizenship by investment programs and donor grants). Government revenue is used to fund expenditure (including public sector wages, public investment in resilience and nonresilience capital, and transfers) and to service public debt. Public investment plays a significant role in this economy and affects the productivity of the manufacturing and agriculture sectors. Government decisions ultimately affect budget constraints and the accumulation of public debt. The model structure is summarized in Annex Table 9.1.1.

## Resilient and Nonresilient Infrastructure

Public infrastructure contributes to the manufacturing and agriculture sector as public capital with sector-specific elasticity of production. In the modeling, we would like to consider the impact from natural disasters and climate change on

[17] This occupational choice captures the brain drain problem faced by many countries in the Caribbean.

**ANNEX TABLE 9.1.1.**

**Model Structure**

| Good | Producer | Input | Use | Commerce |
|---|---|---|---|---|
| Agriculture | Farmers | Unskilled labor and capital | Consumption | Tradable |
| Manufacturing | Entrepreneurs | Skilled labor and capital | Consumption and investment | Tradable |
| Services | Unskilled labor and entrepreneurs | Skilled and unskilled labor | Consumption | Nontradable |

Source: IMF staff, based on country staff report.

infrastructure investment and disaster financing. Therefore, we have two types of infrastructure: resilient $K_t^r$ and nonresilient $K_t^n$. They function the same and depreciate the same in regular time and $K_t^n + K_t^r = K_t^g$. However, when the economy is hit by natural disasters, the resilient infrastructure does not sustain extra damage unless the disaster is large, inflicting damage of more than 20 percent of GDP. Nonresilient infrastructure depreciates more when there is a natural disaster and the additional depreciation depends on the intensity of the disaster. When a unit price of nonresilient infrastructure is set as 1, the unit price for resilient infrastructure is 1.1 in the baseline specification. The price is varied from 1.05 to 1.2 for robustness checks.

## Natural Disaster

A natural disaster generates the separation of both total productivity loss $\theta$ instantly and loss in public capital with a one-time depreciation drop $\delta_d$. The productivity shock is the same for all sectors. The $\theta$ is calibrated for small, middle, and large shocks separately to match the real GDP drop, based on the historical disaster series from the Emergency Events Database (EM-DAT). We define the size of the disaster based on its impact on the damage-to-GDP ratio. If the ratio is below 5 percent, it is regarded as a small natural disaster shock. If it is between 5 percent and 20 percent, it is middle-sized. Otherwise it is a large natural disaster shock. For small states in this study, Table 9.2 shows the frequency of different types of shocks for countries in 20 years.

We assume that GDP would drop 5 percent for large disaster shocks, 1 percent for middle ones, and 0.3 percent for small shocks, based on empirical calculation of the impact of various-sized disasters on growth.

The following depreciation is assumed for when public infrastructure is hit by natural disaster, which varies with the intensity of disaster (Annex Table 9.1.2).

**ANNEX TABLE 9.1.2.**

**Depreciation of Nonresilient and Resilient Infrastructure**
*(By size of natural disaster)*

| | Small | Medium | Large |
|---|---|---|---|
| Nonresilient | 5% | 20% | 40% |
| Resilient | 0% | 0% | 15% |

Source: IMF staff.

## ANNEX 9.2. APPLICATION TO SMALL STATES

The model is calibrated to match the quantitative parameters of the six small states' economies separately. The calibration accounts for sector sizes, labor participation, capital investment, and intersector links, and for the consumption basket for different goods.

*Preferences.* Households' preferences over manufacturing goods ($\psi$) and services ($\gamma$) are calibrated so that consumption shares in the model match those in the consumer price index (CPI) basket, mapping the different types of goods and services to the sectors in the model.

*Labor force.* Labor market parameters, including the distribution of labor across different types of households in the model, are based on data from each country's national administration.[18] Specifically, the sectoral data on employment are allocated as follows (Annex Table 9.2.1): (1) government workers ($\mu^g$): public sector, (2) skilled workers ($\mu^s$): manufacturing, utilities, trade, tourism, and financial sector, and (3) unskilled workers ($\mu^u$): agriculture, fishing, mining, and construction. The remaining sectors are distributed between entrepreneurs ($\mu^e$) and farmers ($\mu^f$). Wages in the United States ($w^{us}$) are calibrated so that remittance flows in the model match the actual data (Annex Table 9.2.2).

*Economic sectors.* The production function is assumed to be Cobb-Douglas. Productivity in the agricultural ($z^a$), formal ($z^{e,s}$), and informal services ($z^s$) sectors is calibrated so that the sizes of the sectors in the model match the national accounts data. Elasticity to private capital ($\alpha^m$, $\alpha^*$) is calculated as the difference between total capital income share and capital income attributed to structures,

**ANNEX TABLE 9.2.1.**

| Parameters | |
|---|---|
| **Parameter** | **Explanation** |
| $\mu^g$ | Share of government workers |
| $\mu^s$ | Share of skilled workers |
| $\mu^u$ | Share of unskilled workers |
| $\mu^e$ | Share of entrepreneurs |
| $\mu^f$ | Share of big farmers |
| $r^*$ | Interest rate in government debt |
| $\beta$ | Discount factor |
| $\bar{c}$ | Lower bound of agricultural consumption |
| $a$ | Emigration elasticity |
| $a^m$ | Tradable elasticity to private capital |
| $a^*$ | Agriculture elasticity to private capital |
| $a^g$ | Elasticity to public capital |
| $\delta$ | Private capital depreciation |
| $\delta_g$ | Public capital depreciation |
| $\delta_h$ | Human capital depreciation |
| $H$ | Human capital stock |

Source: IMF staff, based on country staff reports.

[18] The latest available data are for 2015.

**ANNEX TABLE 9.2.2.**

| Moment Calibration Summary | | |
|---|---|---|
| **Parameter** | **Moment** | **Model=Data** |
| | Preferences (percent) | |
| $\psi$ | Manufacturing share in total consumption | Yes |
| $\gamma$ | Services share in total consumption | Yes |
| | Economic Indicators (percent of GDP) | |
| $z^a$ | Agricultural output | Yes |
| $z^{e,s}$ | Services output | Yes |
| $z^s$ | Informal sector output | Yes |
| $w^{us}$ | Remittances | Yes |
| | Fiscal Policy (percent of GDP) | |
| $\tau^a, \tau^m, \tau^s$ | Revenue from consumption tax | Yes |
| $\tau^w$ | Revenue from personal income tax | Yes |
| $\tau^k$ | Revenue from corporate taxes | Yes |
| $Gr$ | Grants | Yes |
| $NR$ | Nontax revenues | Yes |
| $w^g$ | Public sector wage bill | Yes |
| $T^u, T^s, T^f, T^e, T^g$ | Transfers to households | Yes |
| $\theta$ | GDP deviation from nondisaster period | Yes |

Source: IMF staff, based on country staff reports.

while elasticity to public capital ($\alpha^g$) is assumed to equal capital income because of structures in which capital income shares are estimated by Valentinyi and Herrendorf (2008) (Annex Table 9.2.1). Capital stock is calculated as the stock in the previous period (net of depreciation) increased with investments in which private ($\delta$) and public physical capital depreciation ($\delta_g$) are calculated as the weighted average of depreciation rates by type of capital from Feenstra, Inklarr, and Timmer (2015) with capital income shares estimated by Valentinyi and Herrendorf (2008) serving as weights. Human capital depreciation ($\delta_h$) is calculated based on mortality rates in peer countries (United Nations 2015). Human capital stock ($H$) is normalized to 1.

*Fiscal policy*. Government revenue and expenditure parameters are attuned to central government data (Annex Table 9.2.2). Specifically, consumption ($\tau^a$, $\tau^m$, $\tau^s$), personal income ($\tau^w$), and corporate tax rates ($\tau^k$) are calibrated to yield revenue close to effective revenue collections. Nontax revenues ($NR$) are calibrated to match flows mainly from the government budget plan. Similarly, grants ($Gr$) are aligned with actual current and capital grants. Transfers to households are calibrated to match actual spending on transfers, while public sector wages ($w^g$) are calibrated so that the public sector wage bill is in line with actual compensation of employees. Interest rate on government debt ($r^*$) is set as the implied interest rate on outstanding debt (Annex Table 9.2.1).

## REFERENCES

Arslanalp, Serkan, Fabian Bornhorst, Sanjeev Gupta, and Elsa Sze. 2010. "Public Capital and Growth." IMF Working Paper 10/175, International Monetary Fund, Washington, DC.

Barro, Robert. 1990. "Government Spending in a Simple Model of Endogenous Growth." *Journal of Political Economy* 98 (5): 103–25.

Barro, Robert, and Xavier Sala-i-Martin. 1992. "Public Finance in Models of Economic Growth." *Review of Economic Studies* 59 (4): 645–61.

Bayoumi, Tamim, Saad Quayyum, and Sibabrata Das. Forthcoming. "Growth at Risk from Natural Disaster." IMF Working Paper, International Monetary Fund, Washington, DC.

Bevan, David L., and Samantha Jane Cook. 2015. "Public Expenditure Following Disasters." Policy Research Working Paper 7355, World Bank, Washington, DC.

Cavallo, Eduardo, and Ilan Noy. 2011. "Natural Disasters and the Economy: A Survey." *International Review of Environmental and Resource Economics* 5 (1): 63–102.

Cavallo, Eduardo, Sebastian Galiano, Ilan Noy, and Juan Pantano. 2013. "Catastrophic Natural Disasters and Economic Growth." *Review of Economics and Statistics* 95 (5): 1549–61.

Feenstra, Robert C., Robert Inklaar, and Marcel P. Timmer, 2015. "The Next Generation of the Penn World Table." *American Economic Review* 105 (10): 3150–82.

Futagami, Koichi, Yuichi Morita, and Akihisa Shibata. 1993. "Dynamic Analysis of an Endogenous Growth Model with Public Capital." *Scandinavian Journal of Economics* 95 (4): 607–25.

Government of Fiji, World Bank, and Global Facility for Disaster Reduction and Recovery. 2017. "Fiji 2017: Climate Vulnerability Assessment—Making Fiji Climate Resilient." World Bank, Washington, DC.

Guerson, Alejandro, Wei Guo, Balazs Csonto, and Marina Mendes Tavares. Forthcoming. "A Model for Fiscal Policy Analysis in Small States: An Application to Dominica." IMF Working Paper, International Monetary Fund, Washington, DC.

Guo, Wei, and Saad Quayyum. Forthcoming. "Building Resilience to Natural Disaster in Vulnerable States: Savings from Ex Ante Interventions." IMF Working Paper, Washington, DC.

International Monetary Fund (IMF). 2016. "Small States' Resilience to Natural Disasters and Climate Change—Role for the IMF." IMF Policy Paper, Washington, DC.

IMF. 2018a. "Belize: Climate Change Policy Assessment." IMF Country Report 18/239, Washington, DC.

IMF. 2018b. "Dominica: Staff Report for the 2018 Article IV Consultation." IMF Country Report 18/265, Washington, DC.

IMF. 2019. "Building Resilience in Countries Vulnerable to Large Natural Disasters." IMF Board Paper, Washington, DC.

Knutson, Thomas, Joseph J. Sirutis, Gabriel A. Vecchi, Stephen Garner, Ming Zhao, Hyeong-Seog Kim, Morris Bender, and others. 2013. "Dynamical Downscaling Projections of Twenty-First-Century Atlantic Hurricane Activity: CMIP3 and CMIP5 Model-Based Scenarios." *Journal of Climate* 26.

Lee, Dongyeol, Huan Zhang, and Chau Nguyen. 2018. "The Economic Impact of Natural Disasters in Pacific Island Countries: Adaptation and Preparedness." IMF Working Paper 18/108, International Monetary Fund, Washington, DC.

Loayza, Norman, Eduardo Olaberria, Jamele Rigolini, and Luc Christiaensen. 2012. "Natural Disasters and Growth: Going Beyond the Averages." *World Development* 40 (7): 1317–36.

Marto, Ricardo, Chris Papageorgiou, and Vladimir Klyuev. 2018. "Building Resilience to Natural Disasters: An Application to Small Developing States." *Journal of Development Economics* 135 (C): 574–86.

Noy, Ilan. 2009. "The Macroeconomic Consequences of Disasters." *Journal of Development Economics* 88 (2): 221–31.

Noy, Ilan, and Aekkanush Nualsri. 2007. "What Do Exogenous Shocks Tell Us about Growth Theories?" University of Hawaii Working Paper 07–28, Honolulu.

Raddatz, Claudio. 2009. "The Wrath of God: Macroeconomic Costs of Natural Disasters." Policy Research Working Paper 5039, World Bank, Washington, DC.

Strobl, Eric. 2012. "The Economic Growth Impact of Natural Disasters in Developing Countries: Evidence from Hurricane Strikes in the Central American and Caribbean Regions." *Journal of Development Economics* 97 (1): 130–41.

United Nations. 2015. "World Population Prospects: The 2015 Revision." United Nations, New York.

United Nations Environment Programme. 2016. *The Adaptation Finance Gap Report*. United Nations Environmental Programme, Nairobi.

Valentinyi, Akos, and Berthold Herrendorf. 2008. "Measuring Factor Income Shares at the Sectoral Level." *Review of Economic Dynamics* 11 (4): 820–35.

World Bank. 2016. "Pacific Possible: Climate and Disaster Resilience." World Bank, Washington, DC.

World Bank. 2017. "Pacific Possible: Long-Term Economic Opportunities and Challenges for Pacific Island Countries." Washington, DC.

# PART III

# Building Strong Public Investment Institutions

CHAPTER 10

# Protecting Public Infrastructure from Vulnerabilities to Corruption: A Risk-Based Approach

**Sailendra Pattanayak and Concha Verdugo-Yepes**

## INTRODUCTION

Public investment is prone to corruption particularly when public officials and other actors process information and make decisions at various stages of the infrastructure management cycle for private gain. Several public investment projects have been mired in high-profile corruption scandals. For example, a scandal in Brazil that uncovered illegal payments by companies in return for construction contracts with Petrobras, the majority state-owned company, led to a reduction of 2 percent of GDP in Petrobras investments and a 5 percent reduction in gross fixed capital formation in addition to the embezzlement of about R$6.2 billion (0.13 percent of GDP) during 2004–12 (Costa and Dweck 2019). In Italy, development of the high-speed rail network has been dogged by corruption allegations and an average cost overrun of 216 percent for 13 railway construction projects in 2017, including a 917 percent cost overrun for the Milan–Florence railway line alone (Locatelli and others 2017). A corruption scandal involving private actors and politicians in South Africa has allegedly led to the embezzlement of US$7 billion (2 percent of GDP in 2017) in government funds (Transparency International 2019).

The level of discretion enjoyed by public officials is generally higher for capital expenditure than recurrent expenditure (Mauro 1998). Based on perception data, high-profile scandals, and theoretical considerations, investment in infrastructure is subject to high risks of corruption (Golden and Picci 2005; Kenny 2007). This is because infrastructure development tends to involve projects that are large, long-term, and complex—all fertile corruption grounds. Complex projects are also characterized by high degrees of information asymmetry, which makes it harder to detect misconduct in terms of inflated prices, inferior quality, or sluggish delivery (Golden and Picci 2005; Kenny 2006, 2007). Vulnerability

The authors thank Nestor Sawadogo and Sureni Weerathunga (research assistant) for assistance with data analysis.

**Figure 10.1. PIMA Results versus Corruption Indicators**

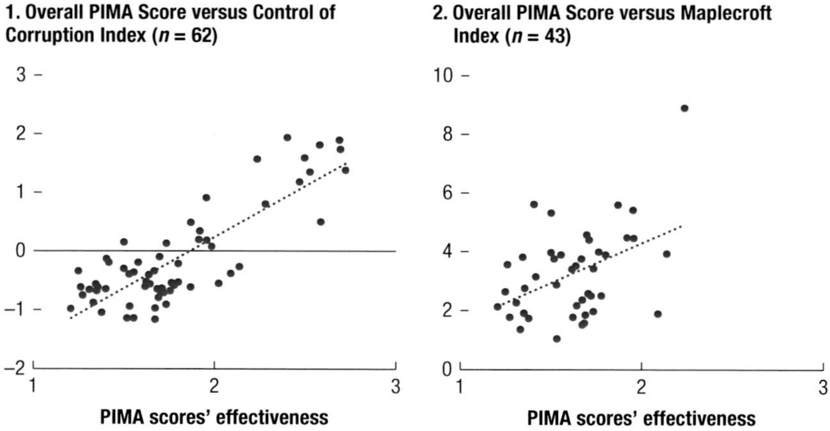

**1. Overall PIMA Score versus Control of Corruption Index (*n* = 62)**



**2. Overall PIMA Score versus Maplecroft Index (*n* = 43)**



Source: IMF estimates based on PIMA databases (2015–18), the Control of Corruption Index from the World Bank Worldwide Governance Indicators (2010–18), and the Maplecroft Index (2016–19).
Note: PIMA = Public Investment Management Assessment.

to corruption is accentuated in countries with weak institutional capacity for public investment planning, execution and evaluation, and lack of transparency in procurement practices, as shown in the case of the Republic of Congo (IMF 2019). There is a positive correlation between different indicators of control of corruption and weaknesses in public investment management institutions (Figure 10.1).

The direct costs of corruption include loss of public funds through misallocations or higher expenses and lower quality of infrastructure. Those who pay bribes aim to recover their money by inflating prices, billing for work not performed, failing to meet infrastructure contract standards, reducing the quality of work or using inferior materials. This results in much higher costs and lower quality of public infrastructure (for example, Lovei and McKechnie 2000; Deiniger and Mpuga 2005; and Hollands 2007).

Assessing the scale and cost of corruption along the public infrastructure cycle is challenging because corrupt behavior is secretive and usually does not leave a paper trail. At the same time, existing literature points to large incidences of corruption at some key stages of public investment. For example, estimates of 20–30 percent of project value lost through corruption are widespread (Stansbury 2005; Søreide and Williams 2014; Wells 2015). The Organisation for Economic Co-operation and Development (OECD) estimates that bribery in government procurement in OECD countries increases contract costs by 10–20 percent, suggesting that at least US$400 billion is lost to bribery every year (OECD 2009; see also OECD 2015a). The 2016 Rand Europe report for the European Parliament concluded that the costs of corruption in public procurement vary considerably between member states and average about €5 billion every year (Hafner and others 2016).[1]

This chapter discusses the types of corruption that generally occur along the public investment cycle and how they result in higher costs and lower quality of public infrastructure, introduces a risk-based approach to identify and analyze corruption risks in the context of specific institutional vulnerabilities, and proposes strategies to tackle corruption risks in infrastructure governance.[2]

## TYPES OF CORRUPTION IN THE PUBLIC INFRASTRUCTURE INVESTMENT CYCLE

Corruption can be defined as the "abuse of public office for private gain." This same definition is used in the IMF's Guidance Note on Governance (IMF 2018a) and is relied on by the World Bank.[3] A specific distinction exists between political corruption and administrative corruption. In the first, the public party involved in the corruption act is an elected official or a senior public servant. In the second, the public party is a less-senior member of the public service. Corruption cases could involve multiple private actors and a public actor.

Corruption can take many forms, ranging from small bribes to kickbacks, fraud, collusion, embezzlement, extortion, influence peddling, and unlawful interest or beneficial ownership (Table 10.1). These activities constitute criminal offences in most jurisdictions although the precise definition of the offense may differ. Each form of corruption differs in its impact at various stages of the investment project cycle and relative to types of projects (Bowen, Edwards, and Cattell 2012; Brown and Loosemore 2015; Transparency International 2016).

**TABLE 10.1.**

Forms of Corruption during the Infrastructure Cycle and Their Fiscal Implications

| Form of Corruption | Examples during Infrastructure Cycle | Fiscal Implication |
|---|---|---|
| *Bribery* refers to giving, promising, soliciting, accepting, or offering a benefit to entice a government official to act in an unethical or illegal manner. Enticements can be in the form of rewards, loans, gifts, donations, special treatment, or services. | Bribes paid by firms to win contracts, approve contract amendments and extensions, and influence auditors; facilitation payments made to speed up an action | Increase in the cost of infrastructure as the payers of the bribe try to recover it in various ways (inflating the price of bids, overinvoicing, supplying low-quality material, and so on) |

*(continued)*

[1] Fazekas and Koscis (2015) constructed an objective measure of corruption in public procurement, making use of a range of public procurement red flags to create a composite measure called the Corruption Risk Index.

[2] We do not discuss ex post legal penal measures, which are beyond the scope of this chapter.

[3] There are various other—but somewhat similar—definitions of corruption. According to public office–centered definitions, corruption in government is generally defined as the abuse or misuse of public office or authority for private gain that occurs when public officials interact with private sector actors.

**TABLE 10.1. *(continued)***

| Forms of Corruption during the Infrastructure Cycle and Their Fiscal Implications | | |
|---|---|---|
| **Form of Corruption** | **Examples during Infrastructure Cycle** | **Fiscal Implication** |
| A *kickback* is payment by a successful bidder to a third party who facilitated obtaining the bid by making a secret payment for a biased decision. | Based on an arrangement before bidding, the winning bid overstates the price to finance kickbacks | Increases the cost of infrastructure as the payers of kickbacks try to recover it in various ways |
| *Fraud* refers to illicit documentary practices or an act of deception with an intention to cheat, with the aim of gaining an illegal or unfair advantage (for example, contract award or financial benefit). | Subverting bid qualification requirements; diverting project assets; setting up front or shell companies[1] to create the illusion of competition or to conceal ownership | Lower quality or higher cost of infrastructure; leakage of public resources without any tangible infrastructure development |
| *Collusion* is an undisclosed arrangement among parties involved—in the private or public sector or both—who conspire with the intention of gaining illegitimate rewards or financial gain. | Bid rigging, when consenting bidders settle on the results of a bid process beforehand; price fixing, when a group of tenderers collude to fix prices; cartelization, when firms agree to fix the prices of goods they control | Higher contract prices and therefore higher costs for implementing an infrastructure project |
| *Embezzlement* occurs when an official misappropriates assets, goods, or funds that were entrusted to him or her and uses them for personal gain. | The most common form is officials who steal from the state budget or extrabudgetary or slush funds and siphon off project funds or materials | Loss of public resources or need for additional allocation to cover lost funds or materials |
| *Extortion* happens when a person in a powerful position, directly or through intermediaries, asks and receives any undue pecuniary or other advantage. | An incumbent political party asking an oil company that participates in public investment for a contribution to finance its election campaign | Diversion of public resources when coercive power is used to distort project planning for private gain |
| *Influence peddling* and *abuse of authority* occurs when a person misuses his or her status or authority over the decision-making process in return for financial favors or other benefits. | A powerful or high-level public official monopolizes key decisions or unlawfully interferes with decision-making at various stages to influence the outcome and so generate private gain | Wrong selection of infrastructure or excessively high prices paid for infrastructure project design and implementation |
| *Unlawful interest* or *beneficial ownership* occurs when a person in public office acts contrary to his or her duty and in breach of public trust. It may also involve a conflict of interest that affects his or her judgement. This includes favoring friends or relatives for public contracts. | A public official secretly owns (or is a director of) a company and wrongly decides in its favor because of a conflict of interest that affects his impartiality; public funds diverted to companies, individuals, or groups in which the public official has unlawful interest | Misallocation and diversion of public resources when infrastructure investment allocation and execution are unduly driven by personal rather than public interest |

Sources: Adapted from Choi and Thum 1998; Paterson and Chaudhuri 2007; Stansbury and Stansbury 2008; Fan, Lin, and Treisman 2010; Financial Action Task Force 2012; OECD 2016a, 2016b; Chan and Owusu 2017; Sobjak 2018; Agence Française Anti-Corruption 2019; and IMF staff.

[1] Front or shell companies refer to limited liability companies or corporations that have no corporal existence regarding jurisdiction and no commercial activities, nor are they made up of any real employees. They are normally established within secrecy for shielding the actual beneficial proprietor from disclosures, taxes, or both.

## CORRUPTION RISKS AT DIFFERENT STAGES OF THE PUBLIC INFRASTRUCTURE CYCLE

This chapter uses an analytical framework that highlights potential risks of corruption at various phases in the public infrastructure cycle and how institutional weaknesses exacerbate vulnerabilities to these risks.

Corruption can occur at any phase of the investment cycle, inflicting different costs and implying different mitigation strategies (Kenny 2006, 2009; Benitez, Estache, and Søreide 2010). Potential risks to corruption arise in five key phases of the public infrastructure cycle (Figure 10.2): (1) infrastructure project identification and preparation, including project planning, costing, and appraisal, (2) project selection and financing, (3) project procurement, (4) project implementation and contract management, and (5) the maintenance of infrastructure assets. These phases in public investment management provide opportunities for government officials, project funders, consultants, contractors, subcontractors, suppliers, joint venture partners, agents, and other actors to take decisions or manipulate information in such a way as to derive undue benefits. Table 10.2 lists specific corruption risks in each of these phases.

**Figure 10.2. Key Phases along the Infrastructure Cycle Posing Corruption Risks**

Source: Adapted from OECD 2015b.

**TABLE 10.2.**

**Specific Corruption Risks in Key Phases of the Infrastructure Cycle**

| Phase | Specific Corruption Risks |
|---|---|
| Project Identification and Preparation | Political influence or lobbying by private firms that introduces bias favoring projects that suit political or private interests; promotion of projects in return for party funds; political influence to favor large projects and new construction over maintenance; underestimated costs and overestimated benefits to get projects approved without adequate economic justification; lack of independent checks on the feasibility of projects; and inadequate project formulation opening the scope of litigation during project execution. |
| Project Selection and Financing | Costly project designs that increase fees and profits of consultants and contractors who may share the gain with public officials; designs that favor a specific contractor during procurement; incomplete designs that leave room for later adjustments that can be manipulated; high cost estimates to provide a cushion for the diversion of funds during project execution; political influence or abuse of authority vested with a senior official to get projects into the budget without appraisal; off-budget financing of infrastructure projects; bilateral funding tied to "sole source" procurement of the project; and pledging future streams of revenue or in-kind payments to secure project financing. |
| Procurement | Bribery to obtain infrastructure project contracts and recovering the cost of bribery during contract execution; collusion among bidders to allocate contracts or raise prices, potentially with assistance from public procurement officials; influence, interference, or manipulation of tender evaluations by public officials to favor specific firms for contract awards; and launching the tender process and signing contracts for projects that are not in the budget, aiming for their regularization later on. |
| Project Implementation | Collusion between the project contractor and supervising engineer that results in the use of lower-quality materials and substandard work or an increase in the contract price, covers losses caused by the fault of the contractor, or recovers money spent on bribes or kickbacks; and false accounting or duplicate invoicing for unlawful payments to contractors. |
| Asset Maintenance | Collusion or agreement by the supervising engineer to accept poor-quality work during maintenance, leading to rapid deterioration of the infrastructure asset; lack of allocated funds for maintenance, as new construction takes precedence over maintenance; and the absence of an updated inventory of assets. |

Source: IMF staff.

The subsequent analysis is based on IMF staff calculations using data from the Public Investment Management Assessment (PIMA) database (2015–18), the Public Expenditure and Financial Accountability (PEFA) assessments database (2008–18), the Control of Corruption Index from the World Bank Worldwide Governance Indicators (average during 2010–18), and the Maplecroft Index (average during 2016–19).[4]

[4] The PIMA is the IMF's key tool for assessing infrastructure governance along the full investment cycle (see Chapter 5 of this book). The PIMA sample used in this chapter includes assessments of 62 countries (52 field assessments and 10 desk-based assessments) and the results use a standardized methodology. The PEFA sample covers 111 countries. The Control of Corruption Index provides a relative measure of perceived corruption that ranges from –2.5 (high corruption) to 2.5 (low corruption). The Maplecroft Index assesses risk by modeling the strength of anti corruption legislation, the efficacy and independence of anti corruption bodies, and the prevalence of corruption from a business perspective; the index ranges from 0 (high risk to corruption) to 9 (less risk to corruption). For further discussion on the Control of Corruption and Maplecroft indexes, see IMF (2017a, 2017b).

## INFRASTRUCTURE PROJECT IDENTIFICATION AND PREPARATION

The infrastructure project identification and preparation phase involves infrastructure planning and project costing and appraisal. Significant opportunities for corruption arise during this phase, particularly when institutions related to identifying, appraising, and prioritizing public infrastructure investment are weak. A positive correlation is found between different indicators of control of corruption and project appraisal (Box 10.1). National and sectoral planning has a positive correlation with the Control of Corruption Index and not with the Maplecroft Index, which may be because whereas many countries have formal national or sectoral plans, they are often fragmented, not properly costed, and do not systematically inform public investment decisions (see IMF 2018b; and Chapter 12 of this book). However, as pointed out in the literature, some of the worst forms of grand corruption and state capture happen at this stage of the project cycle (Wells 2015).

Failures in project preparation, which may be caused by corruption, can also create opportunities for corruption later in the infrastructure cycle. For example, inadequate project preparation increases the risk of arbitration and litigation during the project execution stage. It may also lead to subsequent project implementation delays that may require changes to suppliers' contract or project specifications that can be manipulated for private gain. The cases of Peru and the Republic of Congo illustrate such risks when the formulation and appraisal of infrastructure projects are weak (Box 10.2).

Corruption in the project identification and preparation phase can impact the various forms of investment:

- Bribes to win contracts are often tied to project costs (Locatelli and others 2017), so there is a strong incentive to promote large new projects over small projects such as maintenance and rehabilitation.
- Sectors such as construction, transport, and the extractive industries are typically more vulnerable to rent seeking and corruption (OECD 2014).
- Several studies have shown that countries with high corruption tend to invest less in education and health systems and favor prestigious infrastructure projects that may have low economic and social benefits (Vargas and Sommer 2014).
- The influence of politicians or other stakeholders with vested interests can lead to project appraisals that are manipulated or skewed to justify projects with low rates of return or that are unviable, the so-called white elephants.[5]

---

[5] A white elephant is a project that fails to meet public demand and whose costs of construction, operation, and maintenance are not justified by its ultimate economic and social return.

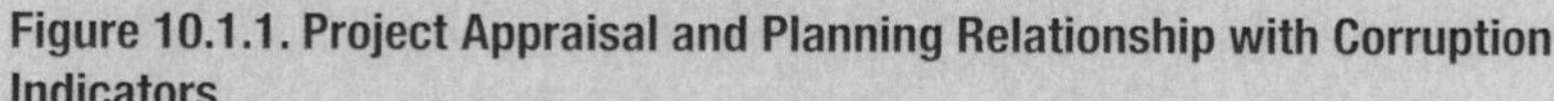

## Box 10.1. Project Appraisal and Planning Relationship with Corruption Indicators

### Figure 10.1.1. Project Appraisal and Planning Relationship with Corruption Indicators

1. Project Appraisal ($n$ = 62)

Control of Corruption Index

PIMA scores' effectiveness

2. Project Appraisal ($n$ = 43)

Maplecroft Index

PIMA scores' effectiveness

3. National and Sectoral Planning ($n$ = 62)

Control of Corruption Index

PIMA scores' effectiveness

4. National and Sectoral Planning ($n$ = 43)

Maplecroft Index

PIMA scores' effectiveness

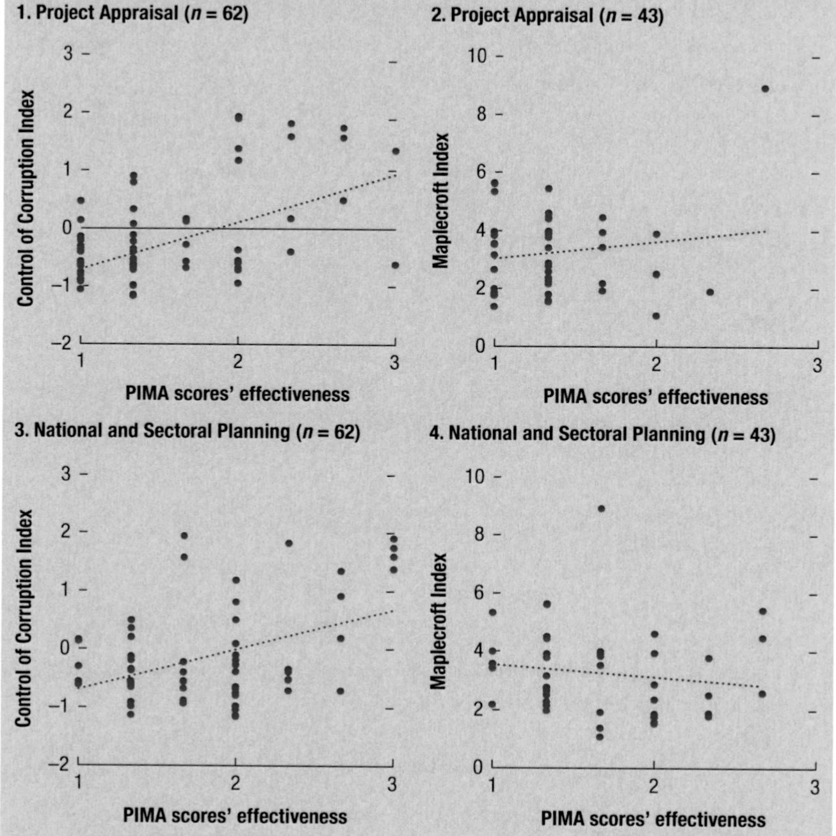

Source: IMF estimates based on PIMA databases (2015–18), the Control of Corruption Index from the World Bank Worldwide Governance Indicators (2010–18), and the Maplecroft Index (2016–19).
Note: In the case of project appraisal, the correlations with corruption indicators are both positive using PIMA indicators. With control of corruption, the PIMA indicator for project selection shows that $r$ = 0.53. With the Maplecroft Index, the PIMA indicator for project selection shows that $r$ = 0.15. In the case of national and sectoral planning, the correlation using PIMA indicators is positive only for the Control of Corruption Index ($r$ = 0.44) but not for the Maplecroft Index ($r$ = –0.14). PIMA = Public Investment Management Assessment.

**Box 10.2. Peru and the Republic of Congo: Project Preparation and Appraisal**

**Peru**

In Peru, deficient specifications for technical studies—including the lack of independent checks on the feasibility of projects—reduced the attractiveness of the public tender, lessening competition and leading to implementation problems. Inadequate project formulation also led to lengthy arbitration and litigation during the project execution stage, increasing the opportunities for corruption. Implementation of the September 2018 legislative decree on the budget system (DL 1440) should strengthen project selection and budgeting. In addition, the authorities are taking steps to make the external audit more effective. The *Contraloria General* (Comptroller General) is starting more proactive monitoring to prevent corruption across all levels of government as effective internal controls are absent. To be effective, however, it will require significant improvements to the capacity of external auditors and a prioritization of their tasks based on a risk assessment.

**Republic of Congo**

In the Republic of Congo, during the infrastructure planning phase, projects are not systematically subject to a rigorous technical, economic, and financial appraisal, which raises concerns about their overall efficiency (Republic of Congo 2018; Melina, Selim, and Verdugo-Yepes 2019) and corruption risks. To the extent that such appraisals are done, they do not undergo independent external review and are not published. Anecdotal evidence suggests that construction contracts are often allocated to members of the governing coalition, particularly if these contracts involve projects that provide high-value consumption goods to the Congolese elite (Bertelsmann Transformation Index 2018).

Sources: Hernandez 2012; Solis 2017; Andina 2018; Republic of Congo 2018; and El Peruano 2019.

## INFRASTRUCTURE PROJECT SELECTION AND FINANCING

This phase involves infrastructure project selection, detailed design, accurate costing, and selecting the type of funding for the project (including allocation through the budget). The parties to project financing transactions include the project owner who is seeking funding for the project, prospective funders, officials and engineers in charge of detailed design, and consultants advising those parties; for example, in relation to the viability of the project. There is a positive correlation between different indicators of control of corruption and project selection (Box 10.3).

Corruption in this phase can take various forms, with different consequences (see Box 10.4):

- Bribery or kickbacks could push projects funded by a donor who selects the construction company as a condition of funding (without tender),[6] or when

[6] For example, during 2014–17, most of the road investment projects in Congo financed within the strategic partnership with China used a restricted call for tender (IMF 2019, 102).

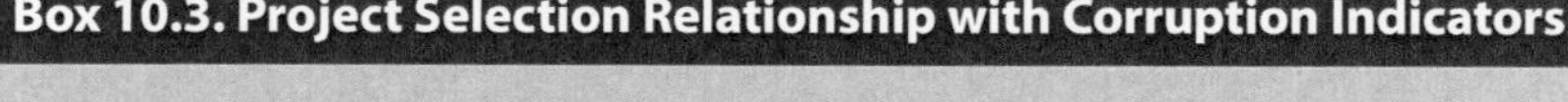

## Box 10.3. Project Selection Relationship with Corruption Indicators

**Figure 10.3.1. Control of Corruption Index and Maplecroft Index: Project Selection**

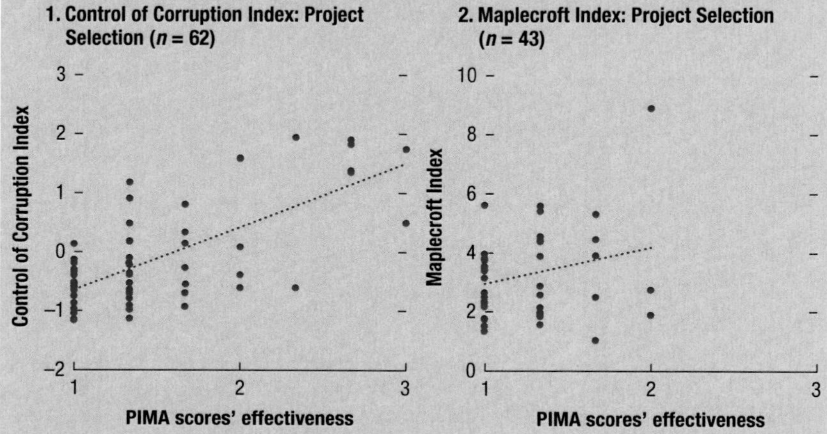


Source: IMF estimates based on PIMA databases (2015–18), the Control of Corruption Index from the World Bank Worldwide Governance Indicators (2010–18), and the Maplecroft Index (2016–19).
Note: In the case of project selection, the correlations with corruption indicators are both positive using PIMA indicators. With control of corruption, the PIMA indicator for project selection shows that $r = 0.70$. With the Maplecroft Index, the PIMA indicator for project selection shows that $r = 0.25$.
PIMA = Public Investment Management Assessment.

projects or public-private partnerships are prioritized by companies that have tendered for the contracts concerned.

- Project appraisals may be manipulated by the deliberate overestimation of benefits and underestimation of costs, so that projects with low economic returns are selected in return for financial favors or other benefits to the official in charge of selection.
- The detailed design of a project may be manipulated. This includes overdesign—increasing the project size or specifications—to prepare high cost estimates that provide a cushion for later diversion of funds and incomplete design that leaves room for changes during project execution. For example, site and soil investigations and environmental impact assessments may be excluded from the initial design, requiring expensive adjustments at later stages.[7]

[7] Although adjustments may occur because of unexpected events or circumstances, even when a project is adequately designed, starting off without a complete plan opens the door to postcontract negotiations and opportunistic behavior.

## Box 10.4. Off-Budget Financing, Influence Peddling, and Manipulating Project Cost-Benefit

### Republic of Congo

The Republic of Congo's weak capacity to reconcile the government's share of oil revenue under various production-sharing agreements and actual revenue received by the Treasury translated into substantial off-budget oil revenue which was used largely to finance infrastructure projects, including a power station (Extractive Industries Transparency Initiative 2015). Because these transactions bypassed the budget process for appraisal and selection and the requirements of the public procurement code, there are concerns about their integrity. As noted in Republic of Congo (2018), this rapid scaling up of public investment has occurred in a nontransparent, inefficient environment amid strong perceptions of corruption.

### Kenya

In Kenya, Burgess and others (2009) found strong evidence that road expansion in any given year is closely related to the home regions of the prime minister and minister for public works and to those of other ethnic groups represented in the Cabinet. One outcome of this phenomenon is deterioration of the road network in areas that lack political connections (Wales and Wild 2012).

### India

In India, Enron's Dabhol Power Corporation signed a deal to produce electricity at a price seven times higher than other providers. This occurred despite warnings from the World Bank that the project was too expensive. It was later alleged that local politicians had been bribed (Kenny and Søreide 2008).

### Uganda

In Uganda, Booth and Golooba-Mutebi (2009) concluded that "the evidence indicates that, under the pre-2008 arrangements, the roads divisions of the Ministry of Works operated as a well-oiled machine for generating corrupt earnings from kickbacks." They then showed how this operated as a complex system of political patronage. Public officials raised money in different ways, including accepting bribes for awarding contracts and signing completion certificates.

### Worldwide

In a review of 258 megatransport projects worldwide, Flyvbjerg (2007) found costs seriously underestimated at the time of the decision to build. He argued that this could not be solely attributed to a lack of experience or to the existence of "optimism bias" among planners and promoters, but in many cases, deception is deliberate and can be traced to political and organization pressures, agency problems, and distorted incentives (see also Flyvbjerg, Garbuio, and Lovallo 2009).

Sources: Extractive Industries Transparency Initiative 2015; Republic of Congo 2018; Wells 2015.

- Influence peddling by high-ranking officials may occur in the selection and funding of projects to achieve personal gain.
- The projects could be financed off budget to circumvent scrutiny procedures (see Box 10.4) or could be implemented through state-owned enterprises, which may have looser selection criteria or be subject to less oversight.

## INFRASTRUCTURE PROCUREMENT

Procurement of public infrastructure is among the government activities most vulnerable to corruption (OECD 2016b). Corruption risks in this phase increase when the central procurement authority is weak and tendering is neither competitive nor transparent. Countries with a higher perception of corruption tend to have a tendering process that is less open and competitive (Box 10.5). In addition to the volume of transactions and the financial interests at stake, corruption risks are exacerbated by processes that are overly complex, and where there is a close interaction and possible collusion between public officials, businesses, and other stakeholders. The OECD's (2014) "Foreign Bribery Report" provides additional evidence that public procurement is vulnerable to corruption. It shows that more than half of foreign bribery cases occurred to obtain a public procurement contract.

Corruption in this phase can take various forms and have different consequences:

- To facilitate rent seeking and corruption, the tendering process may not be open and competitive, leading to a higher cost of procurement and lower quality of infrastructure provision. Box 10.6 discusses the example of Spain, illustrating how lack of transparency in tenders led to corrupt practices, and Korea, where the authorities have introduced measures to ensure procurement is more transparent and competitive.
- Corruption may occur in the awarding of a public procurement contract or a public-private partnership when, for private gain, public officials share inside information with a potential bidder, manipulate the tender evaluation, provide false reasons for a direct award, or allow modifications to the bid parameters in a nontransparent manner that favors the winning bidder.
- Bidders may collude through other mechanisms (for example, bid suppression or bid rotation)[8] to give the appearance of competition. Such collusion and bid-rigging practices are believed to be widespread in many parts of the world, including in some advanced economies. Evidence is difficult to obtain, but the work of the Office of Fair Trading in the United Kingdom and the Charbonneau Commission in Québec, Canada, provide useful insights on this process (Box 10.6).

---

[8] Bid suppression occurs when some of the conspirators agree not to submit bids, allowing another conspirator to win the contract. Bid rotation refers to the practice of competing firms "taking turns" at winning the contract. Bid rotation is in effect a form of market allocation in which competitors enter into an agreement to get a fair share of the industry profits.

## Box 10.5. Infrastructure Procurement Practices and Corruption Indicators

### Figure 10.5.1. Infrastructure Procurement Practices and Corruption Indicators

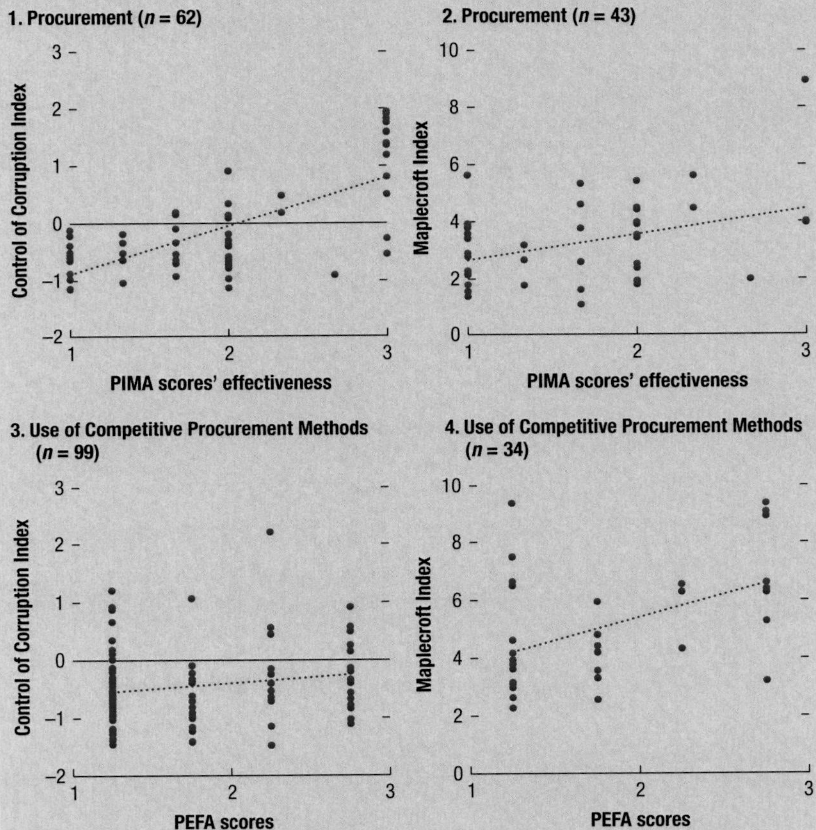


Source: IMF estimates based on PIMA databases (2015–18) and PEFA databases (2008–18), the Control of Corruption Index from the World Bank Worldwide Governance Indicators (2010–18), and the Maplecroft Index (2016–19).

Note: In the case of procurement with corruption, indicators are positive using PIMA and PEFA indicators. For procurement (PIMA scores in effectiveness), the correlation with control of corruption is $r = 0.70$. With the Maplecroft Index, PIMA scores show that $r = 0.36$. In the case of PEFA scores, the indicator more closely related to procurement shows that $r = 0.12$ with control of corruption. With the Maplecroft Index, the PEFA indicator for procurement shows that $r = 0.18$. PEFA = Public Expenditure and Financial Accountability; PIMA = Public Investment Management Assessment.

## Box 10.6. Infrastructure Procurement: Issues and Reforms in Selected Countries

### Spain

In Spain, the government's poorly programmed infrastructure investment during 1995–2016 was accompanied by lack of transparency during the tendering. Recent cases reveal that bid rigging, biased scoring rules in contract assignment, and especially renegotiations after contracts came into force played major roles in facilitating corrupt deals. The government acted to bring more transparency to infrastructure investments and to reduce corruption (Spanish "Comision Nacional de los Mercados y la Competencia; CNMC 2018, 2019). This included measures to sanction bid rigging. For example, the National Commission of Markets and Competition of Spain sanctioned 15 building companies (that had created cartels to distort competition in public tenders) and 14 managers for unlawfully dividing public tenders for electrification and electromechanical systems on conventional and high-speed rail lines. For the first time, the National Commission of Markets and Competition activated the procedure for the prohibition of contracting with the government.

### Korea

In Korea, the implementation of a national procurement system (KONEPs or GePS, in Korean), a one-stop shop for public procurement, has brought notable improvement in the transparency and integrity of the public procurement administration. In 2002, the Public Procurement Service, the central procurement agency of Korea, introduced a fully integrated, end-to-end e-procurement system. This covers the entire procurement cycle electronically (including for one-time registration, tendering, contracts, inspection, and payment), and related documents are exchanged online. All public organizations are mandated to publish tenders through the system, which provides information in real time. In the Fingerprint Recognition e-Bidding system, introduced by the Public Procurement Service in 2010, each user can tender for only one company, by using a biometric security token. Fingerprint information is stored only in the concerned supplier's file, to prevent any controversy over the government's storage of personal biometric information. In 2012, more than 62.7 percent of Korea's total public procurement (US$106 billion) was conducted through the system. Participation in public tenders has increased and transparency improved considerably, eliminating corruption by preventing and detecting illegal practices and collusive acts. This has led to public sector savings of US$1.4 billion (OECD 2016a, 2016b). In addition, the time to process a bid has been reduced from 30 hours to 2 hours (OECD 2016a, 2016b).

### Canada

In Québec, Canada, the Commission of Inquiry on the Awarding and Management of Public Contracts in the Construction Industry (the "Charbonneau Commission") was created in 2011 to examine collusion or corruption in the award or management of public contracts in Québec's construction industry. The report, released in 2015, found that schemes of collusion and corruption were widespread (Charbonneau Commission 2015).

### United Kingdom

In the United Kingdom, the Office of Fair Trading (2009) found that firms colluded in setting artificially high prices in bidding for public infrastructure construction work. Firms would

**Box 10.6 (continued)**

decide which contracts they wanted, and rivals would bid purposefully high prices. This is a practice known as "cover pricing." In 2009, the Office of Fair Trading issued its decision, which saw fines totaling £129.2 million imposed on 103 construction firms that were found to have engaged in bid-rigging activities across 199 tenders from 2000 to 2006. In 11 of these bids, the winning bidder faced no genuine competition as all other bids were cover bids. The Office of Fair Trading also found six instances in which successful bidders had paid an agreed-upon sum of money to the unsuccessful bidder.

Source: OECD 2016b.

## INFRASTRUCTURE PROJECT IMPLEMENTATION

This phase involves project execution and contract management. Corruption risks in project implementation increase when there is weak supervision, monitoring, and enforcement of the related contract. Weak internal controls and oversight arrangements, including internal and external audits, also increase the chances of corrupt behavior by rent-seeking actors. Equally, the presence of corrupt officials may deter governments from introducing and facilitating effective audit procedures.[9] Box 10.7 shows that weak external audit follow-up and ineffective internal audits are associated with a high level of corruption.

Deng and others (2003) reported that the most costly and serious corruption cases may occur after a contract is awarded, during the project implementation stage. Although implementation delays are easy to detect, assessing implementation quality is less straightforward, because the effects may be visible only after many years. Corruption during the procurement phase typically also affects this phase. For example, companies that paid bribes in the procurement process may seek to recover the bribes by inflating the prices of goods and services, submitting invoices for work not performed, and failing to meet contract terms and standards.

During the project implementation phase, corruption can take various forms, with different consequences:

- There may be deficient supervision from public officials or collusion between contractors and supervising officials.[10] Enforcement of the quality standards and performance standards in a contract may be compromised as a result.

[9] For example, finance ministries sometimes set up internal audit units but starve them of information and influence.

[10] Collusion between supervising engineers and contractors is almost always a requirement for corruption during project implementation, as the supervising engineer controls most of the avenues through which corruption occurs.

## Box 10.7. Internal and External Audit Effectiveness and Corruption Indicators

### Figure 10.7.1. Internal and External Audit Effectiveness and Corruption Indicators

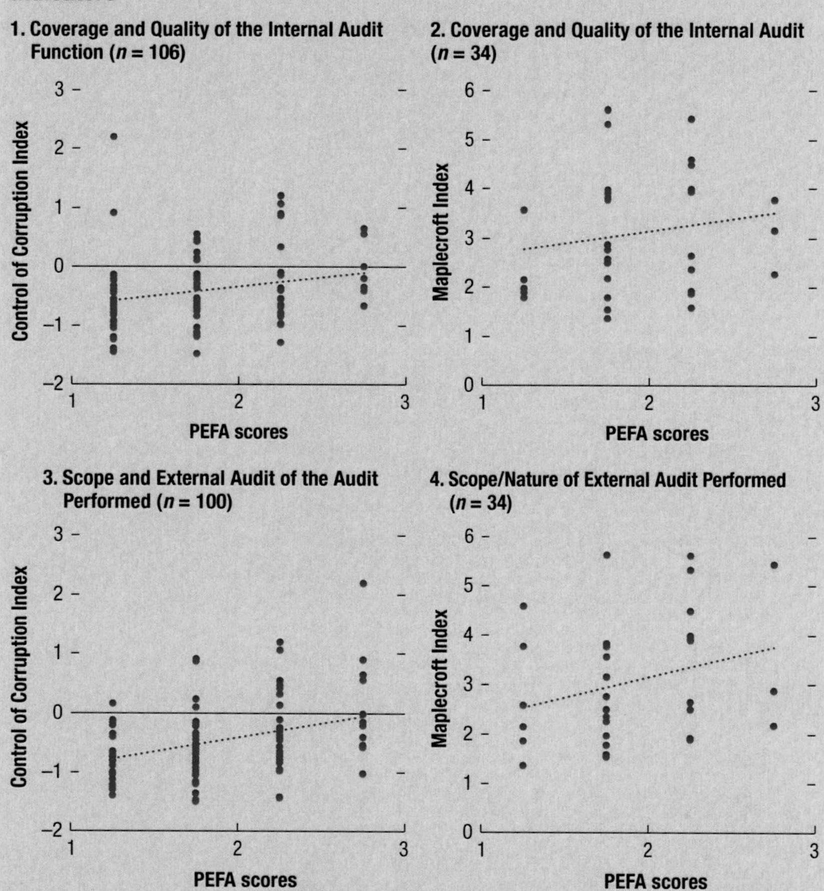


Source: IMF estimates based on PEFA databases (2008–18), the Control of Corruption Index from the World Bank Worldwide Governance Indicators (2010–18), and the Maplecroft Index (2016–19).
Note: In the case of the internal audit relationship with corruption indicators, the correlation with the Control of Corruption Index is 22.8, and the correlation with the Maplecroft Index is 16.1. In the case of external audit, the relationship is stronger with $r = 36.7$ for control of corruption and $r = 22.8$ for Maplecroft index. PEFA = Public Expenditure and Financial Accountability.

**Box 10.8. Brazil: Lack of Internal Controls in State Firms Undertaking Public Investment**

Serious vulnerabilities in the internal control framework of Brazil's national oil company, Petrobras, and weaknesses in its governance structure and operational accountability set the stage for a corruption payment scheme within the company from 2004 to 2012, resulting in about US$2.5 billion of losses in public resources. A group of companies colluded to get contracts with Petrobras, overcharge, and divert some of the funds, partly to illegally finance political parties. A fragmented external oversight system, involving multiple government agencies (the regulatory body, audit institutions, and the supervising ministry), was not able to detect the irregularities. Petrobras subsequently developed control mechanisms and introduced measures to improve its anti corruption standards and increase transparency in reaction to corruption scandals uncovered by the "Car Wash" investigation task force in 2014. It has approved a corruption prevention program (*Programa Petrobras de Prevenção da Corrupção*, or PPPC) that focuses on the prevention, detection, and punishment of acts of fraud and corruption. As a result of the investigations, the Anti-Corruption Law 12.846/2013 and its regulation Decree 8.420/2015 were also enacted, allowing for strengthened external oversight by audit institutions and other external regulatory and supervisory agencies.

Sources: Engel and others 2018; Petrobras 2019.

- Substantial changes in contract conditions may be introduced to allow more time or higher prices for the bidder for private gain (shared between the contractor and corrupt public officials).
- Product substitution or work that fails to meet contract specifications may result from collusion or weak supervision.
- The absence of effective internal control systems creates opportunity for fraudulent practices such as false accounting, cost misallocation, cost migration between contracts, and false or duplicate invoicing for goods and services not supplied. Box 10.8 illustrates how weak internal controls led to massive corruption in public investment by Petrobras, Brazil's national oil company.

The literature also demonstrates costs that may arise from inadequate monitoring of project implementation. For example, based on independent engineers' estimates, increased monitoring of road projects in Indonesian villages led to an approximately 8 percent reduction in unexplained material costs (Olken 2007).

## INFRASTRUCTURE ASSET MAINTENANCE

Infrastructure assets, which are typically of high value, open opportunities for corruption during operation and maintenance, particularly where a sound framework for maintenance management and strong internal control systems are lacking. Such a framework would include an up-to-date register of all public infrastructure assets and regular checks to verify their condition and report damage and lack of proper maintenance.

**Box 10.9. Australia: Corruption in Maintenance of Rail Tracks**

The Independent Commission Against Corruption of Australia investigated state railway operator RailCorp in 2008 and found that employees had improperly allocated contracts worth almost $A19 million to companies owned by themselves, friends, or family in return for corrupt payments totaling more than $A2.5 million. Timesheet manipulation was also widespread in parts of RailCorp and had been for decades. Nicknamed "job and knock," it was most common in services to maintain and repair rail track such as welding. The practice was so pervasive that it was impossible for RailCorp to estimate actual labor requirements for infrastructure maintenance and infrastructure projects. There was evidence that supervisors' tolerance of job and knock allowed it to continue and encouraged new staff to adopt it. A focus on outcomes was used to justify bending rules to get things done so that as long as rail track was being repaired or maintained, management and staff were willing to ignore proper tender procedures and record-keeping requirements.

Source: Independent Commission Against Corruption 2008.

During the maintenance phase, corruption can take forms such as bribery, fraud, collusion, and embezzlement, and have different consequences:

- In the absence of standards and clear guidelines for infrastructure asset maintenance, the estimates and budget allocations for maintenance could be falsified; moreover, it may be difficult to assess later whether assets have been adequately maintained.
- Officials may collude with a third party to submit false or inflated invoices for asset repair and maintenance costs or may purchase resources above actual needs to dispose of the surplus for personal gain (see the example of Australia in Box 10.9).
- Officials may change the status of an asset from current to obsolete without justification or provide for unjustified early retirement or disposal of an asset to aid a third party or for personal gain.
- Officials may deliberately undervalue assets that are to be disposed to aid a third party or for personal gain.
- Maintenance projects may be neglected in favor of inappropriate and extensive new investment projects in which the scope for rent-seeking is much higher.

## ADDRESSING CORRUPTION RISKS IN THE PUBLIC INFRASTRUCTURE CYCLE

Measures to mitigate corruption risks along the infrastructure cycle need to be considered in six areas:

- *A proactive approach to corruption risk management.* This approach would include clear anti corruption policies, with a focus on continual improvement;

strengthening the due diligence and vetting process for contractors and other third parties; communicating and consistently reevaluating ethics and compliance standards for public officials and private actors involved in public infrastructure; and carrying out random anti corruption reviews of infrastructure projects during implementation.

- *Clear delineation of authority for decision-making without conflict of interest.* This may require institutional reforms to assign clear roles and responsibilities, regulate or limit authority for decision-making, and identify and manage conflicts of interest transparently to avoid abuses of office.
- *Transparent frameworks and criteria for making infrastructure decisions.* This includes clear regulatory frameworks and methodologies for processing information to produce key outputs and reports that feed into decision-making on infrastructure and reduce the discretion available to public officials to influence decisions for private gain, including digitalizing the processing of information wherever possible (to reduce the scope for human intervention).
- *Effective arrangements to enforce accountability for decisions taken, backed by sustained anti corruption and anti–money-laundering interventions.* Improving accountability entails efforts to improve both the detection and the sanctioning of corrupt acts, including an alert system to signal corruption risks and suspicious behaviors by relevant actors.
- *A robust and effective framework for transparent reporting and disclosure of relevant information at all key decision points.*[11] This reporting should be timely and complemented by a credible whistleblower[12] system (in both the public and the private sectors).[13]
- *Integrity of transactions of private firms and actors involved in public infrastructure.* Private sector companies and executives should comply with internationally accepted internal control and accounting practices in their transactions with public agencies and officials for public infrastructure development and maintenance. Studies, however, show that infrastructure construction companies have paid inflated contract costs using sham

[11] Key decision points are project identification, selection, financing, procurement, and implementation. For transparent reporting and disclosure, the relevant information should include the cost of the project or the contract, the actors involved in the decision-making, criteria for the decision, the potential conflicts of interest and how they have been addressed, and the relevant public agencies and private firms or actors in charge of processing information for decision-making or project implementation.

[12] A *whistleblower* is any person who exposes or reports an activity that is deemed illegal or unethical.

[13] In several countries, whistleblowers are protected by law. For example, Italy has adopted a new law (No 179/2017 of November 30, 2017) that aims to strengthen protection for whistleblowers in the public sector and adds new protections for those in the private sector. France also recently enacted the Sapin II Act on transparency for tackling corruption, which regulates whistleblowing programs aimed at ensuring protection of whistleblowers.

invoices, recorded these items as legitimate expenses for goods or services, and then consolidated them in their records.[14]

Table 10.3 summarizes key institutional reforms in infrastructure governance to deal with vulnerabilities to corruption, and it proposes some illustrative indicators and "red flags" to alert policymakers and citizens to potential risks and to help them detect corruption. These measures should be backed by (1) strong anti corruption institutions and credible penal actions against corrupt actors (whether in the public or private sector) when corrupt transactions are detected, (2) the development of an anti corruption compliance framework in the private sector, and (3) anti–money-laundering measures (see Box 10.10).

**TABLE 10.3.**

**Measures and Indicators to Prevent and Detect Corruption in Public Infrastructure**

| Stage in Public Infrastructure Cycle | Preventing Corruption: Institutional Reform Measures | Detecting Corruption: Illustrative Indicators/Red Flags |
|---|---|---|
| Infrastructure Project Identification and Preparation | • Integrated infrastructure planning framework<br>• Comprehensive database to forecast the need for new infrastructure projects and maintenance<br>• Clear national, regional, or sectoral objectives for infrastructure<br>• Inclusion of lifetime costs of the project and asset preservation costs in project appraisal<br>• Independent external scrutiny of project appraisal, especially for major projects<br>• Publishing information on originally estimated and updated total cost of projects | • Project planning limited to only one alternative<br>• Absence of economic evaluation/cost-benefit analysis of project<br>• Misrepresentation of costs or benefits to skew the results of economic analysis<br>• High percentage of growth of public investment compared with growth of infrastructure maintenance expenditure |
| Infrastructure Project Selection and Financing | • Clear criteria for project prioritization, selection, and funding<br>• Project costs estimated accurately before funding<br>• Project detailed design reflects the ground reality to prevent unnecessary alterations during implementation<br>• Public and community participation in project design and selection<br>• Credible social, economic, and environmental feasibility studies<br>• Planning and implementing land acquisition and resettlement polices before implementation<br>• Checks and balances to prevent elected officials from choosing projects to benefit firms that contributed to their political campaigns | • Project selection decision taken without feasibility study and project appraisal<br>• Projects funded off-budget<br>• Extrabudgetary funds with earmarked revenue as vehicles for public investment<br>• Failure to budget realistically<br>• Donor funding secured for project by pledging collateralized future revenue<br>• Bids much higher or lower than the estimated project costs<br>• Cost per unit significantly higher than for similar projects |

*(continued)*

[14] For example, the companies Halliburton and Kinross Gold (Canada-based gold mining company) agreed to pay more than US$29.2 million and US$950,000, respectively, as penalty for their failure to implement adequate accounting controls (US Securities and Exchange Commission 2017, 2018).

**TABLE 10.3. *(continued)***

| Measures and Indicators to Prevent and Detect Corruption in Public Infrastructure | | |
|---|---|---|
| **Stage in Public Infrastructure Cycle** | **Preventing Corruption: Institutional Reform Measures** | **Detecting Corruption: Illustrative Indicators/Red Flags** |
| Infrastructure Procurement | • Identifying and reviewing bids for any unusual patterns<br>• Due diligence testing to assure the integrity of bidding companies<br>• E-procurement for bid advertising, acceptance, and reward<br>• Open data and open contracting to provide transparency<br>• Probity advisors and auditors to oversee procurement processes<br>• Noncompetitive procedures not used without proper justification<br>• Project design and specifications not restrictive or tailored to favor a contractor or firm<br>• Random external review of bid specifications<br>• Publishing contract and contract variation information<br>• Establishing complaint mechanisms for reporting procurement fraud and addressing such complaints | • Large difference between contract values and their estimates<br>• Sole-source contracts or contracts with a single bidder, without prequalification, or both<br>• Prequalification standards exclude otherwise qualified contractors<br>• Use of noncompetitive procedures<br>• Splitting up tenders<br>• Reduced timespan for bid submission<br>• Unclear definition of bid amount<br>• Selection criteria not clearly defined<br>• Repeat awards to the same contractor<br>• Public officials or their families acquiring a financial interest or employment in a contracting firm |
| Infrastructure Project Implementation | • Complete records of all decisions and criteria used for work variation orders<br>• Independent external supervisor vets contract variations<br>• Strong accounting practices and regular bank reconciliation of project related financial transactions<br>• Treasury single account to consolidate public funds in the banking system<br>• Strong internal controls and audit capacity to limit risks during project execution<br>• Third-party oversight of large infrastructure projects<br>• Community oversight groups to oversee project implementation | • Projects with high cost overruns<br>• Substantial change in contract conditions during implementation<br>• Failure to maintain records on work progress or work variations<br>• Contract files either incomplete or missing required documents<br>• Failure to monitor contractors' performance<br>• Only one person responsible for multiple functions of contract management<br>• Works or services certified without physical inspections |
| Infrastructure Asset Maintenance | • Central register of infrastructure assets<br>• Regular update of inventories and registries on maintenance<br>• Regular surveys and physical verifications of assets | • High percentage of "poor" condition infrastructure assets<br>• Maintenance expenditure low compared with capital stock |

Sources: Global Infrastructure Anti-Corruption Centre 2008; World Bank 2009; Construction Sector Transparency Initiative 2012; Transparency International Hungary 2015; Wells 2015; Ferwerda, Deleanu, and Unger 2016; OECD 2016a, 2019; and IMF staff.

Note: OECD = Organisation for Economic Co-operation and Development.

**Box 10.10. Anticorruption Framework and Private Sector Integrity Compliance for Infrastructure**

The anti corruption framework for corruption in infrastructure should be applicable to all stages of the public infrastructure cycle. Among other measures, this framework should include (1) enacting an anti corruption law, (2) establishing a national anticorruption agency and vesting it with powers to investigate and sanction corrupt practices, (3) understanding money-laundering risks from corruption and establishing anti–money-laundering measures, (4) identifying and managing conflict of interest situations, (5) providing standards of conduct for the private sector and consultants, (6) regulating and limiting the use of confidential information by public officials, and (7) providing protection for employees who report wrongdoing or breaches of integrity in the public and private sectors.

Sources: Sieber 2012; Financial Action Task Force 2013; OECD 2016a, 2016b; Malgrain, Picca, and Gunka 2018; Agence Française Anti-Corruption 2019; US Department of Justice 2019; and IMF staff.

Note: OECD = Organisation for Economic Co-operation and Development.

## CONCLUSIONS

Public infrastructure development is subject to high risks of corruption as it tends to involve projects that are large, long term, and complex—all fertile grounds for corruption. Countries with weak institutional capacity for public investment management are more vulnerable. Corruption in public infrastructure can take many forms, from small bribes to kickbacks, fraud, collusion, embezzlement, extortion, influence peddling, and unlawful interest or beneficial ownership. Corruption can occur at any phase of the investment cycle, inflicting different costs and implying different mitigation strategies.

The strategy to mitigate corruption risks along the infrastructure cycle should include a proactive approach to risk management in the public and private sectors, clear delineation of authority for public investment decision-making without conflict of interest, transparent frameworks and criteria for making infrastructure decisions, effective arrangements to enforce accountability for decisions taken, a robust framework for transparent disclosure of relevant information at all key stages, and integrity of transactions of private firms and actors involved in public infrastructure.

Specific indicators and "red flags" (as proposed in this chapter) could be used to improve the detection and sanctioning of corrupt acts, alert policymakers and citizens to potential corruption risks and systemic weak points or vulnerabilities, and so take actions to mitigate these risks. Identifying the risks of corruption and taking effective measures to tackle them are vital to a country's development and ensuring value for money in the use of public resources.

## REFERENCES


Agence Française Anti-Corruption (AFA). 2019. "Practical Guide— The Anti-Corruption Compliance Function in the Company." AFA.

Andina. 2018. "Contraloría promueve control ciudadano en lucha anticorrupción" ["Comptroller Promotes Citizen Control in Anti-Corruption Fight"]. https://andina.pe/agencia/noticia-contraloria-promueve-control-ciudadano-lucha-anticorrupcion-729508.aspx.

Benitez, Daniel, Antonio Estache, and Tina Søreide. 2010. "Dealing with Politics for Money and Power in Infrastructure." Policy Research Working Paper 5455, World Bank, Washington, DC.

Bertelsmann Transformation Index (BTI). 2018. "Country Report for Congo (2016–18)." Bertelsmann Stiftung, Gütersloh, Germany.

Booth, David, and Frederick Golooba-Mutebi. 2009. "Aiding Economic Growth in Africa: The Political Economy of Road Reform in Uganda." Working Paper 307, Overseas Development Institute, London.

Bowen, Paul, Peter J. Edwards, and Keith Cattell. 2012. "Corruption in the South African Construction Industry: A Thematic Analysis of Verbatim Comments from Survey Participants." *Construction Management and Economics* 30 (10): 1–17.

Brown, Jeremy, and Martin Loosemore. 2015. "Behavioural Factors Influencing Corrupt Action in the Australian Construction Industry." *Engineering Construction and Architectural Management* 22 (4): 372–89.

Burgess, Robin, Remi Jedwab, Edward Miguel, and Ameet Morjaria. 2009. "Who's Turn to Eat? The Political Economy of Roads in Kenya." Presentation at the Infrastructure and Economic Development Conference, World Bank/TSE, January 11.

Chan, Albert P. C., and Emmanuel Kingsford Owusu. 2017. "Corruption Forms in the Construction Industry: Literature Review." *Journal of Construction Engineering and Management* 143 (8).

Charbonneau Commission. 2015. Charbonneau Commission Report: Volume III—English Translation. International Centre for Criminal Law Reform and Criminal Justice Policy, Vancouver, Canada.

Choi, Jai Pil, and Marcel Thum. 1998. "The Economics of Repeated Extortion." Working Paper 9899–03, Columbia University, New York.

Comisión Nacional de los Mercados y Competencia (CNMC). 2018. "The CNMC initiates disciplinary proceedings against Acciona Construcción, Corsán-Corviam, Dragados, FCC Construcción, Ferrovial Agromán, OHL and Sacyr Construcción." Press release, October 11, 2018.

CNMC. 2019. "The CNMC Sanctions 15 Companies for Forming Several Cartels for the Distribution of the Spanish Rail Infrastructure Company Tenders." Press release, March 27, 2019.

Construction Sector Transparency Initiative (CoST). 2012. http://infrastructuretransparency.org.

Costa, Eduardo, and Esther Dweck. 2019. "Reduction of Petrobras Investments: A Balance of Losses." The Institute for Strategic Studies on Petroleum, Natural Gas and Biofuels Zé Eduardo Dutra (Ineep). https://www.ineep.org.br/post/redu%C3%A7%C3%A3o-dos-investimentos-da-petrobras-um-balan%C3%A7o-das-perdas.

Deng, Xiaomei, Qian Tian, Shizhao Ding, and Bob Boase. 2003. "Transparency in the Procurement of Public Works." *Public Money Management* 23 (3): 155–162.

Deiniger, Klaus, and Paul Mpuga. 2005. "Does Greater Accountability Improve the Quality of Public Service Delivery? Evidence from Uganda." *World Development* 33 (1): 171–191

Engel, Eduardo, Beth Simone Noveck, Delia Ferreira Rubio, Daniel Kaufmann, Armando Larar Yaffar, Jorge Londoño Saldarriaga, Mark Pieth, and Susan Rose-Ackerman. 2018. "Report of the Expert Advisory Group on Anti-Corruption, Transparency, and Integrity in Latin America and the Caribbean." Inter-American Development Bank, Washington, DC.

Extractive Industries Transparency Initiative (EITI/ITIE). 2015. *Report for Republic of Congo December 2015*. Oslo, Norway.

Fan, C. Simon, Chen Lin, and Daniel Treisman. 2010. "Embezzlement vs. Bribery." NBER Working Paper 16542, National Bureau of Economic Research, Cambridge, MA.

Fazekas, Mihály, and Gábor Koscis. 2015. "Uncovering High-Level Corruption: Cross National Corruption Proxies Using Government Contracting Data." Working Paper GTI-WP/2015:02, Government Transparency Institute, Budapest.

Ferwerda, Joras, Ioana Deleanu, and Brigitte Unger. 2016. "Corruption in Public Procurement: Finding the Right Indicators." *European Journal on Criminal Policy and Research* 23: 245–267.

FATF. 2012. "Specific Risks Factors for the Laundering of Money." Financial Action Task Force, Paris.

FATF. 2013. "Best Practices Paper: The Use of the FATF Recommendations to Combat Corruption." Financial Action Task Force, Paris.

Flyvbjerg, Bent. 2007. "Policy and Planning for Large Infrastructure Projects: Problems, Causes, Cures." *Environment and Planning B: Planning and Design* 34 (4): 578–597.

Flyvbjerg, Bent, Massimo Garbuio, and Dan Lovallo. 2009. "Delusion and Deception in Large Infrastructure Projects: Two Models for Explaining and Preventing Executive Disaster." *California Management Review* 51 (2): 170–193.

Global Infrastructure Anti-Corruption Centre (GIACC). 2008. "Examples of Corruption in Infrastructure." Global Infrastructure Anti-Corruption Centre, Chesham, UK.

Golden, Miriam A., and Lucio Picci. 2005. "Proposal for a New Measure of Corruption, Illustrated with Italian Data." *Economics and Politics* 17 (1): 37–75.

Hafner, Marco, Jirka Taylor, Emma Disley, Sonja Thebes, Matteo Barberi, Martin Stepanek, and Mike Levi. 2016. "The Cost of Non-Europe in the Area of Organised Crime and Corruption: Annex II—Corruption." European Union. https://www.rand.org/pubs/research_reports/RR1483.html.

Hernandez, Sandro. 2012. "Structure of corruption networks in the selection processes of public works in the Transport and Communications sector between 2005 and 2010 in Peru." Master's Thesis, Pontificia Universidad Católica Perú, Lima. http://www2.congreso.gob.pe/sicr/cendocbib/con4_uibd.nsf/657A0F017445AEFD052580D6006BB389/$FILE/HERNANDEZ_DIEZ_SANDRO.pdf.

Hollands, Glenn. 2007. "Corruption in Infrastructure Delivery: South Africa—Case Study." The *Partnering to Combat Corruption* series, WEDC, Loughborough University, United Kingdom: pp 143.

Independent Commission Against Corruption (ICAC). 2008. "Investigation into Bribery and Fraud at RailCorp—Eighth Report." Sydney, Australia: 48–50.

International Monetary Fund (IMF). 2017a. "The Role of the Fund in Governance Issues—Review of the Guidance Note–Preliminary Considerations." Washington, DC.

IMF. 2017b. "The Role of the Fund in Governance Issues—Review of the Guidance Note, Preliminary Considerations—Background Notes." Staff Supplement. Washington, DC.

IMF. 2018a. "Review of 1997 Guidance Note on Governance—A Proposed Framework for Enhanced Fund Engagement." Washington, DC.

IMF. 2018b. "Public Investment Management Assessment—Review and Update." Washington, DC.

IMF. 2019. Staff Report for the Republic of Congo—Request for a Three-Year Arrangement Under the Extended Credit Facility, Annex V, page 90–107. Washington, DC.

Kenny, Charles. 2006. "Measuring and Reducing the Impact of Corruption in Infrastructure." World Bank Policy Research Working Paper 4099, Washington, DC.

Kenny, Charles. 2007. "Infrastructure Governance and Corruption: Where Next?" Policy Research Working Paper 4331, World Bank, Washington, DC.

Kenny, Charles. 2009. "Measuring Corruption in Infrastructure: Evidence from Transition and Developing Countries." *Journal of Development Studies* 45 (3): 314–332.

Kenny, Charles, and Tina Søreide 2008. "Grand Corruption in Utilities." Policy Research Working Paper 4805, World Bank, Washington, DC.

Locatelli, Georgio, Giacomo Mariani, Tristano Sainati, and Marco Greco. 2017. "Corruption in Public Projects and Megaprojects: There is an Elephant in the Room." *International Journal of Project Management* 35 (3): 252–68

Lovei, Laszlo, and Alastair McKechnie. 2000. "The Costs of Corruption for the Poor—The Energy Sector." Viewpoint. World Bank, Washington, DC.

Malgrain, Ludovic, Jean-Pierre Picca, and Charlotte Gunka. 2018. "The European, Middle Eastern and Investigations Review 2018." Chapter France. *Global Investigations Review* series, Law Business Research.

Mauro, Paolo. 1998. "Corruption and the Composition of Government Expenditure." *Journal of Public Economics* 69: 263–79.

Melina, Giovanni, Hoda Selim, and Concepcion Verdugo-Yepes. 2019. "Macro-fiscal Gains from Anti-corruption Reforms in the Republic of Congo." IMF Working Paper 19/121, International Monetary Fund, Washington, DC.

Office of Fair Trading. 2009. "Construction Firms Fined for Illegal Bid-Rigging." Press Release 114/09, September 22.

Olken, Benjamin A. 2007. "Monitoring Corruption: Evidence from a Field Experiment in Indonesia." *Journal of Political Economy* 115 (2): 200–249.

Organisation for Economic Co-operation and Development (OECD). 2009. "OECD Principles for Integrity in Public Procurement." OECD Publishing, Paris.

OECD. 2014. *Foreign Bribery Report: An Analysis of the Crime of Bribery of Foreign Public Officials*. OECD Publishing, Paris.

OECD. 2015a. *Consequences of Corruption at the Sector Level and Implications for Economic Growth and Development*. OECD Publishing, Paris.

OECD. 2015b. "Curbing Corruption—Investing in Growth" Background Document, 3rd OECD Integrity Forum, Paris, March 25–26.

OECD. 2016a. *Integrity Framework for Public Infrastructure*. OECD Publishing, Paris.

OECD. 2016b. *Preventing Corruption in Public Procurement*. OECD Publishing, Paris.

OECD. 2019. *Analytics for Integrity: Data-Driven Approaches for Enhancing Corruption and Fraud Risk Assessments*. OECD Publishing, Paris.

Paterson, William D. O., and Pinki Chaudhuri. 2007. "Making Inroads on Corruption in the Transport Sector." In *The Many Faces of Corruption: Tracking Vulnerabilities at the Sector Level*, edited by J. Edgardo Campos and Sanjay Pradhan. Washington, DC: World Bank.

El Peruano. 2019. "Total support to fight against corruption." https://www.elperuano.pe/noticia-apoyo-total-a-lucha-anticorrupcion-74638.aspx.

Petrobras. 2019. Form 20F 2018. https://www.investidorpetrobras.com.br/en/results-and-notices/annual-reports.

Republic of Congo. 2018. "Report on Governance and Corruption." (RGC). Ministry of Economy and Finance. https://www.finances.gouv.cg/fr/rapport-corruption-gouvernance_200618.

Sieber, Niklas. 2012. "Fighting Corruption in the Road Transport Sector: Lessons for Developing Countries." Sustainable Urban Transport Technical Document #10, Deutsche gesellschaft für Internationale Zusammenarbeit (GIZ), Bonn.

Sobjak, Anita. 2018. "Corruption Risks in Infrastructure in Sub-Saharan Africa." 2018 OECD Forum on Anti-Corruption and Integrity, Paris, March 27–28.

Solis, Augusto P. 2017. "Odebrecht and the IIRSA North and South: A Case of Corruption and its Influence on Bilateral Relations with Peru in Infrastructure during the Years 2005–2007." Master's Thesis Repository, Pontifical Catholic University of Peru.

Søreide, Tina, and Aled Williams, eds. 2014. *Corruption, Grabbing and Development: Real World Challenges*. Cheltenham, UK: Edward Elgar.

Stansbury, Catherine, and Neill Stansbury. 2008. *Examples of Corruption in Infrastructure*. Chesham, UK: Global Infrastructure Anti-Corruption Centre.

Stansbury, Neill. 2005. "Exposing the Foundations of Corruption in Construction." In *Transparency International Global Corruption Report 2005*. London: Pluto Press.

Transparency International. 2016. "Anti-Corruption Glossary, Forms of Corruption." Berlin, 10 October.

Transparency International. 2019. "25 Corruption Scandals that Shook the World." Berlin, July 25.

Transparency International Hungary. 2015. "New Warning System for the Identification of Red Flags in Public Procurements (Summary)." Budapest.

US Department of Justice. 2019. "Guidance on Evaluating Corporate Compliance Programs." Washington DC, April.

US Securities and Exchange Commission. 2017. "Halliburton Paying $29.2 Million to Settle FCPA Violations." Press Release 2007–133, July 27.

US Securities and Exchange Commission. 2018. "Kinross Gold Charged With FCPA Violations." Press Release 2018–47, March 26.

Vargas, Mauricio, and Florian Sommer. 2014. "Corruption and the Risks of Losses on Government Bonds." Union Investment Institutional GmbH, Frankfurt, Germany. http://www.union-investment.it/dam/jcr:b8a1689b-18b5-45ef-af0e-31d49f5cf12b/Corruption_and_the_risks_of_losses_on_government_bonds.pdf.

Wales, Joseph, and Leni Wild. 2012. "The Political Economy of Roads: An Overview and Analysis of Existing Literature." Overseas Development Institute, London.

Wells, Jill. 2015. "Corruption in the Construction of Public Infrastructure: Critical Issues in Project Preparation." Anti-Corruption Resource Centre, Chr. Michelsen Institute, Bergen, U4 Issue 2015 (8): 30.

World Bank. 2009. "Deterring Corruption and Improving Governance in Road Construction and Maintenance." Transport Paper TP-27, World Bank, Washington, DC.

CHAPTER 11

# Fiscal Risks in Infrastructure

Rui Monteiro, Isabel Rial, and Eivind Tandberg

## INTRODUCTION

Public infrastructure projects are typically large and complex, with long planning, implementation, and operational periods, and as such they are inherently exposed to uncertainties and risks. However, project risks are often not well integrated in infrastructure governance frameworks and receive only moderate attention during major investment decisions. Governments' decision making is typically shortsighted, and the long-term costs and benefits are poorly reflected in most standard budget systems. Moreover, while planning and monitoring systems may help decision makers get an impression of the long-term effects of infrastructure projects, these systems are often limited in their scope and coverage. As a result, risk management of infrastructure projects remains underdeveloped and project outcomes often deviate significantly from expectations or forecasts.

This chapter advocates that better risk-management practices can improve outcomes in public infrastructure projects. The main sources of risk affecting public infrastructure projects are first reviewed. Then the chapter discusses good practices for assessing and quantifying these risks, and finally suggests potential government actions to better manage them.

The chapter identifies inadequate project design, costing techniques, and risk-sharing arrangements as major sources of cost overruns, project delays, and low social dividends. It finds that all countries, regardless of income, can strengthen their infrastructure governance framework by gradually incorporating a risk-management function. Governments should identify potential sources of risk early in the project cycle to support better-informed policy actions and ensure that fiscal risk assessment becomes an integral part of project management.

## ASSESSING AND MANAGING FISCAL RISKS IN INFRASTRUCTURE

Risks in infrastructure can materialize as large fiscal costs with significant macroeconomic implications. Tables 11.1 and 11.2 summarize cross-country data for large projects in the transport and energy sectors. They show that, on average, governments have paid approximately 33 percent more than originally budgeted for roads, railways, tunnels, and bridges (Table 11.1). Similarly, cost overruns are

**TABLE 11.1.**

**Transportation: Cost Overruns**

| | Range of Estimations | |
|---|---|---|
| **Transportation Asset Type** | **Based on Flyvbjerg (2017)** | **Based on Cantarelli and others (2010)** |
| Roads (average, %) | 24 | 20 |
| Railways (average, %) | 40 | 34 |
| Tunnels and bridges (average, %) | 48 | 33 |
| *Estimations based on:* | | |
| Number of projects | 1,603 | 806 |
| Number of countries | 17 | 20 |
| Sample period | 1927–2013 | 1927–2011 |

Source: IMF staff compilation, based on Flyvbjerg 2017 and Cantarelli and others 2010.

**TABLE 11.2.**

**Energy: Cost Overruns and Delays**

| **Energy Source** | **Cost Overruns** | **Delays** |
|---|---|---|
| **Total energy** | **66** | ... |
| Hydroelectric dam (average, %) | 71 | 64 |
| Nuclear reactor (average, %) | 117 | 64 |
| Thermal plant (average, %) | 13 | 10 |
| Wind farm (average, %) | 8 | 10 |
| Solar facility (average, %) | 1 | 0 |
| Transmission (average, %) | 8 | 8 |
| *Estimations based on:* | | |
| Number of projects | 401 | |
| Number of countries | 57 | |
| Sample period | 1936–2014 | |

Source: IMF staff compilation, based on Sovacool and others 2014.
Note: The ellipses in the "Total energy" row denote that there are no data available for total energy on average delays.

estimated at 66 percent for the average of the energy sector, while project delays can reach up to 64 percent in complex projects such as hydroelectric dams and nuclear reactors (Table 11.2).

Public Investment Management Assessments (PIMAs) conducted so far show that a reactive approach to infrastructure fiscal risks remains the norm, with action taken only after things go wrong. Risk assessments are not systematically included in project appraisal procedures, particularly in low-income developing countries and emerging market economies (Figure 11.1).

## The Nature and Sources of Fiscal Risks in Infrastructure

Infrastructure projects have distinct characteristics that make them particularly risk prone (Figure 11.2). Some sources of risks are project specific; that is, directly linked to project design, construction, and operation. Other sources of risks are market related, such as changes in prices and interest rates. A third source of risks, so-called *force majeure*, transcends projects and markets and would include, for

**Figure 11.1. Risk Assessment in Project Appraisals, PIMA Database**

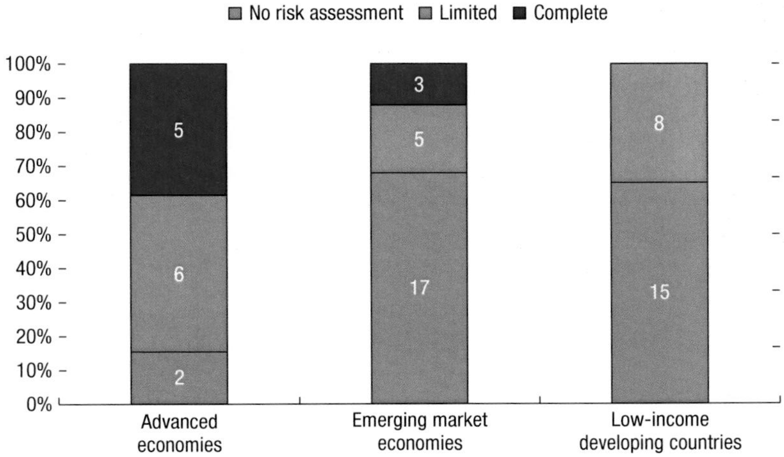

No risk assessment · Limited · Complete

100%
90%
80%
70%
60%
50%
40%
30%
20%
10%
0%

Advanced economies: 2, 6, 5
Emerging market economies: 17, 5, 3
Low-income developing countries: 15, 8

Source: PIMA database, July 2019.
Note: There were 61 total PIMA assessments: 13 in advanced economies, 25 in emerging market economies, and 23 in low-income developing countries. PIMA = Public Investment Management Assessment.

**Figure 11.2. Characteristics of Infrastructure Projects**

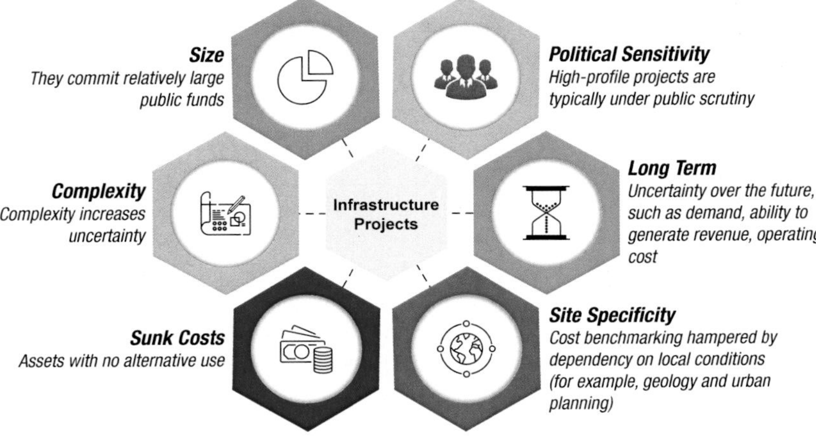


Source: IMF staff.

example, natural disasters and civil disorder. Last, government actions and inactions can also be a major source. Annex 11.1 summarizes main risk factors at each stage of the public investment cycle (planning, allocation, and implementation) classified by these sources of underlying uncertainty.

Fiscal risks frequently originate from weaknesses in the early stages of the project cycle. To illustrate this, 20 infrastructure projects around the world, delivered through both traditional procurement and public-private partnerships (PPPs), were evaluated.[1] Out of this sample, 17 projects faced some type of change from the original plans, which materialized in a combination of cost overruns, project delays, and shortfalls in funding and demand (Figure 11.3; see Annex 11.2 for the list of projects and their main characteristics). More than two-thirds of the deviations originated from the planning and allocation stages and happened because of government actions or inactions related to, for example, unrealistic costing, expansion of project scope, inadequate coordination across levels of government, or weaknesses in appraisals. Deviations originating from the implementation stage, which includes procurement, construction, and operation of infrastructure assets, were more diverse, emanating not only from government actions or inactions, but also from factors outside government control, such as project- and market-related risks or force majeure.

Sources of fiscal risks at different stages of the project cycle are correlated. Risks originating from one stage of an infrastructure project can have significant knock-on impact later in the project cycle. For example, a project with strong political support may be subject to unrealistic costs estimates to avoid rejection at

**Figure 11.3. Identifying Sources of Fiscal Risks**

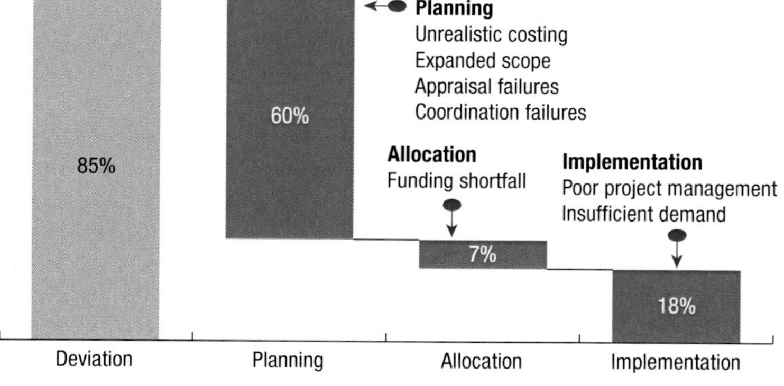


Source: IMF staff estimation based on various sources (for example, audit reports, ex post evaluations).
Note: Percentage is calculated based on the number of projects in the sample ($n = 20$). Details of project sample are shown in Annex 11.2.

[1] The selected project sample comprises infrastructure projects from countries with different development levels, delivered through both traditional procurement and public-private partnerships, and covering various economic and social sectors. Yet, it is not representative, and has been mainly determined by data availability.

the planning stage. Once cost overruns materialize during implementation, it generates funding shortages because the budget allocation is insufficient.

There are also compound sources of risk, such as unsolicited proposals and early contract termination.[2] The acceptance of unsolicited project proposals can create large deviation from strategic priorities and prevent competition during procurement. Low capacity among public procuring entities to identify, prepare, and evaluate infrastructure projects, and the incentive to move projects off budget are often main reasons why unsolicited proposals are accepted (Engel et al. 2019). Another example of compound sources of risks with potentially large fiscal costs is early termination of long-term contracts, such as PPPs. Contract termination can reflect many risk factors, including public entities poorly understanding contractual clauses regulating termination, private partner bankruptcy, or policy changes introduced by government after the contract is awarded.

## Assessing Fiscal Risks in Infrastructure

When assessing infrastructure risks, governments should assess the potential direct and indirect fiscal impact. Cost overruns have direct fiscal impacts, whereas delays, quality shortfalls, or failure to realize benefits may have indirect impacts on fiscal outcomes. Similarly, both traditionally procured projects and PPPs are exposed to risks, although there is sometimes a misperception that PPPs are "risk free" for government. The *composition* of the public sector investment portfolio also affects the magnitude and likelihood of risks materializing. For example, a large share of investment projects linked to one strategic economic sector, such as roads, may excessively expose the government to shocks affecting that sector, with potential spillovers to the rest of the economy.

Assessing fiscal risks in infrastructure is often challenging because information is limited and inaccurate. Data on construction costs and cost overruns are typically scarce, and even when information is available, governments do not necessarily have the skills to put it to good use. In some countries, databases include historical data on road construction costs (for example, Uruguay, Georgia) but they are not used for budgeting road construction costs, nor for estimating possible deviations from the budgeted amounts.[3] Although many governments in recent years have reinforced their fiscal risk teams and included infrastructure in their activities, the methodologies for risk quantification are still underdeveloped.

Assessing complex projects that require forecasts of demand for infrastructure services over the long term is particularly challenging because of uncertainty related to project- and market-specific risks (Box 11.1). It is more difficult to estimate demand for greenfield projects (that is, newly built and with no track record) than

[2] An unsolicited proposal is a proposal made by a private party to undertake a public-private partnership project, submitted at the initiative of the private party rather than in response to a request from the government.

[3] Some techniques for studying deviation and fiscal risk are presented in Irwin (2007).

## Box 11.1. Examples of Challenges in Estimating Demand

Estimating the future demand for an infrastructure asset is a complex task, involving identification of alternative options, analyses of consumer preferences, estimates of relevant prices (for example, gas for cars), and macroeconomic forecasts. These estimations may fail for the ramp-up period after construction, and even fail for the whole life of the asset. Some researchers consider institutional factors affecting demand forecasts, such as the "optimism bias" or the "strategic misrepresentation" of the projects by politicians and public managers willing to maximize the chances of having them approved (see Flyvbjerg 2003). There are several examples of actual demand being much lower than expected demand:

- Roads and highways, such as the Indiana Toll Road (half of forecasted trucks for some time), Madrid-Toledo AP-41 (with only 10 percent of expected demand), Sidney Cross City Tunnel (with a higher-than-50-percent demand shortfall), and several highways in Korea;
- Railways, such as in Korea, where a survey (KOTI 2014) showed that actual ridership of urban railways is only 26 percent of the original estimate, with many lines at around 10 percent of the estimate;
- Metro lines, where, for example, the Busan metro line in Korea had 85 percent fewer passengers than estimates, and the Yongiln Everline light rail metro line in Seoul had 77 percent less, with periods when effective demand reached only 10 to 15 percent of initial forecasts; and
- Airports, where, for example, the Ciudad Real Airport in Spain failed to secure demand forecasts for the project and had to be closed a few years after construction.

The KOTI (2014) survey found that the Seoul Subway Line 9 public-private partnership, with a minimum-revenue guarantee, was receiving compensation from government because, although its demand was 7 percent above contractual expectations, its revenue was just 62 percent of the expected, because of government-determined low fees, losses from free transfers to other lines, and higher-than-expected free ridership.

Source: IMF staff.

for brownfield projects (for example, the replacement of an obsolete power plant or the widening of a highway). *Optimism bias,* such as forecasts that overestimate demand for services to make a project financially viable or underestimate the fees to be paid by users to justify a project and make it politically viable, is not uncommon.

Although these challenges affect all infrastructure projects, PPPs are particularly exposed to optimism bias and undue political interference (Annex 11.3). To help countries to understand, assess, and quantify the costs and risks arising from PPP projects, the IMF and the World Bank have developed the Public-Private Partnership Fiscal Risk Assessment Model, PFRAM 2.0 (Box 11.2).[4] As an analytical tool, PFRAM 2.0 helps country authorities quantify the macro-fiscal implications of PPPs, understand the risks assumed by the government, and identify potential mitigation measures.

[4] PFRAM 2.0 is accessed at https://www.imf.org/external/np/fad/publicinvestment/data/pfram2english.xlsm.

### Box 11.2. The Public-Private Partnership Fiscal Risk Assessment Model

The Public-Private Partnership Fiscal Risk Assessment Model (PFRAM) was developed by the IMF and the World Bank as an analytical tool to assess the potential fiscal costs and risks arising from public-private partnership projects. In many countries, investment projects have been procured as public-private partnerships not for efficiency reasons, but to circumvent budget constraints and postpone recording the fiscal costs of providing infrastructure services. Hence, some governments procured projects that either could not be funded within their budgetary envelope or exposed public finances to excessive fiscal risks.

PFRAM provides a structured process for gathering information for a portfolio of public-private partnership projects in a simple, user-friendly, Excel-based platform, following a five-step decision tree: (1) Who initiates the project? (2) Who controls the asset? (3) Who ultimately pays for the asset? (4) Does the government provide additional support to the private partner? (5) What does the public-private partnership contract risk allocation tell us about macro-fiscal risks?

Based on project-specific and macroeconomic data provided by the user, PFRAM generates standardized outcomes. The outcomes include project cash flows, fiscal tables and charts on a cash and accrual basis, and debt sustainability analysis, with and without the public-private partnerships. Sensitivity analysis of main fiscal aggregates to changes in macroeconomic and project-specific parameters is also carried out, and a summary fiscal risk matrix of the project is produced.

Since it started in April 2016, PFRAM has been used not only in the context of IMF and World Bank technical assistance, but also by country authorities—mainly public-private partnership units in ministries of finance—to better understand the long-term fiscal implications of an individual or a portfolio of public-private partnership projects. As an analytical tool, PFRAM helps country authorities quantify the macro-fiscal implications of public-private partnerships, understand the risks assumed by government, and identify potential mitigation measures.

Source: IMF staff.

Correlations between different risks within a project, and correlations between different projects within a portfolio, are another challenge for risk assessment (Box 11.3). Assessing portfolio risks is more than a simple aggregation of project risks. Correlations can be positive and negative, implying that risks related to the portfolio may be larger or smaller than the sum of the risks related to each project. Some project-specific risks may even be reduced when aggregated in a portfolio because of diversification.

## Managing Fiscal Risks in Infrastructure

How can governments move from an ad hoc reactive behavior to a proactive mitigation strategy for infrastructure risk? Government actions can aim to reduce the likelihood of risks, reduce their potential fiscal impact, or a combination of both. Some countries, mainly advanced economies, have taken steps to incorporate risk management in policies and practices for managing public infrastructure projects, sometimes embedded in dedicated units. For example, the Public and Private Infrastructure Investment Management Center in Korea

### Box 11.3. Correlation of Fiscal Risks in Infrastructure

Materialization of major infrastructure risks is often correlated with main macroeconomic variables. This implies that when those variables move, they impact many infrastructure projects at the same time, amplifying fiscal risks.

There are several examples of many projects being simultaneously affected by macroeconomic volatility. In Mexico, a currency devaluation triggered the materialization of fiscal risks in a large number of road projects. In Colombia, fiscal risks in road projects materialized after a temporary but significant demand reduction caused by economic depression combined with poor internal security. In Spain, several road concessionaires, already suffering from low structural demand and construction cost overruns, went technically bankrupt after the 2008 global financial crisis when highway demand dropped 15–20 percent for several years, and ultimately had to be rescued by government.

Risks may also cancel out. The occurrence of some risks automatically prevents—or reduces the probability of—other risks materializing. For example, a change in law eliminating tolls in road concessions already suffering from low demand and risk of bankruptcy creates a fiscal challenge (compensating the concessionaire for loss of revenue) but eliminates the risks related to demand and revenue generation. Also, a major flooding (or other force majeure event) affecting an independent power producer creates a compensation event but reduces fiscal risk from power-purchase agreements signed with other power producers.

Source: IMF staff.

appraises and manages large public investment projects including PPPs. Since 2005, it has managed to reduce project cost overruns by 82 percentage points. Similar units include the United Kingdom's Infrastructure and Projects Authority and Australia's Infrastructure Australia. Most countries still need to strengthen their risk management to minimize potential fiscal losses and improve project outcomes.

Infrastructure risk management should start at the planning stage early in the project cycle and take a whole life-cycle approach. Table 11.3 identifies key practices to ensure adequate fiscal risk management at the planning phase. It is arguable that the most critical practice is to avoid spending scarce resources on projects that should have been eliminated at an early stage because they do not add value to society (that is, costs are higher than benefits) or do not serve the country's main needs (that is, projects are poorly aligned with government strategies).

Some good risk-management practices at the planning stage have emerged from country experiences. Ireland has strengthened its strategic investment planning through a set of integrated policies.[5] The plan for social housing (Government of Ireland 2016) is a good example of mitigation measures to ensure adequate interdepartmental coordination.[6] Many advanced economies

[5] The National Planning Framework is supported by a 10-year capital plan as an instrument to enable objectives set out in the strategic planning framework.

[6] Designed to tackle some of the most complex issues facing Ireland—housing shortages, rising prices, and homelessness—the strategy has received a strong political consensus. It is well developed with clear targets (to build 47,000 new housing units over 2017–21), a funding envelope of €5.35 billion, an effective system of planning approvals, and a construction pipeline that stretches across local authorities.

**TABLE 11.3.**

## Managing Fiscal Risks in Infrastructure at the Planning Phase

| Action: Planning for Infrastructure | Examples of Good Practices for Fiscal Risk Management | How Are Fiscal Risks Being Mitigated? |
|---|---|---|
| Strengthened investment planning | • Long-term sectoral master plans address current and future needs; medium-term investment plans are aligned to government strategy and Sustainable Development Goals<br>• Medium-term investment plans are developed under an affordable funding envelope and prioritized according to government strategy and Sustainable Development Goals<br>• Mechanisms are in place for experts and decision makers in different ministries and layers of government to coordinate investment plans | • Reduces the probability of later-facing fiscal risks in projects not being perceived as serving real needs and government strategy<br>• Forces line ministries to focus on priority projects, reducing the probability of facing fiscal risks in nonpriority projects<br>• Maximizes synergies in the development of the project pipeline, reducing fiscal risks originating in project changes because of poor coordination |
| Strengthened project appraisal | • Project appraisal includes technical and legal feasibility, financial feasibility (costs and revenues of the project), economic feasibility (costs and benefits for the whole society, including a risk analysis), environmental impact studies (how to mitigate impact on the environment), social impact studies (how to address impact on affected individuals, including resettled persons)<br>• Alternative ways to satisfy needs are always considered, particularly by using the existing assets<br>• Project appraisal is subject to independent review to facilitate reliable demand estimates and realistic fiscal projections | • Increases the consistency of each project proposal, reducing the probability of fiscal risks arising from poor identification of costs, benefits, and risks<br>• Increases the robustness of each proposal, reducing fiscal risk from project changes<br>• Projects submitted for approval will present evidence that benefits outweigh project costs, in most risk scenarios |
| Strengthened framework for infrastructure governance | • Institutions are in place to regulate the quality and price of infrastructure services to end users, and to regulate monopoly and oligopolistic infrastructure markets<br>• All public investment projects, regardless of financing mechanism, funding source, and on-budget/off-budget status, follow equivalent appraisal and approval process<br>• The formal presentation of unsolicited proposals for infrastructure projects is not allowed or is strictly regulated | • Reduces probability and effect of politically induced fiscal risks impacting public-private partnerships and state-owned enterprises<br>• Reduces the probability of fiscal risks being created without adequate identification during the planning and ulterior public investment management phases<br>• Reduces the probability of fiscal risks from nonpriority projects and from lack of competition |

Source: IMF staff.

and, to a lesser extent, emerging market economies and low-income developing countries also assess fiscal risks during project appraisal. Independent review of feasibility studies for large infrastructure projects can strengthen the quality of project appraisal and reduce government exposure to, for example, demand optimism bias and political interference. The United Kingdom's Infrastructure and Projects Authority undertakes assurance reviews on major government projects.[7] Some countries, like Denmark and Germany, include in their budgets a contingency margin for infrastructure projects to deal with uncertainties in project costing.[8]

Adequate fiscal risk management is also critical during the allocation stage (Table 11.4). Given the long-term nature of infrastructure assets, budget allocation should cover not only construction but also the operation of the asset. Delinking budgeting of capital expenditures (construction) from current expenditures necessary to operate them, including maintenance, increases fiscal risks by generating a bias toward approving new projects instead of properly operating and maintaining existing ones. A well-functioning medium-term budget framework allows government to evaluate project costs and risks beyond the annual budget's restrictions and to better consider options around constructing new assets or properly maintaining existing ones. For example, in Estonia the maintenance of strategic public assets, such as roads and railways, is part of the asset management strategy and is prioritized over new construction.[9]

Proactive risk management of projects and contracts at the implementation stage is also essential (Table 11.5). Ministries of finance[10] should have the capacity to stop projects being implemented if they are not fiscally affordable or the government's risk exposure is deemed too high. Ministries of finance also play a large role in ensuring adequate project funding through efficient cash management of domestic and external resources. Similarly, line ministries controlling investment entities should be able to understand fiscal risks when selecting the procurement method for infrastructure assets, such as traditional public procurement or PPP. When risks are not fully understood and properly managed, the probability of risks materializing as project delays or cost overruns during implementation increases dramatically. In turn, once contracts are awarded the governance framework should promote proactive contract management by implementing agencies and a continuous assessment of fiscal risks throughout the project life cycle.

[7] See https://www.gov.uk/government/organisations/infrastructure-and-projects-authority#content.

[8] Denmark includes a 30 percent contingency margin in all infrastructure projects.

[9] As of May 2019, Estonian Railways also has five out of seven projects dedicated to maintenance and renovation (IMF 2019).

[10] In this chapter, the Ministry of Finance is referred to as the central finance authority in the country responsible for public infrastructure. However, in some countries these responsibilities can be shared between the Ministry of Finance and other authorities, for example, a ministry of planning or a ministry of development.

**TABLE 11.4.**

## Managing Fiscal Risks in Infrastructure at the Allocation Phase

| Action: Allocation of Funds | Examples of Good Practices for Fiscal Risk Management | How Are Fiscal Risks Being Mitigated? |
|---|---|---|
| Medium-term budgeting | • The budgeting framework allows for the estimation of medium-term budget ceilings for line ministries | • Helps ministries improve proposals under the ceilings, using a whole-life costing approach |
| | • Projects are included in a pipeline well in advance, allowing the Ministry of Finance to collect and review information on the projects and their fiscal risks | • Allows the Ministry of Finance to understand project's fiscal costs and risks, including implicit liabilities, and their evolution as projects mature |
| | • Ongoing projects are protected and given priority over newly proposed ones | • Reduces the probability of project implementation delays for lack of funding |
| Unity and integrity of the budget | • Discussion of current and capital allocations during budget negotiation follows an integrated process | • Allows and incentivizes line ministries to adopt a whole-life costing approach, integrating capital and recurrent costs |
| | • Reliable recurrent cost estimates, including maintenance and operational costs, are discussed for each project | • Induces ministries to adopt maintenance standards and plans, reducing fiscal risks |

Source: IMF staff.

**TABLE 11.5.**

## Managing Fiscal Risks in Infrastructure at the Implementation Phase: Procurement, Construction, and Operation

| Action: Implementation: Procurement, Construction, and Operation | Examples of Good Practices for Fiscal Risk Management | How Are Fiscal Risks Being Mitigated? |
|---|---|---|
| Strengthened project management and procurement processes | • The selection of procurement mode (for example, traditional, design-build, public-private partnership, management contract, operation and maintenance contract) is reviewed by the Ministry of Finance, and long-term contracting (such as for public-private partnerships) is reviewed to assess fiscal costs and risks | • The fiscal risks created/mitigated by each mode are carefully addressed, identified, and quantified when possible, leading to decisions that do not disregard fiscal risk |
| | • Appraisal, including financial and economic feasibility studies, is reviewed before and during the tendering process | • Project affordability and economic value for society are confirmed, reducing fiscal risk |
| | • Project implementation plans, including procurement strategy, are prepared for each major project; for public-private partnerships, the concessionaire will be implementing but government will need to develop contract management capacity | • Adequate plans and procurement strategy are critical for efficient pricing, cost containment, timely completion, and quality of assets and of service delivery |
| | • Preparation and tendering of each major project are led by a skilled project manager, overseen by a project owner/project committee | • Pre-tender project development and effective tender steering reduce fiscal issues later |

*(continued)*

**TABLE 11.5** ***(continued)***

| Managing Fiscal Risks in Infrastructure at the Implementation Phase: Procurement, Construction, and Operation | | |
|---|---|---|
| **Action: Implementation: Procurement, Construction, and Operation** | **Examples of Good Practices for Fiscal Risk Management** | **How Are Fiscal Risks Being Mitigated?** |
| | • Project management (or contract management in the case of public-private partnerships) is effective; periodic project reports are provided to line ministries and the Ministry of Finance; and potential issues are immediately addressed or raised for superior decision | • Effective project management, with good communication with contractors and effective lines of reporting for decision making, helps prevent or reduce fiscal risks |
| | • Contracts (including public-private partnership contracts and power-purchase agreements) are proactively published in full, and actual payments and project performance are also disclosed | • Proactive disclosure increases pressure for good infrastructure governance; helps users compare costs with actual service performance |
| | • Asset value is recorded and depreciated over time, and asset management function is linked to fiscal risk management | • Allows for effective asset management, reducing global fiscal risk |
| Management of funds disbursement | • Funding plans are integrated with cash management plans; in case of cash rationing, the cost of delaying investment projects is part of decision making | • Reduces the probability of project implementation delays and extra fiscal costs; mitigates fiscal risk in case of cash rationing |
| Contract management, particularly for long-term procurement (for example, public-private partnerships) | • Authorities continuously monitor contract execution and project performance, enforcing contractual agreements | • Reduces the probability of project issues accumulating and leading to major fiscal risks |
| | • Authorities monitor project implementation issues and proactively partner with contractors in finding solutions | • Reduces the effect of project disturbances and consequent fiscal risks |
| | • Authorities continuously assess risks coming from exogenous change and prevent risks or adapt policy | • Reduces the effect of fiscal risks originating in technological, demographic, and other changes |
| | • Authorities continuously assess project risks coming from policy changes, incorporating fiscal cost/risk in decisions | • Reduces the probability of government decisions ignoring fiscal costs and risks |

Source: IMF staff.

## DEVELOPING A RISK-MANAGEMENT FUNCTION FOR PUBLIC INFRASTRUCTURE

A strong infrastructure risk-management function should involve a comprehensive risk-management framework and a clear statement of roles and responsibilities. Risks should be adequately managed over the whole project cycle, from planning to implementation (Figure 11.4), with the cycle being closed by identifying lessons learned and applying them to other projects. A comprehensive framework should comprise management not only of individual major

**Figure 11.4. A Risk-Management Framework for Infrastructure**

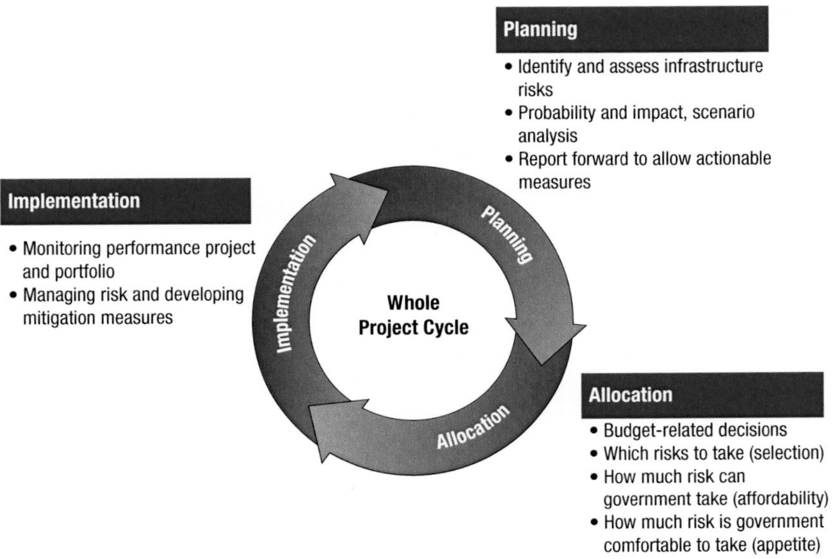


Source: IMF staff.

infrastructure projects, but also of the project portfolio, which—as previously noted—can have a risk profile different than the simple addition of individual projects. Moreover, early identification of the main sources and potential fiscal impact of risks is critical to inform investment decisions and to allow public agencies to manage the risks throughout the project cycle (Figure 11.5).

Infrastructure risks should be centrally managed. Given that the government's portfolio of infrastructure projects is critical to an economy, the overall risk-management function will often rest within or be linked to the ministry of finance and will serve as a center of excellence for capacity development. For example, Portugal has empowered a new department in the Ministry of Finance, *Unidade Técnica de Acompanhamento de Projetos* (Project-Steering Technical Unit), to lead the evaluation and procurement of PPPs and large infrastructure projects, and in Colombia a new *PPP subdirectorate* has been created to support the existing fiscal risks subdirecorate. In addition, experts are needed in the different implementing agencies, and the risk-management function will be dependent on efficient mechanisms for information sharing and coordination across agencies. Because many projects have long-term time frames, it will be important to develop clear procedures for coordination, analysis, and assessment at key milestones of project development, implementation, and operations. Table 11.6 outlines some key practices of the risk-management function.

Some countries with significant infrastructure programs, including Chile, Portugal, South Africa, and the United Kingdom, have created gateway processes to contain fiscal costs and fiscal risks. A gateway process is a sequence of decision points where approval by the finance minister is required. It provides a space for

**Figure 11.5. The Timing of Fiscal Risk Management Decisions**

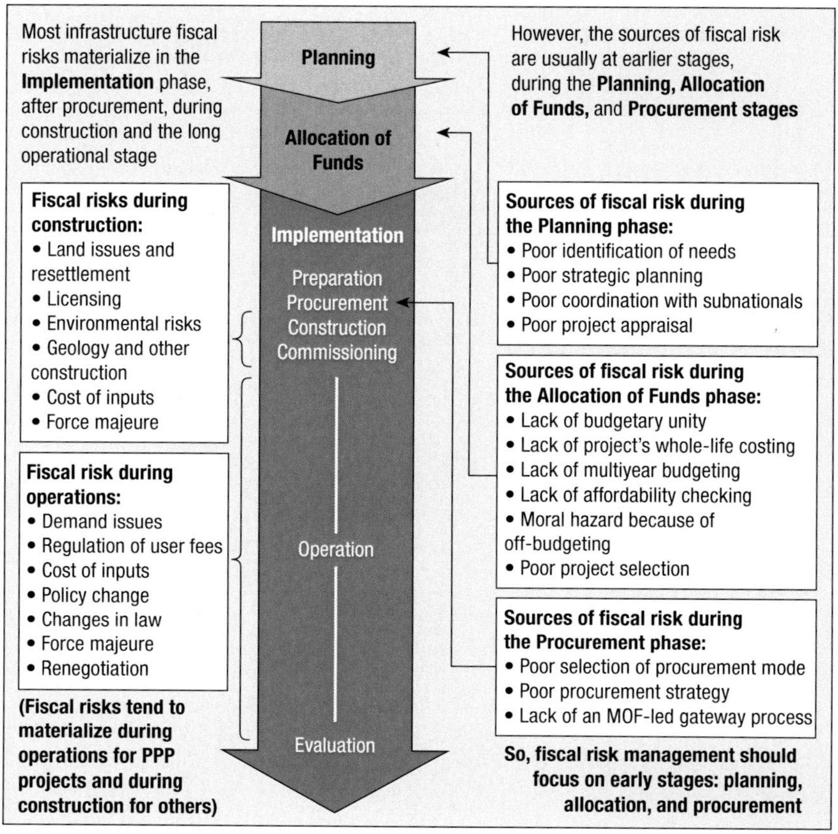

Source: IMF staff.
Note: MOF = Ministry of Finance; PPP = public-private partnership.

evidence-based decisions and allows the finance minister to have effective veto power over infrastructure projects or decisions that may jeopardize fiscal sustainability, while sectoral policy responsibility remains in the hands of line ministers (Table 11.6).

Data sharing among decision-making entities is critical to inform the selection of policy options for project design as well as risk management at the operational level. A risk-management framework for decision-making purposes should comprise detailed and frequently updated information. This enables intragovernmental cooperation and ensures alignment of goals and processes. Information should cover the full range of relevant explicit and implicit risks, including those for which it is difficult to assess likelihood and probability and those assessed through a qualitative approach, and it should cover both projects and the overall portfolio. This type of information is intended for internal use and typically not published.

**TABLE 11.6.**

## Managing Fiscal Risks in Infrastructure along the Whole Project Cycle

| Action | Examples of Good Practices for Fiscal Risk Management | How Are Fiscal Risks Being Mitigated? |
| --- | --- | --- |
| Fiscal rrisk management function | • Infrastructure fiscal risk managers identify portfolio risk correlation and the bidirectional links between infrastructure and macroeconomic variables | • Mitigates infrastructure fiscal risks linked to specific variables that affect other areas (for example, exchange rates), when jointly managed |
| | • Infrastructure fiscal risk managers coordinate with project managers, analyze periodic reports, update the risk registry, and participate in preventive/corrective decision making | • Allows for preventive measures reducing probability and impact of risk, and for corrective measures mitigating impact |
| | • Infrastructure fiscal risk management is integrated with general fiscal risk management (subnationals, state-owned enterprises, pensions, financial system, and so on) | • Allows for effective understanding of the full impact for fiscal risks related to macroeconomic variables and for effective risk-edging measures |
| | • Contingency plans and risk-mitigation measures are in place for each major macroeconomic shock and for natural disasters, and government practices and public-private partnership contracts are designed in ways that mitigate global fiscal risk | • Requires development of a global, integrated perception of fiscal risks, and corresponding risk-acceptance and risk-mitigation strategies, reducing global fiscal risk |
| | • Major policy changes and project scope decisions are reviewed ex ante by the Ministry of Finance, identifying fiscal risk impact | • Reduces the probability and impact of fiscal risks created by government action |
| | • Infrastructure fiscal risk managers have a continuous tracking of major fiscal risks, proactively inviting project managers and other decision makers to address fiscal risks | • Reduces the probability and impact of fiscal risks created by government action or inaction, or by legislative action or inaction |
| Effective gateway process for major projects | • Ministry of Finance is directly involved in steering public-private partnerships and major projects | • Allows Ministry of Finance to assess fiscal risks |
| | • Ministry of Finance reviews documentation of public-private partnerships and major projects | • Allows Ministry of Finance to assess fiscal risks |
| | • For long-term projects such as public-private partnerships, the Ministry of Finance explicitly reviews fiscal risks, including the ones originating from land issues, construction, environment | • Allows Ministry of Finance to assess fiscal risks before core decisions, making it possible to block a project or to redesign contractual risk allocation |
| | • For public–private partnerships, the finance minister has veto power regarding the call for tender, the contract close, and any decision on change orders, renegotiation, termination, or similar | • Allows Ministry of Finance to assess fiscal risks before core decisions, making it possible to block a project or to redesign contractual risk allocation |
| | • In case of public-private partnership renegotiation, termination, or a similar event, Ministry of Finance is in the negotiation team | • Adds bargaining power and therefore reduces probability and impact of fiscal risk |
| | • In case a project is affected by demand issues (scarce demand or excessive use), Ministry of Finance engages with the line ministry to discuss solutions | • Adds bargaining power and therefore reduces probability and effect of direct fiscal risk, and of indirect fiscal risk through political risk |

Source: IMF staff.

The government should disclose key information about fiscal risks related to the infrastructure portfolio as part of a comprehensive fiscal risk statement. This would serve two different but overlapping objectives: first, to inform decision making regarding fiscal risks in infrastructure projects and programs; and second, to contribute to overall fiscal transparency, which allows participants and other stakeholders to make informed assessments of the government's fiscal policies. Because risks related to public infrastructure often are correlated with other important fiscal risks, disclosure of portfolio risks is needed for the public and financial markets to have a complete picture of the government's overall risk position.

In general, public risk disclosure will be more aggregate and qualitative than in the government's internal risk-management framework, and the focus will be on explicit risks. A fiscal risk statement will usually be updated and published once a year.

## CONCLUSIONS

Although risks cannot be fully eliminated in infrastructure projects, governments can manage them to minimize their fiscal impact. Governments can influence the probability that some risks—particularly those under their control—will happen, assess their fiscal impact, and prepare to cope with the residual risks. In doing so, they need a strong infrastructure governance framework. All countries, regardless of income or development level, can strengthen their infrastructure governance framework by gradually incorporating a risk-management function. It is critical to identify sources of fiscal risks early in the project cycle to support better-informed policy actions, with the focus not only on projects, but also on the overall infrastructure portfolio, to take advantage of project synergies and correlations. Effective data sharing and disclosure mechanisms are also important to ensure that fiscal risk assessment becomes an integral part of project management.

Government should have the capacity and framework in place to monitor and manage different risks accruing from individual projects, and to identify the correlation among these risks and among projects within the overall investment portfolio. Both are relevant from a fiscal risk management perspective and should be dealt with in an integrated and consistent way.

Special attention should be given to infrastructure risks that originate early in the project cycle because of government action or inaction. Although infrastructure risks typically materialize as cost overruns and project delays once projects are being implemented, underlying risk factors are often linked to weaknesses in infrastructure governance at the planning and allocation stages. Inadequate project design, costing techniques, and risk-sharing arrangements are prominent sources of cost escalation, project delays, and low social dividends. Yet, these sources of risk all depend on decisions and actions taken by government, and therefore are under a government's control.

## ANNEX 11.1. MAIN SOURCES OF FISCAL RISKS IN INFRASTRUCTURE OVER THE PROJECT CYCLE

**ANNEX TABLE 11.1.1.**

## Main Sources of Fiscal Risks in Infrastructure over the Project Cycle

| Sources of Risk | How Does Fiscal Risk Materialize? | Project Specific | Market Related | Force Majeure | Government Action |
|---|---|---|---|---|---|
| | | Source Type | | | |
| **Planning for Infrastructure** | | | | | |
| Unrealistic planning envelope | Planning of investment projects is not constrained by realistic fiscal projections and the volume of projects submitted for approval is excessive | | | | ✓ |
| Projects with low strategic value | Project concepts and plans are not effectively aligned with key national and sector priorities and user needs, and so additional projects are needed | | | | ✓ |
| Poor coordination | Projects by different levels of government overlap or do not maximize synergies | | | | ✓ |
| Poor choice of concept | Project concepts are chosen prematurely, without thorough analysis, and subsequent changes in scope or restructuring may increase costs, benefits, and risks | | | | ✓ |
| Poor project appraisal | Allowing project to move forward without evidence that benefits outweigh costs | | | | ✓ |
| Poor regulation | Poor competition, quality, or price of services requires government intervention | | | | ✓ |
| Off-budget financing | Infrastructure undertaken by state-owned enterprises, public-private partnerships, and other off-budget projects does not receive adequate project appraisal and fiscal risk oversight | | | | ✓ |
| Unsolicited proposals | Compound all the above risks | | | | ✓ |
| **Allocation of Funds** | | | | | |
| Lack of multiyear budgeting | Insufficient funds for the timely completion of the project, forcing the government to delay it, change its scope, or delay some other project | | | | ✓ |
| Unrealistic costing estimates | Biased capital cost estimates result in requests for additional budgetary funds, project delays, or changes in scope | | | | ✓ |
| Unrealistic estimate of recurrent costs | Lack of reliable recurrent cost estimates results in inability to fully maintain and operate the infrastructure and accelerates the reduction in its value | | | | ✓ |
| Lack of maintenance standards and plans | Lack of maintenance standards and plans inhibits effective maintenance and prevents adequate funding for proactive maintenance | | | | ✓ |
| No prioritization of ongoing projects | New projects are initiated while ongoing projects are delayed | | | | ✓ |

*(continued)*

**ANNEX TABLE 11.1.1.** ***(continued)***

## Main Sources of Fiscal Risks in Infrastructure over the Project Cycle

| Sources of Risk | How Does Fiscal Risk Materialize? | Project Specific | Market Related | Force Majeure | Government Action |
|---|---|---|---|---|---|
| | | Source Type | | | |
| Confusing project financing with budget funding | Financing for infrastructure projects is available (for example, bilateral, private) so projects are approved and proceed to construction, even when budget funding for recurrent expenses during operation is not secure; risks materialize because of a lack of budget funding for operating the project (that is, maintenance costs, availability payments) | | | | ✓ |
| **Implementation: Project Procurement, Construction, and Operation** | | | | | |
| Inappropriate procurement mode | The selected procurement mode (for example, traditional, design-build, PPP, management contract, operations and management contract) leads to excessive fiscal costs or risks | | | | ✓ |
| Poor procurement strategy | Inadequate procurement strategy results in poor competition and inefficient pricing | | | | ✓ |
| Poor implementation | Inadequate implementation plans prevent timely and efficient project implementation | | | | ✓ |
| Poor contract management | Poor monitoring leads to low outcome quality, and poor management of contract changes prevents effective actions to mitigate shocks affecting the project | ✓ | ✓ | ✓ | ✓ |
| Financing issues and funds disbursement | Inadequate financing and funding plans, and poor management of funds disbursement originate project implementation delays and additional fiscal costs | | | | ✓ |
| Change orders | Additional costs resulting from changes in design and scope during construction | | | | ✓ |
| Land cost | Additional costs arising from land acquisition | ✓ | | | |
| Land availability | Construction delays resulting from untimely availability of land | ✓ | | | |
| Change in land use | Additional costs for people resettlement and relocation of activities | ✓ | | | |
| Geological issues | Additional costs resulting from significant geological issues during construction | ✓ | | | |
| Environmental issues | Additional costs resulting from significant environmental protection issues | ✓ | | | |
| Input prices | Additional costs resulting from significant changes in input prices | | ✓ | | |
| Other construction | Additional construction costs resulting from delays and other issues | ✓ | ✓ | | |

*(continued)*

**ANNEX TABLE 11.1.1. *(continued)***

Main Sources of Fiscal Risks in Infrastructure over the Project Cycle

| Sources of Risk | How Does Fiscal Risk Materialize? | Project Specific | Market Related | Force Majeure | Government Action |
|---|---|---|---|---|---|
| | | Source Type | | | |
| Exchange rate issues | Additional costs resulting from significant increase in nominal exchange rate | | ✓ | | ✓ |
| Force majeure | Additional costs resulting from force majeure events (for example, natural disasters, war, civil unrest) | | | ✓ | ✓ |
| Change in law/policy | Additional costs resulting from changes in legislation, regulations, and policy | | | | ✓ |
| Demand shortfall | Low use reduces revenue stream and challenges cost recovery | ✓ | ✓ | | ✓ |
| Renegotiation or contract termination | Government low bargaining power or poor negotiating skills leads to efficiency losses; early termination is not well prepared and effectively managed, leading to costs for government | | | | ✓ |
| Lack of disclosure | Lack of proactive disclosure of costs and performance reduces governance | | | | ✓ |
| Poor asset monitoring | Poor information on value and status of assets prevents effective asset management | | | | ✓ |
| Poor management of the asset portfolio | Lack of a broad picture, with interproject risk correlations, prevents integration of infrastructure in overall fiscal risk management strategy and processes | | | | ✓ |
| Renegotiation or contract termination | Government low bargaining power or poor negotiating skills leads to efficiency losses; early termination is not well prepared and effectively managed, leading to costs for government | | | | ✓ |
| Lack of disclosure | Lack of proactive disclosure of costs and performance reduces governance | | | | ✓ |
| Poor asset monitoring | Poor information on value and status of assets prevents effective asset management | | | | ✓ |
| Poor management of the asset portfolio | Lack of a broad picture, with interproject risk correlations, prevents integration of infrastructure in overall fiscal risk management strategy and processes | | | | ✓ |

Source: IMF staff.

## ANNEX 11.2. SAMPLE OF PROJECTS

Annex Table 11.2.1 presents estimates of risks materialized in selected projects through cost overruns, project delays, shortfall in demand compared with initial estimates (once projects become operational), and inadequate budget funding to operate the assets after construction.

## ANNEX 11.3. ASSESSING FISCAL RISKS IN PUBLIC-PRIVATE PARTNERSHIPS

Assessing fiscal risks in infrastructure built through public-private partnerships is particularly challenging, given that they allow governments to transform short-term fiscal costs into medium- to long-term fiscal risks (and vice versa). Using public-private partnerships, a government can convert some fiscal risk (future contingent liabilities) into direct fiscal liabilities (predetermined payments to a public-private partnership concessionaire). In principle, this contractual arrangement could be used for reducing fiscal risk, with government paying the corresponding premium. In practice, it may create more fiscal risk rather than reduce it.

There are two main reasons for this, with both under control of government:

- First, as long-term contracts, public-private partnerships create significant risks when applied to projects and sectors with policy volatility or subject to significant change in the medium to long term (for example, technological change, demographic evolution, change in user preferences, change in management practices). For example, the volume of costs and issues created by public-private partnerships involving information and computing technologies led the British parliament to approve a recommendation for government not to use public-private partnerships for this.
- Second, public-private partnership contracts increase fiscal risk when contractual design is not based on a sound business plan—for example, when requiring levels of government payments that jeopardize fiscal sustainability, or when authorizing tolls and other fees that users cannot afford (or government cannot politically sustain), or when assuming unrealistic levels of demand. Portugal had to cancel several public-private partnership contracts during its 2010–14 crisis (paying compensation to concessionaires); Korea had to lower tolls and pay compensation regarding several public-private partnership highways; and Box 11.1 presents several examples of unrealistic passenger-traffic forecasts, many of them leading to fiscal costs.

For these two reasons, instead of being known for their fiscal risk–reduction characteristics, public-private partnerships are seen in some parts of the world as generators of fiscal surprises, as Augusto de la Torre noted in his 2015 paper on public-private partnerships in Latin America (de la Torre 2015).

Public-private partnerships are particularly exposed to optimism bias and political interference. Confidence in optimistic demand forecasts can make governments

**ANNEX TABLE 11.2.1.**

## Estimates of Risks Materialized in Selected Projects

| Project | Type | Sector | Cost Overrun (Percent) | Delay (Percent) | Demand Shortfall (Percent) | Funding Shortfall | Main Drivers |
|---|---|---|---|---|---|---|---|
| Boston Big Dig (Central Artery/Tunnel Project, CA/T), United States | TPP | Road-Tunnel | 478 | 114 | No | No | Unrealistic initial cost estimate and expanded scope; failure to assess unknown subsurface conditions; environmental and mitigation costs |
| Golden Gate, Chicago, United States | TPP | Bridge | –5 | 0 | No | No | On budget and ahead of schedule. |
| Port La Union, El Salvador | TPP | Port | 55 | 80 | Not operational | Yes | Expanded scope; sedimentation exceeding the original forecast; steep rise of equipment and material prices. Lack of budget funding for recurrent dredging expenditures. |
| Berlin Brandenburg Airport (ongoing), Germany | TPP | Airport | 125 | 180 | No | No | Change in design required new permits, causing significant delays owing to unresolved safety issues; poor project management |
| ICE Frankfurt-Cologne, Germany | TPP | Railway | 116 | 75 | No | No | Changes in project specifications and design; changes in environmental and safety requirements; delays from court challenges and geological problems |
| Kuala Lumpur Airport (KLIA2), Malaysia | TPP | Airport | 114 | 200 | No | No | Scope changes (longer runway, automated baggage system, more parking stands) |
| High speed railroad Madrid-Valencia, Spain | TPP | Railway | 269 | . . . | Yes | Yes | Changes in prices, fiscal austerity force to changes in design. Changes in design to lower costs resulted in lower demand |
| Couva Hospital, Trinidad and Tobago | TPP | Hospital | 0 | 0 | No | Yes | Chinese company financed the construction and transferred the hospital fully equipped to government, but government lacked the budget for operating it |
| Sydney Cross City Tunnel, Australia | PPP | Tunnel | 0 | 0 | 71 | No | The tollway became insolvent because of low traffic volumes. It has been sold several times. |
| Forrest Highway, Australia | TPP | Road | 406 | . . . | No | No | Changes in scope, design, change in materials |

*(continued)*

**ANNEX TABLE 11.2.1.** ***(continued)***

Estimates of Risks Materialized in Selected Projects

| Project | Type | Sector | Cost Overrun (Percent) | Delay (Percent) | Demand Shortfall (Percent) | Funding Shortfall | Main Drivers |
|---|---|---|---|---|---|---|---|
| Barts and Hear Hospitals, London, United Kingdom | PPP | Health | . . . | . . . | No | Yes | Insufficient budget funding resulted in one and two hospital floors closed (mothballed) after building |
| Busan metro line, Korea | PPP | Railway | . . . | . . . | 85 | No | Overly optimistic demand forecasts |
| Everline light rail train, Korea | PPP | Railway | . . . | 60 | 77 | No | Delays in other related projects (transfer stations) Overly optimistic demand, improvements in other competing projects |
| Ciudad Real Airport, Spain | PPP | Airport | 0 | 0 | 100 | No | Ceased operations in April 2012 because of operator bankruptcy after failure to secure demand for the project |
| West Rail, Hong Kong | TPP | Rail | –27 | 0 | No | No | Under budget and on time. Effective control, value engineering and lower prices resulting from a competitive market. |
| A8 Augsburg-Munchen, Germany | PPP | Road | –23 | . . . | No | No | First public-private partnership in Germany |
| Eurotunnel, France-United Kingdom | PPP | Road | 100 | 0 | 67 | No | Overestimated market share gain in freight and passengers by 200 percent |
| Highway Madrid-Toledo, Spain | PPP | Road | . . . | . . . | 90 | No | Insufficient traffic volume |
| Desalination plants, Australia | PPP | Water | . . . | . . . | Yes | No | Insufficient demand caused by environmental changes and cheaper supply alternatives |
| Izmit water plant, Turkey | PPP | Water | 0 | 0 | Not operational | No | Demand for water dropped because of environmental changes and cheaper supply alternatives. Is no longer operational |

Source: Authors.

Note: Ellipses indicate information not available. ICE = InterCityExpress; PPP = public-private partnership; TPP = traditional public procurement.

feel comfortable in providing guarantees on demand (expecting a low likelihood they will be called out). Similarly, private companies may be willing to accept too much demand risk that they may ultimately not being able to afford if expected demand does not materialize. Thus, optimism bias creates explicit and implicit fiscal risks, and their expected value cannot be easily computed for a project (even scenarios are hard to compute, except for the worst-case scenario, the upper bound on demand risk). Therefore, public-private partnerships require strong public investment management institutions and adequate fiscal risk management, to restrict the use of public-private partnership procurement to the projects in which it can deliver efficiency, and to assess and manage their fiscal risks effectively.

Public-private partnerships have the potential for reducing fiscal risk but do increase it when poorly structured and when used for the wrong projects. When well designed and for the right projects, public-private partnerships can reduce fiscal risk by delegating to a private entity the responsibility for implementing the project, with a credible threat of financial punishment in case of poor performance. But, being long-term contracts, public-private partnerships may create government commitments that are not politically or fiscally sustainable over time, leading to renegotiations that affect efficiency and change risk allocation.

Badly structured public-private partnership contracts also create fiscal risks beyond those in traditional procurement. That happens when the business case is not sound or when the private partner is given unfettered power to influence demand, affecting fiscal cost and the quality of public service. For example, contracts for public hospitals need to be designed in such a way that private companies cannot distort the contractually prescribed delivery of service, by denying it or by promoting abusive use of service. Usually, public-private partnership contracts for hospitals pay for availability of infrastructure (independent of volume of use) and (when clinical services are added) include a set of incentive mechanisms, preventing perverse behavior (see Barros and Monteiro 2015). Similarly, public-private partnership prisons are paid according to availability and not volume of use; public-private partnership concessionaires should not have an interest in higher criminality. A famous pathological case (created by corrupt officials) is the kids-for-cash scandal in Luzerne County, Pennsylvania, where judges were receiving kickbacks for sending juvenile offenders to prison, even for minor crimes, because the local public-private partnership prison was paid according to the number of inmates.

## REFERENCES

Barros, Pedro, and Rui Monteiro. 2015. "Public-Private Partnerships." In *World Scientific Handbook of Global Health Economics and Public Policy*, edited by Richard M. Scheffler. Singapore: World Scientific.

Cantarelli, Chantal, Bent Flyvbjerg, Eric Molin, and Bert van Wee. 2010. "Cost Overruns in Large-Scale Transportation Infrastructure Projects: Explanations and Their Theoretical Embeddedness." *European Journal of Transport and Infrastructure Research* 10 (1): 5–18.

Engel, Eduardo, Fischer, Ronald, and Alexander Galetovic. 2019. "When and How to Use Public-Private-Partnerships in Infrastructure: Lessons from the International Experience."

NBER Working Paper Series, National Bureau of Economic Research, Cambridge, MA. http://www.nber.org/papers/w26766.

Flyvbjerg, Bent. 2003. *Megaprojects and Risk*. Cambridge: Cambridge University Press.

Flyvbjerg, Bent. 2017. *Oxford Handbook of Megaproject Management*. Oxford: Oxford University Press.

Government of Ireland. 2016. *Rebuilding Ireland: Action Plan for Housing and Homelessness*. Dublin.

International Monetary Fund (IMF). 2019. "Estonia: Technical Assistance Report—Public Investment Management Assessment." IMF Country Report 19/152, Washington, DC.

Irwin, Timothy. 2007. *Government Guarantees: Allocating and Valuing Risk in Privately Financed Infrastructure Projects*. Washington, DC: World Bank.

KOTI, Korea Transport Institute. 2014. "Korea's Railway Public-Private Partnership Projects." KOTI Knowledge Sharing Report 11, Korea Transport Institute, Sejong City.

Sovacool, Benjamin, Alex Gilbert, and Daniel Nugent. 2014. "An International Comparative Assessment of Construction Cost Overruns for Electricity Infrastructure." *Energy Research and Social Science* 3: 152–60.

CHAPTER 12

# Integrating Infrastructure Planning and Budgeting

**Richard Allen, Mary Betley, Carolina Renteria, and Ashni Singh**

## INTRODUCTION

Efficient and well-integrated planning and budgeting functions are key for building quality infrastructure. Planning establishes a framework of national, sectoral, and subnational government goals, policies, and targets. Budgeting puts these policies into a defined fiscal space and resource envelope, thus allowing policymakers to move from aspiration to action. In many countries, however, strategic planning and budgeting systems are neither efficient nor well integrated. Planning systems are often poorly designed and largely aspirational in focus, while decisions on major infrastructure projects can be dominated by short-term political and electoral considerations. Budgeting is often separate from the planning process, undermined by weak enforcement of fiscal and budgetary rules, and affected by poor control in budget execution, so that the annual budget lacks credibility.

What are integrated planning and budgeting functions and why does integration matter? At one level, "integration" amounts to little more than loose coordination between the government ministries and agencies responsible for planning and budgeting. At the other extreme, it means full integration of the tools and decision-making processes that encompass planning and budgeting. Between these two extremes, a variety of intermediate approaches can be observed. Approaches to planning and budgeting that are not well integrated frequently result in plans for infrastructure investment that are aspirational or overambitious, continuous improvisation in project selection, delays and cost overruns in project implementation, and weak accountability for results.

This chapter defines the concepts of planning and budgeting, sets out a brief history of the evolution of these two key functions of government, and analyzes how well they are integrated, drawing on evidence from the IMF's Public Investment Management Assessment (PIMA) database. It considers some possible mechanisms—notably medium-term budget frameworks and public investment

The authors are grateful to Patrick Ryan (research assistant, Fiscal Affairs Department, IMF) for his valuable assistance.

programs—to better integrate planning and budgeting functions. The chapter discusses whether an optimal organizational structure for planning and budgeting exists and, to achieve better integration, the relative advantages and disadvantages of establishing a single ministry or entity responsible for both planning and budgeting or separating these functions. Last, the chapter examines the role of national infrastructure commissions and other specialized government agencies recently established in advanced economies such as Australia, New Zealand, and the United Kingdom to provide a strategic approach to planning and financing infrastructure projects and technical support for line ministries.

A key message is that most countries are still struggling to find efficient mechanisms for linking their medium- and long-term infrastructure plans within a sustainable fiscal framework. The chapter offers some suggestions for moving forward. Second, the chapter argues that establishing efficient and effective planning and budgeting functions is much more important than their organizational form, for which solutions are country dependent. Although centralized agencies can play a useful role in the strategic planning of infrastructure and mitigating the influence of political factors and the electoral cycle on infrastructure investment, capacity constraints and data requirements may limit the applicability of such innovations in many low-income developing countries.

## DEFINITION OF BUDGETING AND PLANNING FUNCTIONS

The concept of budgeting is relatively straightforward. Elements of modern budgeting practices can be traced back to ancient Greece, Rome, Mesopotamia, and China. In more recent times, de Renzio (2013, 137) referred to a French law of 1862 and an earlier British practice from the mid-1700s defining the budget as "a document that forecasts and authorizes the annual receipts and expenditures of the state" and the related processes and procedures. Since then, budgets have developed, from plans of a government's revenues and expenditures for a period of generally one year ahead into comprehensive systems for allocating and managing public resources over the medium term. In some systems, the capital or investment budget is separately identifiable from the budget for wages, goods and services, interest payments, and other current spending. In other systems, capital investment projects may not be identified separately but are subsumed within the spending programs of sectors (or regions or municipalities). In many low-income developing countries, however, the capital budget is replaced by a development budget that comprises both capital and recurrent expenses (Allen and others 2017).

The core of the budget function is the allocation of fiscal resources across public services and public investments. The budget envelope for the year ahead is derived from forecasts of government revenue and other financing available. The task of allocating this finite sum across government functions and alternative public investments, which typically compete for funding, then becomes a critical aspect of the budget function. This involves prioritizing among uses of public resources and between alternative infrastructure investment opportunities, within and across sectors. Thus, in its most comprehensive sense, budget preparation comprises a determination of the macroeconomic and fiscal framework, the preparation and issuance of budget instructions, the preparation and examination of budget proposals, negotiations on those proposals, the prioritization of competing proposals for funding, and the submission of these proposals for legislative approval (Schiavo-Campo 2007).

A concise definition of planning is more difficult to find in the literature because the concept embraces many ideas and approaches and has evolved considerably over the years. Waterston (1969, 28), for example, defined the planning process as "an organized, conscious and continual attempt to select the best alternatives to achieve specific goals." In many countries, by long tradition, planning is associated with a government-prepared national development plan, but these have many different dimensions and variants. Most commonly, plans are aspirational or visionary documents with a time horizon stretching forward 10 or more years and with titles such as "Vision 2050."[1] Medium-term national development plans typically look four or five years ahead and are usually underpinned by electoral or presidential cycles, organizational structures, and a decision-making process—typically defined in a country's constitution or the supporting legal framework—designed to prepare and implement a governmental political agenda to improve economic and social outcomes. Other forms of strategic planning are outside the scope of this chapter.[2]

Notwithstanding its developmental origins, the planning function is not confined to low-income developing countries and emerging market economies. Some wealthier countries (examples include Australia, Austria, France, Ireland, and New Zealand) have used national development plans to reorient the focus of economic strategy, such as to improve national competitiveness, diversify the economy from dependence on a single sector, or realize a major transformative initiative. Others have used planning to focus on thematic or sectoral priorities, such as bridging the infrastructure gap, improving connectivity, and reducing regional inequality (OECD 2017).

In practice, very few national and sectoral plans are costed and constrained by an effective fiscal framework. Planning involves the identification of national policy objectives, and the preparation of national and sectoral strategies to realize these objectives. It is performed at multiple levels: typically a central agency in the case of the national plan, and by sectors or line ministries in the case of sectoral plans. The planning function provides important support to a strategic medium-term approach to policymaking and resource allocation (Diamond

[1] Among many examples, see World Bank and the Government of Rwanda (2018). This report explores Rwanda's goal to become a middle-income country by 2035 and a high-income country by 2050.

[2] For example, the important field of spatial planning (a branch of geography) focuses on the distribution of people and activities in urban and other physical spaces of diverse sizes.

2013). However, a distinction should be made between plans that are fiscally constrained and the majority, which are not. The absence of costing and weak links to the fiscal framework are among the most important shortcomings of national development plans. A recent survey by Chimhowu, Hulme, and Munro (2019), for example, showed that out of 107 national development plans studied, 79 had "no specific costing associated with the plan implementation save for vague references to domestic and foreign sources [of finance]." While some national development plans do include estimates of the cost of projects, the figures are rarely broken down by year and are frequently out of date or unreliable (see the subsequent discussion of public investment programs and in Chimhowu, Hulme, and Munro 2019).

An integrated approach to planning and budgeting is especially important in relation to public infrastructure projects. Table 12.1 shows some examples of planning and budgeting functions and key areas in which these intersect. Where national development plans and budgets are not guided by a unified framework of macroeconomic assumptions and projections and a coherent and credible fiscal framework, the likelihood of the plans being implemented or of the budgets being sustainable may be severely reduced. The project appraisal (cost-benefit analysis), prioritization, and selection functions are other key intersections of the planning and budgeting functions. Projects selected through a clearly defined appraisal process, having been included in the budget, need to be funded to completion, including for their associated operations and maintenance expenditures. Infrastructure clearly risks being degraded when the budgetary provision for operations and maintenance expenditure is inadequate, thus requiring much

**TABLE 12.1.**

Selected Examples of Planning and Budgeting Functions

<table>
<tr><th>Planning</th><th>Budgeting</th></tr>
<tr><td colspan="2">National Policy Objectives<br>Reflected in national and sectoral plans<br>Guiding resource allocation through the budget process</td></tr>
<tr><td colspan="2">Macroeconomic and Fiscal Framework<br>National plans constrained by a resource envelope derived from the medium-term fiscal framework<br>Sectoral plans constrained by sectoral allocations consistent with the medium-term budget framework<br>Annual budgets aligned with the medium-term fiscal framework and medium-term budget framework</td></tr>
<tr><td>National Development Plan</td><td>Medium-Term Budget Framework</td></tr>
<tr><td>Thematic and Sectoral Plans</td><td>Budget Proposals by Sectors</td></tr>
<tr><td>Project Identification</td><td>Budget Review by Ministry of Finance</td></tr>
<tr><td>Project Appraisal</td><td>Budget Consultations and Negotiations</td></tr>
<tr><td colspan="2">Project Appraisal and Selection<br>Prioritization and selection from appraised projects<br>National and sectoral plans reflecting only projects that have been screened<br>Annual budgets including only screened and appraised projects drawn from the pipeline</td></tr>
<tr><td>Pipeline of Appraised Projects</td><td>Budget Submission and Approval</td></tr>
</table>

Source: Authors.

greater expenditure later on (Heller 1982). Similarly, multiannual commitments made by donors and domestic suppliers through infrastructure contracts approved during the planning process need to be properly recorded and monitored in the budget so that arrears do not arise.

## HISTORICAL DEVELOPMENTS

The historical development of planning systems can be traced to two main roots. First is the former Soviet Union model that originated in the late 1920s (for example, see Nove 1961; Agarwala 1983; and Ericson 1991). The Soviet planning system comprised a series of nationwide centralized economic plans, based on the theory of productive forces that was central to the communist ideology. An elaborate structure of more than 20 centralized state committees—including *Gosplan* (planning), *Gossnab* (materials and equipment supply), and a state bank (*Gosbank*)—administered the plan until the Gorbachev era (Nove 1986; Ericson 1991). Alongside the planning of all physical activity and production ran a parallel process of budgeting and financial planning managed by the Soviet Ministry of Finance.

The second root is the French model of "indicative" planning developed after World War II, which quickly spread to other European countries such as Belgium, the Netherlands, Norway, and Italy (see, for example, Waterston 1969). As noted by Kindleberger (1967, 125), the French approach to planning was "indicative, rather than imperative . . . that is, it shows the directions in which an economy ought to go, rather than (as in the Soviet model) providing specific targets for individual plants and firms." By the late 1960s, strongly influenced by the Soviet or French models, development planning had spread to most developing countries, as well as to many emerging market economies and advanced economies (see Waterston 1969; and Caiden and Wildavsky 1974).

Although in some countries traditional planning systems may be waning, in others they remain strong or are enjoying a revival. One recent study shows that the number of countries with a national development plan increased from 62 to 134 between 2006 and 2018, partly because of the need to plan for the internationally agreed-upon Sustainable Development Goals (see Chimhowu, Hulme, and Munro 2019). In some countries, however, all-embracing planning institutions have been replaced by a policy-oriented process that focuses on specific areas or sectors (defense, social security, health care, and so on) and on infrastructure requirements. Once a bastion of traditional planning in its most elaborate form, India in 2018 abolished its once all-powerful Planning Commission and terminated production of its monumental and byzantine five-year national development plan. Indian states are following suit. This has helped create a policy vacuum, without clearly defined mechanisms to set strategic priorities or to coordinate and finance the sector plans that remain.

In many (mostly lower-income) countries, national development plans have evolved in response to demand from international financial institutions and other development partners who wish to influence decisions on infrastructure investment. Their involvement represents an additional challenge to planners who must balance their own domestic requirements and the perceived preferences of the donors when raising finance for infrastructure. As an example, in the late 1990s and early 2000s, poverty-reduction strategy papers—national development plans with a different name and focus—were used as a condition for countries demonstrating both need and eligibility for debt relief under the Heavily Indebted Poor Country initiative and its successor, the Multilateral Debt Relief Initiative. Challenges with costing and prioritization, as well as the credibility of the underlying macroeconomic frameworks, are often said to have undermined the practical value of poverty-reduction strategy papers (World Bank and IMF 2005). National development plans, however, continue to be a powerful mechanism to attract donor funding, which in many low-income developing countries represents a large proportion of public investment, as high as 80–90 percent in some countries.[3]

The adoption of the Millennium Development Goals and the Sustainable Development Goals that replaced them is another example of externally driven demand for planning, notwithstanding domestic ownership of the associated planning frameworks. The Sustainable Development Goal process includes annual voluntary national reporting on progress with the goals. The progress reports typically include a description of steps taken to align development plans and strategies with the Sustainable Development Goals (United Nations 2017). As a result, several countries have developed national plans either targeting these goals or ensuring alignment. More recently, recognition of the shortcomings of these plans in the absence of robust costings has led to efforts to develop and apply more rigorous costing methodologies, including by the IMF (Gaspar and others 2019). Studies have showed that implementing the Sustainable Development Goals in low-income developing countries cannot be achieved without massive additional resources from domestic sources, the capital markets, development partners, and the private sector. However, the well-integrated planning and budgeting mechanisms required for delivering these resources have not yet been established (see also Chapter 4).

In some advanced economies, planning systems have survived and are even enjoying something of a revival, even as they take a different form than traditional models. As noted earlier, the resurgence of national planning is not confined to low-income developing countries and emerging market economies but includes advanced economies in Europe and Australasia (Chimhowu, Hulme, and Munro 2019). An Organisation for Economic Co-operation and Development (OECD) study (2017), however, notes most advanced economies

[3] In The Gambia, for example, the authorities presented their national development plan financing strategy at an international conference in Brussels in May 2018. The strategy costed 21 priority projects with a value of $2.4 billion, of which $750 million was committed by the donors, leaving a $1.6 billion shortfall to be met by additional donor support, domestic funding, or public-private partnerships. See IMF (2019).

do not have a coherent long-term framework for national infrastructure planning. Infrastructure is planned mostly at the sector level and is informed by cost-benefit assessments that do not necessarily factor in cross-sector interdependencies or wider developmental issues that may be signaled in the Sustainable Development Goals (such as climate change, resilient infrastructure, and gender equality). Many projects are dictated by reactions to urgent needs or short-term political interests rather than by long-term and comprehensive strategies. To anticipate an important conclusion of this chapter, the planning process is continuing to evolve and can retain its relevance if focused on key economic and social objectives and applied with flexibility.

Budgeting systems have developed on largely independent lines from planning systems as budgets have taken a much larger share of national resources since the early 20th century (de Renzio 2013). The original focus of budgeting up to the 1930s was on the proper accounting and recording of expenditure and revenue transactions. Over the past 90 years, budget systems in advanced economies have developed a stronger emphasis on the outputs and results of public expenditure, a medium-term focus, a gradual decentralization of budget responsibilities to spending ministries, and greater transparency. Developing countries have followed suit, with varying degrees of success, under pressure from development partners and peers (de Renzio 2013). However, with the exception of a focus on institutional arrangements, and some attempts to integrate the planning and budgeting of infrastructure through public investment programs, links between planning and budgeting functions and processes have remained essentially unchanged.

Planning and budgeting institutions also evolve as countries develop. As explained in Chapter 5, the PIMA framework is a comprehensive approach for analyzing public investment institutions. Figure 12.1 sets out an analysis of PIMA data for the five institutions relating to the coordination of planning and budgeting functions.[4] It finds that, on average, low-income developing countries implement planning functions about as well as budgeting functions. On the other hand, emerging market economies and advanced economies tend to implement budgeting functions better than planning functions (both lie above the 45° line). This result is in part because of the relative strength of spending controls and budget institutions in most advanced economies and emerging market economies. There are, however, some exceptions—for example, the IMF's PIMA database identifies Mexico as an emerging market in which planning institutions have retained their importance and advanced budget institutions are still developing. Looking across all countries, one can see a broad spectrum of policies and instruments related to planning and budgeting, and strong variations among countries at different levels of development.

[4] The five institutions concerned have separate responsibility for national and sectoral planning, coordination between entities, multiyear budgeting, budget comprehensiveness and unity, and budgeting for investment.

**Figure 12.1. Relationship between Planning and Budgeting (Effectiveness)**

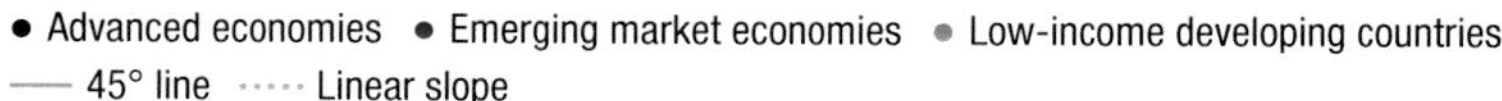


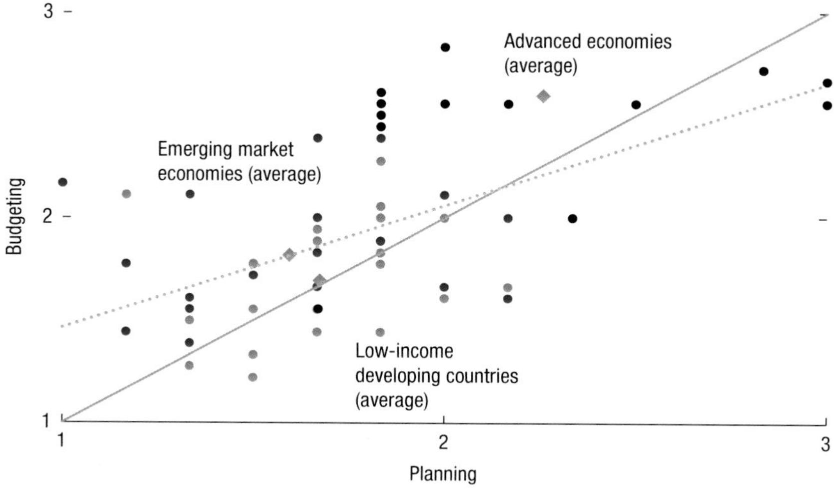


Source: Authors' calculations based on the PIMA database.
Note: PIMA = Public Investment Management Assessment.

Strong links between plans and resources may arise among countries that are members of an economic and monetary union or that receive substantial external resources for infrastructure investment. An example is the structural and investment funds of the European Union.[5] These funds are the EU's main policy tool for planning public investment in member states. Each eligible country negotiates a partnership agreement with the European Commission on access to and use of the structural and investment funds. The agreements covering 2014–20 set out priorities, expected results, and a budget for each of the funds. These agreed-upon spending envelopes allow beneficiary countries to plan their expenditure, part of which is capital infrastructure, within a known resource constraint. The mechanism is not perfect, however. For example, absorption of EU funds can be delayed significantly, leading to a rush of project spending at the end of each programming period, creating inefficiencies and potentially bad implementation decisions. Anecdotal evidence also suggests that EU funds in some member states are managed outside the national budget process, with separate project pipelines and appraisal methodologies (in Serbia, for example).

[5] There are three main funds: the European Regional Development Fund, the European Social Fund, and the Cohesion Fund. In addition, there are other funds set up under the EU's Common Agricultural Policy.

# HOW TO BETTER INTEGRATE PLANNING AND BUDGETING

## Planning within a Defined Fiscal Constraint

As noted earlier, of the many features of a modern national development plan, integration of the planning process with the provision of financial resources from the budget and external sources is arguably the weakest link (Chimhowu, Hulme, and Munro 2019). Are there any public financial management tools for building stronger links between planning and budgeting functions? The answer is yes, and foremost among them is the medium-term fiscal framework. Close integration of planning and budgeting requires the national development plan to be subject to the reality of a fiscal constraint, which is determined by such a framework. To ensure that national development plans provide meaningful guidance to the budget process, they need to be costed at least indicatively and constrained to fit within the aggregate resources (fiscal space) that are forecast to be available over the medium-term planning horizon.

## Medium-Term Budget Frameworks

The medium-term budget framework[6] has also often been suggested as a potential bridge between planning and budgeting functions. These frameworks have a multiannual perspective, include expenditure ceilings, and increasingly adopt a programmatic classification of spending, which ideally should be (though in practice is frequently not) a common element in both modern planning and budgeting systems (Harris and others 2013). Nevertheless, even in advanced economies with relatively strong public financial management practices, there are frequent challenges in linking the medium-term budget framework to a country's medium- and long-term strategic development objectives and its national infrastructure plan (if one exists). An integrated approach to planning and budgeting requires that annual budgets and medium-term budget frameworks are credible: namely, that both reflect and are executed in line with the plan. This is not the case in many low-income developing countries and emerging market economies, and medium-term budget frameworks and national development plans often lack a consistent programmatic structure (Allen and others 2017). Thus, the financial base for good planning is often absent or weak.

Medium-term budget frameworks are also prepared on different assumptions and classifications compared to a country's national development plan. For example, these budget frameworks often have a different time horizon than the planning

[6] The medium-term budget framework differs from the medium-term fiscal framework in that the latter only provides projections of the main fiscal aggregates (revenue, expenditure, borrowing, and debt) with minimal disaggregation. In contrast, the medium-term budget framework provides a much more detailed breakdown of spending.

framework and are prepared on a rolling basis,[7] whereas many national development plans cover a fixed 4/5-year period. They may also use a different system for classifying projects and investment spending. For example, many low-income countries, in preparing their national development plans, use the concept of a "development budget" and "development projects" rather than capital investment projects.[8] As a result it may not be possible to identify infrastructure projects within the national development plan or annual budget documents. Countries need to establish a consistent set of assumptions and classifications, aligned with international benchmarks, if a reliable bridge is to be built between the planning framework and the budget.

Other features of public financial management systems can help improve the link between planning and budgeting. These are more widely applied in advanced economies and emerging market economies, which generally have more efficient decision-making processes and higher capacity than low-income countries. For example, if countries have put in place a program- or performance-based management system (Curristine and Flynn 2013), it is helpful to include a framework for measuring outputs, outcomes, and other aspects of performance that is common to the annual budgets, the medium-term budget framework, and the national development plan. In practice, however, different concepts and definitions are frequently used, even in more developed economies. In advanced economies and some emerging market economies, spending reviews applied to sectors or state enterprises with heavy infrastructure needs (for example, energy, transport, and water) can also provide a useful bridge between planning and budgeting.

## Public Investment Programs

Another widely used tool to help integrate planning and budgeting is a public investment program. At its simplest, a public investment program comprises a list of projects, small or large, a country wants to implement to meet the goals and objectives of its national development plan. Some countries provide rough estimates of the total cost of these projects, sometimes broken down by year, but the quality of these projections varies widely. In more advanced systems, the public investment program includes a pipeline only of projects that have been subject to

[7] A rolling framework (covering, for example, four years) is one in which, at the end of each year, the first year of the framework is moved forward by one year to become the new base year, and one year is added to the end of the four-year period.

[8] The concept of the "development budget," widely used in Africa and Asia, often includes both current and capital expenditure. To get around this problem, it is common for countries to report development spending using the economic classification to identify current and capital expenditure. However, this is not the same as identifying individual capital projects, with their unique demands for appraisal, selection, monitoring, and management. Many budget and supporting information systems found in low-income countries do not currently identify capital projects within their development budget.

a feasibility study and cost-benefit appraisal, have been selected to be included in the medium-term budget framework, and are based on more reliable cost estimates. Ideally, public investment programs should provide robust resource projections for investment projects over the medium term, but this objective is rarely met in practice.

Public investment programs emerged initially in the 1970s and 1980s and were expanded in the 1990s, accompanying multiyear national or strategic development plans (Jacobs 2008). Economic growth models popular at that time helped stimulate interest in the development of public investment programs by providing a simple justification for increased public investment.[9] This basic prescription underpinned recommendations supported by development partners for governments to introduce lists of investment projects (basic public investment programs), funded by the domestic budget or (mainly) by external finance. The Public (Sector) Investment Reviews, popular in the 1980s and often carried out by World Bank–funded teams, were a by-product of this approach (Jacobs 2008).[10]

A key objective of introducing public investment programs, for both governments and external partners, was to provide a tool for the coordination of overseas development assistance. The disbursement of resources on projects supported by development partners could help governments with their planning and their requests for additional external support, including technical assistance. The literature cites numerous examples in which public investment programs were used to facilitate coordination between the government and development partners. For example, coordination was an explicit rationale given by the Kenyan government for introducing a public investment program, specifically "to become a tool for better aid coordination to assist in the matching of Government investment needs with donor financing opportunities" (Kenya National Treasury).[11]

How useful are public investment programs as a tool of infrastructure planning? An analysis of 218 countries and independent territories by the authors

---

[9] The implied, simplistic message of the celebrated Harrod-Domar model, for example, was that a higher rate of economic growth could be achieved by increasing capital investment. Furthermore, if domestic savings rates were insufficient to generate the investment required to achieve the desired growth rate, the thinking was that foreign savings (external financing) should be used (Rosenstein-Rodan 1961).

[10] Jacobs (2008) noted that there was a symbiotic relationship between Public Investment Reviews and public investment programs. Eventually, the analysis in the Public Investment Reviews expanded beyond just investment to include all public expenditures, resulting in their transformation into Public Expenditure Reviews. Over time, the influence of these simplistic models has waned, as there has been little evidence that the linear relationship between growth and investment worked as supposed (Burnside and Dollar 2000).

[11] Kenya National Treasury, "Public Investment Programme." Accessed in November 2018 from http://www.treasury.go.ke/28-departments/79-public-investment-programme.html.

**Figure 12.2. Classification of Use of PIPs**

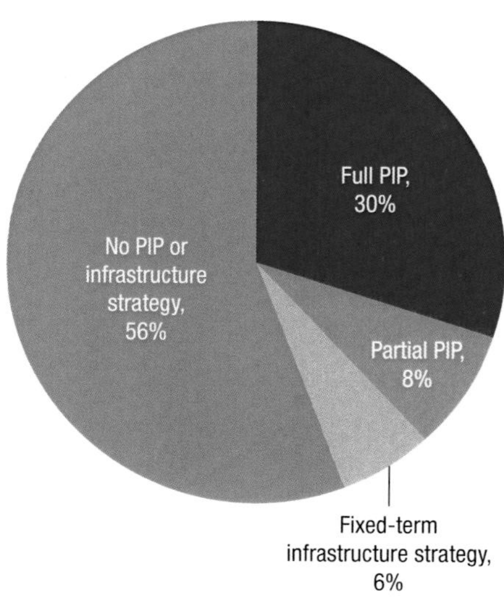


Source: IMF staff calculations, based on online searches for 218 countries and independent territories.
Note: A full PIP refers to a rolling multiyear list of public investment projects that have been selected for inclusion in a multiyear budgetary framework. A partial PIP has some elements of a full PIP but is not part of a multiyear budgetary framework. PIP = public investment program.

(summarized in Annex 12.1) suggests that, globally, around one-third of countries currently have in place multiyear rolling public investment programs, while a further 8 percent have some elements of a public investment program in their budgets (Figure 12.2).[12] The prevalence of public investment programs is much higher in low-income developing countries than in advanced economies or emerging market economies (Figure 12.3). This is not surprising because the former group is generally much more dependent on projects financed by development partners. The regional distribution of public investment programs largely reflects income levels across regions (Figure 12.4).[13]

Public investment programs need to be appropriately designed to serve as an effective link between infrastructure plans and budgets. Countries should aim to ensure the following:

[12] This survey, and the survey of organizational arrangements for planning and budgeting discussed in the "Organizational Arrangements" section of this chapter, was carried out by Mary Betley and is based on publicly available information.

[13] Further details of this analysis are provided in the companion working paper.

**Figure 12.3. PIP Prevalance, by Income Group**
*(Percent)*

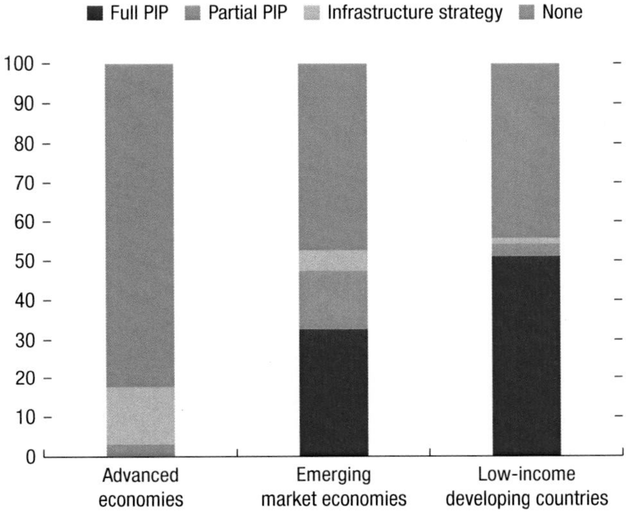

Source: IMF staff calculations, based on online searches for 218 countries and independent territories.
Note: A full PIP refers to a rolling multiyear list of public investment projects that have been selected for inclusion in a multiyear budgetary framework. A partial PIP refers to a PIP with some elements of a full PIP but not part of a multiyear budgetary framework. PIP = public investment program.

- The resource framework for the public investment program is realistic, particularly in terms of forward projections and the planning of projects, which are due to start in the later years of the medium-term period;
- The public investment program is not simply an unconstrained wish list of poorly prepared and unscreened or weakly screened projects searching for domestic or external funding;
- The public investment program pipeline includes both ongoing projects and new projects being planned for the medium term, ideally with regularly updated estimates of their total cost; and
- An appropriate link exists with the government's strategic/results framework on the one hand and with the medium-term budget framework on the other hand.

Most public investment programs also do not provide any mechanism for incorporating the recurrent costs associated with infrastructure costs (for example, the costs of equipping and staffing a hospital). Lack of integration of current and capital spending is exacerbated to the extent that public investment programs were, and in some countries still are, associated with separate development budgets.

**Figure 12.4. PIP Prevalence, by Region**
*(Percent)*

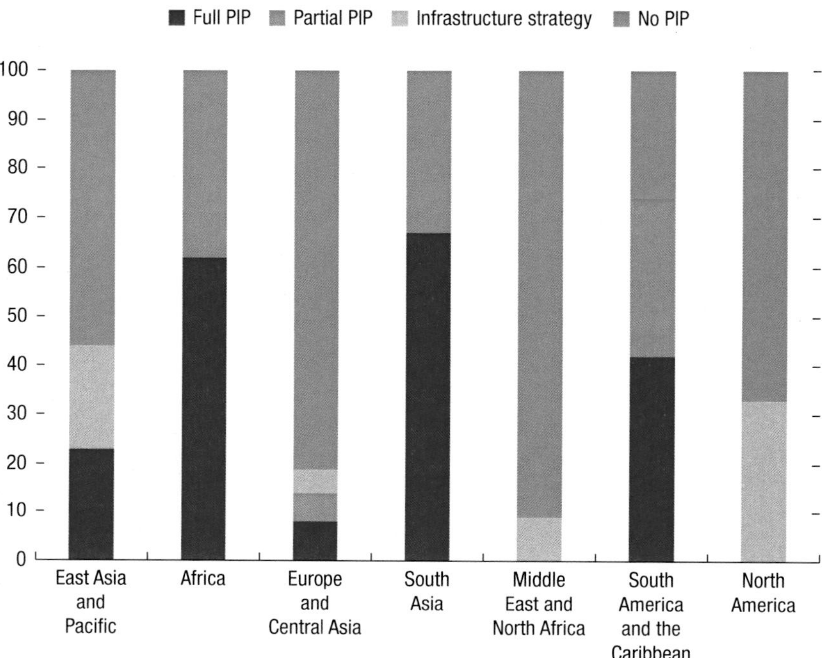


Source: IMF staff calculations, based on online searches for 218 countries and independent territories.
Note: A full PIP refers to a rolling multiyear list of public investment projects that have been selected for inclusion in a multiyear budgetary framework. A partial PIP refers to a PIP with some elements of a full PIP but not part of a multiyear budgetary framework. PIP = public investment program.

## ORGANIZATIONAL ARRANGEMENTS

A crucially important issue that remains unresolved in the literature and in practical application is the organizational arrangements for planning and budgeting. There is no uniformity of practice across countries. Broadly, the arrangements fall into the following three categories: (1) separate entities—the central functions of planning and budgeting are undertaken by two separate ministries or agencies, (2) a single central ministry (typically the finance ministry) is responsible for both planning and budgeting functions, and (3) there is no agency undertaking a central planning function.

The authors analyzed the organizational responsibilities for planning and budgeting in 218 countries and independent territories (see Annex 12.2). Table 12.2 summarizes the results (see also Figures 12.5 and 12.6). Of the countries surveyed, 37 percent have established a single organization for both functions, in most cases a ministry of finance and planning or a ministry of finance with a distinct planning section. In some, line ministries are responsible for preparing strategies or plans at the sector, ministry, or program level, and the central budgeting institution or

**TABLE 12.2.**

Summary of Organizational Arrangements for Planning and Budgeting

| | Single Planning and Budgeting Entity | Separate Planning and Budgeting Entities | No Central-Level Planning Entity |
|---|---|---|---|
| Advanced economies | 15% | 26% | 59% |
| Emerging market economies | 39% | 56% | 5% |
| Low-income developing countries | 47% | 53% | 0% |
| All countries | 37% | 49% | 15% |

Source: Authors.

Note: The data shown exclude Syria. The classification of countries by income group is based on the list in the IMF's April 2019 *World Economic Outlook*.

ministry of finance is responsible for certain functions, such as project selection or the independent review of cost-benefit analyses. Almost half the countries surveyed have established separate entities (such as a ministry of finance or ministry of the budget and a ministry of planning or economic development), which carry out the government's planning and budgeting functions. The remaining 15 percent do not have a central organization responsible for national development planning.

The pattern of institutional arrangements varies widely across countries and regions. Nearly all low-income developing countries and emerging market economies have established a single or separate planning agency at the center of government, but this pattern is less common in advanced economies, where nearly

**Figure 12.5. Organization of Responsibilities for Planning and Budgeting**
*(Percent)*

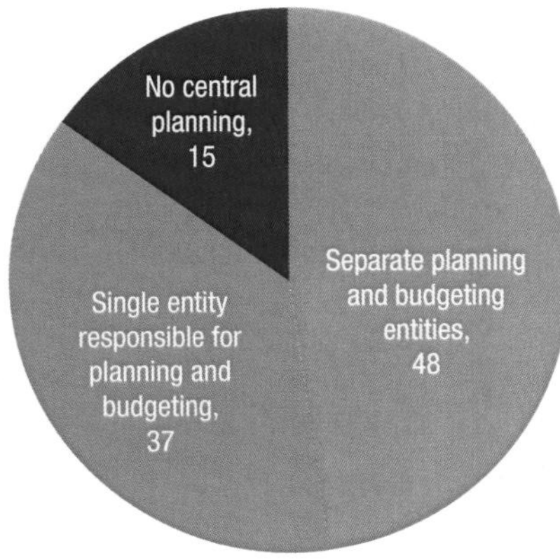


Source: Authors, based on online searches for all 218 countries.

**Figure 12.6. Organizational Responsibilities, by Income Group**
*(Percent)*

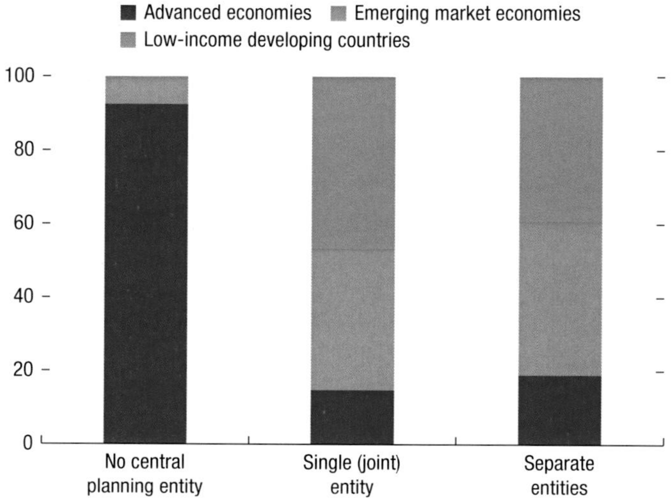

Advanced economies
Emerging market economies
Low-income developing countries

100
80
60
40
20
0

No central planning entity
Single (joint) entity
Separate entities

Source: Authors, based on online searches for all 218 countries.

60 percent of countries have no central planning agency. Many advanced economies and some emerging market economies have decentralized their planning functions to line ministries—and thus away from the center. They also have no (or little) need to manage externally financed infrastructure projects or to use a national development plan to mobilize resources from development partners. Figure 12.7 shows the distribution of organizational arrangements by region, which varies widely according to the mix of advanced economies, emerging market economies, and low-income developing countries in the region. For example, both in Latin America and the Caribbean and in the Middle East and North Africa region, all countries surveyed have some type of planning entity.

The organizational arrangements for planning and budgeting described previously have been fluid in many countries. The survey shows that many countries have changed their organizational arrangements for planning and budgeting at least once over the past couple of decades, either splitting out planning functions from a single ministry that originally covered both finance and planning functions into a separate ministry or agency, or consolidating these functions into a single entity (such as the finance ministry). Some large countries (for example, Brazil, Kenya, Korea, Nigeria, and the Philippines) have experienced three or more such back-and-forth iterations over the past 20 years. The effect of these changes on the efficiency and effectiveness of planning and budgeting processes has not been assessed.

This instability largely reflects political economy factors. Where planning and budgeting functions are situated in separate ministries, the minister of planning's role has some of the characteristics of a line minister as the proponent of new policies and projects. In contrast, one of the finance minister's key roles is to

**Figure 12.7. Organizational Responsibilities, by Region**
*(Percent)*

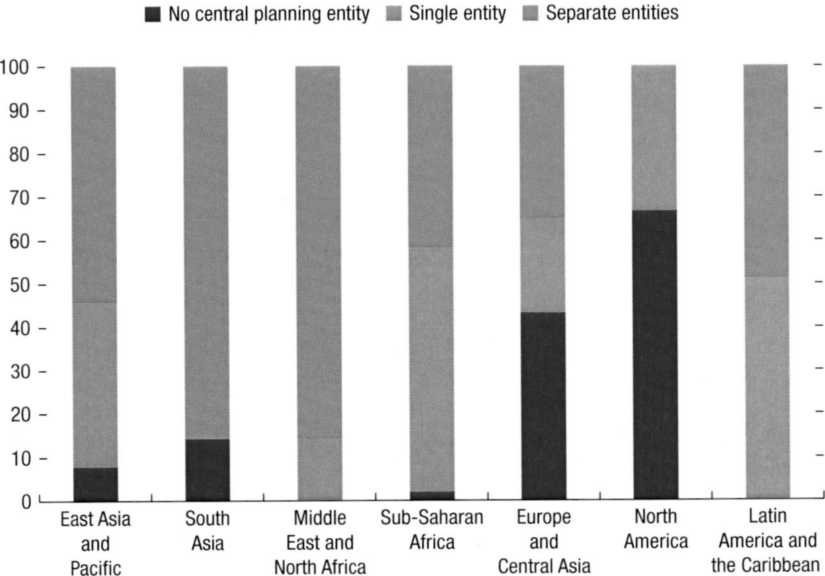


Source: Authors, based on online searches for all 218 countries.

eliminate ideas for new projects that do not create economic or social value, find savings in ministers' spending programs, or cut out waste. As Schick (1966, 243) put it, "planning and budgeting have run along separate tracks and have invited different perspectives, the one conservative and negativistic, the other innovative and expansionist . . . in its extreme form, the one measures saving, the other spending." A similar tension may arise when separate units within the same ministry perform planning and budgeting functions, and where the minister of finance and planning wears two hats that do not fit comfortably on one head.

The inherent tension between the planning and budgeting functions does not necessarily have a negative effect on the efficiency of decision-making about infrastructure investment. If properly harnessed, it can serve a useful role in creating a symbiotic relationship between the functions. Thus, finance officials can challenge the proposals for new infrastructure put forward by the planning ministry to ensure they are economically and financially robust. Similarly, planners can challenge budget officials to ensure fiscal space is allocated in a manner that allows policy objectives and plans to be realized. Countries where such a symbiotic relationship exists are not easy to find but include Colombia, where planning and budgeting are closely coordinated both at the working and political levels, and Ireland, whose new planning framework includes medium- and long-term projections of infrastructure requirements prepared by the finance ministry in close coordination with the planning ministry.

Government decisions on whether to combine or separate planning and budgeting functions, and on the appointment of the heads of the responsible agencies, often signal the views of the political leadership on how much power to vest in a single minister or whether to operate a policy of "divide and rule." In many instances, a key consideration is the need to balance the ambitions of the planning function and the fiscal conservatism of the budget function. Institutional rivalries tend to prevail.[14] Some countries have attempted to use interministerial committees and commissions to better coordinate the work on planning and budgeting and to achieve a balance between the competing policy objectives noted previously. An example is Colombia. A high-level committee composed of cabinet ministers (*El Consejo Nacional de Política Económica y Social,* CONPES), chaired by the president, approves the national development plan, the medium-term fiscal framework, and the annual budget, after the latter has been reviewed by the CONFIS (*Consejo Superior de Política Fiscal*). CONFIS is chaired by the Minister of Finance with full participation of the National Planning Department.

## THE ROLE OF SPECIALIZED INFRASTRUCTURE AGENCIES

Political economy factors can influence decisions on infrastructure investment in various ways. Most investment projects have multiyear fiscal implications and larger projects often have fiscal and economic consequences that extend beyond a single electoral cycle. Gupta, Liu, and Mulas-Granados (2016), for example, have documented the strong effect of the political cycle on public investment activity across different country groups.[15] In advanced economies, older democracies, and countries with very efficient management systems, fluctuations in public investment tend to be linked less to electoral cycles. Williams (2017) used project data to examine investment efficiency through noncompletion rates, and attributed observed inefficiencies at least partially to the political process, noting also that the effects of political failure could be mitigated by stronger fiscal institutions.

Some countries have aimed to establish institutional arrangements to reduce the effect of the political cycle on public investment decisions. In recent years, especially in advanced economies, some entities have been set up to address the reality of the political cycle and its effect on public investment (for a full discussion, see OECD 2017).[16] These agencies, which typically have a lot of operational independence, are

---

[14] As Caiden and Wildavsky (1974) note, "The relationship between planning and finance is generally one-sided. Finance usually holds most of the cards. It will allow planning influence up to the point of actual decision, but it will keep for itself the power to make decisions on resources. . . This is one reason why planners have found it hard to make the budget carry out the plans."

[15] The results show that—for a sample of 67 advanced economies, emerging market economies, and low-income developing countries—the growth rate of investment is larger at the beginning of a government, peaks at about 28 months before an election, and declines fast as the election approaches.

[16] See OECD (2017) for a review of experiences with strategic infrastructure planning in a selection of OECD countries.

designed to help improve the efficiency and effectiveness of public investment, and to protect infrastructure to the extent possible from short-term political influences and the electoral cycle. Some centralized agencies also provide technical support services to line ministries (such as on the appraisal and selection of projects).

Infrastructure Australia, for example, is responsible for conducting strategic audits of nationally significant infrastructure projects and developing 15-year rolling infrastructure plans that specify national and state priorities. The agency also determines which nationally significant projects are included in Australia's Infrastructure Priority List. It enjoys operational independence from the executive by law. In the United Kingdom, a National Infrastructure Commission was established in 2015 to review the country's infrastructure needs and provide advisory services to government agencies. A separate agency, the Infrastructure and Projects Authority, monitors progress in implementing major projects. In New Zealand, the Infrastructure Transactions Unit in the Treasury helps deliver major infrastructure projects (New Zealand Treasury 2018).

Another approach followed in some countries has been to establish an infrastructure "delivery" unit at the center of government, sometimes in the president's or prime minister's office. Examples include the Performance Management and Delivery Unit (PEMANDU) in Malaysia and the United Kingdom's former Prime Minister's Delivery Unit. Units such as these track strategically important investment projects and may take remedial action if the projects go off track or underperform. Some delivery units may also provide technical support to line ministries (for example, the *Escritório de Gestão de Projetos* in some Brazilian states and the Office of *Proyectos México* [Mexico Projects], which is under the auspices of the government's development bank [*Banobras*] and provides technical support on public-private partnerships).

The goal of these specialized agencies at the center of government is not to undertake or duplicate functions that could be better performed at ministry level. Rather, they are designed to help create a coherent long-term strategy for national infrastructure planning, and account for economic and social interdependencies and Sustainable Development Goal priorities such as climate change and gender equality. The effectiveness of these arrangements, however, has yet to be assessed comprehensively.

At the same time, the emergence of new and nontraditional investors in infrastructure is challenging traditional planning and budgeting institutions. China, for example, has become the largest source of infrastructure financing in Africa in recent years (McKinsey 2017), and its Belt and Road Initiative is expected to transform transcontinental infrastructure.[17] The large volume of resources now available, combined with strong supply-side incentives to execute

[17] In Africa, for example, at least five countries have had their rail transport systems financed by China (Angola, Djibouti, Ethiopia, Kenya, and Nigeria). At the close of the 2018 China-Africa Forum for Cooperation Summit held in Beijing, the Chinese government announced that it had set up a new fund of 900 billion Yuan ($60 billion) intended for Africa's development. This fund covers telecommunications, roads, bridges and ports, energy, human resources development, government buildings, and other infrastructure.

projects and disburse funding quickly, has made it possible for many poor countries to finance megaprojects for which funding would previously have been unavailable. It is important to ensure that these new sources of finance, and an analysis of the associated projects, are brought within the scope of a country's planning and budgeting processes to ensure that investments are fiscally sustainable and consistent with a country's priorities for economic and social development.

## CONCLUSIONS

The main conclusions of this chapter are as follows.

First, planning functions have evolved over the years, from the historic Soviet and French models, in diverse ways across countries and regions. Norms and standards that define how planning should be carried out and by which entity are rare. Some countries continue to prepare full-blown national development plans, while others—more typically several advanced economies—rely on systems in which sectors play a dominant role in decision making, notably on infrastructure investment. A flexible approach to planning, focused on key economic and social objectives, can achieve better results than traditional methods.

Second, good integration of planning and budgeting functions is key to quality infrastructure, although difficult to achieve in practice. The absence of a resource envelope for capital projects that is binding and built into the planning process is a serious challenge in most countries. Medium-term budget frameworks and public investment programs can provide a bridge between planning and budgeting functions, if designed properly, and the chapter provides general guidance on how these mechanisms can be improved.

Third, planning and budgeting functions are based on fundamentally different objectives, approaches, and skills. There is a creative tension between the two functions that in principle can lead to better decisions on the management of public investment, yet often does not in practice. It is much more important for countries to ensure that their planning and budgeting functions are carried out efficiently and effectively than that they take a specific organizational form, for which no unique model exists.

Fourth, the recent establishment of semiautonomous agencies at the center of government has helped mitigate the influence of the electoral cycle of political opportunism on infrastructure decisions. These entities are designed to provide strategic oversight of infrastructure planning and deliver technical services to line ministries on the appraisal, selection, financing, and monitoring of infrastructure projects. Some emerging market economies and low-income developing countries may be able to learn from these initiatives, while noting that they require a high level of skilled capacity and access to plentiful and reliable data.

**ANNEX TABLE 12.1.**

## Typology of Public Investment Program, by Country/Territory and Income Category (Selected Countries)

| Country | Full Public Investment Program | Partial Public Investment Program | Fixed-Term Infrastructure Strategy | No Public Investment Program or Infrastructure Strategy |
|---|---|---|---|---|
| **Advanced economies** | | | | |
| Australia | | | × | |
| Austria | | | | × |
| Canada | | | × | |
| France | | | | × |
| Japan | | | | × |
| Korea | | | | × |
| United Kingdom | | | × | |
| **Emerging market economies** | | | | |
| Angola | × | | | |
| Armenia | | | | × |
| Brazil | | × | | |
| Colombia | | × | | |
| Egypt | | | | × |
| Hungary | | | | × |
| Indonesia | | | | × |
| Iran | | | | × |
| Kosovo | × | | | |
| Mexico | | × | | |
| Mongolia | × | | | |
| Russian Federation | | | | × |
| South Africa | | | | × |
| Ukraine | | | | × |
| **Low-income developing countries** | | | | |
| Bangladesh | | | | × |
| Cambodia | × | | | |
| Ethiopia | | | | × |
| Rwanda | × | | | |
| Senegal | × | | | |
| Tajikistan | | | | × |

Source: Authors.

Note: This annex presents a selection of data from the full analysis of 218 countries and territories prepared by the authors. The countries and territories are based on the World Bank's classification, defined as those in which the authorities report separate social or economic statistics. Further details are available on request. A full public investment program refers to a rolling multiyear list of public investment projects included in a medium-term budget framework. A partial public investment program has some elements of a full public investment program but is not part of a medium-term budget framework.

**ANNEX TABLE 12.2.**

**Typology of Planning and Budgeting Institutions, by Country/Territory and Income Category (Selected Countries)**

| Country | Single Planning/ Budgeting Entity | Separate Planning/ Budgeting Entity | No Central Planning Entity |
|---|---|---|---|
| **Advanced economies** | | | |
| Australia | | | × |
| Austria | | | × |
| Canada | | | × |
| France | | | × |
| Japan | | | × |
| Korea | × | | |
| United Kingdom | | | × |
| **Emerging market economies** | | | |
| Angola | | × | |
| Armenia | | × | |
| Brazil | | × | |
| Colombia | | × | |
| Egypt | | × | |
| Hungary | × | | |
| Indonesia | | × | |
| Iran | | × | |
| Kosovo | | × | |
| Mexico | × | | |
| Mongolia | | × | |
| Russian Federation | × | | |
| South Africa | | × | |
| Ukraine | | × | |
| **Low-income developing countries** | | | |
| Bangladesh | | × | |
| Cambodia | | × | |
| Ethiopia | × | | |
| Rwanda | × | | |
| Senegal | × | | |
| Tajikistan | | × | |

Source: Authors.

Note: This annex presents a selection of data from the full analysis of 218 countries and territories prepared by the authors. The countries and territories are based on the World Bank's classification, defined as those in which the authorities report separate social or economic statistics. Further details are available on request. The category of a single planning/budgeting institution includes countries where there is no separate planning entity, but some planning functions are carried out by the finance ministry or the institution responsible for budgeting.

## REFERENCES


Agarwala, Ramgopal. 1983. "Planning in Developing Countries: Lessons of Experience." World Bank Working Paper 576, World Bank, Washington, DC.

Allen, Richard, Taz Chaponda, Lesley Fisher, and Rohini Ray. 2017. "Medium-term Budget Frameworks in Sub-Saharan African Countries." IMF Working Paper 17/203, International Monetary Fund, Washington DC.

Burnside, Craig, and David Dollar. 2000. "Aid Policies and Growth." *American Economic Review* 90 (4): 847–68.

Caiden, Naomi, and Aaron Wildavsky. 1974. *Planning and Budgeting in Poor Countries.* New York: Wiley.

Chimhowu, Admos, David Hulme, and Lachlan Munro. 2019. "The New National Development Planning and Global Development Goals: Processes and Partnerships." *World Development* 120: 76–89.

Curristine, Teresa, and Suzanne Flynn. 2013. "In Search of Results: Strengthening Public Sector Performance." In *The Emerging Architecture of Public Financial Management*, edited by Marco Cangiano, Teresa Curristine, and Michel Lazare. Washington, DC: International Monetary Fund.

de Renzio, Paolo. 2013. "Assessing and Comparing the Quality of Public Financial Management Systems: Theory, History and Evidence." In *The International Handbook of Public Financial Management*, edited by Richard Allen, Richard Hemming, and Barry H. Potter. Basingstoke, UK: Palgrave Macmillan.

Diamond, Jack. 2013. "Policy Formulation and the Budget Process." In *The International Handbook of Public Financial Management*, edited by Richard Allen, Richard Hemming, and Barry H. Potter. Basingstoke, UK: Palgrave Macmillan: 4.

Ericson, Richard E. 1991. "The Classical Soviet-Type Economy: Nature of the System and Implications for Reform." *Journal of Economic Perspectives* 5 (4): 11–27.

Gaspar, Victor, David Amaglobeli, Mercedes Garcia-Escribana, Delphine Prady, and Mauricio Soto. 2019. *Fiscal Policy and Development: Human, Social and Physical Investment for the SDGs*. Washington, DC: International Monetary Fund.

Gupta, Sanjeev, Estelle X. Liu, and Carlos Mulas-Granados. 2016. "Now or Later? The Political Economy of Public Investment in Democracies." *European Journal of Political Economy* 45: 101–14.

Harris, Jason, Richard Hughes, Gösta Ljungman, and Carla Sateriale. 2013. "Medium-term Budget Frameworks in Advanced Economies: Objectives, Design and Performance." In *The Emerging Architecture of Public Financial Management*, edited by Marco Cangiano, Teresa Curristine, and Michel Lazare. Washington, DC: International Monetary Fund.

Heller, Peter. 1982. "The Problem of Recurrent Costs in the Budgeting and Planning Process." In *The Recurrent Costs in the Countries of the Sahel.* Paris: Club du Sahel/CILIS.

International Monetary Fund. 2019. "The Gambia: Technical Assistance Report—Public Investment Management Assessment." IMF Country Report 19/277, International Monetary Fund, Washington, DC.

Jacobs, Davina. 2008. "A Review of Capital Budgeting Practices." IMF Working Paper 08/160, International Monetary Fund, Washington, DC.

Kenya National Treasury. nd. "Public Investment Programme." http://www.treasury.go.ke/28-departments/79-public-investment-programme.html

Kindleberger, Charles. 1967. "French Planning." In *National Economic Planning*, edited by Max F. Millikan. New York: National Bureau of Economic Research.

McKinsey and Company. 2017. *Dance of the Lions and Dragons: How Are Africa and China Engaging, and How Will the Partnership Evolve?* New York: McKinsey.

New Zealand Treasury. 2018. *A New Independent Infrastructure Body—Background Papers.* Wellington: Government of New Zealand.

Nove, Alec. 1961. *The Soviet Economy.* London: Routledge.

Nove, Alec. 1986. *The Soviet Economic System*. 3rd edition. London: George Allen and Unwin.

Organisation for Economic Co-operation and Development (OECD) and National Infrastructure Commission: International Transport Forum. 2017. *Strategic Infrastructure Planning: International Best Practice*. OECD, Paris.

Rosenstein-Rodan, Paul. 1961. *International Aid for Underdeveloped Countries.* Cambridge, MA: MIT.

Schiavo-Campo, Salvatore. 2007. "Budget Preparation and Approval." In *Budgeting and Budgetary Institutions*, edited by Anwar Shah. Washington, DC: World Bank: 2–5.

Schick, Allen. 1966. "The Road to PPB: The Stages of Budget Reform." *Public Administration Review: Planning-Programming-Budgeting Systems: A Symposium* 26 (4): 243–58.

United Nations. 2017. *High-Level Political Forum on Sustainable Development: 2017 Voluntary National Reviews Synthesis Report*. New York: United Nations.

Waterston, Albert. 1969. *Development Planning: Lessons of Experience*. Washington DC: World Bank.

Williams, Martin. 2017. "The Political Economy of Unfinished Development Projects: Corruption, Clientelism, or Collective Choice?" *American Political Science Review* 111 (4): 705–23.

World Bank and the Government of Rwanda. 2018. "Future Drivers of Growth in Rwanda: Innovation, Integration, Agglomeration, and Competition." World Bank Working Paper 131875, World Bank, Washington, DC.

World Bank Operations Evaluation Department and IMF Independent Evaluation Office. 2005. *The Poverty Reduction Strategy Initiative: Findings from 10 Country Case Studies of World Bank and IMF Support.* Washington, DC: World Bank and International Monetary Fund.

CHAPTER 13

# Best Practices in Project Appraisal and Selection

**Robert Taliercio and Eduardo Andrés Estrada**

## INTRODUCTION

Project appraisal and project selection are key functions in the planning and allocation stages of public investment. Effective appraisal supports decision making for optimization of project design and impact and is critical in selecting projects that yield the highest social and economic returns. Project appraisal and selection have vital roles for infrastructure governance because they serve a gatekeeping function, ensuring in principle that only socially and economically viable projects reach the implementation stage. Moreover, good appraisal and selection methods increase the probability of maximizing net benefits to society, including by scrutinizing investment and operational costs to avoid unfinished projects or inefficient operations (Rajaram and others 2014).

Good project appraisal and selection requires institutions capable of designing appraisal methodologies and having procedures in place for sound project selection. Inaccurate and unrealistic appraisal may lead to inefficiency and wastage of resources through cost overruns during implementation, or even to incomplete projects. Furthermore, poor project selection can result in overprogramming of projects or wasteful white elephant projects with limited social and economic value (Rajaram and others 2010). Examples include grandiose presidential palaces, vast university campuses, or unnecessarily large airports (Mauro 1997).

The IMF's Public Investment Management Assessment (PIMA) framework assesses whether countries have a project appraisal system that ensures major project proposals are subject to rigorous appraisal using standard methodology and taking account of potential risks, systematic vetting processes for project selection based on published standard criteria, and inclusion in a pipeline of approved projects (see Figure 13.1; IMF 2018). Often, this is not the case: project appraisal and

This chapter was drafted with funding support from the Korea Development Institute School Partnership Trust Fund. The authors thank Jim Brumby (Senior Advisor, World Bank), Carolina Renteria (Division Chief, IMF), Ceren Ozer (Senior Governance Specialist, World Bank), and Ian Hawkesworth (Senior Governance Specialist, World Bank) for their overall support and guidance; Isabel Rial (Senior Economist, IMF) for assistance with navigating the PIMA data set; and Jay Hyung-Kim (Advisor, World Bank) and Xingjun Ye (Research Analyst, World Bank) for useful inputs.

**Figure 13.1. Average PIMA Scores for Project Appraisal and Selection**

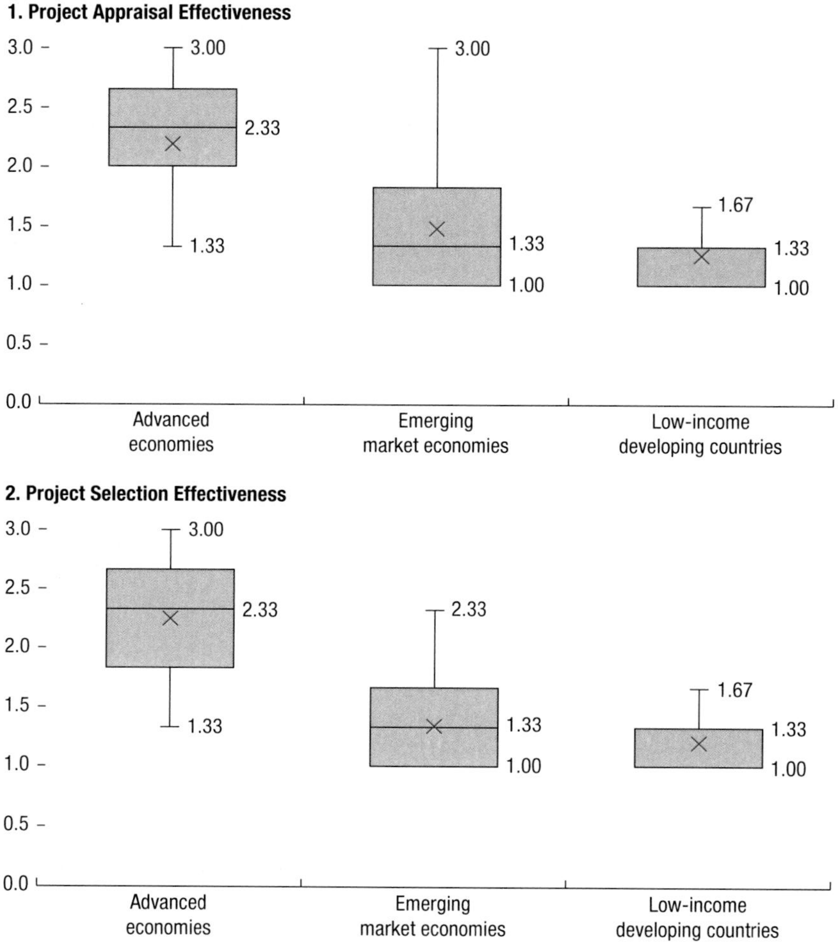

Source: World Bank and IMF staff calculations using the PIMA data set.

Note: PIMA = Public Investment Management Assessment. Dispersion of PIMA scores for project appraisal and selection effectiveness by income level. Values displayed for the minimum, average, and maximum scores by income level; median displayed with an ×.

selection generally score quite poorly in institutional design (de jure) and effectiveness (de facto) in comparison with the other public investment management practices covered in PIMA, particularly in low-income developing countries and emerging market economies. Given the critical importance of project appraisal and selection in infrastructure governance, this is an issue of great concern.

This chapter assesses good practices in project appraisal and selection. It discusses the defining characteristics of an effective project appraisal function, including types of evaluation, appraisal methodologies, and safeguards against undue political interference. Then it examines how to link project appraisal and project selection to the budget cycle. The chapter finds that a clear, well-supported appraisal methodology and published project selection criteria with well-defined processes for project selection are critical for good infrastructure governance. Undue political influence is an issue in many countries and should be mitigated through rigorous analysis, scrutiny by a central ministry using clear and transparent procedures, and an independent review of projects before they are included in the budget. In low-capacity countries, outsourcing of project appraisal could be considered but should be balanced with the need for in-house capacity building and the development of practical know-how.

## CHARACTERISTICS OF THE PROJECT APPRAISAL FUNCTION

### Types of Evaluation and Their Application

Four main types of evaluations are used in project appraisal (Box 13.1). In general, all countries rely to a great extent on cost-benefit analysis, although they also complement it in specific cases with other methodologies. In the United Kingdom, cost-benefit analysis is the default, whereas in Korea, which uses

### Box 13.1. Main Types of Evaluation Used for Project Appraisal

**Cost-Benefit Analysis**

This technique is used to compare the total costs of a project with its total benefits. It provides the net cost or benefit associated with a given project. Alternatives are appraised and compared to select the best approach, the one that yields the most benefits relative to the costs (Kaplan 2014a). The intellectual and conceptual underpinnings of cost-benefit analysis are robust as it is based on principles of applied welfare economics, which provide a clear and rigorous framework for assessing the "social" (or economic) value of projects. However, it requires capacity in advanced economics, and some variables (such as more intangible benefits or costs) can be difficult to estimate.

**Cost-Effectiveness Analysis**

This is an alternative to cost-benefit analysis that compares the relative costs of two or more courses of action with their related outcomes. Cost-effectiveness analysis is more commonly used when it is not possible to carry out cost-benefit analysis, in instances when quantifying the benefits is difficult (Kaplan 2014b), or when outputs are standardized. The benefit of cost-effectiveness analysis is its simpler methodology.

**Multicriteria Analysis**

This uses weighting and scoring of the most important project impacts. It is often used when quantification of costs and benefits is not pursued. Multicriteria analysis can be used to compare alternative actions based on the aggregation of criteria, which can be qualitative or quantitative. Multicriteria analysis can be easy to apply. However, it lacks theoretical

**Box 13.1. (*Continued*)**

or conceptual underpinnings for investment appraisal. The approach relies on decision makers having a high degree of discretion and creates the risk of preferences driving the analysis.

**Simplified Methodologies**

Simplified methodologies attempt to evaluate a project using techniques that are simpler in scope. These are used for back-of-the-envelope analysis of low-cost investments and could include simplified templates for cost-benefit analysis or cost-effectiveness analysis, or simplified multicriteria analysis using a few weights with a basic rating scale. These approaches can be used when more rigorous methods are infeasible or too costly.

Source: Authors.

*multicriteria analysis*, cost-benefit analysis is the most heavily weighted component of the analysis. In Ireland, the methodological choice depends on the type, scale, and complexity of the project, with cost-benefit analysis used wherever possible. It is worth noting that in some countries, such as the United Kingdom, cost-benefit analysis is being used more today than in the past because there have been concerns about inefficiencies resulting from the use of methods in which economic efficiency has less weight.[1]

The main phases of evaluation encompass the following:

- *Prefeasibility* (also known as options appraisal in some systems), under which a study is prepared presenting the relevant alternatives to solve a given problem, risks are identified, and preliminary estimates of costs and benefits are provided; and
- *Feasibility*, which expands on the prefeasibility phase by refining data collection, providing detailed estimates of costs and benefits for the selected alternative, performing a detailed assessment of risks, and assessing environmental and social impacts (Rajaram and others 2010).

In some countries, detailed project designs and tender documents are also subject to evaluation. Reappraisal may be carried out if project assumptions change after approval, or at the end of the construction phase or during operation of the project, mainly for monitoring purposes.[2,3]

---

[1] See the new Green Book (HM Treasury 2018).

[2] A unique characteristic of project appraisal in Korea is the use of a Reassessment Study of Feasibility, which is triggered when cost overruns exceed 20 percent of planned costs (for certain types of projects). Project costs are monitored through a management system. In a few instances, projects were canceled because the Reassessment Study was applied (Kim 2012).

[3] Another form of evaluation is retrospective analysis, which is conducted at the end of the project (Florio and Vignetti 2013). This type of evaluation compares the outputs and outcomes of a project with the objectives envisioned at the design stage (Rajaram and others 2014). Technically, analysis after the fact is not part of project appraisal, but it provides a feedback loop with lessons learned from concluded projects that ideally would feed into the design and appraisal of new projects.

Conditions for application of the appraisal system vary widely between countries. Decision rules around cost thresholds and exemptions govern whether project proposals are subject to appraisals and, if so, which types of appraisals are to be used. In principle, all projects should be covered by an economic appraisal. However, in practice, given resource and capacity constraints, countries limit how and under which conditions different appraisal techniques are applied. In some countries, such as Norway, Canada, and Korea, only larger projects are subject to rigorous cost-benefit analysis. In other countries, such as Ireland, the appraisal methodology depends on the type, scale, and complexity of the project (Box 13.2).

The share of the public investment budget that is subject to project appraisal is determined largely by the thresholds applied in the appraisal system. Yet, no established best practice exists when it comes to using such thresholds, which

## Box 13.2. Thresholds for Requiring Application of the Appraisal System

Examples illustrate the wide variation between countries in conditions for application of the appraisal system in terms of threshold values and exempted sectors or areas.

- In Chile, all investment initiatives financed by the government, regardless of the amount, are subject to technical and economic analysis. This includes municipal projects financed with capital transfers from the central government, provided the transfers cover more than 50 percent of project costs (Ministry of Social Development and Ministry of Finance 2018).
- In Korea, the threshold is W50 billion ($43 million) for central government projects, and W30 billion ($26 million) for subnational government projects or projects with private participation receiving a central subsidy equal to or greater than that amount (Kim 2012).
- In Canada (Québec), the threshold is Can$50 million ($38 million) for all projects, except for those related to the maintenance or improvement of transport infrastructure, in which case the threshold is Can$100 million ($76 million), according to Samset and others (2016).
- In Norway, the threshold for central government projects is NKr750 million ($84 million), according to Samset and others (2016).
- In Ireland, the appraisal methodology to be used depends on the type, scale, and complexity of the project:
  - For project proposals below €10 million ($11 million), approving authorities should engage with sponsoring agencies as to whether an economic appraisal is required and what type of economic appraisal is appropriate.
  - For all other project proposals, approving authorities and sponsoring agencies should engage on the choice of the appropriate appraisal methodology in line with sectoral guidance. Wherever possible, cost-benefit analysis should be used. In cases where this may not be possible or desirable, cost-effectiveness or multicriteria analysis may be used.
  - Cost-benefit analysis is used for all projects more than €100 million ($111 million) (Department of Public Expenditure and Reform 2019).

Source: Authors.

**TABLE 13.1.**

**Appraisal Thresholds Normalized by GDP**

| Country | 2018 GDP ($ billion) | Project Cost Threshold ($ million) | Threshold/GDP (× 1,000) | Normalized Threshold/GDP (Relative to Ireland) |
|---|---|---|---|---|
| Canada | 1,713 | 38 | 0.022 | 0.77 |
| Ireland | 382 | 11 | 0.029 | 1.00 |
| Korea | 1,619 | 43 | 0.027 | 0.92 |
| Norway | 434 | 84 | 0.193 | 6.73 |

Source: World Bank staff calculations using GDP estimates (current US dollars) from the World Development Indicators.

have a large range, even if normalized by GDP (Table 13.1). This indicates that appraisal is operationalized very differently across countries. Thresholds are usually determined through considerations about capacity, assessment of the risk of poor project proposals, and the size of the budget. Many low-income developing countries would find it practical to set a higher initial threshold when capacity is low and gradually lower it as the capacity of the system matures.

In practice, no single appraisal system covers all public investment. For example, a central project appraisal system might not cover subnational spending or spending by state-owned enterprises. Also, some sectors could be exempted.[4] Again, there is no best practice on decision rules for jurisdictional and sectoral coverage, but they should be based on an assessment of the risk of low- or negative-value projects by sector, appraisal capacity, and the overall size of the portfolio. In general, countries should aim to expand coverage of their appraisal system. In some countries, line ministries also play a technical oversight role in relation to subnational investment and can provide technical support for their project preparation (Box 13.3).

In principle, all investment projects should undergo the same appraisal process, regardless of funding and procurement modalities, although in many countries that is not always the case. The decision on whether to realize a project through budget funding, donor funding, or a public-private partnership should be taken after the project has been determined to be a government priority and appraised.

## Decision Rules for Project Appraisal

Project appraisals consider many dimensions related to project proposals, from policy relevance and economic rationale to social and environmental impacts.

[4] In Chile, the appraisal system excludes large items such as housing subsidies and municipal investment, with some exceptions (see Box 13.2), and state-owned enterprises are covered only if the public sector has a capital contribution greater than 50 percent of state-owned enterprises' social capital. Moreover, defense and spending on natural disaster–related emergencies and reconstruction are exempted. So are public infrastructure conservation projects, but they must be recorded in the country's Integrated Project Bank (Ministry of Social Development and Ministry of Finance 2018).

### Box 13.3. Strengthening Subnational Project Preparation and Appraisal in Colombia

In Colombia, subnational governments—especially small municipalities—have limited capacity to prepare and appraise projects. Analyses have shown that public investment portfolios at the subnational level are fragmented and not aligned with strategic planning. In some cases, municipalities propose small projects only because of their lack of capacity to identify and prepare bigger projects. The general adjusted methodology for project preparation and appraisal does not differentiate between projects with different levels of complexity or risks. Moreover, projects financed by royalties from nonrenewable natural resources often do not consider operations and maintenance costs, which undermines the long-term sustainability of investments. The National Planning Department has designed a series of toolkits and technical assistance mechanisms to help municipal governments improve project preparation and appraisal. Colombia is also advancing a series of policy reforms aimed at strengthening collaboration among subnational governments in public investment and promoting development of high-impact regional investments.

Source: Authors.

They delve into the technical design and engineering of the proposed solutions and assess whether financial arrangements are sound and affordable, including whether to use commercial opportunities. They also consider whether projects are achievable from a project management perspective. Ideally, they also assess whether potential risks have been adequately identified and mitigated, or at least minimized (see Chapter 11 of this book).

Evaluation of proposed solutions to a problem should explore a variety of alternatives, such as whether to use new, refurbished, or used equipment; or whether to rent, purchase, or build an asset. It should consider variations in scale and timing, the output to be produced, and the intended service quality. Combinations of recurrent and capital inputs should also be considered, along with whether project services should be outsourced, the alternatives for location and sites, and regulatory issues.

These myriad considerations, when contextualized in specific countries, result in a variety of approaches to decision making. For example, key process responsibilities at the prefeasibility stage vary. In Chile, the line ministry is in charge of proposing and appraising projects, while reviewing is the responsibility of a central evaluation unit within the Ministry of Social Development. The ministry provides a recommendation, and its decision stands unless it is overruled by the president.

In Korea, the line ministry submits a list of projects that are candidates for a Preliminary Feasibility Study to the Ministry of Economy and Finance. The preliminary study helps the economy and finance ministry assess the validity of public sector projects (Korea Development Institute 2016b). The ministry selects these projects on the basis of rationale, relevance, and affordability, among other things. The study is the responsibility of the economy and finance ministry but is undertaken by the Public and Private Infrastructure Investment

Management Center, an independent professional entity within the Korea Development Institute.[5]

The United Kingdom and Ireland offer a contrast to Korea and Chile in that their central evaluation units play less of a gatekeeper function. Their role is more advisory than regulatory, and the line ministry has more authority. For example, in Ireland the central unit does not do appraisals but only reviews cost-benefit analysis for the largest projects before they go to the cabinet. Furthermore, it has less control over the methodological framework.

## APPRAISAL METHODOLOGIES

The methodological foundations of project appraisal in welfare economics are broad and deep. Most project appraisal methodologies in use today reflect this academic pedigree (for example, Harberger 1972; Jenkins, Kuo, and Harberger 2011). The following are three notable good-practice country experiences:

- Chile's methodological approach, the General Methodology for the Preparation and Evaluation of Projects, is one of the most comprehensive and transparent in use (see Ministry of Social Development 2013). The methodology, as well as nationally applied parameters (such as the economic cost of foreign exchange) and sectoral conversion factors (such as the economic cost of unskilled labor) calculated from it, are well developed, and most of the methodological work (and the conversion factors) are available online.[6] Chile's system also applies social cost-benefit analysis as the default mode of analysis for public investment.
- Korea's multicriteria analysis uses a decision-making technique that treats economic analysis (largely cost-benefit analysis) as a core factor but also considers others, including policy analysis and regional development analysis.[7] These three main factors are weighted according to government priorities and have been revised over time. Historically, economic analysis has been weighted at 40 percent to 50 percent, making it the most significant factor in the overall analysis.
- The United Kingdom's system, which is laid out in the HM Treasury Green Book (2018), is perhaps the most widely emulated methodology and one of the longest in use (Box 13.4). The Green Book recommends social cost-benefit

[5] A key metric to determine whether the appraisal function of a country is robust is the rejection rate (that is, what percentage of projects are accepted versus rejected). In Korea, during 1999–2018, 64.2 percent of projects were deemed feasible (KDI PIMAC 2019). This means that more than one-third of project proposals were rejected. In many developing countries, the rejection rate is not tracked.

[6] Conversion factors convert market prices to economic prices, eliminating distortions and accounting for externalities.

[7] Policy analysis considers aspects such as consistency with policy and risk factors in pursuing the project. Regional development analysis reviews the level of regional development and ripple effects on the regional economy. See Korea Development Institute (2008) for more details.

**Box 13.4. Appraisal and Evaluation in the United Kingdom**

The Green Book is the United Kingdom's central government guidance on how to appraise and evaluate policies, programs, and projects. Developed by the Treasury, it applies to all proposals about public spending in the country. It provides approved guidance and methods, recommended tools for developing options, and standard values for use across government. The aim of the Green Book is to help officials develop objective advice to support decisions across government. It is geared to a variety of users, from policy officials to analysts.

The Green Book provides a high-level overview of appraisal and evaluation and describes how appraisal fits within the government decision-making processes. For practitioners, it provides more detailed information on how to generate options and undertake long-list appraisal, followed by how to undertake social cost-benefit analysis of a short-list of options. It sets out the approach to valuation of costs and benefits and outlines how to present appraisal results. Finally, the Green Book sets out the approach for monitoring and evaluation, including different types of evaluation and uses before, during, and after evaluation. It contains a variety of annexes with further technical information and values for use in appraisal across government.

Source: Authors, based on HM Treasury 2018.

analysis as the approach to detailed comparison of the short-list of options, while social cost-effectiveness analysis is also used in some circumstances. The Green Book no longer recommends the use of multicriteria analysis.

Robust appraisal methodologies provide for centrally calculated national economic parameters, including shadow prices. Key parameters include the economic (or social) discount rate and conversion factors for labor and foreign exchange, as well as other input costs (energy, transportation, and so on), the social value of time, the statistical value of life, and the social price of carbon emissions. It is important for a central oversight agency, such as a finance ministry or a planning agency through a specialized unit, to provide these parameters for all stakeholders in the public investment system. Chile provides and publishes many of these parameters (Ministry of Social Development 2018). More recently, the Ugandan Ministry of Finance has published national economic parameters and a commodity-specific database of economic conversion factors, which is innovative because it allows users to adjust or update for market distortions (regarding tax and subsidy rates) easily as needed (Ministry of Finance, Planning and Economic Development 2018). This approach allows the appraisal system to be managed more sustainably because it keeps down the costs of updating the large set of conversion factors (Jenkins, Kuo, and Harberger 2011).

To be useful, the general methodology must also be complemented by specific sectoral guidelines or applications. The specific aspects of applying an appraisal methodology to different sectors will vary, even among subsectors. Good-practice systems produce detailed guidance on how to apply the general methodology; for example, how to calculate economic (social) benefits by sector. In Chile and Korea the sectoral guidelines are prepared by the central oversight agency, whereas in the United Kingdom and Ireland they are prepared by spending units, consistent with the general methodology (and central units providing advice and guidance as needed). Chile has published more than 20 sector-specific methodologies, including for water, transport, energy, communications, education, health, justice, sports, and public buildings (Ministry of Social Development 2019b). Korea has about a dozen sector-specific methodologies, including for airports, ports, information technology, roads and railways, social welfare, health, and industrial complexes (Korea Development Institute 2016a).

A core element of a well-developed appraisal methodology should be the requirement to conduct risk analysis (Chapter 11). The main techniques for managing uncertainty in project appraisal are *sensitivity analysis*, which identifies key risk variables through determining their impact on project outcomes; *scenario analysis*, in which multiple variables are altered simultaneously to demonstrate the combined impacts of particular scenarios (for example, best case and worst case); and the *Monte Carlo analysis*, in which risk variables (identified from the sensitivity analysis) are modeled as probability distributions, which generate project outcomes as expected values (Jenkins, Kuo, and Harberger 2011). Risk analysis is required by the guidelines in Chile, Colombia, Ireland, Korea, and the United Kingdom, among others.

More recently, research on *optimism bias*, which shows that project costs and completion times tend to be systematically higher and longer, respectively, than initially projected, has motivated some governments to adopt methods to control ex ante for such biases (Flyvbjerg 2006). The United Kingdom's Green Book recommends applying adjustments for optimism bias and provides adjustment factors for different generic categories of spending (for example, for capital costs, adjustment factors for buildings, civil engineering, equipment, and so on). The Green Book also recommends reviewing the optimism bias adjustment at different stages of appraisal. Procedures for this include the Gateway Review process (Box 13.5).

### Box 13.5. The United Kingdom's Gateway Review Process

The Gateway Review process, which was introduced by the Office of Government Commerce, requires examination of a program or project at key decision points in its life cycle to provide assurance that it can move successfully from one stage to the next. The process is mandatory for procurement, IT-enabled, and construction programs and projects in the United Kingdom. The reviews are structured as "peer reviews," in which independent practitioners examine the progress and likelihood of successful delivery of the program or project.

The reviews provide valuable perspective to internal teams and also serve as an external challenge to the robustness of plans and processes. They help to bring realism to estimated completion times and cost targets. In the case of projects, the process examines five delivery areas beyond project appraisal: (1) business justification, (2) the delivery strategy, (3) the investment decision, (4) readiness for service, and (5) an operational review and benefits realization.

Source: Authors, based on Office of Government Commerce (2007).

One unsettled aspect of appraisal methodologies is how to treat equity effects. In cost-benefit analysis, costs and benefits are typically aggregated across individuals, without taking into consideration who receives the benefit or who pays the cost.[8] The methodological foundation of distributive analysis in project appraisal is to acknowledge that any economic externalities from a project accrue to different stakeholders, whether consumers (that is, project beneficiaries), producers, labor, or government (Jenkins, Kuo, and Harberger 2011). Some countries, such as the United Kingdom and New Zealand, require distributional analysis, in which, at a minimum, appraisers quantify how project costs and benefits accrue to different socioeconomic groups. These systems also recommend that distributional weights (for example, that benefits for low-income groups receive higher weight) should be used where possible. The use of distributional weights, however, is not widely accepted because of the potential for inefficiencies to be generated and greater discretion in decision making to be introduced.

## Undue Political Influence in Project Appraisal and Selection

Political influence is a defining factor in the allocation of public resources at both the appraisal and selection stages of public investment management. Political considerations are important for determining investment priorities and the types of projects that fit national, regional, and sectoral plans. However, political influence can sometimes also be used to override the technical appraisal, and this can generate significant inefficiencies. In many cases, political decisions are opaque, which limits accountability and likely results in inefficiencies that include decisions to undertake white elephant projects.

Countries have adopted different approaches to factor in political priorities in decision making. In Chile, the government aims to maintain the technical purity of its rigorous cost-benefit analysis approach, but it makes a formal provision for the president to override the appraisal to account for political priorities. Projects can be designated as Presidential Priorities, with the ability to veto appraisal results vested in the president, although this practice is becoming less common. The advantage of the system is that it is formalized, transparent, and can contribute to accountability as the president is associated with those projects. Korea takes a different approach by formally incorporating variables for policy priorities and equitable territorial development directly into the multicriteria analysis.[9] One of the political pressure points in Korea is the impetus for more equitable regional development, so the Korean system attempts to quantify a project's ability to address regional needs. This factor is then weighted and, along with the

[8] See Department of the Prime Minister and Cabinet (2016) for guidance from Australia on how to account for equity within cost-benefit analysis.

[9] As described previously, Korea's multicriteria analysis combines quantitative and qualitative criteria for decision making. Economic analysis (largely cost-benefit analysis) is the most heavily weighted component. Projects are also evaluated from policy analysis and regional development perspectives, which are given different weights.

cost-benefit analysis, incorporated into the formal appraisal. Challenges with this approach include the generation of pressures to increase the weight of this factor in decision making. Moreover, most low-income developing countries would not have the technical capacity needed to implement the approach. That said, the Chilean and Korean examples show how transparent decision rules can improve outcomes.

### Capacity Development Approaches

It is not surprising that the best-performing systems—in terms of analytically rigorous methods and their consistent implementation—have taken systematic approaches to building public sector capacity through significant investment over several decades. Both Chile and Korea are cases in point. Chile, for example, has been providing training since the mid-1970s and the responsible ministry continues to offer basic, intermediate, and advanced diploma courses in social project evaluation, as well as specialized courses. Hundreds of officials are trained each year.[10] Korea has also invested significantly in developing its methodologies and training its officials.

In low-capacity countries, external consultants could play an important technical role in project appraisal. The disadvantage of this approach is that it engenders possible conflicts of interest (consultants may have incentives to provide project sponsors with the results they would like to see) and a lack of incentives to develop capacity in house. Outsourcing appraisal functions may also mean that public officials do not develop the skills needed to be intelligent consumers of consultants' reports. Taking time and dedicating the resources to developing capacity to design and implement a project appraisal system is a critical and very likely high-return investment.

## CONSIDERATIONS FOR PROJECT SELECTION

The decision to proceed with a project[11] can be quite contentious politically. As such, it is important to clarify institutional roles and establish clear processes for project selection. Several European countries have introduced tools such as models, criteria, or scoring grids to strengthen their project selection functions.[12]

The IMF has identified several practices and procedures for strong project selection, which are outlined in the revised PIMA framework. All major projects, regardless of whether they are financed by the government's own resources or

---

[10] In Chile, about 550 public sector officials are trained per year in formal courses and 600 in other project training as needed (Ministry of Social Development 2019a).

[11] A decision to proceed would not in itself guarantee that funding will be obtained. Securing funding for a project occurs through the budgetary process (Kim and others 2020).

[12] See Burduja and others (2014) for an overview of project selection models used in Estonia, Germany, Ireland, Italy, Lithuania, Poland, Slovenia, and the United Kingdom related to the use of funds from the European Union's Regional Operational Program.

whether they are donor funded or are public-private partnerships, should be reviewed by a central ministry. Ideally, independent experts or organizations provide input into the process before the decision to include a project in the budget. The revised PIMA framework also highlights the importance of governments publishing standard criteria for project selection, outlining a process for the selection of projects, and making the selection through the given process (IMF 2018).

The PIMA framework also suggests that the government should maintain a pipeline of appraised investment projects, which should be used for selecting projects that will be included in the budget (IMF 2018). In Chile, for example, the government has developed a pipeline of appraised and approved projects that are eligible for budget funding (Rajaram and others 2014). In Ireland, the government recently expanded the functionality of its Capital Tracker database to improve the inventory of the pipeline of capital investment projects with a medium-term horizon (Department of Public Expenditure and Reform 2018).[13]

Colombia is a good example of a country with a database that supports project selection. Sponsoring agencies and line ministries conduct a formal project review, which is then subjected to independent review from the National Planning Department (World Bank 2018). The department determines which projects are feasible and can be preselected for inclusion in the Bank of National Investment Programs and Projects, the country's project database. Line ministries propose which projects should be financed from the national budget from those that have been included in the database. Together with the National Planning Department, they decide which ones to include in the Public Investment Program (IMF 2017). Projects financed by royalties go through a different process.

Australia has gone a step further and has developed an Infrastructure Priority List, a publicly available list of nationally significant infrastructure investments that the country needs over the next 15 years. The Priority List is updated regularly, includes projects with a full business case that have been assessed by the independent Infrastructure Australia Board, and guides decisions on how best to allocate resources. An infrastructure priority map available at Infrastructure Australia's website presents information about projects and initiatives (early-stage solutions without a full business case) that have received a positive evaluation (Infrastructure Australia 2019).

Project selection criteria should be clear and transparent (IMF 2015). A good example of project selection criteria comes from the Slovak Republic, which uses a scorecard with 23 criteria for prioritizing projects organized across three principles. The projects are reviewed by the Ministry of Finance, which scores them according to the criteria. The three principles include an assessment of the strategic relevance of the project, a review of the economic appraisal and fiscal affordability of the project, and an assessment of the maturity of the project and its related implementation plan (IMF 2019).

---

[13] According to the 2017 Ireland PIMA, a pipeline of approved projects was available at the department level, but not at the national level.

### Linking Project Appraisal and Selection to the Budget Cycle

Decisions on which projects to pursue should be an integral part of the budget process, and strong infrastructure governance systems link project appraisal and selection to the budget cycle. Looking at the institutional arrangements, this implies having a well-defined process for project appraisal and transparent criteria for project selection. Project appraisal and selection should perform a gatekeeping function, ensuring that only projects that have gone through the process (and have been independently reviewed) are selected for funding in the budget. The budget preparation process should also adequately integrate projects' recurrent and capital expenditures (that is, should consider projects' capital outlays and the funds needed for operations and maintenance). A key consideration is the affordability of projects, ensuring that sufficient budget funding is available for the selected projects (Rajaram and others 2014); or, to put it another way, which projects to select, given the budget envelope. If too many projects vie for finance through the budget, prioritization should be based on the projects' net present value, pursuing those with the highest value given the budget constraint.[14]

Kazakhstan has a three-stage upstream public investment management process for project proposal, appraisal, and selection, which is conducted through the annual budget. A key feature of the process is that to be eligible for inclusion in the draft budget, projects must have completed a feasibility report and received a positive appraisal and a positive decision from the relevant budget committee. The criteria for project proposal, appraisal, and selection is clearly outlined in the country's budget code (Kim and others 2020).

## CONCLUSIONS

A clear, well-supported appraisal methodology and published project selection criteria with well-defined processes for project selection are the foundations of a good infrastructure governance system. This includes having a clear methodology with national and sectoral guidelines for project appraisal. A management or research unit employing robust methodology is also important. Where it should be housed (the finance or planning ministries, or an affiliated think tank) would depend on the country setting.

In practice, the appraisal and selection process cannot be reduced to a purely technical exercise. Political influence exists in developing, emerging, and advanced systems and this affects (or even determines) how projects are ultimately decided. This is the main limitation of the technical work. Advanced systems are designed and negotiated to channel politics transparently and in a structured manner. Political influence can be an issue in project appraisal and selection in both weak and strong infrastructure governance systems, but it can be tempered through

[14] Projects with a positive net present value increase social welfare and are generally preferred over those with a negative net present value, which should be avoided (Office of Management and Budget 1992).

rigorous analysis, scrutiny by a central ministry using clear and transparent procedures, and an independent review of projects before they are included in the budget.

Capacity development, as illustrated by the Chilean and Korean experiences, is an expensive, long-term undertaking. In low-capacity settings (low-income developing countries and fragile and conflict-affected states), outsourcing or using consultants for core functions are possible alternatives, but they must be balanced with sustained investments in capacity building and the development of practical know-how. History shows that all project appraisal and selection systems adapt over time, and while some improve, some also deteriorate. As such, there is a need for constant vigilance to ensure that systems adopt relevant new techniques while also preventing backsliding.

## REFERENCES

Burduja, Sebastian Ioan, Florian Gaman, Victor Giosan, Graham Glenday, Eric Nolin Huddleston, Marcel Ionescu-Heroiu, Elena Iorga, and others. 2014. *Identification of Project Selection Models for the Regional Operational Program 2014–2020.* Washington, DC: World Bank.

Department of the Prime Minister and Cabinet. 2016. *Cost-Benefit Analysis.* Canberra: Department of the Prime Minister and Cabinet.

Department of Public Expenditure and Reform. 2018. "Minister Donohoe Updates Cabinet on the Ongoing Delivery of Project Ireland 2040." Press release, Gov.ie, September 19.

Department of Public Expenditure and Reform. 2019. *Public Spending Code: Guide to Evaluating, Planning and Managing Public Investment.* Dublin: Department of Public Expenditure and Reform.

Florio, Massimo, and Silvia Vignetti. 2013. *The Use of Ex Post Cost-Benefit Analysis to Assess the Long-Term Effects of Major Infrastructure Projects.* London: Centre for Industrial Studies.

Flyvbjerg, Bent. 2006. "From Nobel Prize to Project Management: Getting Risks Right." *Project Management Journal* 37 (3): 5–15.

Harberger, Arnold C. 1972. *Project Evaluation: Collected Papers.* London: Palgrave Macmillan UK.

HM Treasury. 2018. *The Green Book: Central Government Guidance on Appraisal and Evaluation.* London: HM Treasury.

Infrastructure Australia. 2019. *Infrastructure Priority List.* Sydney: Infrastructure Australia.

International Monetary Fund (IMF). 2015. *Making Public Investment More Efficient.* Washington, DC: IMF.

IMF. 2017. "Ireland: Technical Assistance Report—Public Investment Management Assessment." International Monetary Fund, Washington, DC.

IMF. 2018. "Public Investment Management Assessment—Review and Update." International Monetary Fund, Washington, DC.

IMF. 2019. "Slovak Republic: Technical Assistance Report—Public Investment Management Assessment." International Monetary Fund, Washington, DC.

Jenkins, Glenn P., Chun-Yan Kuo, and Arnold C. Harberger. 2011. "Cost-Benefit Analysis for Investment Decisions." Development Discussion Papers, 2011–5.

Kaplan, Josiah. 2014a. *Cost-Benefit Analysis.* Melbourne, Australia: BetterEvaluation.

Kaplan, Josiah. 2014b. *Cost-Effectiveness Analysis.* Melbourne, Australia: BetterEvaluation.

Kim, Jay-Hyung. 2012. *The Republic of Korea: PIM Reform after the Financial Crisis.* Washington, DC: World Bank.

Kim, Jay-Hyung, Jonas Alp Fallov, Simon Groom, and Marin Darcy. 2020. *Public Investment Management Reference Guide.* Washington, DC: World Bank.

Korea Development Institute Public and Private Infrastructure Investment Management Center (KDI PIMAC). 2019. 2018 *PIMAC Annual Report.* Sejong: Korea Development Institute.

Korea Development Institute. 2008. *General Guidelines for Preliminary Feasibility Studies*, 5th edition. Sejong: Korea Development Institute.

Korea Development Institute. 2016a. *Preliminary Feasibility Study Guidelines*. Sejong: Korea Development Institute.

Korea Development Institute. 2016b. *Public Institution Evaluation*. Sejong: Korea Development Institute.

Mauro, Paolo. 1997. "Why Worry about Corruption?" Economic Issues, International Monetary Fund, Washington, DC.

Ministry of Finance, Planning and Economic Development. 2018. *Commodity-Specific Economic Conversion Factors Database for the Republic of Uganda*. Ministry of Finance, Planning and Economic Development, Kampala, Uganda.

Ministry of Social Development. 2013. *General Methodology of Project Preparation and Evaluation*. Santiago, Chile: Ministry of Social Development.

Ministry of Social Development. 2018. *Social Prices 2018*. Santiago, Chile: Ministry of Social Development.

Ministry of Social Development. 2019a. *Training for the National Investment System*. Santiago, Chile: Ministry of Social Development.

Ministry of Social Development. 2019b. *Requirements by Sector for Project Formulation—Current Classification*. Santiago, Chile: Ministry of Social Development.

Ministry of Social Development and Ministry of Finance. 2018. *Norms, Instructions, and Procedures for the Public Investment Process (NIP)*. Santiago, Chile: Ministry of Social Development, Ministry of Finance.

Office of Government Commerce. 2007. *OGC Gateway Process: Review 0–Strategic Assessment*. London: Office of Government Commerce.

Office of Management and Budget. 1992. "Guidelines and Discount Rates for Benefit-Cost Analysis of Federal Programs." Circular A-94. Washington, DC: Office of Management and Budget.

Rajaram, Anand, Kai Kaiser, Tuan Minh Le, Jay-Hyung Kim, and Jonas Frank. 2014. *The Power of Public Investment Management: Transforming Resources into Assets for Growth*. Washington, DC: World Bank.

Rajaram, Anand, Tuan Minh Le, Nataliya Biletska, and Jim Brumby. 2010. *A Diagnostic Framework for Assessing Public Investment Management*. Washington, DC: World Bank.

Samset, Knut F., Gro Holst Volden, Nils Olsson, and Eirik Vårdal Kvalheim. 2016. *Governance Schemes for Major Public Investment Projects: A Comparative Study of Principles and Practices in Six Countries*. Trondheim: Norwegian University of Science and Technology.

World Bank. 2018. *Public Investment Management in Colombia*. Washington, DC: World Bank.

CHAPTER 14

# Maintaining and Managing Public Infrastructure Assets

**Andrew Blazey, Fabien Gonguet, and Philip Stokoe**

## INTRODUCTION

Chapter 3 focused on how improving infrastructure governance to produce better outcomes from existing assets is among the critical ways to close the global infrastructure gap. To improve these outcomes, countries should look to both maintain their assets—routinely preserve the quality of individual infrastructure assets and renovate them in good time and with the right amount of funding—and manage their portfolio. This chapter turns to how a life-cycle approach to the development and use of public assets is key to their management, along with optimizing balance sheets to maximize returns. Asset maintenance and management needs are particularly salient in a context of aging infrastructure, especially in some advanced economies (IMF 2014b), where large infrastructure networks were developed during the second half of the 20th century.

The main focus in this chapter is on maintenance. The concept, as used in the Public Investment Management Assessment (PIMA) framework, covers two categories of spending: *routine maintenance* to ensure that infrastructure assets operate as initially intended in a long-lasting manner, and *capital maintenance*, performed to rehabilitate or renovate assets to extend their lives and capacity.

Maintenance has often been neglected for the following:

- *Political economy* reasons—governments will opt for ribbon cutting rather than maintaining existing assets, with the widespread perception that the former will draw more votes than the latter;
- *Fiscal* reasons—budget funding for operations and maintenance is prone to be cut when fiscal space is limited, in favor of nondiscretionary spending;
- *Institutional* reasons—in many countries, separate agencies still prepare investment and current expenditure budgets (routine maintenance being included in the latter and capital maintenance in the former) without an integrated medium-term perspective, leading to a mismatch over time between infrastructure assets and the need for their operation or maintenance; and
- *Capacity* reasons—up-to-date information on the state of assets may not be readily available, particularly in low-income countries, and the measure-

ment of maintenance needs is difficult, because of lack of standard methodologies (see Box 14.1 for more details on the definitional and data-related challenges posed by maintenance) and because the slow effects of asset depreciation may not be immediately visible.

There is also considerable margin for better *asset management.* Many countries lack a life-cycle view of infrastructure in design, build, and maintenance.

## Box 14.1. The Challenge of Defining and Measuring Maintenance Spending

Identifying what governments spend on repairs and maintenance is a challenge. Documents such as the IMF *Government Finance Statistics Manual 2014* (GFSM 2014; IMF 2014a) provide for the separate identification of important areas of government expenditure, such as the government compensation of employees, interest, subsidies, or social benefits. However, maintenance spending is not recorded separately as a major expenditure item but is subsumed within other spending items. Most frequently, maintenance spending will be contained within the use of goods and services, alongside spending on utilities or other goods and services (if maintenance is outsourced), but it can also be lumped in with compensation of employees (if maintenance is undertaken directly by government employees). Of course, maintenance may be taking place in both of these spending lines. That said, many governments have a chart of accounts that distinguishes between different types of expenditure on goods and services and does identify maintenance spending, which enables this to be quantified and analyzed by the ministry itself or those with access to this data.

However, there is a more fundamental issue. GFSM 2014 (§8.25, page 222) recommends a distinction be drawn between repairs and maintenance on one hand and major renovations, reconstructions, or enlargements of existing fixed assets on the other, with the latter recorded as the acquisition of fixed assets or capital investment. In practice, this line is not so easy to draw. Consider roads. Some simple repairs, like filling in a pothole, are clearly maintenance spending, but what about the resurfacing of extensive sections of road? Should this be considered a major renovation and recorded as capital investment? What if the resurfacing is accompanied by road widening? What if this spending is mixed together in a single budget allocation, such as a highway budget that contains both maintenance and repair *and* new road projects? Reporting units across and within countries may differ in their decisions to record these expenditures either as repair and maintenance or as the acquisition of new assets.

Even if data on maintenance spending were readily available, in aggregate these do not provide sufficient information to determine if enough money is being spent on the right assets, in the right way, to combat wear and tear. Indeed, how does a government know what the depreciation rate is for a specific class of asset and what the right amount to spend is? Most governments still follow cash-based accounting, meaning they do not record depreciation of their fixed assets, which may indicate the spending required to keep assets in good condition.

The question of whether governments are spending enough to maintain existing infrastructure can be complicated further by infrastructure being held by entities and institutions outside the government. Water, gas, electricity, and telecommunications infrastructure, and sometimes road and rail infrastructure, are often not recorded on the government balance sheet, and instead sit on those of public or private companies. These data might be compiled in aggregate. More commonly, these data will be available only in individual financial statements.

Source: Authors.

Data challenges are often cited as the key bottleneck to enhancing asset management—in practice, few governments manage their wealth using balance sheets. Yet, such tools, even in simplified forms, could be within reach for most countries and help lower costs and increase returns on investment (IMF 2018).

This chapter first describes the theoretical rationale for maintaining infrastructure, illustrating this with empirical evidence. Then it explores the approaches to ensuring proper funding and monitoring of maintenance needs and argues that knowledge about the portfolio's condition and performance can yield better decision making and optimize the use of resources. Last, the chapter provides an overview of good practices developed by the New Zealand Transport Agency to manage road infrastructure.

The chapter concludes with key findings:

- Country examples and empirical evidence show that the benefits associated with maintaining and renovating assets include longer asset life spans, reduced fiscal costs in the medium and long terms, and economic and social benefits for users.
- A variety of tested mechanisms exists to properly provide resources for the maintenance of infrastructure assets, from dedicated funding arrangements to wider asset management frameworks.
- The success of maintenance mechanisms relies on the ability of governments to assess the maintenance needs of an asset from its conception, to regularly review its performance, and to adjust actual maintenance spending in a timely manner.

## WHY MAINTAIN EXISTING INFRASTRUCTURE?

Theoretical models have been developed to explore the mechanisms through which maintenance spending can affect economic growth.[1] Models demonstrate that neglecting maintenance holds back the economic outcomes provided by infrastructure, and that there is an optimal ratio of maintenance to new investment to maximize economic growth.

Little empirical research has been conducted, however, on the actual effects of maintenance—the main limitation being the difficulty to access quality data on maintenance spending. Only a handful of advanced economies, such as Canada (Annual Capital and Repair Expenditures Survey), produce exhaustive maintenance expenditure data on a regular basis. Most empirical studies focus on the transportation sector thanks to better data availability, including at a cross-country level, available from an Organisation for Economic Co-operation and Development (OECD) database.

In this section, country examples and empirical evidence (often from the transportation sector) are used to argue that the key reasons for giving priority to

[1] Building on Barro (1990), these models (Rioja 2003; Kalaitzidakis and Kalyvitis 2004) turn the depreciation rate of infrastructure to an endogenous variable, which depends negatively on maintenance spending: the higher the maintenance, the lower the depreciation rate.

maintenance are as follows: (1) to increase the efficiency of infrastructure investment, (2) to reduce the burden of repair for future generations, and (3) to reduce several negative externalities associated to insufficient maintenance.

## Maintenance Alleviates the Effect of the Gradual Wear of Infrastructure Assets

All infrastructure assets are subject to gradual wear or aging. This depreciation in the value of the asset occurs at varying speeds, depending on its nature. Although maintenance is needed to mitigate the effects of aging and offset the loss in asset value associated with it, many countries do not make it the priority it warrants. Many advanced economies, which accumulated large asset bases in the decades following World War II, can provide good illustrations of this lack of maintenance. Assets are now nearing the end of their life spans and are sometimes still in use while known to be obsolete or in dire need of maintenance and improvement. For example, in the United States (American Society of Civil Engineers 2017), where 44 percent of bridges are 40 years or older, about 9 percent of all bridges are considered to be structurally deficient (that is, requiring significant maintenance, rehabilitation, or replacement).

Without maintenance, infrastructure will go into decline, leading to poorer outputs and outcomes over time: effective access to infrastructure will gradually decrease (for instance, in terms of the number of users the infrastructure can tackle) and service quality will also fall. In France, lack of maintenance spending on the rail network since the late 1970s (and a concomitant focus on the development of high-speed trains) has led in the past 10 years to the paradoxical doubling of the share of the network where trains can only move at low speed, creating delays and suboptimal traffic (Spinetta 2018). Poor maintenance of transmission lines has also historically been one of the possible reasons cited for causing electricity blackouts globally (Yu and Pollitt 2009).

Spending on the maintenance and improvement of existing infrastructure assets supports their performance over time and sustains their quality, as perceived by the public and business leaders. With respect to road infrastructure in advanced economies with well-developed networks, a correlation exists between public maintenance spending and sustained quality of service (Figure 14.1). Higher maintenance spending allows the gradual loss in quality associated with the aging of roads to be limited.

Overall, the quality of infrastructure is improved when maintenance spending is aligned to the use of the asset and is reviewed at regular intervals. In this regard, the economic life of a maintained asset is likely to be longer than the accounting (depreciation) period of the asset.

## Delaying Maintenance Increases Fiscal Costs in the Short and Long Terms

Postponing maintenance spending results in a fiscal cost: subjecting maintenance activities to budget cuts in the short term may lead to greater costs in later years

**Figure 14.1. Roads in Advanced Economies with Well-Developed Networks: Maintenance Spending versus Improvement in Perceived Quality**

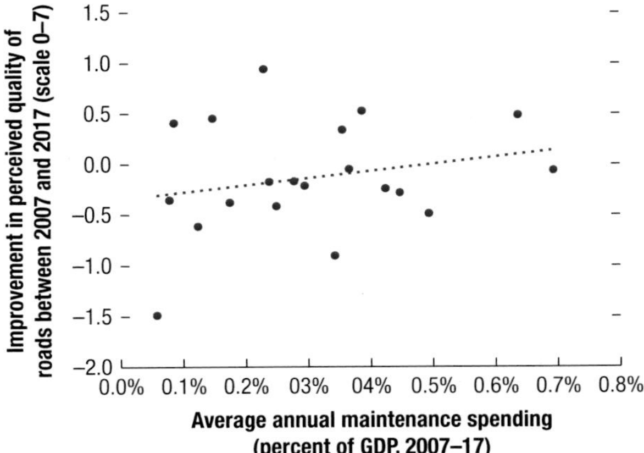


Source: Authors' calculations, based on OECD and World Economic Forum data.
Note: The figure shows advanced economies in which the road and motorway network density has increased by less than twice the OECD average over the 2000–17 period. Road maintenance covers public spending on preservation of the existing road network. OECD = Organisation for Economic Co-operation and Development.

(IMF 2018). In the transportation sector, the aging of infrastructure is not linear: it is only after a long period of barely visible deterioration that the condition of the asset may begin to drop more significantly. The US Federal Aviation Administration[2] assesses that $1 spent for preventative maintenance early in the airfield pavement life is equivalent to $4 or $5 spent later, making it more economical to spend on maintenance when the condition of the asset is relatively good. Spending on maintenance and rehabilitation early in the life of an asset is usually also cheaper and prolongs its life span.

Timely spending on maintenance can also lead to sustained efficiency gains. In Peru, a large-scale rural road rehabilitation and maintenance program initiated in the mid-1990s, funded by the World Bank and led by local communities, has reduced the cost of routine road maintenance from $1,200 to $750 per kilometer over the duration of the program (Rioja 2013). In a context of limited financing, the maintenance argument has resounded as a missed opportunity for several

[2] https://www.faa.gov/airports/central/airport_compliance/pavement_maintenance/. The ratio is also valid for road pavement: every $1 of deferred maintenance on roads and bridges costs an additional $4 to $5 in needed future repairs (TRIP 2018).

decades. According to World Bank (1994), timely road maintenance expenditure of $12 billion in Africa in the mid-1980s could have prevented a $45 billion reconstruction cost in the subsequent decade.

Insufficient maintenance spending also increases fiscal risks related to infrastructure. When maintenance is low, vital infrastructure assets such as power plants, highways connecting major cities, or international airports are more fragile and exposed to hazards and disasters (see Chapter 9). The temporary or permanent closure of strategic assets bears significant fiscal costs, both direct (the need to repair or rebuild the asset) and indirect (negative impact on economic activity, hence on tax revenue). Furthermore, without strong public investment management practices, urgency surrounding replacement or rebuilding may lead to ill-designed, ill-advised infrastructure, hence perpetuating the fiscal costs of not maintaining the assets in the first place.

## Limited Maintenance Leads to Negative Externalities for Users

The costs of delaying or avoiding maintenance spending go well beyond the fiscal sphere.

- *User costs.* The cost of using infrastructure networks can increase dramatically when networks are badly maintained. According to a survey by the National Transportation Research Group, the average motorist in the United States loses about $600 annually in additional vehicle operating costs from driving on roads in need of repair—up to $1,000 in some areas of California. Further, some empirical studies suggest that better-maintained infrastructure assets improve economic welfare. The rural road rehabilitation program in Peru increased nonfarm income of households near maintained roads above the estimated income they would have earned in the absence of rehabilitation, mostly thanks to easier access to towns (Escobal and Ponce 2003).
- *Human costs.* Infrastructure failing because of a lack of maintenance can lead to injury and even death. This is especially clear for transportation infrastructure, which can place users at risk. In Minnesota, after years of being rated as "structurally deficient" by federal agencies, yet the rating not leading to any significant maintenance or improvement effort, the Mississippi River Bridge collapsed at rush hour in 2007, killing 13 and injuring 145. Maintenance can save lives: data on highway infrastructure across US states suggests that the higher the maintenance spending, the lower the number of road fatalities per driven mile (Figure 14.2).
- *Ecological costs.* Ecological waste is associated with poor maintenance. According to World Bank (2006), the water lost daily in the developing world from leaks could meet the needs of 200 million people. Extending the life of road pavement with early maintenance could reduce the greenhouse gas emissions associated with road use by 2 percent, thanks primarily to a

**Figure 14.2. US State Highways: Maintenance Spending and Road Fatalities, 2012–15**

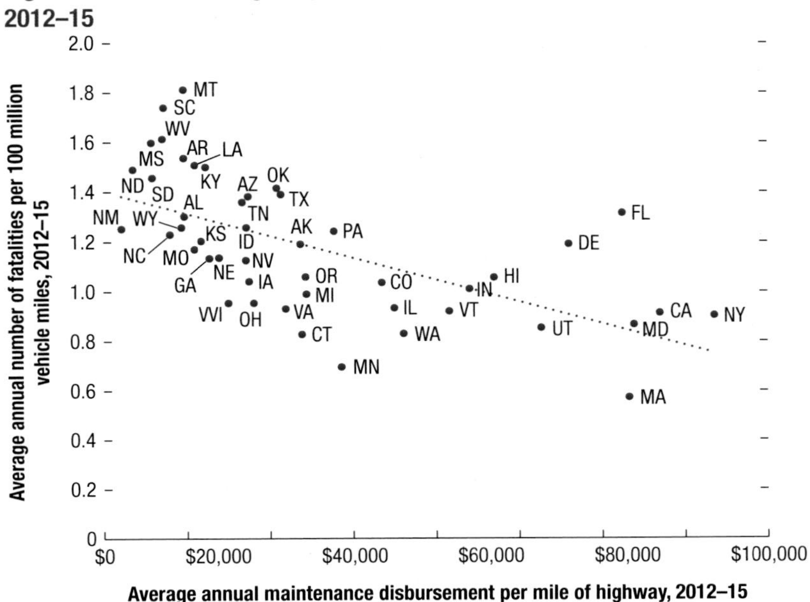


Source: Authors' calculations, based on data from Annual Highway Reports, Reason Foundation.

decrease in road roughness (Wang and others 2019). And spending $1 million to reduce transmission losses on power lines could save $12 million in power generation (World Bank 1994). Increasing infrastructure maintenance is part of more economical, more resilient approaches for the planet and its depleting resources.

## HOW IS PROPER FUNDING OF MAINTENANCE ENSURED?

The estimated needs to cover maintenance costs are significant. Rozenberg and Fay (2019) estimates that between 1 and 3 percentage points of GDP of annual maintenance spending will be needed to reach the Sustainable Development Goals in key infrastructure sectors by 2030 (Figure 14.3). Important steps are needed to ensure proper funding of maintenance. The discussion now turns to these requirements, including the capacity to assess the needs of each asset early on, to guarantee consistent and sustainable access to funding, to monitor public assets, and to collect and analyze data relating to asset performance.

**Figure 14.3. Average Annual Maintenance Costs to Reach Sustainable Development Goals in Key Infrastructure Sectors**
(percent of GDP, average for 2015–30)

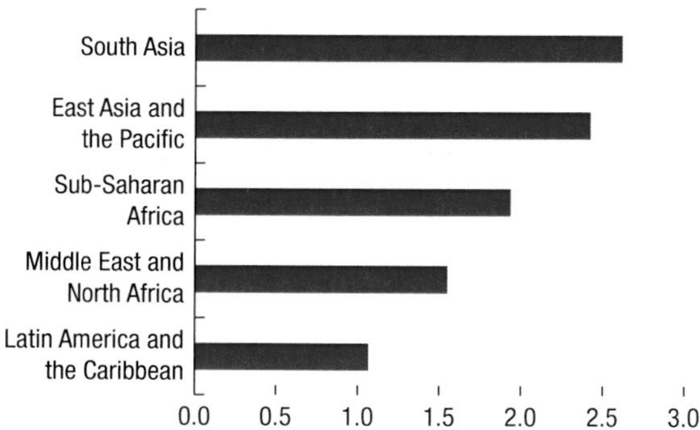


Source: Rozenberg and Fay 2019.
Note: Key infrastructure sectors include transportation, electricity, water supply and sanitation, and irrigation and flood protection.

## Identify Maintenance Requirements as Part of the Investment Decision

The requirement for maintenance to support the operation and planned life of a public infrastructure asset should be fundamental to the decision to invest in that asset. Maintenance often makes up a substantial proportion of the cost of an infrastructure investment over its operational life span. The advanced practice of the PIMA framework (see Chapter 5 of this book) requires standard methodologies to be used to assess the needs for both *routine* and *capital* maintenance and that these needs be accounted for in national or sectoral planning documents. However, identifying, measuring, and managing maintenance requirements can be difficult when the demand or use of an asset across its life span is uncertain (Parlikad and Jafari 2016).

Maintenance costs should be considered through a cost-benefit analysis (CBA) during the appraisal that informs the public investment decision. Identifying maintenance costs in a CBA contributes to the composition of a budget. A budget would be incomplete without the provision of maintenance costs. CBAs should account for changes in the maintenance requirements depending on use of the asset and its age (OECD 2001). Calculation of the whole-of-life cost of an asset is meant to include all costs related to the operations and maintenance of fixed assets, including the environmental and social costs of maintenance, such as the disposal of by-products created from maintenance processes.

Identification of maintenance requirements and costs leading up to the investment decision helps identify the revenue sources and capabilities needed to ensure

**Box 14.2. Maintenance Guidelines for Public Infrastructure in South Africa**

South Africa has established guidelines and standards for maintenance of public infrastructure to ensure maintenance levels sufficient to avoid deterioration of public asset values. A national infrastructure maintenance strategy was approved by the cabinet in 2007, containing an infrastructure maintenance budgeting guideline.

The guideline provides a comprehensive infrastructure asset management system. It focuses on effective and efficient service delivery, ensuring that adequate infrastructure maintenance can be planned and funded, taking into account all factors that influence the life-cycle costs of infrastructure, such as the current and future demand for services requiring infrastructure to support their delivery, the current technology being used, the current condition of available infrastructure, current operating and maintenance costs, the potential remaining useful life of the infrastructure, and the replacement and disposal strategy for existing infrastructure.

The guideline includes a table that provides a macrobudgeting guide for indicative budgetary costs of maintaining different types of assets, based on key assumptions about the types of repairs likely needed. It also provides an estimation of the period after which replacements or major rehabilitations are warranted.

The macrobudgeting guide is used as a starting point to tackle the maintenance requirements. The guideline neither substitutes for proper infrastructure maintenance nor can be simply applied across the board to maintenance planning. In South Africa, the Ministry of Public Works has a lead role in implementing the strategy, which includes indicative budget requirements for maintenance of different types of assets.

Source: Construction Industry Development Board 2007.

an infrastructure asset will deliver public services as expected. Some governments provide indicative maintenance and rehabilitation needs based on the specificities of each asset class. South Africa, for instance, has established guidelines for maintenance, providing an estimation of routine maintenance needs for each specific type of infrastructure and the average frequency of major rehabilitation works (see Box 14.2).

The quantum and source of revenue can change, just as maintenance activities can change as an asset ages. As such, the responsibilities for managing a sustainable source of revenue and its application should be established at the time the source of revenue is identified. Management responsibilities include planning, forecasting, and reporting on the revenue received and how it is applied. These functions are governance arrangements to support the delivery of maintenance in a transparent and quality-informed manner (OECD 2011).

## Ensure Sustainable Access to Funding for Maintenance

A government's annual budget often provides most of the funding to maintain public infrastructure. Yet, governments also employ other mechanisms to provide a sustainable source of revenue to fund maintenance activities, and to establish a performance framework to support the efficient and effective

**TABLE 14.1.**

**Modalities to Fund Infrastructure Maintenance: Strengths and Weaknesses**

| | Strengths | Weaknesses |
|---|---|---|
| Direct funding modalities | | |
| Appropriation in annual budgets | • Is simple<br>• Is subject to budget accountability mechanisms | • Involves volatility through annual decisions and many other competing budget priorities |
| Dedicated maintenance funds | • Secures funding for a multiannual period<br>• Is overseen by an entity whose principal purpose is to carry maintenance | • Faces governance issues on the stewardship of the responsible entities<br>• Involves integrity issues on operational decisions, particularly on procurement practices |
| User charges | • Is able to be set at a rate proportionate to the costs generated from the use of infrastructure | • Assumes charges are collectable, affordable, and equitable across different types of users |
| Asset management modalities | | |
| Auxiliary business activities | • Optimizes the value achievable from surplus and supporting assets connected to a core infrastructure asset | • Does not specifically provide for maintenance, but the revenue generated is to support the sustained operation of infrastructure |
| National wealth funds | • Places the operation of infrastructure at arm's length from political decisions<br>• Incentivizes the provision of maintenance to sustain the value of the infrastructure | • Does not specifically provide for maintenance |
| Holding companies | • Places the operation of infrastructure at arm's length from political decisions<br>• Incentivizes the provision of maintenance to sustain the value of the infrastructure | • Does not specifically provide for maintenance |

Source: Authors.

delivery of maintenance. Table 14.1 summarizes the relative strengths and weaknesses of these funding modalities, drawing a distinction between modalities that directly fund maintenance and those that include asset management incentives.

- *Dedicated funds.* Since the 1990s, so-called road funds have been a way for countries in Africa, Latin America, and other regions to ensure sustainable funding to maintain road networks. In Tanzania, the Roads Fund gets most of its revenue from fuel levies and road charges, which are applied to meet routine, periodic, and emergency maintenance needs (Tanzania Road Funds Board 2016). Road funds are independent entities, usually established through legislation, with a board of directors and obligations associated with planning, reporting, and audits. Dedicated funding secures revenue to fund maintenance but does not remove all the challenges of maintenance functions. Indeed, experiences in Tanzania and other African countries show that maintenance needs exceed the available funding and criteria are needed to prioritize maintenance activities (African Development Bank 2015). Operational constraints, such as timely procurement processes, the availability of equipment, and access to trained staff, extend beyond the availability of funding. Road funds have also been criticized for governance and management weaknesses in that the relationship between a fund and a country's consolidated financial statements is not always clear and procurement practices can give rise to integrity concerns, while funds may not be subject to the same level of scrutiny as other government spending. However, assistance from the World Bank and other organizations has helped to improve the design and operation of the funds, leading to a second generation of funds, with enhanced governance and operational obligations (Zietlow 2004).

- *User charges.* In circumstances when infrastructure is operated in a commercial environment, revenue from user charges may provide funding for the operator to carry out maintenance. For example, where a toll road is operated through a public-private partnership, the private partner may be contractually responsible for upkeep of the road using the revenue generated from tolls. In other cases, potential sources of revenue through user charges may remain an option available to a government. This is relevant for subnational governments that might not have existing funding sources to support the upkeep of roads, though it requires the capacity to collect fees and to forecast user demand for the service (Bova and others 2013; Potter 2013).
- *Auxiliary business activities.* Infrastructure assets often include land and other asset categories that are connected to but not directly used in providing the core services delivered by an infrastructure asset. By way of example, airport entities earn concession revenue from food and beverage services, duty-free sales, car parking, airport hotels, and so on. All are additional to revenue generated from aircraft landing and take-off fees. Commercial business practices for auxiliary business activities apply to a range of infrastructure assets, including seaports, railways, and motorways, although the percentage of revenue generated is typically lower than achieved at airports. Revenue from auxiliary activities does not directly relate to or contribute to maintenance expenses, but by increasing the overall returns from infrastructure assets, it creates potential for increased funding for maintenance (World Economic Forum 2014).
- *National wealth funds.* About 21 funds across 16 countries, mostly in East Asia and North Africa and the Middle East, provide a means to manage public assets using an asset manager to help maximize the portfolio value and other objectives of public infrastructure assets. The wealth of a fund is the net value of a portfolio of publicly owned assets and the manager is charged with responsibility to achieve specified results. These goals provide incentives for the asset manager to consider maintenance to maximize the portfolio value of the assets through the optimized operation of the assets (Detter and Fölster 2015).

- *Holding companies.* A number of countries have established holding companies to own and govern a portfolio of infrastructure assets at arm's length from the government. Examples include Khazanah Nasional (Malaysia), Mumtalakat (Bahrain), and Temasek (Singapore). The entity form of the companies differs across countries, but their principal purpose is to contribute to the long-term wealth of the country. As with national wealth funds, the holding company aims to maximize the value of its asset portfolio. The companies can define the use of dividends, including reinvestment into businesses. A pure application of a holding company would see that it can buy and sell businesses to maximize value, but certain businesses, such as airlines, might be in the national interest to always retain, suggesting that there can be limits on the company's ability to exit an investment (Detter and Fölster 2015). Furthermore, the recourse to such holding companies calls for a high degree of accountability and transparency and for a careful definition of corporate governance mechanisms (OECD 2015; IMF 2019).

By way of illustrating a variation of a dedicated maintenance fund, the United Kingdom operates specific-purpose funds with the objective of spurring innovation and achieving targeted improvements to maintenance outcomes (Hayden 2019). The Department of Transport is responsible for the funds, including the Local Highways Maintenance Challenge Fund and the Local Highways Maintenance Incentive and Efficiency Fund. Both funds reward councils that guard affordability and value for money when carrying out maintenance. The funds are to incentivize good practice, rewarding local government where results are achieved. Other examples of special purpose funds in the United Kingdom include the Pothole Action Fund, the Safer Roads Fund, and the National Productivity Investment Fund, which aims to reduce congestion and improve maintenance.

## Monitor the Condition of Infrastructure Assets

Keeping records on public assets up to date is a blind spot for many governments. It is a technically demanding task, involving valuation and revaluation of nonfinancial assets. In spite of having elaborate financial and accounting systems, most countries do not reflect nonfinancial assets in the government's financial statements. Only a few countries that undertook a PIMA, such as Estonia and Ireland, produce comprehensive asset registers.

The absence of comprehensive records or asset registers, indicated by a low PIMA score on the Monitoring of Public Assets institution, usually goes together with insufficient maintenance (Figure 14.4). Without a clear view of the age profile and quality of the asset base, a country is unable to budget appropriately for maintenance funding. Thus, lack of monitoring of the existing asset base exacerbates the bias against maintenance, contributes to a declining capital stock, and raises the cost of future replacement as the asset is gradually run down.

**Figure 14.4. Maintenance and Monitoring of Public Assets of 27 Countries: PIMA Scores**

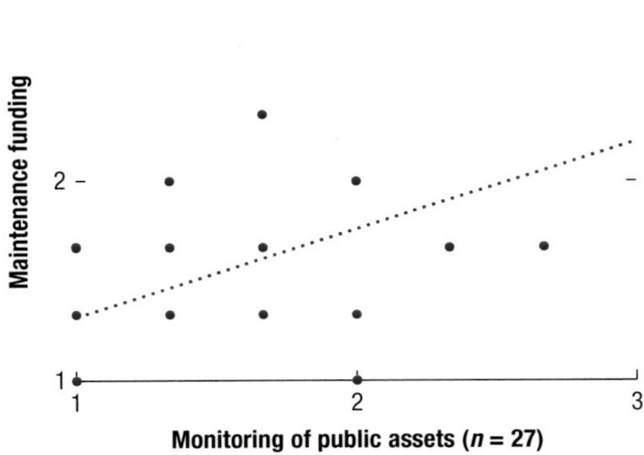


Source: PIMA scores (effectiveness).
Note: A data point on the graph can represent more than one country with the same scores. PIMA = Public Investment Management Assessment.

## Collect Sound Performance Data to Underpin Maintenance Results

Four important aspects are related to generating, analyzing, and disclosing performance data to underpin maintenance results: a systemwide (portfolio) perspective, the operational approach connecting data to maintenance results, the role of technology, and the use of standards to support the delivery of results.

A systemwide perspective is necessary to look at the condition across multiple individual assets when aiming to achieve the desired service outcomes across a network of roads or similar infrastructure assets. *Network effects*, such as a bridge connecting a road to a highway, means that the condition of one asset, a bridge, can affect the quality of service from many assets, a network of roads.

An operational approach that enables the collection, analysis, and reporting of performance-based data is the foundation of any assessment of maintenance needs. Research suggests there is no single assessment methodology superior to another in maintaining infrastructure assets, such as roads; the critical elements are the planning and operational systems that support a methodology (International Transport Forum 2012). Similarly, the OECD assessed standardized performance indicators in the road sector and concluded that a client-focused approach by a road agency to manage and maintain roads is a significant determinant to the results achieved relative to any specific indicator. Of note is the role performed by long-term plans to identify the funding required over a multiyear period for maintenance, recognizing that the funding of the cost of maintenance can vary over time (OECD 2001).

Technology plays an important role in the collection of data and provides data sets for multiple purposes, including simulation analyses to inform maintenance needs, based on possible changes to demand and conditions. Technology automates the collection of data on the number and weights of vehicles using a bridge, weather and air quality readings, and the condition of asphalt for cracks and other impairments. The cost of collecting data for such systems is insignificant relative to the results the data can have on maintenance budgets and the quality of a road network (National Cooperative Highway Research Program 2012). Data on the condition of a road have progressed from human surveyors and directional sensors to multisource data modelling. Examples of advanced practices include a trial funded by the Innovation Fund Denmark for cars to self-report the condition of the roads they drive along. In doing so, cars are collecting data in real time (Reeh 2019).

While comprehensive systems and robust data are fundamental, these elements need to be supported by asset and maintenance standards. Variations in the quality and functionality of an asset should be measured against standards to enable the estimated cost of maintenance to be calculated. For example, in Australia, Austroads has developed data standards for such things as pavements, road barriers, and street lighting. These, in turn, are used to measure the value of road maintenance and renewal work, to link maintenance to performance outcomes, and to help inform investment decisions (Opus International Consultants 2016; Austroads 2018). The use of standards supports the regulatory environment of an infrastructure asset and the operational policies relating to infrastructure, such as procurement, by providing a baseline against which the measurement and comparison of results is possible.

## Unlock Potential for the Active Management of Infrastructure Assets

Beyond the critical need for micro-level data on the performance and maintenance needs of individual assets, there is much to gain from looking at the overall infrastructure asset portfolio and managing it through a government balance sheet. Though this may require accounting and data capacity efforts, balance sheet management extended to the whole public sector can help governments optimize their returns and to better oversee risks (IMF 2018).

This is true for all types of public sector assets. According to IMF (2018), improved management of financial asset holdings and of nonfinancial public corporations could yield a revenue gain of 3 percent of GDP per year—equivalent to corporate income tax revenue in advanced economies. Gains from better management of nonfinancial assets as a whole or within sectors can also be significant, though harder to estimate: higher returns could be obtained from the more active management of governments' heavily underestimated real estate portfolios (Detter and Fölster 2015). Such returns can then be used to fund the maintenance of assets.

## CASE STUDY: THE NEW ZEALAND TRANSPORT AGENCY

Unlocking the potential to improve the efficiency and effectiveness of services provided by public infrastructure assets is demonstrated through the governance arrangements and the performance expectations that an entity sets out to meet. The expectations are informed by law, regulations, operating standards, public expectations, and financial constraints. Transport entities such as the New Zealand Transport Agency (NZTA) provide good examples of sound practices for the active management of road infrastructure.

The NZTA is established in primary legislation as a public entity, wholly owned by the Government of New Zealand and governed by a board of directors. The NZTA receives hypothecated funding from fuel excise levies, vehicle registrations, license fees, and related sources. It is responsible for the funding of the land transport system, the management of regulatory requirements for land transport, the state of the highway system, and the investigation and review of accidents. The agency's function is to contribute to an effective, efficient, and safe land transport system that is in the public interest.

When determining whether to invest in road infrastructure, the NZTA carries out a CBA of a potential infrastructure investment and ranks the results. Projects with the highest cost-benefit ratio are funded first. The assessment is performed for all potential investments to ensure equal treatment in the assessment of projects, regardless of whether a project is arranged at a national or subnational level. The NZTA annual report compares the cost-benefit ratio of a particular activity and for each major region across the country.

The NZTA measures its performance against criteria like road safety, reviewed and reported in the agency's annual report. Measures for maintenance include the delivery of activities to agreed-upon standards, safety outcomes, surface condition, availability of the network after unplanned road closures, and maintenance cost per kilometer. The New Zealand Treasury provides guidance to government entities such as the NZTA on the categories of asset performance measures for annual reports to support measurement of nonfinancial considerations such as the use, condition, and functionality of an asset. These measures help identify the results achieved from maintenance and operation of assets. Of note, the financial statements in the NZTA annual report include the value of the road assets. The road network is valued using an optimized depreciated replacement cost methodology, based on the estimated current cost of building the existing asset, reduced by factors that include the age, condition, and the performance of the asset. The estimated cost is expected to change over time and is calculated by qualified independent valuers. Information in the report and related documents enables comparison between the cost of maintaining the asset and its value (New Zealand Treasury 2016; NZTA 2018).

The NZTA illustrates a model in which investment decisions for new roads and the use of funds for the upkeep and safety of existing roads is at steps removed from political decisions, while retaining state ownership of the road network.

The model does not overcome issues such as whether the hypothecated funding is sufficient or whether the construction and maintenance sectors meet New Zealand's infrastructure and maintenance needs. In this regard, the challenges facing New Zealand in road infrastructure are similar to many other countries.

## CONCLUSIONS

Suitable maintenance spending can extend the life span of assets and can reduce intertemporal costs for the government as well as for the users. Yet, despite this strong rationale, maintenance continues to be an "unloved line item" with low strategic priority. This chapter has provided examples of ways to ensure funding for maintenance while addressing critical capacity and data issues. In that regard, policymakers should look to (1) identify funding sources for maintenance and the responsibilities to perform maintenance at the time a public infrastructure investment is initiated, to ensure the sustainability of the investment to provide services over the life of the asset, and (2) establish a requirement to review funding and maintenance regularly to account for performance information and changes to the institutional arrangements over the life of an asset.

Yet, the maintenance challenge can only be fully tackled by going beyond technical solutions. A strong governmental commitment for maintenance is required to ensure that public infrastructure is more durable, more sustainable and, over time, more economical.

## REFERENCES

African Development Bank. 2015. *Transport in Africa: The African Development Bank's Intervention and Results for the Last Decade.* Summary Evaluation Report, African Development Bank, Abidjan, Côte d'Ivoire.

American Society of Civil Engineers. 2017. *Infrastructure Report Card.* American Society of Civil Engineers, Reston, VA.

Austroads. 2018. "Measuring and Reporting the Value of Road Maintenance and Renewal Work." Austroads, Sydney, Australia.

Barro, Robert J. 1990. "Government Spending in a Simple Model of Endogenous Growth." *Journal of Political Economy* 98 (S5): S103–S125.

Bova, Elva, Robert Dippelsman, Kara Rideout, and Andrea Schaechter. 2013. "Another Look at Governments' Balance Sheets: The Role of Nonfinancial Assets." IMF Working Paper 13/95, International Monetary Fund, Washington, DC.

Construction Industry Development Board. 2007. "National Infrastructure Maintenance Strategy: Infrastructure Maintenance Budgeting Guideline." Construction Industry Development Board, Pretoria, South Africa.

Detter, Dag, and Stefan Fölster. 2015. *The Public Wealth of Nations.* Palgrave Macmillan: London.

Escobal, Javier, and Carmen Ponce. 2003. "The Benefits of Rural Roads: Enhancing Income Opportunities for the Rural Poor." Working Paper 40, Grupo de Analysis Para el Desarrollo (GRADE), Lima, Peru.

Hayden, Andrew. 2019. *Local Roads Maintenance in England.* House of Commons Library, London.

International Monetary Fund (IMF). 2104a. *Government Finance Statistics Manual 2014.* Washington, DC: IMF.

IMF. 2014b. *World Economic Outlook: Legacies, Clouds, Uncertainties.* Washington, DC, October.

IMF. 2018. *Fiscal Monitor: Managing Public Wealth*. Washington, DC, October.

IMF. 2019. *Fiscal Monitor: Curbing Corruption*. Washington, DC, April.

International Transport Forum (ITF). 2012. *Performance Measurement in the Roading Sector: A Cross-Country Review of Experience*. Paris: ITF.

Kalaitzidakis, Pantelis, and Sarantis Kalyvitis. 2004. "On the Macroeconomic Implications of Maintenance in Public Capital." *Journal of Public Economics* 88 (3–4): 695–712.

National Cooperative Highway Research Program. 2012. "Best Practices in Performance Measurement for Highway Maintenance and Preservation." NCHRP Project 20–68A, Scan 10–03, Lawrenceville, NJ.

National Transportation Research Group (TRIP). 2018. "Bumpy Road Ahead: America's Roughest Rides and Strategies to Make Our Roads Smoother." Washington, DC, October.

New Zealand Transport Agency (NZTA). 2018. *Annual Report 2017–18*. Wellington, New Zealand.

New Zealand Treasury. 2016. *Asset Performance Measures, Guidance for Annual Reports*. Wellington, New Zealand: New Zealand Treasury.

Organisation for Economic Co-operation and Development (OECD). 2001. *Performance Indicators for the Roading Sector*. Paris: OECD.

OECD. 2011. *OECD Framework for the Governance of Infrastructure*. Paris: OECD.

OECD. 2015. *Guidelines on Corporate Governance of State-Owned Enterprises*. Paris: OECD.

Opus International Consultants. 2016. "Data Standard for Road Management and Investment in Australia and New Zealand." Austroads, Sydney, Australia.

Parlikad, Arjith Kumar, and Moshen A. Jafari. 2016. "Challenges in Infrastructure Asset Management." *IFAC Papers* 49 (28): 185–90.

Potter, Barry. 2013. "User Charging." In *The International Handbook of Public Financial Management*, edited by Richard Allen, Richard Hemming, and Barry Potter, 496–512. London: Palgrave Macmillan.

Reeh, Line. 2019. "Cars to Report on Road Condition." Technical University of Denmark, Lyngby, March 5.

Rioja, Felix. 2003. "Filling Potholes: Macroeconomic Effects of Maintenance vs. New Investment in Public Infrastructure." *Journal of Public Economics* 87 (9–10): 2281–2304.

Rioja, Felix. 2013. "What Is the Value of Infrastructure Maintenance? A Survey." In *Infrastructure and Land Policies*, edited by Gregory Ingram and Karen Brandt. Cambridge, MA: Lincoln Institute of Land Policy.

Rozenberg, Julie, and Marianne Fay, eds. 2019. *Beyond the Gap: How Countries Can Afford the Infrastructure They Need While Protecting the Planet*. Sustainable Infrastructure Series. Washington, DC: World Bank.

Spinetta, Jean-Cyril. 2018. *L'Avenir du Transport Ferroviaire [The Future of Rail Transportation]*, Report to the French Prime Minister, Paris, France, February.

Tanzania Road Funds Board. 2016. *Annual Report 2015–16*. Dodoma, Tanzania.

Wang, Hao, Israa Al-Saadi, Pan Lu, and Abbas Jasim. 2019. "Quantifying Greenhouse Gas Emission of Asphalt Pavement Preservation at Construction and Use Stages Using Life-Cycle Assessment." *International Journal of Sustainable Transportation* 13, London, United Kingdom.

World Bank. 1994. "Infrastructure for Development." *World Development Report*, Washington, DC.

World Bank. 2006. *The Challenge of Reducing Non-Revenue Water (NRW) in Developing Countries - How the Private Sector Can Help: A Look at Performance-Based Service Contracting*. Water Supply and Sanitation Board Discussion Paper Series No. 8. Washington, DC.

World Economic Forum (WEF). 2014. *Strategic Infrastructure: Steps to Operate and Maintain Infrastructure Efficiently and Effectively*. Geneva: WEF.

Yu, William, and Michael Pollitt. 2009. "Does Liberalisation Cause More Electricity Blackouts? Evidence from a Global Study of Newspaper Reports." EPRG Working Paper 0827, Energy Policy Research Group, University of Cambridge, United Kingdom.

Zietlow, Gunter. 2004. "*Road Funds in Latin America*." Paper presented for the Senior Road Executives' Programme, Road Financing and Road Fund Management, University of Birmingham, United Kingdom, April 26–30.

# CHAPTER 15

# Building Resilience in Infrastructure to Climate Change

Tuan Minh Le, Wei-Jen Leow, and Fabian Seiderer

## INTRODUCTION

Governments face growing economic and fiscal liabilities because of the increased scope and scale of climate change and the disasters it induces. While the many spillover effects cause damage to private property, public infrastructure, and services such as communications, transportation, and utilities, the economic losses can well exceed the cost of replacement. A road bridge that is washed away not only drains resources to replace it and hits economic activity, but where alternative transportation routes are minimal or costly, the net private benefit to bridge users is also lost. The longer it takes to repair the bridge or provide alternative transport routes, the more the economic loss accumulates.

Worldwide, the expected annual damage for transport infrastructure alone is in the billions of dollars, with more damage expected among advanced economies, given their larger capital stock (Figure 15.1). Transport infrastructure damage first increases with income growth and then decreases. Damage to other infrastructure facilities, like energy and water systems, only adds to the total cost.[1]

One would expect that specific project locations with a history of hazards and known exposure to climate change will attract less investment interest. Yet this does not always happen. Look no further than the unabated trend of beachfront development and the supporting public infrastructure for that. The reality is that climate and disaster risks are not fully encoded into public and private investment decisions at all levels. In developing countries, capacity and institutional processes to screen public projects for climate-induced risks are often lacking. Private investment decisions rarely account for these risks, often because they are heavily discounted to favor short-term profit. Consequently, large amounts of capital continue to flow into hazard-prone areas, leading to significant increases in the value of exposed economic assets. This amounts to a "fiscal time bomb" of explicit and contingent liabilities on the government when climate change manifests.

In response, governments need robust infrastructure governance frameworks to strengthen climate resilience. In the opening example of a road bridge, the losses could

[1] Chapter 9 also provides additional information on total costs of natural disasters.

## Figure 15.1. Expected Annual Damage to Transport Infrastructure per Hazard, by Country Income Group

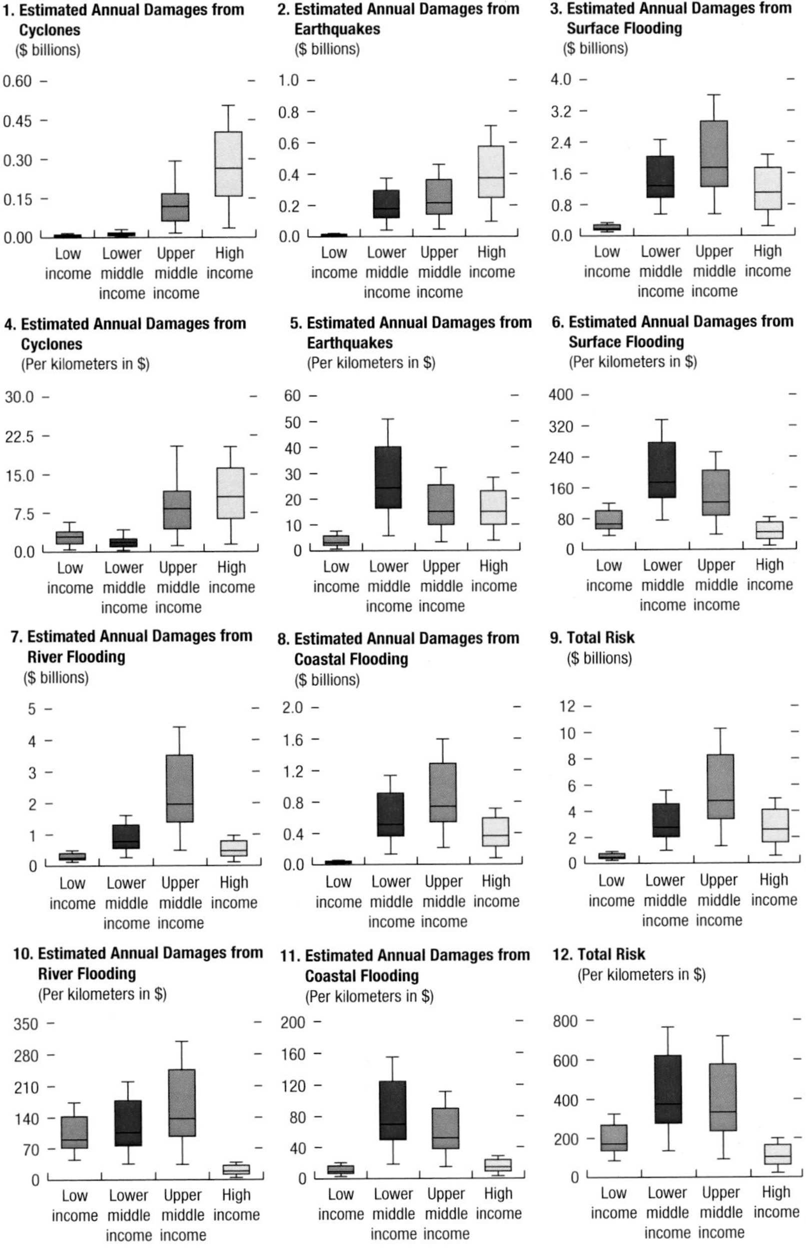


Source: Hallegatte, Rentschler, and Rozenberg 2019.

have been prevented or minimized had the government designed and built a more resilient bridge, planned for alternatives in the event of collapse (the use of military pontoon bridges, for example), or developed rapid repair or replacement capacities. Responses should also include risk management, through investing in adaptation measures, as well as the resilience financing strategies explored in Chapter 9.

This chapter provides guidance on how to integrate considerations of climate-related risks into infrastructure governance, focusing on the planning, design, appraisal, selection, and financing of public investments. It begins by looking at the frequency and growing severity of climate-related disasters, the rising cost of damage and losses, the expected trends in extreme weather, and an assessment of the resilience and vulnerability of countries and regions to climate-related disasters. It then presents an approach for governments to integrate climate considerations into the upstream stages of infrastructure governance, including in project planning and appraisal. With this new approach in hand, the chapter proposes some country-based enhancements to the IMF Public Investment Management Assessment (PIMA)[2] framework and the World Bank PIM diagnostic assessment frameworks (presented in Rajaram and others 2010 and Rajaram and others 2014), combining climate-specific dimensions with quantitative measures of risk based on data on past damage.

## THE EFFECTS OF CLIMATE CHANGE ON ECONOMIES AND INFRASTRUCTURE

### Past Hazards: Frequency and Severity

A large body of evidence supports the existence, causes, and ramifications of climate change, as collected by the United Nations' body of climate experts (Intergovernmental Panel on Climate Change, IPCC). World Bank (2014) provides a summary of the key climate impacts caused by tropical storms, wind, drought, heat extremes, floods, and landslides across regions over recent decades (Annex 15.1). Among the main issues it highlighted were the early onset of climate impacts, their uneven regional distribution, and interaction among impacts, which accentuates cascade effects.

The cost of climate-related disasters has also increased, with water-related damage being a dominant component. A review of the Emergency Events Database (EM-DAT)[3] over the past six decades shows that natural disasters increased sixfold from the 1960s to after the turn of the century.

Climate change elevates the risk profile of many countries, given their historical record of climate-related disasters. In the long term, many countries risk being hit by at least one severe climate disaster. Figure 15.2 shows to what extent

[2] The Public Investment Management Assessment framework also aims to accommodate the World Bank's diagnostic assessment frameworks (Rajaram and others 2010 and Rajaram and others 2014).

[3] Emergency Events Database (EM-DAT) by the Centre for Research on the Epidemiology of Disasters at the Université catholique de Louvain: https://www.emdat.be.

**Figure 15.2. Global Climate Risk Index**

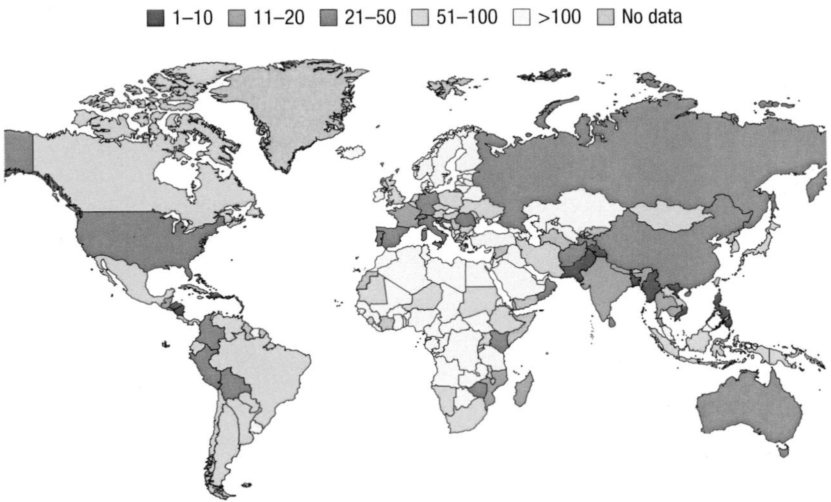


Source: Global Climate Risk Index 2019, https://germanwatch.org/en/cri.
Note: The boundaries, colors, denominations, and any other information shown on the map do not imply, on the part of the International Monetary Fund, any judgment on the legal status of any territory or any endorsement or acceptance of such boundaries.

**Figure 15.3. Economic Damage from Climate Disasters**
(Percentage of GDP)

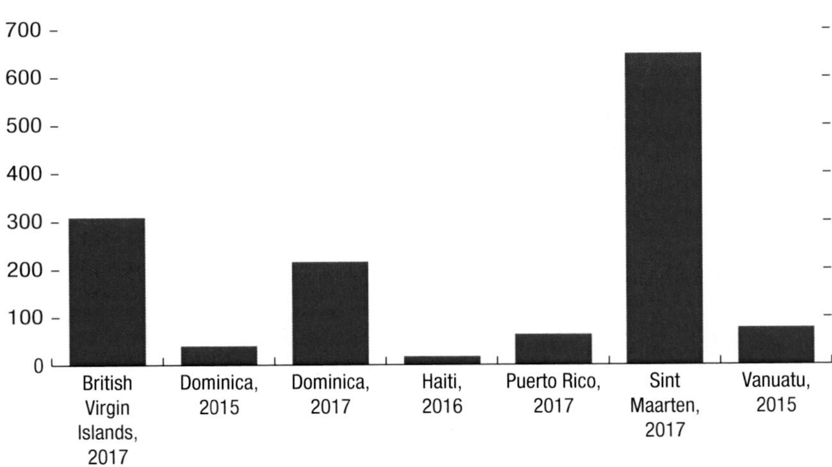


Sources: World Bank staff calculations, based on Acevedo 2016 and UNISDR 2018.
Note: Acevedo (2016) notes that the 20 largest of 148 hurricane disasters to Caribbean islands over 1950–2014 caused losses averaging 81.7 percent of GDP, with five causing losses of more than 100 percent of GDP. UNISDR (2018) reports the top 10 climate-related disasters ranked by loss as a share of GDP; all 10 are Caribbean islands with losses ranging from 69 percent to 797 percent of GDP.

countries and regions have been affected by weather-related loss events (storms, floods, heat waves, and the like). The annual climate risk index[4] ranks almost one-third of countries as worst affected. Many of these are developing countries, with Caribbean nations among those suffering climate disasters with high frequency over the long term, as seen in Chapter 9. Damages can be extraordinarily severe for small countries (Figure 15.3).

## Worrying Trends in Climate Change Hazards

The provisional 2019 statement by the World Meteorological Organization confirmed the global warming trend reported in its 2018 assessment: 2019 is likely to be the second- or third-warmest year on record. Greenhouse gas concentrations in 2018 reached new highs, with carbon dioxide, methane, and nitrous oxide all reaching record levels. The ocean heat content in 2019 surpassed the level in 2018, and the daily Arctic Sea ice extent in the month of October was at a record low. In autumn 2019, the global mean sea level reached its highest value since the beginning of high-precision altimetry records (January 1993).

The warming trend is set to continue, and even in the best scenario, the frequency and severity of extreme weather will increase. The IPCC *Special Report on Global Warming of 1.5°C* reported that the average global temperature for 2006–2015 was 0.87°C above the preindustrial baseline (IPCC 2018).[5] With a global target of limiting global warming effects to 1.5°C by 2050, even in the "best case" outcome, the report expects extreme weather (including tropical cyclones, extreme rainfall or drought, and extreme temperatures) will increase in frequency and intensity, and that sea levels will rise, along with damage inflicted on terrestrial and ocean ecosystems.

## Vulnerability and Resilience of Infrastructure to Disasters Induced by Climate Change

The extent of actual damage to infrastructure and, more widely, to an economy depends on the vulnerability and resilience of the country in question and its location. A severe storm can wreak more economic losses on one country than another, depending on locational factors such as physical geography (for example, whether an area is already flood prone), population density, physical resilience of the infrastructure, and the preparedness and actions of the population

[4] The climate risk index is a measure computed from a weighted average of a country's rankings on four indicators (deaths, deaths per inhabitant, US dollar losses, and losses as a share of GDP) caused by weather-related events in a particular year.

[5] The IPCC Special Report's Technical Summary noted that "Human-induced warming reached approximately 1°C (±0.2°C likely range) above preindustrial levels in 2017, increasing at 0.2°C (±0.1°C) per decade (high confidence)." It also noted that "Since 2000, the estimated level of human-induced warming has been equal to the level of observed warming with a likely range of ±20 percent accounting for uncertainty due to contributions from solar and volcanic activity over the historical period (high confidence)."

**Box 15.1. Infrastructure Washed Away: A Case from Kerala**

The increasing frequency and severity of floods caused by climate change have a particularly devastating impact on countries' infrastructure and assets as seen in 2018 in Kerala. The Indian state is a climate change hotspot relative to the rest of India, as measured by Verisk Maplecroft's Climate Change Vulnerability Index.[1] The index for the state in 2018 stood at 2.09 out of 10 (which is the lowest vulnerability). The total loss from the 2018 floods was estimated at 2.6 percent of state GDP, which is higher than the total annual capital budget (2.3 percent of GDP). The recovery needs are estimated at $3.5 billion. The infrastructure sector was the most affected by the floods and has the highest share of total recovery needs ($2.2 billion). In response the government has adopted the Rebuild Kerala Initiative, with a focus on enhancing the state's resilience anchored upon rebuilding better institutions for public investment management.

Source: World Bank public investment management diagnostic and 2019 development policy operation, "First Resilient Kerala Program DPO (P1699074)."

[1] The Verisk Maplecroft's Climate Change Vulnerability Index measures the susceptibility of populations to climate change and shocks on a scale of 0–10, where 0 is the highest risk and 10 the lowest risk. https://www.maplecroft.com/insights/analysis/84-of-worlds-fastest-growing-cities-face-extreme-climate-change-risks.

and authorities in response to the storm threat. These "resilience" factors contribute to the true vulnerability of a location and its infrastructure, and may attenuate the actual number of affected lives, value of property damage, and days of service disruption.

These developments call for urgent infrastructure governance to account for the losses that an investment may suffer over its operating life because of compounded climate-related weather disaster risks. Accounting for losses will naturally reduce the expected net economic benefits that give rationale to the project, and so impacts project planning and appraisal. At the same time, this should also prompt infrastructure governance to be improved to ensure that it systematically encourages consideration of adaptation solutions in design and in cost-benefit assessments. Box 15.1 discusses how the State of Kerala of India decided to develop a climate-informed public investment management after a severe flood.

## INTEGRATING CLIMATE CHANGE CONSIDERATIONS UPSTREAM IN PUBLIC INVESTMENT MANAGEMENT

This section provides guidance for mainstreaming climate screening and techniques in the upstream stages of public investment management, specifically project identification, prescreening, project appraisal, and selection[6] It discusses

[6] Climate sensitivity has to recognize both the climate impacts of projects and their adaptation to minimize the economic costs of expected and possibly worsening damage from natural hazards. Each of these two considerations requires the public investment management system to be climate informed.

the main dimensions (including the main climate hazards, risk identification and vulnerability assessment, climate-informed cost-benefit analysis, and climate impact of projects) that underpin the mainstreaming of climate change in the upstream stages of the public investment management cycle (Glenday and others 2019). These are followed by a discussion on the challenges and policy considerations involved in such an approach.

## Climate-Informed Project Planning, Identification, Guidance, and Screening

The first challenge is to account systematically for the climate impacts of projects and their vulnerability to climate risks, and for their necessary adaptation. This requires developing an understanding of (1) the climate impact of large projects (such as greenhouse gas emissions), (2) the sources, types, and sizes of damage and economic losses from climate events, (3) how these relate to the size or strength of different natural hazards, and then (4) how to analyze the historical record and use models to predict the frequency of natural hazards of different strengths.

As part of the screening or preappraisal, project proposals should meet broader criteria of consistency with sustainable development goals that in turn should be addressing service delivery shortages, growth promotion, and distributional goals. However, these goals are impacted by climate change and related extreme weather events, as seen above. Consideration of these climate impacts and risks needs to be built into the public investment management framework and considered early in the project identification and design stage. As these are often new and complex dimensions for developing countries to consider, it is recommended to prioritize climate-informed public investment management modules in countries considered climate hotspots or for large infrastructure projects.

The first stage of a public investment management assessment involves the screening of project proposals to detect any potential major climate impact or risk from or vulnerability to natural hazards, especially climate- or weather-induced hazards. This should be part of the overall screening of infrastructure projects in feasibility studies, design, and selection for budgeting. Climate-sensitive screening of the project pipeline requires that projects identify potential climate impacts and exposure to natural hazards, and that some assessment of vulnerability to risks is provided.

Tools to support climate-informed project screening have been developed to a sophistication that is applicable to major transportation projects (Ebinger and Vandycke 2015). For example, a generic "traffic signal" guide that could rate the preliminary risk of hazards to specific sectors is shown in Figure 15.4.

The risk categories should be country specific and clearly identified, based on historical hazard and loss data and by disaster risk management and climate models. They should include more refined and sector- or location-specific quantitative criteria and data, vetted by central planning and finance agencies and requiring decisions in project preparation, such as reject, redesign, and reevaluate. Generally, the no- or low-risk cases could be ignored for the small, medium, and

**Figure 15.4. A Traffic Signal Rating of Hazard Risks**

| | |
|---|---|
| **Insufficient Understanding** | Greater familiarity with the sector and/or hazards is needed. This rating should be revised once there is sufficient understanding. |
| **No Risk** | The hazard does not pose a risk to the sector and/or region and will not affect the achievement of development goals and priorities. |
| **Low Risk** | The hazard could have a modest negative effect on the sector, but the country and/or sector has sufficient institutional capacity to respond to the hazard. |
| **Moderate Risk** | The hazard could have a considerable negative effect on the sector, and institutional capacity to respond to the hazard might not be sufficient; this risk has the potential to affect the ability of the country to meet its development objectives. |
| **High Risk** | The hazard is likely to have a considerable negative effect on the sector, and institutional capacity to respond to the hazard will not lessen the impact; this risk will likely affect the country's achievement of development goals and priorities. |

Source: Rating Guide of the World Bank Climate and Disaster Risk Screening Tool (https://climatescreeningtools.worldbank.org/content/risk-rating-popup).

repetitive projects, and result in some reduction in the expected net benefits of large projects being subjected to full cost-benefit analysis. Moderate- and high-risk cases for large projects would be handled at the stage of project appraisal, whereby adaptive measures should be considered to mitigate the risks and lower the expected losses.

## Climate-Informed Project Appraisal

While portfolio screening (mentioned previously) is relatively light and manageable for most governments, climate-informed project appraisal can be more demanding and so needs to be prioritized to prevent overwhelming already-limited appraisal capacity. A first set of criteria is the size, the unique characteristics, or the strategic importance of the project. A second criteria is potential impact and loss, in the expected number of people affected and expected value of the damage to project assets (infrastructure, buildings, inventories). Where the number of people affected or the share of project asset damage is high, a more in-depth climate-informed project appraisal is warranted. Specific, transparent thresholds for such filtering and differentiated appraisal methods need to be enacted as part of public investment management governance.[7]

[7] In the case of small and medium-sized repeat projects, the resources used to screen and select them can be streamlined, in terms of both the appraisal process and the approval authority. Large and complex projects often need to be subjected to full cost-benefit analysis, including financial, economic, distributional, and climate risk appraisal and need to be vetted by central or independent planning and finance institutions.

**Figure 15.5. Components of the Climate-Sensitive Cost-Benefit Analysis**

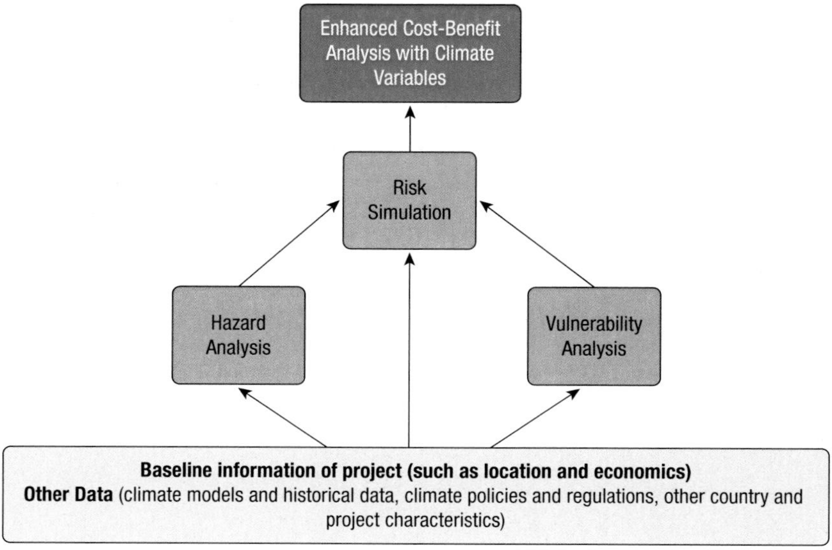

Source: Adapted from Fernholz and Erdem 2019.

## Methodology for Climate-Informed Project Appraisal

As indicated, all new, large, or complex projects should be subject to full-fledged cost-benefit analysis that integrates climate change impacts into the economic analysis. Figure 15.5 shows the components of the enhanced cost-benefit analysis for climate change considerations.

As indicated in Figure 15.5, climate-sensitive cost-benefit analysis is anchored in three building blocks (Fernholz and Erdem 2019). They are as follows: hazard analysis, vulnerability analysis, and risk simulation. All rely on the baseline information gathered for the projects supplemented by other data, for example, climate models and historical data.

- *Risk identification.* Based on past records, expert opinions, and probabilistic modeling, the potential costs of damage need to be assessed along with the vulnerability of the project to damage from different intensities of risks.
- *Hazard analysis.* For an infrastructure or facilities project that is potentially vulnerable to climate-related hazards (such as a road or a bridge that could be damaged by flooding), the project appraisal must account for projected hazards that may damage the asset and its ability to generate expected services and a return on investment.
- *Vulnerability analysis.* This type of analysis focuses on estimating loss functions. It would help clarify the economic impact of climate parameters at different intensities on specific infrastructure assets and property, or the whole economy.

Techniques of varying complexity can be applied depending on the importance of the project, risk, and country capacity and data availability. Ministries can be asked to consult with planning and disaster management departments to build some simplified climate risk assumptions and shock scenarios into their standard cost-benefit analysis. For large projects and climate hotspots, hazard and climate models can be used. First, this requires estimating the threshold strength for a hazard in a location that will bear significant damage, and then estimating the probabilities that hazards above the threshold could occur. This "exceedance" probability distribution then needs to be linked to damage and loss estimates. Second, differently costed risk-mitigation measures for the project, such as more resilient infrastructure design, redundancies, and asset insurance schemes, can be factored in to the project cost-benefit analysis. In addition, net economic losses that can be expected until the infrastructure or facility services are restored have to be assessed and also factored in. The overall economic loss of a disaster varies with the intensity of the hazard, the ability of the infrastructure to withstand it, the government's capability to reduce the hazard (for example, to divert or dam flood-waters), and the speed with which the government can restore the infrastructure services or provide alternatives.

The next step is to consider whether modifications can be made to the new infrastructure investment (a road system, say) that will make it more resilient while improving the expected net benefits. The approach here refers to real options analysis.

Real option analysis, in a nutshell, extends the conventional cost-benefit analysis. By taking into consideration future costs and benefits, it explores the opportunities to delay full implementation of adaptation measures until better information becomes available and allows resolution of uncertainty about climatic impacts.[8] The real option can include provisions in design and construction that accommodate adaptive reinforcement of structural elements in the future. As such, a so-called real option is the right but not the obligation to adjust the infrastructure system in ways likely to be more resilient, as needed for the infrastructure to to continue to function as expected in the face of change.[9]

## Incorporation of Project Climate Impacts in Economic Appraisal

A key aspect of a climate-smart system is the inclusion of the evaluation of climate impacts of changing greenhouse gas emissions arising from a project. This may be either a direct impact from emissions reduction through expanded green power supply in place of fossil fuel–based power, or an indirect impact through changes in forest coverage or management that impact the carbon sequestration capacity of the country or the local climate. The climate change impacts of changing the level of carbon dioxide and other greenhouse gas emissions have

[8] Chapter 5 in Rajaram and others (2014).

[9] For an example of real options analysis, see Gersonius and others (2013).

both domestic and international economic values to be taken into account in economic analysis of a project. The two most common methods of estimating the emissions externality are either by estimating the added economic costs of damage from added carbon dioxide emissions[10] or by estimating the value of carbon emissions rights traded in an open market.[11] The challenge to cost-benefit analysis from an economic perspective is that the reduction of greenhouse gases is a global public good because benefits accrue nationally and to the rest of the world.

## Challenges and Policy Considerations for Mainstreaming Climate Screening and Appraisal in Public Investment Management

Making public investment management climate smart is a new and important demand on the institutional capacity of a government. It requires gathering and managing the information on current and past natural hazards, forecasting the future occurrence of natural hazards or extreme climate events, and tracking the nature and costs of natural disasters as they occur. While this is increasingly done by countries' disaster risk management agencies, it often remains outside of public investment management institutions and processes. Conversely, these agencies are rarely informed at the planning stage about additional infrastructure investments, compounding locational climate vulnerabilities and risks. To succeed, integrating the adaptation to natural hazards—or accounting for the climate change impact of public investments—would require the combination of information, greater coordination, incentives, and disciplines.

## Collection of Required Data and Information

Identification of natural hazards requires the accumulation of meteorological, geological, and other data to analyze and develop models to forecast the probabilities of extreme natural hazard events that can lead to significant damage and economic loss. Data for temperature and precipitation have been collected for more than 100 years; the density of earth-based weather stations has been increasing and has been supplemented by data from satellite-based platforms since the 1980s. This has allowed the development of sophisticated weather models for forecasting climate events in most regions of the world. These data and models have allowed access to climate event data provided by major international and national agencies. The challenge, however, comes in linking natural disaster data to the actual historical and projected potential disaster information by country, location, and sector. This requires a greater integration of national and international climate and disaster risk management

[10] Current estimates in the United States of the economic costs of an added ton of carbon dioxide emissions are $42 per ton (National Academies 2017).

[11] The value of carbon traded on the European Union emissions trading system as of March 2019 is $25 per ton.

databases and competencies in upstream public investment management functions and frameworks.

## Institutionalization of Climate-Informed Public Investment Management

Policymakers determine four sets of actions to mainstream the collection and use of information into public investment management. First comes institutionalization of the channels and governance structure, leveraging national and international climate and disaster databases and models. Second, development of mechanisms and procedures to ensure climate screening, vetting, and amendment of project options and designs. Third is capacity building, and fourth, the appropriate treatment of the climate change impact of publicly financed projects. Some highlights of the authors' analysis along these four dimensions of policymaking are summarized in this section.

### *Institutionalize the Channels and Governance Structure for Climate-Sensitive Public Investment Management*

Typically, countries face institutional fragmentation as a perpetual problem, which is intense for cross-cutting government functions such as public investment management and disaster risk management. It is critical, therefore, to develop channels by which information on natural hazards flows into government planning and can help guide investment design, selection, and budgeting.

Institutionalized processes and division of labor, a transparent accountability mechanism, and appropriate institutional incentives to reward cross-agency collaboration are ingredients critical for making public investment management sensitive to climate change. Countries can build on their experience with the environmental impact assessments done on most large projects. Therefore, functions that need to be allocated to specific government agencies—and coordinated and managed by sector and central ministries—include the following:

1. Building databases of the historical occurrence of natural hazards and predicting the strength and frequency of hazards.
2. Documenting and analyzing the damage and economic losses caused by past disasters by sector and location, and predicting the potential damage and economic losses by sector and location over time.
3. Establishing climate-sensitive construction regulations by sector and location.
4. Screening projects for climate impact and natural hazard vulnerability.
5. Developing climate-sensitive project designs for vulnerable projects and appraising them.
6. Selecting and financing projects, including the possible added climate adaptation costs, and sustaining appropriate levels of operations and maintenance financing.
7. Monitoring and evaluating project performance, particularly for climate-related impacts and valuation of disasters (to feed these observations back into the disaster damage prediction in point 2).

The coordination and aggregation function demands active involvement and direction from the central planning and finance agencies, thus the need to include these functions in regulations and processes for public investment management.

### *Develop Mechanisms or Procedures to Ensure Climate Screening, Vetting, and Amendment of the Investment Design*

Climate screening needs to be included in a country's legal and regulatory framework for public investment management in the same manner as environmental impact assessments. Appropriate vetting and disclosure processes need to be in place to ensure screening is properly done and to inform the cost-benefit analysis and design (or design change) for large projects as warranted. This can be complemented by sector or through construction regulations that are location specific. Regulations are appropriate where a hazard is expected frequently and where the regulations can be applied to a wide range of investment types in a specific sector and location.[12] For example, minimum road drainage standards may be required where significant rainstorms occur regularly. Public disclosure of climate-informed public investment screening, feasibility studies, and construction permits enhances compliance and accountability.

### *Build Capacity*

Developing countries and emerging economies face a significant lack of capacity to capture information on the damage estimates that would need to be collected by a combination of disaster risk management agencies and local governments and sector agencies (typically those responsible for transportation, environment, and agriculture).[13]

While initial qualitative and expert assessments can be carried out, a gradual buildup of quantitative methods of analysis (cost-benefit analysis and risk simulation) is required in government ministries responsible for planning and budgeting, focusing on the key tasks in points 1 to 7, leveraging knowledge and competencies across a government and globally. It is therefore essential that the reform—with support and commitments by donors in the case of developing countries—includes a proper training and capacity-building plan to ensure the climate-sensitive public investment management framework can be implemented effectively.

### *Assess Climate Change Impacts in Public Investment Management*

Large projects or projects that are expected to impact environmentally sensitive areas such as forests, wetlands, and coastal zones are required to undergo some level of environmental impact assessment to identify vulnerabilities and the possible adaptations required to minimize the environmental impacts of a project.

---

[12] Ideally, as with any regulation, climate-sensitive construction codes should be subjected to cost-benefit analysis to ensure that the costs of compliance are expected to result in cost savings when the construction is exposed to a natural hazard.

[13] Damage estimates are available in 98 percent of the occurrences in Australia and New Zealand, but only 12 percent of the occurrences in sub-Saharan Africa. Moreover, damage estimates are available in less than 50 percent of the countries in Latin America and the Caribbean and South Asia.

These environmental impact assessments are typically conducted as an early input into the appraisal of the project. The assessment of the climate impacts of the project should be part of that process. Clearly, where a country has no process for doing environmental impact assessments, special regulations or directives are needed so that climate impacts can be routinely assessed as part of project screening, appraisal, and approval.

## DIAGNOSTIC PROMISE OF CLIMATE MODULE IN INFRASTRUCTURE GOVERNANCE

Existing infrastructure governance diagnostic tools have established a solid framework for assessing public investment management systems, but they were not specifically designed to deal with climate change impacts on public investments. The proposed climate module presented in Annex 15.2 aims to complement infrastructure governance diagnostic assessment tools or traditional diagnostic frameworks such as the PIMA and the World Bank's eight "Must-Haves" diagnostics (Rajaram and others 2010, 2014), as well as the Public Expenditure and Financial Accountability (PEFA) framework. It provides a more climate-informed assessment of countries' upstream public investment policies and actual practices. It asks the basic question of whether a public investment management system is climate sensitive or blind. It follows a PEFA/PIMA-type of questionnaire (and heatmap system) with the focus on the five core dimensions of public investment management (Table 15.1).

**TABLE 15.1.**

**Mapping a Climate-Related PIM Module to the PIMA and PEFA Frameworks**

| Climate-Related Public Investment Management Module | Relevant Institutions in the PIMA Framework | Corresponding PEFA Indicators and Dimensions |
|---|---|---|
| 1. Climate-sensitive legal and regulatory framework | Cross-cutting issue on the legal framework | Cross-cutting in respective dimensions |
| 2. Climate-informed investment planning and guidance | Institution 2: National and Sectoral Planning | 16.2: Alignment of Strategic Planning and Medium-Term Budgeting<br>17.2: Budget Preparation |
| 3. Project identification and prioritization considering climate risks (portfolio level) | Institution 4: Project Appraisal (Prefeasibility stage) | 11.2: Investment Project Selection |
| 4. Climate-informed project appraisal and selection (project level) | Institution 4: Project Appraisal (Feasibility)<br>Institution 5: Budgeting<br>Institution 10: Project Selection | 11.1: Economic Analysis |
| 5. Climate-informed state-owned enterprise investments and public-private partnerships | Institution 5: Alternative Infrastructure Financing | 10.1: Monitoring of Public Corporations |

Source: Authors.

Note: Numbers represent the respective PIMA and PEFA indicators. PEFA = Public Expenditure and Financial Accountability; PIMA = Public Investment Management Assessment.

## CONCLUSIONS

Governments are having to deal with growing economic and fiscal costs and risks from the increasing frequency and severity of climate-related extreme weather. Over the last four decades, natural disasters have increased sixfold and done significant damage to developing and emerging economies. Fixed capital accumulation, including in disaster-prone areas, exponentially increases the risk exposure, particularly as these climate and fiscal risks are rarely considered in investment decisions. Given the high stakes, mainstreaming climate-informed public investment management, including through the Helsinki principles adopted by the Coalition of Finance Ministers for Climate Action, is a priority for the international community.

This chapter proposes an approach governments could use to adapt their infrastructure governance frameworks to strengthen climate resilience in the upstream stages of public investment management: project planning, design, appraisal, selection, and financing. Some caution for policymakers is worth highlighting. First, to avoid overwhelming already-stretched public investment management systems, an upstream and differentiated approach is recommended to assess and mitigate the most severe climate risks and impacts for the most important public investments. Different qualitative and quantitative approaches and tools exist for climate risk identification and vulnerability assessments, portfolio and project screening and appraisal, and mitigation measures. They have yet to be further tested and incorporated in a country-specific public investment management framework. Second, upgrading a national system to factor in and mitigate growing climate risks requires a sequenced but holistic approach, including regulatory, institutional, and operational reforms and adequate capacity building. To improve the national climate-sensitive public investment management systems efficiently, it is imperative that government vision fits a comprehensive plan, with realistic milestones and timelines. And third, greater institutional cooperation serves as one of the major preconditions for a functional climate-sensitive public investment management system.

## ANNEX 15.1. OVERVIEW OF CLIMATE CHANGE IMPACTS ACROSS REGIONS

The following is an overview of some of the climate change impacts (excluding storm- and flood-related impacts) across regions identified in the World Bank report *Turn Down the Heat* (2014):

1. *Unusual and unprecedented heat extremes.* These are expected to occur far more frequently and cover much greater land areas, both globally and in the three regions (Latin America and the Caribbean, North Africa and the Middle East, and Europe and Central Asia) examined. Heat extremes in Southeast Asia are projected to increase substantially in the short term and would have significant adverse effects on humans and ecosystems under 2°C and 4°C of warming.
2. *Rainfall regime changes and water availability.* Even without any climate change, population growth alone is expected to put pressure on water resources

## ANNEX 15.2.

**ANNEX TABLE 15.2.1**

Climate PIM Module: Questionnaire

| Dimension | Question | A | B | C | D |
|---|---|---|---|---|---|
| 1. Climate-sensitive legal and regulatory framework | Does the government have an explicit legal or regulatory framework expressing the climate mitigation objectives or the adaptation requirements for programs and projects? How comprehensive is this framework? Does it apply to all levels of government? | The PFM/ PIM legal or regulatory framework does explicitly address both mitigation and adaptation and covers the entire public sector.<br>Strong compliance: applied to more of 75 percent of the major public sector project sample.[1] | The PFM/ PIM legal or regulatory framework either (1) addresses only one climate dimension (mitigation or adaptation), or (2) limits its scope to the central government.<br>Medium compliance: applied to 50 percent to 75 percent of the major public sector project sample. | The legal or regulatory framework does include some modest climate provisions, applicable only to the central government.<br>Limited evidence of compliance: 25 percent to 50 percent of the major central government project sample. | None of the previous situation.<br>No such legal framework or weak compliance. Less than 25 percent of the major central government project sample. |
| 2. Climate-informed Investment planning and guidance | Do PIPs or sector strategies include the country's climate objectives (NDCs) and evidence-based vulnerability assessments? | PIP or sector strategies exist, include the country's main NDCs, and consider the vulnerability of its major sectors and public investment (more than 75 percent of capital budget) based on adequate hazard and exceedance data. | PIP or sector strategies include some NDCs and consider the vulnerability of some sectors and public investment (between 50 percent and 75 percent of the capital budget) based on hazard and exceedance data. | PIP or sector strategies either include the country's main NDCs or consider the vulnerability of its major sectors and public investment (less than 50 percent of capital budget) based on hazard and exceedance data. | None of the above. |
| 3. Project identification and prioritization considering climate risks (portfolio level) | Are there climate-informed project selection and prioritization criteria and are large or new projects screened for their climate impact and resilience? | The government has published climate assessment and prioritization criteria for large or new public investments. The assessment covers the climate impact of the project and its exposure to climate risks, based on adequate hazard and exceedance data.<br>Strong compliance: applied to more than 75 percent of the major public sector project sample. | The government has climate assessment and prioritization criteria for large or new public investments. The assessment covers either the climate impact of the project or its exposure to climate risks, based on hazard and exceedance data.<br>Medium compliance: applied to 50 percent to 75 percent of the major public sector project sample. | The government accounts for the impact of large projects on climate change but not the climate risk exposure of major projects.<br>Compliance is limited, and it is applied to less than 50 percent of the central government sample of major projects, or there is no or limited evidence it contributed to project prioritization. | None of the above. |

Source: Authors.

*(continued)*

[1] Large projects are defined per the country's thresholds. The sample is expected to cover at least 1 percent of the capital expenditures.

**ANNEX 15.2. (*continued*)**

| Climate PIM Module: Questionnaire | | | | | |
|---|---|---|---|---|---|
| **Dimension** | **Question** | **A** | **B** | **C** | **D** |
| 4. Climate-informed project appraisal and selection (project level) | Do project appraisal guidelines exist that (1) mandate the evaluation of climate change impacts for large projects and provide a methodology or (2) require the real options or adaptation measures to be considered in project design to mitigate known climate risks. | Project appraisal guidelines (1) mandate the evaluation of climate change impacts for large projects and provide a methodology or (2) require the consideration of real options or adaptation measures in the project design to mitigate known climate risks. They are applied for large projects and compliance is vetted and high (more than 75 percent of the major project sample). | Project appraisal guidelines (1) mandate the evaluation of climate change impacts for large projects but do not provide a methodology or (2) do not mandate consideration of real options and adaptation measures in project design to mitigate climate risks are not systematic.<br>Enforcement is medium: applied to 50 percent to 75 percent of the central government's major project sample, and vetting is limited. | Basic guidelines exist to incorporate the evaluation of climate risks and mitigation measures for major projects. Enforcement and vetting are limited (less than 50 percent of the central government large project sample). | None of the above. |
| 5. Climate-informed state-owned enterprise investments and public-private partnerships. | Are there policies or guidelines mandating state-owned enterprises and public-private partnerships to assess the climate risk and include mitigation measures in the designs/contracts.<br>Is there an independent review and vetting mechanism in place to ensure enforcement and accountability? | Specific polices or guidelines mandating state-owned enterprises and public-private partnerships to evaluate and mitigate major known climate risk for major investments, according to robust prescribed methodologies, exist.<br>Compliance is high: more than 75 percent of the sample of major state-owned enterprise and public-private partnership projects apply these guidelines and are independently vetted. | Specific polices or guidelines mandating the evaluation and mitigation of the climate risk for their major investments exist for either state-owned enterprises or public-private partnerships. Methods are not specified or robust.<br>Compliance is medium: 50 percent to 75 percent of the sample of major state-owned enterprise or public-private partnership projects apply these guidelines and are vetted. | Consideration of climate impact and risk in state-owned enterprises, investments, or public-private partnerships is nascent and compliance is limited: less than 50 percent of the sample of major state-owned enterprise or public-private partnership projects apply these guidelines. | None of the above. |

Note: NDC = nationally determined contribution; PFM = public financial management; PIM = public investment management; PIP = public investment plan. The ranged colors mimic the traffic lights showing the various degrees of efficiency. Color scale: green (4); yellow (3); orange (2), red (1).

in many regions. With projected climate change, however, pressure on water resources is expected to increase significantly.

- Declines of 20 percent in water availability are projected for many regions under 2°C warming and of 50 percent for some regions under 4°C warming. Limiting warming to 2°C would reduce the global population exposed to declining water availability to 20 percent.
- South Asian populations are likely to be increasingly vulnerable to the greater variability of precipitation changes, in addition to disturbances in the monsoon system and rising peak temperatures that could put water and food resources at severe risk.

3. *Agricultural yields and nutritional quality.* Crop production systems will be under increasing pressure to meet growing global demand in the future. Significant crop yield impacts are already being felt at 0.8°C warming.
   - While projections vary and are uncertain, clear risks emerge as yield-reducing temperature thresholds for important crops have been observed, and improvements appear to have been offset or limited by observed warming (0.8°C) in many regions. There is also some empirical evidence that higher atmospheric levels of carbon dioxide could lower protein levels of some grain crops.
   - For the regions studied in this report, global warming above 1.5°C to 2°C increases the risk of reduced crop yields and production losses in sub-Saharan Africa, Southeast Asia, and South Asia. These impacts would have strong repercussions on food security and are likely to shrink economic growth and poverty reduction in the impacted regions.
4. *Terrestrial ecosystems.* Increased warming could bring about ecosystem shifts, fundamentally altering species compositions and even leading to the extinction of some species.
   - By the 2030s (with 1.2°C to 1.3°C warming), some ecosystems in Africa, for example, are projected to experience maximum extreme temperatures well beyond their present range, with all African ecoregions exceeding this range by 2070 (2.1°C to 2.7°C warming).
   - The distribution of species within savanna ecosystems is projected to shift from grasses to woody plants, as carbon dioxide fertilization favors the latter, although high temperatures and precipitation deficits might counter this effect. This shift will reduce available forage for livestock and stress pastoral systems and livelihoods.
5. *Rising sea levels.* Sea level rise has been occurring more rapidly than previously projected, and a rise of as much as 50 centimeters by the 2050s may be unavoidable because of past emissions: limiting warming to 2°C may limit the global sea-level rise to about 70 centimeters by 2100.
   - As much as 100 centimeters sea-level rise may occur if emissions increases continue and raise the global average temperature to 4°C by 2100 and

higher levels thereafter. While the unexpectedly rapid rise over recent decades can now be explained by the accelerated loss of ice from the Greenland and Antarctic ice sheets, significant uncertainty remains as to the rate and scale of future sea-level rise.

- The sea level nearer to the equator is projected to be higher than the global mean of 100 centimeters at the end of the century. In Southeast Asia for example, sea-level rise is projected to be 10–15 percent higher than the global mean. Coupled with storm surges and tropical cyclones, this increase is projected to have devastating impacts on coastal systems.

6. *Marine ecosystems.* Substantial losses of coral reefs are projected by the time warming reaches 1.5°C to 2°C from both heat and ocean warming.

## REFERENCES

Acevedo, Sebastian. 2016. "Gone with the Wind: Estimating Hurricane and Climate Change Costs in the Caribbean." IMF Working Paper 16/199, International Monetary Fund, Washington, DC.

Ebinger, Jane Olga, and Nancy Vandycke. 2015. *Moving Towards Climate Resilient Transport: The World Bank's Experience from Building Adaptation into Programs.* Transport & ICT Global Practice. Washington, DC: World Bank.

Fernholz, F., and O. Erdem. 2019. "Climate-Sensitive Public Investment Appraisal: General Methodology and an Application to St. Lucia." Duke University and World Bank.

GermanWatch. 2020. "Global Climate Risk Index 2020: Who Suffers Most from Extreme Weather Events? Weather-Related Loss Events in 2018 and 1999 to 2018." Briefing Paper, Bonn.

Gersonius, Berry, Richard Ashley, Assela Pathirana, and Chris Zevenbergen. 2013. "Climate Change Uncertainty: Building Flexibility into Water and Flood Risk Infrastructure." *Climatic Change* 116 (2): 411–23.

Glenday, Graham, Tuan Minh Le, Wei-Jen Leow, and Fabian Seiderer. 2019. "A Proposed Climate-Informed Public Investment Management Framework". Unpublished.

Hallegatte, S., J. Rentschler, and J. Rozenberg. 2019. *Lifelines: The Resilient Infrastructure Opportunity.* Washington, DC: World Bank.

Intergovernmental Panel on Climate Change (IPCC). 2018. *Global Warming of 1.5°C.* Geneva: IPCC.

National Academies of Sciences, Engineering, and Medicine. 2017. *Valuing Climate Damages: Updating Estimation of the Social Cost of Carbon Dioxide.* Washington, DC: National Academies Press.

Rajaram, Anand, Tuan Minh Le, Nataliya Biletska, and James Brumby. 2010. *A Diagnostic Framework for Assessing Public Investment Management.* Working Paper 5397, World Bank, Washington, DC.

Rajaram, Anand, Tuan Minh Le, Kai Kaiser, Jay-Hyung Kim, and Jonas Frank, editors. 2014. *The Power of Public Investment Management: Transforming Resources into Assets for Growth.* Washington, DC: World Bank.

Seiderer, Fabian. 2019. *Kerala Public Investment Diagnostic.* Washington, DC: World Bank.

United Nations Office for Disaster Risk Reduction (UNISDR) and Center for Research on the Epidemiology of Disasters (CRED). 2018. *Economic Losses, Poverty and Disasters, 1998–2017.* Geneva: UNISDR.

World Bank. 2014. *Turn Down the Heat: Confronting the New Climate Normal.* Washington, DC: World Bank.

World Meteorological Organization (WMO). 2019. "The State of the Global Climate in 2019." WMO Provisional Statement, December 3.

# Index